The People's Lawyer

THE PEOPLE'S LAWYER

*The Colorful Life and Times
of Julian L. McPhillips, Jr.*

Carroll Dale Short

REVISED EDITION

with a 2005 update
By Julian L. McPhillips, Jr.

NEWSOUTH BOOKS
MONTGOMERY | LOUISVILLE

NewSouth Books
P.O. Box 1588
Montgomery, AL 36102

Revised Edition, 2005
ISBN 1-58838-069-6

This book was originally published in 2000 in hardcover with the Library of Congress Cataloging-in-Publication Data:

Short, Carroll Dale.
The people's lawyer : the colorful life and times
of Julian L. McPhillips, Jr. / Carroll Dale Short.
p. cm.
Includes index.
ISBN 1-58838-004-1
1. McPhillips, Julian L., Jr. 2. Lawyers—Alabama—Biography.
I. Title
KF373.M397 S55 2000
340'.092—dc21
[B]

Design by Randall Williams

Printed in the United States of America

Contents

Part I: Roots and History

Part II: The Practice of Law

Preface to the 2005 Edition

Julian L. McPhillips, Jr.

MUCH HAS OCCURRED in the past five years, since the first edition of this book went to press in August 2000. At that point, I was preparing to attend the National Democratic Convention in Los Angeles.

Leslie, Grace, and David accompanied me on that trip, which was marked by revelry, family fun, and, for me, political possibilities.

There was mission and purpose aplenty. Renewing old friends, enjoying new friends, focusing on the national issues—such was the brick and mortar of this pre-campaign. I felt called to run for the United States Senate. Chairing Bill Bradley's 2000 presidential campaign in Alabama, while falling short of its goal of getting him the Democratic nomination, nonetheless set the stage for my own Senate run two years later.

Jimmy Carter had proved that an evangelical, pro-life Democrat from the South could win politically. Perhaps it helped that he had a head full of hair, a smile the size of a half-moon, and was a farmer.

But that was in 1976, before conservative Democrats, especially white males, poured into the red-state column in a seismic political shift. In Alabama, that move was hastened by the Democratic party's 1983 hand-picking scheme and the Baxley-Graddick fiasco of 1986. No wonder Democratic Senator Richard Shelby, following his self-preservation instinct, switched parties in 1994. And Jeff Sessions, the incumbent I wanted to oust, was only the second Alabama Republican elected U.S. Senator since Reconstruction when he won in 1996. (Former P.O.W. Jeremiah Denton, also of Mobile, had been the first.)

I admit that it was bold to run for the U.S. Senate in 2002, without previously holding public office. My only direct political experience was my run for state attorney general in 1978. I was then the youngest of nine candidates, the most liberal in the race, and with 85 percent of the newspaper endorsements, the "darling of the press."

While my views on civil rights, consumer and environmental protection, health insurance reform, public education, social security, and medicare were then and are still doctrinaire Democrat, in the intervening years I had become more evangelical, charismatic, and pro-life.

My views on these spiritual matters were of sincere conviction, not political expediency. In 2000, as I moved toward a 2002 campaign, I realized my beliefs might hurt me in the Democratic primary, yet possibly help me in the general election. I decided the only course was to let the chips fall where they may.

Armchair critics might call my campaign presumptuous, pretentious, or foolhardy. They said much the same thing about John Edwards. Yet I reasoned that if Edwards, a plaintiff's lawyer from North Carolina, could successfully parlay his legal experience and progressive ideas into a seat in the U.S. Senate, why couldn't I, a plaintiff's lawyer from Alabama, do the same? Of course, Edwards is better-looking than I am— for that matter, than most other men in U.S. politics, the women in my family point out.

I might not have held public office, but I had accumulated a wealth of experience in public life. As a plaintiff's lawyer, I had years of practice speaking for people, being an advocate for their issues and causes, in courthouses all across my native state.

The practice of law is a profession, yes, but it is also a calling. And when you specialize in representing those who are often poor and powerless, you have a window into a lot of the same issues that are wrestled with in Congress.

My dear father, a retired Episcopal priest, had encouraged me into law practice in the first place. He also strongly supported my running for the U.S. Senate and was enormously helpful in the early stages of the race, despite his pressures of having to deal with my mother's advancing Alzheimer's disease.

SO, AS THIS BOOK was first being published in 2000, I was preparing to run for the Senate. Both my parents were still alive. The horrors of September 11, 2001, were yet unimaginable.

Obviously, a lot can happen in five years. Campaigns come and go. Beloved parents can leave this existence and move on to their next glorious one. Children grow older, marry, enter into their own new jobs and missions. New legal cases keep coming.

The first printing of *The People's Lawyer* sold out, a statistic which makes me proud, and its publisher did not want to reprint without an update. Although the book is a biography told in the third-person, it was an authorized one, and I had worked closely with and become friends with its writer, Carroll Dale Short, who has also moved on to other projects. The book's editor, Randall Williams, suggested that I just write the update myself, in the first person, which I have done in a new Part V of this edition. I am grateful to Randall for his editorial insight, sensitive nurturing of this project, and his friendship.

The 2005 update covers my parents and my family, the Senate campaign, the ongoing legal work of myself and my law partners, and the extracurricular activities of myself and my wife, Leslie.

The ups and downs, the curves and twists, the issues and personalities, and yes, the shenanigans of the campaign make for a beguiling story, especially if you like politics. Similarly, the catalog of cases gives a snapshot of some of the continuing issues which arise regularly and which have to be resolved within our legal system of judges, juries, evidence and advocates, all working conscientiously to find the truth, or as close to it as we can hope to get.

Much of the new material has involved local history, some Alabama history, and my cases with the Chicago Cubs and Richard Scrushy had national consequences.

Finally, at my age and stage, thirty-four years out of law school, fifty-eight years out of the womb, I have reached some conclusions about "the best things in life." I hope you, the reader, will appreciate what I have to say in this new section of the book.

Foreword to the 2000 Edition

I AM honored that I was asked to write a foreword to *The People's Lawyer,* the biography of Julian McPhillips, not only because of my long friendship with Julian, but also because of the important issues which have been at the heart of his life and legal service.

As well as Julian's biography, this book is a history of the socio-political evolution of Montgomery, Alabama. The city has been at the crossroads of some of the most critical points in the nation's history; and Julian was there, too, working in his own way toward a more just America.

As a lawyer, Julian has been a tireless advocate for the underdog, the underprivileged, the abandoned, and the abused. He takes on cases that other lawyers won't touch. And most impressively, at a time when lawyers seem to rank very low in the eyes of the public, Julian is the kind of advocate to whom other lawyers can point with pride.

Julian and I have known each other since 1964, when we met at Princeton University. We have remained in contact over the years, whether as fellow Princeton alumni, or through our involvement in Democratic Party politics. Together with his lovely wife, Leslie, Julian has shown a remarkable consistency in his commitment to social and economic justice.

Throughout my years in the Senate, I regularly corresponded with Julian — although almost every letter from Alabama concluded with him encouraging me to run for the Presidency! But when I decided to enter the race in December 1998, one of my first calls was to Julian. And Julian was as good as his word, organizing the state of Alabama, serving as my chairman there, and helping raise money throughout the South.

Whether standing up for those in need, or helping my campaign in the South, Julian's actions speak louder than words. His career has lived up to the highest ideals of public service, even though most of his career has been in the private practice of law. In these pages, we see the foundation of his determination and his character, and we see the colorful and complex backdrop of history and politics against which his life has unfolded.

I commend it and him to you.

Author's Preface to the 2000 Edition

ONE OF the first times I drove down to Montgomery to follow Julian around for a day, I turned off of Interstate 65 and — not uncharacteristically, for me — despite very clear directions, got hopelessly lost. As an alternative strategy, I consulted my computer-generated trip maps, and couldn't make heads nor tails of them, either. Finding places easily does not run in my family.

In desperation, I stopped to ask for advice at an auto-parts store in an older, and slightly run-down, part of Montgomery.

The man at the front counter was extremely cordial, even before I laid my cards on the table for him: "Sir? I'm lost real bad. I need some help."

"I'll try," he said. "What are you looking for?"

I searched my memory for some general landmark near Julian's and Leslie's house.

"I know it's in the Old Cloverdale neighborhood," I told him, confidently.

His facial expression showed he was very much underwhelmed by this clue. "Whew," he whistled, with both lips, around the cigarette stub in his mouth. "Cloverdale covers a whole lot of ground. What place are you talking about in particular?"

I wracked my brain for landmarks, again. "The Cloverdale Baptist Church?" I offered. I knew the historic church was less than a mile from Julian's and Leslie's house. If only I could get there, I would certainly remember the rest of the route.

The counter man shouted back into the depths of the warehouse shelves, where several young men were searching for auto parts to fill the computerized order lists they held in their hands: "Do any of ya'll know where the Cloverdale Baptist Church is?"

They all shook their heads in unison.

"What highway is that on?" the man asked me, with the patience of a lifelong mechanic accustomed to fending off false leads, automotive and otherwise. I surprised myself by remembering, without the help of notes.

"It's on East Fairview," I said triumphantly.

This response was clearly no improvement over "Old Cloverdale."

"Whew," the man said. "That East Fairview covers a whole lot of ground. What part of it are you taking about, in particular? Like a cross street, or something?"

I searched my memory, but this time came up blank. He took mercy on me, as career mechanics sometimes do.

"Just who are you going to see, in particular?" he asked me, in a confidential tone.

"Julian McPhillips," I told him.

The posture of both his face and dwindling cigarette showed great relief. He shouted to the ceiling-high shelves in the back of the warehouse, "He's going to see Julian."

The deliveryman nearest the counter strode up, nodding, his basket of auto parts in hand. "Are you going to Julian's house, or his office?"

"House," I said.

"Aw, hell!" the man said, with a wide smile, "I'm about to pass right by there. You want to follow me?"

I nodded my assent, and ten minutes later — thanks to a wave and a friendly honk from my escort — pulled into Julian's and Leslie's driveway, in the historic Old Cloverdale neighborhood.

MY FIRST meeting with Julian McPhillips, in the winter of 1998, came about through the most long-shot of scenarios. A long-time friend of mine in Tuscaloosa, Lydia Smith, was doing research for a paper on the history of Cullman, Alabama, and set out to track down Julian's father, the Rev. Julian McPhillips, Sr., for an interview. Directory assistance instead gave her the younger Julian's number.

After Julian supplied her with the Reverend's correct phone number, he and Lydia struck up a long conversation, as Southerners will, about their mutual roots in Cullman. He invited her and her family down to Montgomery for a visit, and for a tour of the Scott and Zelda Fitzgerald Museum, a historic home that he and Leslie had saved from the wrecking ball more than a decade earlier.

The following Monday, I got an excited phone call: "You've got to see this place," Lydia told me. I was not hard to convince. I arranged a meeting with Julian at the Museum, and ended up enjoying an afternoon of his and Leslie's considerable hospitality.

I confided to Julian that for a number of years I'd wanted to write a book-length work of narrative non-fiction in the tradition of some of my literary heroes of that genre, which included John McPhee, Tracy Kidder, and Dennis Covington, among others. I also told him I'd long been intrigued by the legal profession, and was curious about the day-to-day emotional life of a practicing trial attorney.

Over the next few weeks, as the pieces of the project began to fall into place, it was increasingly clear to me that I'd found my subject: an unlikely combination of political insider and folk hero, the equivalent of a walking paradox.

Looking back, it would be an understatement to say neither Julian nor I had a twinkling of what we were getting ourselves into with this little experiment.

The year-and-a-half odyssey that followed took me from small-town courthouse to big-city political rallies, from library and newspaper archives to a faith-healing church on the outskirts of Charlotte, North Carolina, and through far more hours of courtroom proceedings and intrigues than is healthy for a non-practitioner of the law.

Among the many things I learned on this journey is that the old aphorism "familiarity breeds contempt" is not always true. Friction, definitely. And in mine and Julian's case, that time spent together has also bred a complicated mix of close friendship interspersed with the necessary antagonisms of passionate advocacy (his for the law, mine for literature), as well as a deep and growing respect — albeit at times a grudging one — for one another's wildly divergent personalities, professional skills, and personal styles. Suffice it to say for now that the process was a major education for both of us, in every sense of the word. And one for which I'm grateful.

THIS BOOK would not have been possible without the hospitality, patience, and many kindnesses of Julian and Leslie, and the acceptance, openness, and faith of the Rev. Julian McPhillips and his wife Eleanor.

I am likewise thankful to Lydia Webb Smith for her continuing friendship, for contributing the Sewanee and Cullman chapters of this book, and for her advice, guidance, and listening ear throughout.

Thanks are also due to the wonderfully welcoming congregation of Christ the Redeemer Episcopal Church; to evangelists Bonnie and Mahesh Chavda and the congregation of All Nations Church; to Julian's friends and colleagues, including but not limited to Dr. Wesley Newton, Bobby Segall, Frank McPhillips, Page McKee, Les Faucette, and the indefatigable and imperturbable Amy Strickland; to Yvonne Crumpler, Jim Pate, and the staff of the Southern Collection of the Birmingham Public Library; to Suzanne La Rosa and Ben Beard of NewSouth Books; and to Randall Williams for his editorial integrity, wisdom, and surety of touch.

I'm also indebted to the writings of Dr. Wayne Flynt and Kathryn Tucker Windham on the history of Montgomery.

The People's Lawyer

A Case In the Making:
PeeWee Takes a Hit

PEEWEE'S Tuesday has been unusually good, so far. His life has taken some very wrong turns, but in trying to clean up his act, it dawned on him recently that since driving is one of his favorite things to do, he may as well get paid for it. He's just finished up a six-week training program to qualify for a Commercial Driver's License, and tomorrow, at the age of twenty-six, he starts interviewing around the Montgomery area for a job in the trucking business.

To celebrate the hopeful turn of events, PeeWee – whose real name is Reginald Jones – is having his car washed and is planning to go out with some friends in the evening. Residents of the midtown low-income housing project known as Trenholm Court don't have to go to the car wash – it comes to them. One of their neighbors makes extra money by going door-to-door with his pitch: "Wash your car? How about I wash your car?" he'll say, smiling. "Person just feels better, in a clean car."

PeeWee won't realize until several hours from now, when he's trying to help locate witnesses to what's about to happen, that he doesn't even know the man's name. "Everybody I know calls him by his nicknames," Reginald will tell his lawyer: "Just 'Lump' or 'Car Wash.'"

It's a clear day and milder than usual for January, even in the deep South, though a jacket still feels good. The sunlight is so brilliant on the bare trees that the limbs look as if they're ready to bud. It's a little after 3 p.m. and children are walking home from

elementary school. Reginald, while getting out his billfold, is looking at the gleaming blue hardtop and commenting to Lump on the
good job he's done.

But as he's counting off seven one-dollar bills in payment, he
hears a harsh voice behind him:

Hey! Come here . . .

Reginald spins around and sees a late-model black Suburban
jumping the curb. In the front seat are two grim-faced white men,
one of them pointing at him through the rolled-down window.

"The first thing I thought was 'drive-by,'" Reginald will recount
later. In any event, he takes off running. As he sprints down the
sidewalk, the driver of the Suburban wheels the vehicle around in
pursuit. To evade him, Reginald leaves the sidewalk and runs
through the grass courtyards that separate the rows of one-story
apartment buildings. But as he turns the corner of one building, he
spots another white man, this one in some type of uniform, racing
toward him on foot.

Stop! a voice shouts.

Reginald takes off running again.

"I know I shouldn't have," he'll say later. "But it happened so fast
I wasn't thinking very clear." Actually, he *was* thinking clearly
about one thing – a couple of weeks earlier, he'd had a heated
argument with his older sister and afterward she'd signed a warrant on him, and he now understandably assumes that particular
piece of trouble may be what this is about.

Reginald looks over his shoulder for an escape route, but sees
only the wide brick front of one of the buildings.

Suddenly, from the opposite direction, the roar of an engine
catches his attention. The Suburban he saw earlier has now leaped
across the curb onto the grass and is quickly bearing down on him.

Surrounded, he backs up against a small tree and raises both
hands high in the air.

Out of the corner of his eye he sees neighbors watching from
their doors, a crowd beginning to gather outside. But as he glances
back toward the moving Suburban, what he sees is bad: it's only a

few feet away from him, and it isn't slowing down. The truck hits him, driving him into the tree.

The next thing he remembers is looking up and seeing the dark underside of the vehicle's chassis where blue sky should be. The Suburban's axle has both him and the tree pinned to the ground. He feels a burning numbness in his lower legs, and he can't move them to crawl away.

"The driver jumped out, then," Reginald remembers, "and started hollering at me. He was saying 'nigger' this, and 'nigger' that, and telling me I'd better get up."

"I hollered back at him, 'How the hell I'm gone get up with your car sitting on top of me?" and then finally he gets in and backs it off of me, so I can move. And all this time the other policemen are just looking at him and shaking their heads, like, 'Man, I can't believe you done this.'"

What comes afterward is mostly a blur to Reginald, until an ambulance arrives. At the emergency room, X-rays determine that, miraculously, he has no broken bones; but from the waist down he's badly banged up and bruised, his legs too much in pain to bear his weight. On a nearby table are his corduroy pants, caked with dirt and blood, that the paramedics had to cut away to treat him.

When things settle down a bit, Reginald phones his older brother Spence, who works as a medical assistant at the same hospital. "They tried to kill me, man," he tells Spence. "They run over me and then they didn't arrest me. They didn't even charge me with nothing."

(Later, the Police Department will say that the officer saw money changing hands and assumed the two black men were transacting a drug deal.)

Spence tells him he needs to find a lawyer.

"I don't know no lawyers," Reginald says.

Spence says he'll ask around.

A COUPLE of miles away, on tree-shaded South Perry Street, the late afternoon sun glazes a conservative white wooden sign that reads

McPhillips, Shinbaum & Gill, L.L.P. A former residence, built in 1870, the three-story brick building is one of many professional offices along the street. Nearby is a black Pentecostal church, and less than ten blocks away are the gleaming white buildings of the State Capitol complex, the church where Martin Luther King, Jr., preached, and the First White House of the Confederacy, a wooden frame building – now a museum – where Jefferson Davis briefly lived at the beginning of the Civil War.

In a front corner office, the firm's founding partner, Julian L. McPhillips, Jr., shuffles a stack of pink phone messages and sets about returning calls. Before the day is out, he will have spoken with an Episcopal priest, a college history professor, a wrestling coach, a Christian faith healer, a presidential candidate, the executive director of the city's Scott & Zelda Fitzgerald Museum, members of a Princeton University alumni reunion committee, an abortion counselor, an art dealer, a high school honors student, and a South American missionary – even a number of actual law clients.

Even in a city where the eccentricities of politicians are legendary, McPhillips often seems a walking contradiction: a former member of state government who has won high-profile cases against three Alabama governors, several cabinet members, a state attorney general, a U.S. Congressman, and the city of Montgomery's police department and its mayor.

He's also a small-town white Southerner from a family of civil rights activists who have rubbed shoulders with Martin Luther King's family and Mother Teresa; an activist in the Vietnam War peace movement who attended military school; a supposed member of the establishment who takes on government agencies and large corporations for age, race, and gender discrimination; a political maverick and Ivy League college grad who's a fervent anti-abortion crusader; a scholar of international affairs who helped found a local charismatic church that practices faith healing; a tenacious former prosecutor who questions capital punishment in many cases; a wrestling champion who's also a patron of the arts; and coincidentally, in his spare time, as this was written, Alabama campaign manager for then-presidential candidate Bill Bradley.

Over the years, McPhillips's predilection for taking the side of the underdog against powerful government and business interests has prompted news commentators to refer to him as "the private attorney general," "the public watchdog," and "the people's lawyer." Columnist Joe McFadden of the *Montgomery Advertiser* wrote: "His heart is with the cases that bug the establishment, that right some wrong, and that rarely pay enough to attract most lawyers."

Another columnist, profiling him ("A Good Battle Delights Julian McPhillips") in Columbia University Law School's alumni magazine in 1984, said:

> McPhillips is an imposing man. At first glance, in fact, he seems almost *too* imposing; in some ways, he just doesn't *look* like a lawyer. He stands about an inch over six feet, is powerfully built, and he advances straight at you with a slight stoop of the shoulders and gleam in his eye that calls to mind Robert Duvall's chipper helicopter commander from the movie *Apocalypse Now*. In fact, McPhillips *looks* like he might well be a lieutenant colonel in the Marines, a happy warrior ready to cry havoc and cheerfully let slip the dogs of war.
>
> Looks are not entirely deceiving, but in McPhillips's case, their testimony must be weighed against his manner. He is, a new acquaintance quickly notices, almost insistently courteous, betraying traces of Southern gallantry in his demeanor and accent. And, while he observes of himself that he "likes standing up to bullies," he insists that he is now – and has always been – a mild, peaceable fellow.
>
> Hearing him talk, a listener might well conclude that McPhillips is a stickler for both detail and proper behavior. Each impression – that he loves a good struggle, and that he insists upon decorum – is correct. Consider for example, his college athletic career and his behavior during the Columbia student unrest in the spring of 1970. At Princeton, where he earned his bachelor's degree in history, McPhillips distinguished himself at wrestling, a sport

which pits brute force against brute force, cunning against cunning, with such carefully restrictive rules that its injury rate is lower than basketball's.

McPhillips flourished as a wrestler. In college, he was an All-American heavyweight and was undefeated in four years of league competition; he continued to wrestle while at Columbia Law School and afterward, placing fourth in the National Amateur Athletic Union Championship tournament during his last year of law school and almost made the Olympic team in his first year as an associate at the Wall Street law firm of Davis Polk & Wardwell.

At Columbia, McPhillips found himself supporting many of the goals espoused by student radicals, but fiercely opposed to their disregard for what he saw as the very basis of civilized behavior. Looking back, he characterizes himself as having had "leftist sympathies and a rightist manner." He took to working for a greater student voice in university government and, as chairman of the Law School Senate, became chairman of the Law School Coalition Against the War after the invasion of Cambodia. "We took a much more mature, constructive, and peaceful tack than the undergraduates did," he recalls . . .

In 1998, McPhillips was the first attorney in Alabama – and possibly the nation – to officially represent in court what he called "the ultimate underdog," an unborn child whose under-age mother had decided to have an abortion. In earlier years, he successfully represented a different type of underdog – scoring acquittals in all five murder cases he tried, four of which involved capital murder charges, which could have put the accused in Alabama's electric chair.

McPhillips has also been a major thorn in the side of former Montgomery mayor Emory Folmar, whom he's battled over many issues, including an alleged pattern of police misconduct. During one city election season a friend of both men jokingly asked Folmar if he had received a campaign contribution yet from Julian. Folmar reportedly responded, "I'd rather accept money from the Viet Cong."

The long-term mayor was both mercurial and a loose cannon, a condition which sometimes made even his supporters wince when he was in command of a microphone. As the local chief of President Bush's re-election campaign in 1992, Folmar once told a Montgomery crowd to consider the alternative:

"If Bill Clinton were to somehow get elected," Folmar told the crowd, "he would pick Jesse Jackson as his running mate, Julian McPhillips as his attorney general, and they would buy everybody in the United States a new Cadillac."

But still fresh in Julian's memory is the occasion, during his 1978 campaign for Alabama attorney general, when one of his opponents attacked him as " . . . another wealthy Northeastern establishment liberal, just like the Kennedys."

Today, Julian shakes his head in disbelief and laughs about it. But at the time, for a boy who grew up in the north Alabama town of Cullman, this particular political salvo was one of several attacks that carried a sting, but which he chose to rebut with a shrug and a chuckle.

"True, I did go to Princeton and Columbia Law School, and true, I'm not presently hurting for money" – though nothing on the scale of the Kennedys, he quickly adds. "But the one thing *nobody* can call me," Julian says passionately, "is a doctrinaire liberal."

The bombastic rhetoric of his opponents during stump speeches is one of the few aspects of the troubling 1978 campaign McPhillips laughs about. In an election plagued by "irregularities" at the polls, McPhillips's approximate 6,000-vote lead over state senate president Joe Fine on election night mysteriously evaporated into a 5,000-vote deficit three days later, costing McPhillips his run-off spot. It also landed him more than $40,000 in personal debt, and a recount – which he eventually decided against – would have cost another $200,000.

In a different – and bizarre – turn of events, winning candidate Charles Graddick catapulted over both Fine and McPhillips in the waning weeks of the campaign by proclaiming his rabid support of capital punishment. At one point, Graddick was quoted, "I'll cram them into the electric chair and fry them until their eyeballs pop out, until their skin burns, and smoke comes out of their ears."

WHETHER Alabama's capital city is a regional hotbed (no pun intended) of get-tough-on-crime sympathizers is still a matter of debate, but a tremendous amount of press coverage during recent years seems to weigh in on the side of the critics.

In an influential series of investigative reports by the *Birmingham Post-Herald* in May 1991, staff writer Nick Patterson noted that, "In some respects, the city of Montgomery is as genteel as Southern hospitality and magnolias. But beneath its charm lies something less genteel: allegations of police brutality."

"Many public officials, including the county district attorney and assistant state attorney general, say they have no evidence to substantiate claims that Montgomery's police department has a brutality problem. But many other officials cite a growing list of allegations as evidence of such a problem . . ."

One article in the series was dominated by a poignant four-column picture taken by staff photographer Karim Shamsi-Basha at a Montgomery funeral home. The photo showed an elderly black woman sobbing beside the casket of her grandson, a thirty-seven-year old mental patient, whom she claimed was wrongfully killed by city police officers.

After Patterson's list of the most recent, and most blatant, citizen complaints, he quoted various attorneys on the subject. David Schoen says, "My experience indicates to me that Montgomery has the most brutal department and seems to be the least interested in doing anything about it."

And Julian told Patterson, "There's a serious problem, especially among young officers, both black and white, who come in with the mentality of 'Hey, this is just like the military. We're going to kick some butt and teach them a lesson.' It's a sort of macho, Rambo mentality that is usually rewarded by higher-ups in the department and in the city administration."

McPhillips and Schoen were by no means alone in their allegations. Former Montgomery City Councilman Mark Gilmore said, at the time, "We have some problems. There's no use in denying that. We get this every day from our constituents. We get people saying the police beat them up, and saying they don't trust them (the police)."

State Representative Alvin Holmes, a Montgomery resident, agreed, "The mayor of the city of Montgomery has a military-type personality, like the Montgomery Police Department is at war with the public, or at war with the blacks."

The U.S. Civil Rights Commission did a study of police and community relations in Montgomery. Their 1986 report said the study was prompted by "the alarming number of complaints received by committee members alleging abusive and discriminatory conduct by members of the Montgomery Police Department." The mayor took exception to some of the details of the study, but wouldn't comment on others.

Charlie Graddick – who was, by this time, serving as the county's district attorney – likewise downplayed the significance of the Commission's study. "I haven't had any reason to believe that there's any evidence at all of police brutality," Graddick told the press. "If somebody presented me evidence, you can rest assured it would be scrutinized very closely and appropriate action would be taken. But that hasn't been the case."

At one point, the study cited the appointment of Police Chief John Wilson as a significant step forward for community relations. Others disputed that contention, pointing out that Wilson had been quickly catapulted from Folmar's personal bodyguard, to corporal, then police chief, and claimed he was not only insensitive to minority concerns, but condoned, along with Folmar, the practice of rough-house tactics by the police.

The chief refused to comment when approached in 1991 by the *Post-Herald* reporter. But he did furnish Patterson with copies of departmental memos he had written. One was from the previous March, in the wake of the Rodney King case:

"The acts shown on national television ... hurt me deeply," Wilson wrote, "as they should everyone connected with police work ... We have had our share of trouble with officers straying outside the standards set for this department. Some officers have been convicted, some are awaiting trial and some are still being investigated ..."

"If any officer of this department has any doubt of the consequences of an act such as the one shown on national television, let me set the matter straight right now. Punishment for such actions will be swift and sure, including criminal prosecution."

A second memo, from 1987, said he had heard that complaints by victims of alleged brutality within the department were largely from black citizens.

As Patterson concluded his report, "While progress arguably has been made, some observers say Montgomery has a long way to go to lose its negative reputation."

After the *Post-Herald's* investigative series, the issue died down somewhat. But never for very long.

Of the many claims of brutality and excessive force McPhillips has filed on behalf of his clients over the years, one 1995 case involved five high-school honor students from Prattville (all black) driving to a Scholar's Bowl competition who were stopped by police, searched, and made to lie on the ground at gunpoint – one of them on top of an ant bed. Police later said they were acting on a tip from an informer that the students were transporting drugs, but the person who had given the supposed tip was never found or identified.

On the evening of January 13, 1999, it's clear that the issue still hasn't gone away. The lead-off team on the nightly TV news shows Julian and Reginald Jones sitting behind a row of microphones at a press conference, holding up for display the torn and soiled trousers Reginald was wearing when the automobile hit him.

"It's a case of adding insult to injury," Julian tells the reporters.

"Or injury to insult, if you will. He had his hands up, he was standing still, the Suburban was yards away. The police officer had several choices at that point. He could have gotten out and shouted, 'You're under arrest.' He could have pulled his gun if he wanted to, and apprehended him. Mr. Jones certainly wasn't going anywhere. But instead, the officer chose to run over him."

If Julian comes across as calm and confident with TV reporters, there's a reason. He's gotten more airtime, over the years, than any other private attorney in town. His record so far is seven interviews on six straight nights (in April 1985) – one night he was interviewed twice, on different cases – on a Montgomery TV station, the state's largest NBC affiliate.

(Once a local judge, who was hoping to have a private hearing on a particular matter, looked down the building's hallway and saw TV reporters setting up their gear. "All right," he wearily chided, tongue-in-cheek, the two attorneys who were to appear before him. "Who called the TV stations? Julian's not even involved in this case.")

"McPhillips is seeking $100,000 in damages," the reporter is saying in a voice-over as the camera returns to Reginald, "and perhaps more in punitive damages. He's called upon Mayor Folmar, the district attorney, and the attorney general to investigate."

Now Reginald is describing the incident on camera. "It was like . . . *bam*," he says, slamming his fist into the palm of his hand. "He didn't just bump me, he ran over me. All I could think of was, 'He's trying to kill me.'"

The TV anchor says, "And we'll be back, after these messages . . ."

JULIAN TAKES his status as a public figure in Montgomery seriously. His home telephone number is, however unexpectedly, listed in the phone book. But, he points out, so is his supposed arch-rival Emory Folmar's. Julian gives Emory a lot of points for that concession.

Julian also seems to have an encyclopedic recall of names, faces, and family histories, which comes in very handy for a politician.

Today, as he and associate Sim Pettway – a clean-cut, stylish young black man in his late twenties – grab a quick plate lunch at the Farmer's Market Restaurant with client Reginald Jones and his brother Spence, other diners wave occasionally from nearby tables, or stop by to say hello before paying their checks. Julian introduces them around, one and all, briefly bragging on some recent accomplishment in their career and/or thanking them for their help with some past project.

Afterward, Julian, Sim, and the Jones brothers drive the short distance to the Trenholm Court housing project for a walk-through of the area where Reginald was run over, several weeks earlier.

It's a sunny, pleasantly mild day, and a few of the trees are budding out. Reginald, walking somewhat unsteadily on a new cane, leads the way to the large grass courtyard where the incident happened.

In early afternoon the place at first looks deserted, but eventually a couple of neighbors peer out their windows, see the men, and drift out hoping for news of Reginald's case. Despite the city's foot-dragging on the release of documents Julian has asked for, a few facts have come to light: one of the first policemen on the scene has been identified as a Corporal Steelman, and the officer driving the Suburban when it hit Reginald is a Corporal DeJohn. The latter has been the subject of earlier complaints of excessive force, which include firing his pistol into the automobile of a man who was driving while intoxicated.

Reginald stands looking at the ground, shaking his head.

"What are you thinking, Reggie?" Sim asks him.

"There ain't even no trace of it left," Reginald answers. "There's no sign of what happened. See, this is where the tree was . . ." He jabs the cane in the dirt, where the stump of a small tree has been cut almost even with the dry surface of the soil. A passerby would never notice it.

"The tree you were backed up against when you were run over," Julian supplies. Reginald nods. He goes through the scenario from the beginning again, pointing across the way to where his freshly washed car had been sitting when the officers first drove up, and describing the route that he ran before being backed against the tree. Julian and Sim listen, take notes, ask questions.

After several minutes, there seems nothing left to be discussed. Reginald looks at the tiny stump again, shaking his head.

"So," Sim says brightly, to Spence, "your brother tells me you work as a medical assistant. Do you like it?

"Yeah, I do," Spence says. "But I'm still going to school, some. You know, trying to work my way up in my job."

"It's a good field to be in," says Sim. "No matter what the economy does, there'll never be a shortage of people getting sick or hurt."

To which a bystander adds dryly, "Not as long as officer DeJohn is on the job, anyway."

The four men in the courtyard share a spontaneous, rich, freeing laughter. There is no way for them to know that it will be the last time they laugh together for a very long while.

I.

Roots and History

1

The Forebears

I F THE tragedy known as the American Civil War had a "ground zero," you can stand beside it on the west portico of the state capitol, where a bronze star, no larger than a dinner plate, marks the exact spot where Jefferson Davis stood in 1861 when he took the oath of office as the first (and only) president of the Confederate States of America.

Formerly a high-ranking United States Senator, and Secretary of War under President Franklin Pierce, Davis resigned from the Senate when the coming war appeared inevitable. He moved back to his home in Mississippi, then to Montgomery to form the new secessionist government.

Today, the view across the hillside is sedate office buildings, parking meters, and the cars of government employees. On the day that Davis took his oath, this same broad space was filled with cheering crowds. Few people remember, now, that Herman Frank Arnold's Southern American Band was the group chosen to play for the occasion.

A couple of months before, H. F. Arnold had attended a minstrel show where he'd heard a new song that he couldn't get out of his head. He contacted the song's composer, Daniel Decatur Emmett, and got the rights to orchestrate it for the Confederacy's inauguration ceremony.

The name of the song was "Dixie." And the rest, as they say, is history.

What history *doesn't* tell you—or at least, you have to search very hard for it—is that "Dixie" was also a favorite song of Abraham Lincoln's. When the Union's military band took requests, even in the darkest days, Lincoln often asked for "Dixie." He once said, "It's got the catchiest tune I've ever heard."

Many commentators ask, "What is it, about the Civil War?" Millions of people come on pilgrimages to battleground national parks. Countless groups from across the U.S. hold annual re-enactments of portions of the war, complete with horses, uniforms, and firearms. There are more volumes in libraries about the Civil War than on any other subject except the Bible.

Among the Earliest Settlers

Julian McPhillips, both by ancestry and interest, is a product of those early times. His forebears settled in Alabama before it became a state.

His great-great-grandfather James McPhillips, Sr. landed in Mobile during the 1850s, having emigrated as a boy from Ireland to New York during the disastrous potato blight of the 1840s. During the Civil War, James served as a baker in the Confederate Army, stationed in Mobile and at Fort Morgan. Julian has copies of paperwork reflecting James's Civil War assignments.

As the original McPhillips in Alabama, and a good Catholic, James attended the Cathedral of Mobile, where in 1867 he met an attractive young organist named Rose Woodworth. They were married within the year.

And history took its course. Between 1868 and 1891, James and Rose had ten children, with four sons and four daughters living into adulthood, giving rise to eight branches of the family. By 1996, their number had swollen to 435 descendants in thirty-five states and three foreign countries. Three of the sons—James Jr., Joe, and Harry—remained in Mobile, running the prosperous family wholesale and retail grocery and liquor business. Genealogical research by Julian and his family reflect that approximately ninety-five percent of the McPhillips families in Alabama in the late 1990s descended from one of these three branches.

The oldest son, James McPhillips, Jr., became Julian's great-grandfather. In 1894 he married Petronella "Mare" Greenwood, who was descended on her mother's side from a Spanish lady, Rosena Sierra, who was descended from earlier Spanish settlers of Florida, when Mobile was a Spanish territory. Sierra's forebears included Don Manuel Gonzales, an early Spanish colonial governor of Florida. Sierra's father, Ignacio Sierra, the 1790s' harbormaster of Mobile-Pensacola, is the subject of a 1987 biography. On her mother's side, Rosena Sierra's forebears included French explorer Jean Baptiste Baudreau and a Choctaw Indian named Ocqui, daughter of a chieftain.

James McPhillips, Jr., and "Mare" had three sons: Manning, Julian and Jamo. The middle son, Julian Byrnes McPhillips, became Julian's grandfather. He was—due to a mispronunciation by the family's maid—nicknamed "Jutes." (Grandfather Jutes was delighted when Eleanor and Julian Sr. in 1946 nicknamed their first son "Jutsy" in his honor. Far less thrilled, says Julian, was his fiancé Leslie when she learned of the family nickname. She remarked that it sounded like the name of a French poodle.)

Julian B. "Jutes" McPhillips was a shrimp exporter during the 1920s and 1930s and a vegetable canning executive from the forties to the seventies, thus being the third generation of the McPhillips family in the food business in Alabama. He married Lilybelle McGowin, who was descended from a Scottish family that came to Georgia in the mid-1700s and migrated to Alabama in the late 1700s and early 1800s. Her grandfather, Jacob Lewis McGowin, served in the Confederate Army. Her father, Ernest Lenwood McGowin, was a lumber baron from Brewton, Alabama.

Thus we reach the three Julians who carried forth the McPhillips name in Alabama in the twentieth century: Julian Byrnes, born in Mobile in 1897; Julian Lenwood, Sr., born in Mobile in 1920; and Julian Lenwood, Jr., born in Birmingham in 1946.

JULIAN'S mother's ancestors include ten Revolutionary War soldiers and several Confederate soldiers, including Howard Poole, whose family is now fifteen generations old in America. Several played significant roles in the colonial and pioneer days. Great-great-grandfather David Davidson Sanderson grew up in Perry County, Alabama, in the 1820s and 1830s, and graduated from Princeton's college in 1845 and its seminary in 1848. Sanderson ministered at First Presbyterian Church of Eutaw, in Greene County's plantation-based economy, from 1860 to 1891.

Together with his best friend Charles Alan Stillman, Sanderson co-founded the Tuscaloosa Black Preacher's College, now Stillman College, just after the Civil War.

In 1987, a distant relative gave Julian original portraits of both the co-founders, and Julian donated Stillman's portrait to the college—the only likeness of the founder that the college has. The artist, by coincidence, was none other than Julian's great-grandmother Ellen Gilmer Bocock, originally of Virginia.

Julian's maternal great-great-grandfather, Henry Flood Bocock, was clerk of the Appomatox County Courthouse just before Lee's surrender to Grant in 1865. Henry's brother Thomas was speaker of the Confederate House of

Representatives, and another Bocock brother served as a Virginia Supreme Court Justice during the Civil War. Yet another brother, Willis Bocock, was the attorney general of Virginia during the Civil War, after which he moved to Alabama and now rests in a cemetery in Greensboro in Hale County. All four were the sons of John Thomas Bocock (1773–1845), Julian's triple great-grandfather.

In the 1880s Ellen Gilmer Bocock married James Alexander Sanderson of Eutaw, Alabama, and they moved to French Camp, Mississippi, setting in motion the journey of Julian's maternal family to New Orleans.

Ellen and James Sanderson's daughter Stuart—Julian's maternal grandmother—was an Annie Oakley type. She met Frank Dixon at Ole Miss during the nineteen teens, where they both enjoyed William Faulkner's friendship. Grandfather Dixon founded the Great Southern Box Company, which merged with Continental Can Company in the late 1920s. A smoker, he died of lung cancer in 1937 at forty-five, but Stu lived to be ninety, before dying in 1987. Grandmother Stu was a very positive influence on her grandson Julian, he says, inspiring him with her "generous and kind spirit."

Stuart and Frank Dixon were, of course, the parents of Eleanor Dixon, born in New Orleans in 1920, who brings the maternal line down to her second child, Julian L. McPhillips, Jr.

DESPITE a lifelong love of history and genealogy, Julian says he's amused by Southerners' propensity to attach great social value to their lineage. He doesn't hesitate to point out, though, that his distant blood relatives include Winston Churchill, Robert E. Lee, Patrick Henry, and James Buchanan. It was not until April 2000, through a genealogist brother-in-law, that Julian discovered his paternal great-great-great-grandfather George Woodworth (father of Rose McPhillips) was directly descended from James Chilton of *The Mayflower*, making Julian a Mayflower descendent as well. (Julian's father's take on this development was, "I guess this means we must be related to everyone else in the country.")

The younger Julian also enjoys telling the story of how a family friend, an Episcopal priest in Birmingham, once nominated Julian—despite some resistance on Julian's part—for membership in the Sons of the Revolution.

The membership application had apparently stayed on hold for most of a year when the priest called, embarrassed, and said Julian had been blackballed. It seems they didn't question his credentials, but some of the members strongly disliked Julian's political leanings. The priest and another family friend resigned from the Sons of the Revolution in protest.

The Immediate Forebears: A Sixty-Year Romance

This much of the story, at least, is undisputed:

On a muggy September day in New Orleans, in 1939, Tulane University held its first day of classes for the school year. Into a classroom of the College of Commerce walked two juniors: a nineteen-year-old girl from New Orleans and a nineteen-year-old boy from Mobile. Being strangers, they nodded at one another politely and found their seats—which, purely by chance, happened to be in the same part of the room.

The boy, seeing a friend already seated, said "Hi, Gus." The girl, seeing a friend already seated, said "Hi, Gus." Or, vice versa, depending on who tells the story.

After this point, the accounts vary.

And although two of the professions—theology and law—that are recurring threads woven through the McPhillips family tree both have as their goal, via different approaches, the arrival at truth, the only person in a position to know the exact details of the Tulane scenario maintains that his memory is permanently fuzzy on that point.

Gus Lorber—a fraternity brother (DKE) of Julian Lenwood McPhillips, Sr. at Tulane and a former high school classmate of Eleanor Dixon—does remember that after he introduced the two of them that morning, he got to do very little talking for the rest of the day. He wouldn't necessarily label the incident "love at first sight," but to say that Julian and Eleanor were "comfortable" together was an understatement.

They coincidentally began taking Coke breaks at the same time, soon discovered they lived within blocks of one another and began walking home together in the afternoons. They also had a great excuse—their class assignments—for long talks on the phone.

But they were far from intellectual clones. Their opinions on lecture material often varied significantly (another good reason for extended conversations) and their classroom personalities were virtually opposite. Julian eagerly took part in the discussions, while Eleanor mostly kept her own counsel and took meticulous notes.

When grades were returned on the first exam, Eleanor's was higher. Slightly. But though Julian could be competitive on occasion, he found this disparity no problem. Life was good.

"A romantic interest? Oh, no," Eleanor would say, some forty years later, when she and Julian sat down to write their joint autobiography, *The Drummer's Beat: Our Life and Times*. Technically, both were "pinned" at the time to sweethearts at other universities.

Then came Halloween, a special tradition for the DKEs. Julian "surprised himself" by inviting Eleanor to go with him to the party, and she "surprised herself" by accepting.

As they dressed for the party—Julian as a country farmer, in overalls and a shaggy straw hat, Eleanor as a peasant girl in a pink and white dirndl skirt—they had no idea they were setting off on a joint odyssey that would take them a number of times around the world—as activists for causes ranging from peace to civil rights—through some of the most tumultuous years of American history, and through a series of tragedies and triumphs that even a gifted screenwriter would have found hard to envision.

What they *did* know was that the party's punchbowl that night seemed to hold a special attraction for all the guests. The flavor was "purple passion," served in a huge bowl with orange slices floating on top, and the taste had an unusual edge. A few people winked and made obscure references to a secret ingredient.

Meanwhile, Julian's farmer costume was quickly becoming a hit—as was his thick Alabama accent, which students from some parts of the country had never heard in person. When they asked him about his background, he started to give them the straight facts of his Mobile upbringing but instead found himself spinning taller and taller tales (in retrospect, helped along by the fact that the punch's secret ingredient was pure grain alcohol) about growing up in the remote town of "Chittlinswitch, Alabama."

After Julian had walked Eleanor home that night (no kiss at the door, just a friendly good-bye) she woke up her mother to tell her, "I don't believe I've ever had so much fun."

JULIAN Sr.'s and Eleanor's wedding photo — dated November 4, 1941 — shows, against a background of greenery, a confident young man in black tuxedo and white tie, his arm interlinked with a beaming, dark-haired young woman in lacy dress and veil. She is slightly tilting her head toward him, and firmly holding her bouquet in just the right spot to balance the composition of the photograph.

The promise of their lives together seemed limitless—and continued to, for thirty-three days. Julian and Eleanor were attending a friend's debutante party in Houston on a Sunday afternoon when news came over the radio that Japanese planes had bombed Pearl Harbor.

"It was a while before we could talk to each other about the war," Eleanor remembers, "even though in the back of our minds we both knew it was virtually certain he'd have to go."

It was during their Christmas shopping that year that they first broke the ice on the subject. They knew it was one of the most difficult decisions they would ever have to make.

Conscience and Duty: Eleanor And Julian Sr. in the War Years

In the wake of Pearl Harbor, the fighting steadily escalated on many fronts. Though they didn't talk often about the subject, Eleanor and Julian Sr. both knew that his draft notice might arrive at any time. Their emotions were badly torn—not just from the uncertainty that the country, and the world, faced in the years ahead, but also by the fact that while Julian felt obligated to help defend the U.S. after the unconscionable Pearl Harbor attack, as Eleanor writes in their memoir, "The thought of having to kill another human being was abhorrent to him."

The compromise they struck in this moral dilemma was that Julian would volunteer for Navy duty, where there would be less chance for person-to-person combat. He was appointed to the rank of Ensign, and his commission was dated January 28, Eleanor's twenty-second birthday. His initial training would be at the Naval Gun Factory in Washington, D.C. They had thirty days to prepare for leaving.

It was about this time that they learned Eleanor was expecting their first child, which changed their plans considerably. The doctor advised her against taking a long trip, and they also found that accommodations in Washington for couples were almost non-existent. As a result, Eleanor would stay with Julian's parents in Metairie, Louisiana, just outside of New Orleans, for the six weeks of his training.

At the Navy school, Julian found that he was one of thirty naval officers who would be assigned to supervise the arming of merchant vessels in the principal ports of the U.S. When the time came for assignments, Julian happened to be away from the barracks. Upon his return, his heart sank to learn that the other officers had already chosen their ports and he would be left with the one assignment nobody else had wanted.

To his surprise, by grace and chance the assignment happened to be Mobile, the city where he'd grown up. "The other officers told him he'd be disappointed with the duty there," Eleanor remembers. "They had no idea how much it meant to him to return to his hometown at that point."

But once there, he found it wasn't the same city he had left, years before. The housing shortage meant there was a waiting list, and in the meantime they had to stay in Julian's grandmother's apartment. A heat wave that summer, in the days before air-conditioning, made for miserable weeks late in Eleanor's pregnancy. It was a lonely time as well, as nearly all Julian's friends and cousins were away fighting the war.

Their apartment was ready in late September. At around midnight on October 13, 1942, Eleanor went into labor and was taken to Mobile Infirmary. After a hard night, their daughter was born at 8 a.m. the next day. They named her Sandra Stuart. As she was the first great-grandchild in either family, her arrival was big news, and relatives came from far away to take a look.

On the war front, though, things were not going well for the U.S. It was Julian's job to place hundreds of Navy men on former merchant ships bound for the fighting. With increasing frequency, many of the ships never made it, being torpedoed by German submarines with great losses of life.

By the next May, Julian and several of his colleagues decided that they couldn't, in good conscience, keep sending young men out on high-risk assignments while they themselves stayed safely in port. Julian asked for duty on a destroyer. It was immediately approved, and he was transferred to a naval training school at Treasure Island, near San Francisco.

With their household belongings in storage, and a small blue Ford Club Coupe jammed with baby equipment and supplies, they set out on the seven-day drive to San Francisco. It would be the first of many such scenarios, as Julian's assignments took the family to Miami, then Norfolk, Virginia, then Orange, Texas—where Julian would join the crew of a newly built destroyer-escort.

From Texas, Julian's ship would take a shake-down cruise to Bermuda for more training, then return to Boston for its first battle assignment, as one of a convoy of vessels headed for the war zone in Italy. Eleanor left Sandy with Julian's parents and flew to Boston for his return.

"We had a wonderful hotel room downtown," Julian Sr. recalls. "The officers could spend nights on shore with their wives, and then report aboard ship each morning." But it was also a stressful and anxious time. For reasons of security, none of the crew knew in advance when the ship would leave for the war. Each morning when the couple said good-bye, they both knew all too well it might be for a very long time.

But once again, fate appeared to be on their side. One day Eleanor received a phone call from the executive officer of the ship, Herbert Shriver—the brother of Sargeant Shriver, whom they would know in later years as director of the Peace Corps and a vice-presidential candidate in the McGovern campaign—telling her that Julian had been detached from the ship to undergo eight weeks of specialized training at St. Simon's Island, Georgia.

When the U.S.S. *Edwin A. Howard* sailed for the Mediterranean, Julian and Eleanor's car was once again loaded and on the road—first to New Orleans to pick up Sandy, and then on to Sea Island, near St. Simon's, where they had been able to rent a large beach house facing the Atlantic.

Eleanor remembers that time as a halcyon stretch. After Julian finished each day's training, the two would sometimes dance under the stars until midnight, go swimming in the ocean, and lie peacefully on the beach. But it was a time that had to run out, and it did.

Julian completed his training just two days before the wedding of his only brother, Warren, in Birmingham. Eleanor and Julian drove into town just in time for the rehearsal of his "best man" duties. After the next day's ceremony, though, Julian had to leave the wedding supper early to catch a plane to New York, in preparation for shipping out to the South Pacific. Eleanor and Sandy, after seeing him off at the airport, boarded a train to New Orleans.

ELEANOR and Julian exchanged long, detailed letters during his time in the Pacific theatre. But the medium was less than ideal. Sometimes his ship would go for weeks without spotting land, and his letters home would pile up until the crew made port again. Eleanor remembers the days when the accumulated mail would arrive as being "like Christmas: sometimes there was a dozen or more at once." But there was also the eerie feeling of getting envelopes that had already been opened, and which had long passages blanked out, courtesy of military censors.

Some of the most memorable letters were Julian's descriptions of what it was like to "stand watch" on the top deck of the ship, along with the sky and ocean. His favorite time to stand watch was nights, he told her, when he would often feel a transcendent peace and calm, even during a storm—a foreshadowing, in retrospect, of the spiritual path he would take in coming years.

Once in a violent typhoon with waves twice the height of the ship, two vessels in his group sank without a trace. It was the closest he would come to death during his tour of duty, though there were other dangerous assignments: skirmishes with Japanese submarines and aircraft during the invasion of the Philippines, and the invasion of Borneo, in which his ship was one of the few sent to pave the way of the main force, putting it under fire by the Japanese shore battery.

It was one of the most intense periods of the war for Eleanor, as well. Julian's letters stopped coming for six weeks, and as she read accounts of the invasion in *Time* magazine, she remembers an almost supernatural certainty that he was part of the operation, though censorship regulations prevented him from telling her.

"I was near the breaking point," she said, "and then one day I got twenty of his letters at once. I remember Sandy hugging the mailman that day. She was very young, and sometimes it seemed she almost believed the mailman *was* her father, because seeing him always made her mother happy."

Eleanor found consolation in friends and neighbors, other young mothers whose husbands were away in the war. She remembers how solemnly that group gathered after the news that nuclear bombs had been dropped on Hiroshima and Nagasaki.

"It was incomprehensible to us," she recalls. "We knew the devastating effect on the Japanese civilian population, but at the same time it meant that our husbands were coming home, and everything else was way down the list of importance."

After the surrender, Julian's ship was assigned to escort the first convoy into Tokyo Bay. After several days at anchor, the officers and crew were allowed to go ashore. Eleanor still remembers the alarm she felt on receiving a letter from Julian postmarked from Tokyo. "I knew the resentment toward Americans was great, and I had these terrible visions of him being knifed in the back on a crowded street."

The Tokyo days passed safely, though, and before long Julian was promoted to executive officer of his ship—succeeding Herbert Shriver as second-in-command after Shriver received a new assignment. As happy as he was over the promotion, the down side was that he would almost certainly be responsible for bringing the ship back to the U.S., meaning a long delay in returning home. But at the last minute, the U.S.S. *Howard* was ordered to remain in the Philippines, and in December 1945, Julian was allowed to come home ahead of his ship on an aircraft carrier.

On December 20, Eleanor picked up the morning newspaper and read that the particular aircraft carrier was due to arrive in San Francisco that same day. Like magic, the telephone beside her rang. A voice on the other end said, "Is this my wife?"

They planned a reunion midway of the continent, in Houston. The travel schedules went like clockwork, she says, "and it didn't take long at all for the strangeness to wear off. It was like we had never been apart."

Eleanor says she wonders how they weathered the war years as well as they did: "We were almost children ourselves when it started. We grew up with a big leap, knowing that we had to accept life as it comes, take responsibility for our actions, and make the best of it together. It awakened us, too, to a real spiritual presence. Neither of us believed in war, and the reports of enemy soldiers being killed in action never became just numbers, but were real human beings. We came up with a watchword for ourselves that we've used ever since: 'We do our best, and to God we leave the rest.'"

2

Cullman: The Foundational Years

I N THE 1950s, Cullman, Alabama, could almost have passed for the fictional American small town of Pleasantville as depicted in the popular movie of the same name. Firemen not only responded to major emergencies, but were also glad to rescue a cat caught in a tree.

There's no shortage of trees in Cullman. They line the streets, along with pastel flowers that border two-story white houses accented with gingerbread trim. The unusually wide streets and large lots are the legacy of Colonel Johann Gottfried Cullmann, the civil engineer and political exile from Bavaria who started the town in 1873 when he brought five German families there from Cincinnati. He envisioned the town as "Alabama's garden spot." At first, the soil seemed unfruitful for the familiar growing techniques they had learned in Europe. But when the Germans and Scotch-Irish settlers collaborated, they eventually created what's now the county seat of Alabama's top agricultural county in a number of categories, including total farm income.

It was into this world—on November 13, 1946, his father Julian's twenty-sixth birthday—that Julian L. McPhillips, Jr., was born and grew up. By and large, it was an "Ozzie and Harriet" life, where "real" men held real jobs, and real housewives wore real lipstick.

Julian recalls his hometown as "a wonderful, wonderful place. In fact, whenever I go back there, it's like stepping into a time machine. A whole flood of memories just come tumbling back, and most of them are good ones. It was a great place for a child to grow up. It was just a clean-cut, wholesome, positive sort of environment. I'm not saying there weren't the little fights and misunderstandings that kids anywhere will have. But you could ride your bicycle from one side of Cullman to the other without worrying about being safe. You probably still can. For a kid, the town seemed like one big playground."

Children were encouraged to be heard, not just seen, and felt at home in the stores and markets as well as their neighbors' houses. Julian and his brother David were avid coin collectors, and routinely swapped their stock of pennies, nickels, and dimes for more vintage ones with downtown business owners. Their mother, Eleanor, frequently picked up homemade potato salad from Wertz's Delicatessen, owned and run by one of the original German families.

The McPhillipses' house, at 402 Fourth Avenue Northeast, had a large backyard—which came in handy, because Eleanor and Julian Sr. had five children. Sandy was born in 1942, Julian (known from childhood as "Jutsy"— pronounced JOOT-see) in 1946, David in 1948, Betsy in 1949, and Frank in 1954. Jutsy, David, and Betsy, three kids in three years, were also known in the McPhillipses' home as "the three musketeers" in their early years, as they frequently ran around together. The welcome mat was always out, and neighboring kids often came in swarms. Jutsy's childhood friend and next-door neighbor, Don Weaver, remembers that "Julian's mother and dad were always nice to me. In a way, they were like my secondary parents. I think I spent more time at Julian's house than I did at my own."

Eleanor McPhillips remembers the time similarly. "Wherever your children were," she wrote in her autobiography, "there was always someone who knew them. If they overstayed their welcome, and it was time for them to come home, you could be sure somebody would send them there. In a sense, we were all our 'neighbor's keeper.'"

"It was a great satisfaction to know that if an illness in the family, or trouble of any sort arose, our friends stood by us in a real way. They would come to our home with food, look out for our children, and do anything else that needed to be done."

Edna Earl Arnold, who for decades was—along with her husband—editor of *The Cullman Tribune*, remembers Eleanor as "not just a friend, but a counselor. She was easy to talk to, and children and adults alike came to her when they had trouble. She just had a kindness about her, an understanding of other people's needs."

Her main memories of Julian Jr. are that he was "sweet to the little people." He helped younger kids find Easter eggs, and when the church had its annual rummage sale in the city park, Julian "was the one who fetched things. I think he inherited his mother's love of doing things for people."

But coming to the town of Cullman was also, to some degree, a culture shock for both of Julian's parents, who had grown up in much more urban and sophisticated locales: Julian Sr. in Mobile and Eleanor in New Orleans.

"We were told to go the Eureka Hotel," Eleanor recalls, "where a room was awaiting us. The hotel was straight out of the movies, a little country hotel. The desk clerk sat at his desk with a green visor over his eyes. In the lobby, a bunch of men were talking, laughing and chewing tobacco. In fact, [four-year-old daughter] Sandy barely missed a wad of flying tobacco juice aimed at a spittoon as she ran by . . ."

The "redeeming feature" of the hotel was its dining room, "where wonderful country-style cooking was served, and large bowls of fresh vegetables were passed."

Those vegetables were what had brought the McPhillipses to Cullman in the first place. Following his return from World War II duty in the South Pacific, Julian Sr. took over from his father the management of King Pharr Canning Company, which processed locally grown vegetables and sold them nationwide. With the McPhillips family as majority stockholders, King Pharr canned and distributed thirty-three different varieties of vegetables. There were additional canning operations in Selma and Uniontown, Alabama, as well as Georgia and Louisiana. In its heyday—the 1950s and '60s—the company was Cullman County's largest employer, with some one thousand workers.

Vegetables, Julian remembers, were a large part of the fabric of his childhood: "One of my earliest memories is going out with Dad in his pickup truck, visiting farmers he would contract with to buy their vegetables. It seems like we went down every dirt road in north Alabama, leaving a cloud of dust behind our pickup.

"Canned vegetables were a large part of what we grew up on. In fact, the canning plant was just two blocks from our house."

Cullman native Rachel Howard Trinchitella, an elementary-school classmate of Julian's, still recalls the long lines of farmers' trucks, loaded high with fresh produce, along the neighborhood streets leading to the plant: "I can smell those peppers 'til this day!" she says. But King Pharr wasn't the only business to share in the agricultural bounty. Next door to the plant was the popular "Nell's Cafe," where nobody ever had to ask if the vegetables were fresh. Before

Julian started to school, he'd often walk over to Nell's to eat lunch with his father.

Julian and younger brother David envisioned that when they grew up, they would be in the business, too.

LIFE WAS good. During the late 1960s, in fact, a conglomerate in Texas offered to buy the plant for some $6 million, but the owners declined. In retrospect, it was a bad call. By the mid-1970s, market forces the equivalent of the Biblical plagues of Egypt—the popularity of frozen foods, Richard Nixon's price controls, federal red tape, and the burgeoning fast-food industry—combined to send King Pharr into a tailspin from which it wouldn't recover. (In a self-liquidation in 1975, the bondholders and creditors were paid off, but the stockholders got nothing.)

NOT MANY people actually *recall* wearing diapers, but Julian swears he does. He says he remembers the joy of jumping up and down in his baby bed. But another childhood memory is far darker: the time in 1948 when he ran from his family's front yard alongside Highway 278 (now Guntersville Highway) into the path of an eighteen-wheeler. The driver stopped just in time, and a neighbor, Mrs. Frances Ponder, saw the incident and rushed to make sure Julian was all right. It wasn't long before his parents moved the family to a quieter street, with a sturdy white picket fence around their yard.

Next door, however, lived a four-year-old Janie Young, who dumped a bucket of green paint on Julian's head when he was only two. The next year, at three, Jutsy and his big sister Sandy resolved to ride to Decatur—forty miles away—on their respective tricycle and bicycle. A few blocks down the street, reality dawned and the journey ended.

Julian also recalls with relish his kindergarten days at Miss Johnson's across the street from the home of his best friend at the time, Courtney McKoy. Every year a new group would take off for school and "Jutsy" got left behind, until finally, nearing the age of seven, Julian started to school. A strapping kid "just touching 5 feet and 105 pounds," legend has it that young Julian took on two fourth-grade bullies in his first year and subdued them.

Like any child, young Julian sometimes tested his mother, who would resort to the "switch bush" for a disciplinary tool. As a big-for-his-age preschool child, Julian once grabbed a switch from his mother's hand, broke it in two, and laughed. It was no laughing matter to his mom, however, who got Julian Sr. to take matters into his hands, giving Julian Jr. the spanking he deserved.

During summers and AEA holidays of the early 1950s, the McPhillips and McKoy families, each with four similarly aged kids, frequently vacationed together at Gulf Shores and Daytona Beach, Florida.

Beverly McKoy, mother of the four young McKoys says "he (Jutsy) was always such an honest, fair person . . . I always felt like he had a strong faith, a belief in God, as he grew up. Julian was always kind to people, but his whole family is like that."

Like many Southern towns of that era, Cullman's virtually "white-only" society gained a reputation for racism. Allegedly (or perhaps apocryphally; historians' accounts are divided) there were signs posted at the county line, reading "Nigger, Don't Let The Sun Set On Your Ass In Cullman County."

In the 1950s, the vast majority of Cullman residents were either German Catholic, German Lutheran, or White Anglo-Saxon Protestant. There were a couple of Italian families, and one or two Oriental families. During the 1970s, *The Cullman Times* boasted a Jewish reporter. In the mid-1960s, at the height of the civil rights movement, many Cullman families began to hire black people as domestic workers and gardeners. Most of them came from areas known as the "Colony" (now an incorporated town), about fifteen miles south of Cullman. Julian's parents had been far ahead of the curve, hiring a girl named Patty Lou to work for them in the 1950s.

Dr. Henry Frank Arnold, now an English professor at the University of the South, in Sewanee, Tennessee, is a Cullman native whose parents were editors of the *Tribune*. He says the town still has a place in his heart. "Except for the racism," he says, "Cullman had a real sort of commitment to democracy. I truly believe that Cullman took the notion of democracy seriously, and in many ways was very idealistic about what a government ought to be."

The community's spirit and sense of cooperation, and its family-friendly environment, is where young Julian developed his populist instincts. The king of populism in those days, of course, was the legendary "Big Jim" Folsom, a two-term governor of Alabama and a champion of equal rights who raised campaign "stumping" to a high art form. Born in the south Alabama town of

Elba, he moved to Cullman and considered it his home as well as headquarters for his campaign forays.

To underscore his pledge to clean up the supposed corruption and shady dealings in Alabama's capital, Folsom traveled the state with a mop and a scrub-bucket which he placed alongside the podium whenever he made a speech. He also brought along his country/bluegrass band known as "The Strawberry Pickers" to warm up the crowd.

And, Folsom was far from alone. The list of politicians from Cullman County reads like a virtual "Who's Who" of Alabama government, a fact that is not lost on its contemporary population. Bob Bryan, a former publisher of *The Cullman Times*, once said—probably with tongue lodged firmly in cheek—that "Most of the people here are either farmers or politicians, and politics is easier." And, as *Times* columnist Mickey Clem has written: "There's not a hell of a lot to do in Cullman. Some people run for office out of sheer desperation to leave."

Opinions aside, the historical record speaks for itself. In addition to "Big Jim," there was his son "Little Jim" Folsom, who served variously as lieutenant governor, interim governor and gubernatorial candidate, and his wife, former Congressional candidate Marsha Folsom. Others include Billy Joe Camp, a former secretary of state; Tom Drake, speaker of the House from 1983-86; Don Hale, who chaired the Senate Rules committee in the early 1990s; Jimmy Knight, state Democratic Party chairman in the early 1980s; Roy Drinkard, member of the state's Pardon and Parole Board during "Big Jim's" administration; the late Finis St. John, president pro tem of the state Senate in the early 1980s; Chris Doss, a former Jefferson County commissioner; Wayne Teague, a former gubernatorial candidate who retired as head of the state's Department of Education; former Governor Guy Hunt, ousted for ethics violations; Paul Hamrick, chief of staff of Governor Don Siegelman; and Phillip Kinney, executive director of the Alabama Democratic Party.

To name a few.

Cullman attorney John David Knight (classmate of Julian's sister Sandy growing up in Cullman) believes the area is an ideal breeding ground for politicians in general. "The whole population participates in government," Knight says. "So our many successes in state politics really come from the grassroots."

The city apparently inherited this quality from its founder. Reportedly, founding father John Cullmann, while living in his native Bavaria, tried to free his kinsmen of their oppression by attempting (unsuccessfully) to assassinate Bismarck, the Prussian chancellor, at which point America began to seem to Cullmann, more than ever, the land of opportunity.

But whether the present-day town of Cullman's native political savvy is in the water, the land, or the people, Julian sees growing up there as a major formative experience. Both in his political and professional work, he says, the town has influenced him more than any other place he's lived—including educational opportunities that many people don't ordinarily connect with small-town public schools.

"The foundation I got in Cullman's schools was superb," Julian says. "And my mother was great, too, about helping us all read at an early age. She'd read stories to us until we could read them back to her."

But of all the teachers, he says, it was the late Helen Vines—who taught him in sixth grade—who was the greatest influence. "A tremendous part of being a lawyer is communication, and when I say Mrs. Vines 'instilled' grammar in me, I mean she was absolutely superb. We would diagram sentences endlessly, with the stress on syntax—putting words into the proper tense and into the proper person."

"Today, when I hear poor grammar, it goes through me like fingernails on a chalkboard. And I hear it constantly, from people who, based on their education, should know better."

One of his partners in sentence-diagramming was the aforementioned Rachel Howard Trinchitella, a cute blond who sat behind him in Mrs. Vines's classroom. "I was impressed with his brain," Rachel remembers, "but he also had the biggest feet I think I've ever seen. I mean, they were *huge*. I thought, 'He's going to grow up to be a big guy,' but I also thought he was going to do big things. He was always laughing and cutting up, but underneath it you could tell how determined he was, to go places."

Julian's main academic competition—albeit a friendly one—in elementary school was Gloria King Bush, now a high school librarian in Mobile, Alabama. They were the only two students to maintain "straight-A" averages in all six grades. "Julian was industrious," Gloria recalls. "He was very focused. But at the same time, he was a lot of fun to be around."

Childhood friend Don Weaver agrees. "We were very different in personality," he says. "Julian was more organized, more of a 'detail' person than me. I was more of a free-wheeling sort of guy. But it seemed that Julian always had a plan, as to where he wanted to go, and I knew he would get there. I'm proud of what he's achieved."

Besides the educational skills, kids who grew up in Cullman during those days apparently got a strong dose of idealism as well. An unusually high percentage of his classmates went on to careers in "people-helping" professions. Rachel, unconventionally, went on to graduate from a traditionally all-black college—Hampton Institute in Virginia, near where her husband was stationed in the military—and majored in Home Economics. "It was a beautiful place, and the people were so nice," she says. "I picked Home Economics because everybody's gotta have a home, and it's important to be happy in it."

After college, she went to work at an inner-city service program teaching health, nutrition, and consumer education to pregnant teenage girls who were forced to drop out of regular classes.

Keith Carter, another childhood friend and neighbor of Julian's, graduated in secondary education from the University of Alabama and came back home to teach children of migrant workers in Cullman County. In 1970 he took a job teaching sixth grade in the Birmingham City School system, where he was the only white male on the staff.

"I didn't exactly go out *looking* for a job in a black school," Carter says. "But after I accepted the position, I saw my assignment as an opportunity to help kids of a minority race."

Surprisingly, he says, the racial aspect of the job never created any significant problems for him. "I guess," he says, "the reason that I—and many other people who grew up in Cullman during that era—*didn't* have a lot of racial prejudice is that we were hardly ever around black people." But being aware of racial prejudice sort of second-hand, by reading about ugly incidents in larger, and more integrated, cities "only made me want to see blacks succeed, after all the mistreatment they'd received over the years."

Julian looks back similarly on that time. "Growing up in Cullman," he said, "I can truthfully say that I never heard a racial slur. Nobody used the 'n' word. Maybe it was just because there weren't any 'n's' to talk about." In the years since, as racial slurs of all types became a matter not just of decency but of law, he's regularly come face-to-face with the matter in dozens of employment discrimination cases.

During the civil rights era, Cullman was often referred to as the "City of Churches; one on every block," as the saying used to go. While that was somewhat of an exaggeration, it's true that every Christian denomination was exceedingly well-represented in the city. Baptists and Catholics have traditionally held the strongest influence. At one time the city was home to both a two-year liberal arts Catholic college, Sacred Heart, and a four-year one, St. Bernard. (One now serves as a retreat center, the other as a college preparatory school.) Also within the city, Catholics and Lutherans have their own parochial schools.

It was in Cullman that Julian's father—who had descended from a long line of Catholics—broke with the church. Julian Sr. wanted his children to attend public schools, and didn't believe the bishop should have the right to dictate a parochial education instead. Julian's mother, raised Presbyterian and descended from a long line of Presbyterian ministers, had begun attending an Episcopal church during her high school and college days in New Orleans.

In 1950, when an Episcopal congregation was forming in Cullman, Julian Sr. and Eleanor naturally gravitated toward it—first attending services in the city of Decatur, to the north, but finally joining in to build a new church facility in Cullman.

Julian was not yet four years old when the foundation for Grace Episcopal Church was poured, only a block from his house, and one of his strongest memories is walking over to watch the carpenters at work, nailing boards together for the frame as, week by week, the structure came together. (He couldn't have predicted that he would someday play a role in building two other Episcopal churches; Julian and Leslie were involved with Julian's parents in the genesis of the Church of St. Simon Peter in Pell City in 1975, and were founding members of Christ Redeemer Episcopal in Montgomery in 1980.)

As Edna Earl Arnold recalls it, the McPhillipses were "pillars of the church"—not only spiritually, but materially as well. Eleanor's father had recently died, willing his family a considerable fortune earned from his New Orleans business. His widow, Stu Dixon, donated money to the fledgling Episcopal church, which allowed them to add, among other things, a rector's home and a parlor-style fellowship room at the church.

As Eleanor McPhillips writes in her memoirs, "The McPhillips family filled a whole pew, and we were a noisy bunch. But the church membership loved our family, and the children loved them. We were active participants, down to the last child, and at that time very few of the other families had children as young as ours." Her daughter Sandy became known as "the fainter," for her tendency to sometimes fall out into the aisle. Young "Jutsy," meanwhile, once chased a grasshopper down the aisle and proudly held it up by the rail for the congregation to admire.

Julian's mother calls Grace Episcopal "a vital force in the collective life of our family." She writes, "We had family prayers in our home on a regular basis during this period. Moreover, with the church only a block from our home, almost every day some member of our family was over at the church doing something."

Mrs. Arnold remembers that the couple had a sort of "extended" church family, as well: "They had all these cute little children, but it was amazing how Eleanor would bring so many unchurched children from the neighborhood, too. Whenever she found out some child didn't have a church, she'd volunteer to pick them up and bring them to Sunday School."

Another fertile field for Eleanor's "ministry" was the Cub Scout troop for which she served as den mother. Between those tasks, and being a perpetual homeroom mother at school, she found time for her two favorite hobbies, golf and swimming.

"Mother just always had a heart for people," Julian says, "especially for the disadvantaged and less fortunate in the community . . . I didn't grow up as a 'preacher's kid,' but I *did* grow up with a strong enthusiasm for the Christian faith. Especially the hymn-singing, that was so Spirit-filled. 'I Sing a Song of the Saints of God' and 'Onward Christian Soldiers' were two that especially moved me."

Life was good—and seemingly very stable. Julian's parents had acclimated extremely well to the small-town community, were active in both church and civic affairs, and loved long summer vacations in the 1950s at nearby Lake Guntersville with their five thriving youngsters—often joined by Uncle Warren, Aunt Sara Frances, and their equal number of children. But as it happened, Julian Sr.'s earlier decision to break with Catholicism on a matter of principle was a foreshadowing of a far more significant turning point in the family's history.

In 1958, despite a secure corporate job, Julian's father began to feel an unyielding call to enter the ministry. When he confided this to Eleanor, she writes, "We got down together on our knees, turned the decision over to God, and left it with Him. At the end of the year, the feeling was just as strong as ever, and Julian Sr. was convinced that the matter was out of his hands."

But far more than an ordinary "job change," becoming an Episcopal priest was no decision to be taken lightly. Or, as Eleanor would write, "From the outside, it just didn't make sense for a man who was president of a large corporation, a leader in the community, and 'on top of the world' in many respects, to just ditch it all. Why go back to school, when he would have to start again, from square one, in a whole new field? But that was the view of people who saw things in terms of dollars and cents. Our close friends, and our church members, didn't question it. They understood that it was the Lord's will for him."

In the summer of 1959, they took the leap in earnest. They packed up some of their belongings, put the rest in storage, and moved from Cullman—their home of thirteen years—to Sewanee, Tennessee, where Julian Sr. would spend the next three years working on a seminary degree. They took with them all the kids but "Jutsy," who stayed with relatives that summer to finish out the season playing in the Cullman County Little League.

The separation was indicative of the fact that sports were serious to Julian—and still play a large role in his life and his identity today. One of his teammates from that time, John Shaw, remembers a vacant lot of "more than half of a city block, it seemed like, behind Julian's house. There was room to play any kind of ball you wanted to play. He had a basketball court. We played football, baseball, cork ball, every kind of ball you can think of."

"And we played constantly. It was primarily what we did with our time, back then. It's hard to convey just how important baseball, in particular, was for boys in the 1950s and '60s. It was extremely important, extremely meaningful."

The last year John and Julian played Little League together, Julian was the pitcher and John the catcher. "Truth is," Shaw recalls, "Julian today is not much bigger than he was at thirteen and fourteen years old. He just towered over everybody else. I mean, *today* I wear a size twelve shoe. But he did, back *then*. Biggest feet of any kid I ever saw. He was a really big guy. And he could really throw a fastball. He threw so hard it kept my hands bruised, catching it.

"I respected his baseball arm, obviously, but he also seemed like an ethical person. He trained hard, and he played clean. Even today, I think he has a knack for seeing things as they really are, as opposed to just what's on the surface."

Their Little League coach in those days was Dafford Smith, a phys-ed teacher who was a favorite of kids who weren't even involved in organized sports. Smith led his Little Leaguers, including Julian, to win the county title. And he was no slouch as a ballplayer, himself. Soon after Julian's last Little League Year, Smith signed with the Detroit Tigers farm team. In the early 1980s, with baseball behind him, Smith went back to school and earned a law degree.

"Julian was one of the most dominant players in the league," Smith recalls. "He was a big, strong boy, and the best pitcher in the league. I always had a high regard for him. He wasn't a show-off. He tended to his own business. An intelligent kid, too. I thought he had a lot of potential in life, and obviously he's proven me right."

McPhillips and Shaw give Smith high marks, as well: "Coach Smith just had a 'spirit' about him that nobody else did," says Shaw. "All the different personalities, the different classes of people, made no difference to him whatsoever. He treated everybody exactly alike. He was just a good person. If you could play, you were welcome on his team. Heck, even if you just *wanted* to play, you were welcome."

The coach also set his own standards. He believed, for instance, that pitchers that young had no business throwing curve balls, because it might damage their arms. Many of the team's opponents, though, had no such restrictions and brought a varied repertoire of curves, knuckles, and sliders to the field—making Cullman's one-shot arsenal of Julian's fastball even more important to the team's strategy. And Shaw's catching hand took a beating.

"The mitt I had was old and worn out," he says. "Coach Smith tried all different kinds of padding in it, but nothing worked very well." Then a sudden blessing came—in the form of a brand-new Wilson catcher's mitt, supposedly provided by the team's sponsor, the local Kiwanis Club. "They sold for around

$10," Shaw says, "which was pretty big bucks, back then."

Some thirty years afterward, Shaw moved to Montgomery and one day ran into Julian at a streetcorner. "He and Leslie had me over for supper a few days later, and after we ate he was showing me around his house. He said, 'John, I think I've got something in this closet you might remember.' So he pulls out two old baseball gloves, his glove and my catcher's mitt. The inside of that mitt was as black as coal, from being hit so hard. And that's the first time I realized that it wasn't the Kiwanis Club who bought me the mitt—it was Julian's dad."

THOUGH Julian was a sixth-grader his last year in Cullman, his height led to his being drafted into service by the junior high's basketball team.

But his teachers made sure sports didn't interfere with his academic life. Sewanee Military Academy began with the eighth grade, and Julian was just finishing the sixth. Julian's parents gave their blessing to his being double-promoted, a rare event in 1959. His favorite teacher, Mrs. Vines, gave Julian extra work—including a reading list of nearly a hundred books, from novels to biographies—and during the second semester Mrs. Vines tutored him privately, in her spare time, with the seventh-grade curriculum, including higher math.

Mrs. Vines's strategy worked. That spring, despite the accelerated curriculum, Julian brought home an all-A report card, and was officially "skipped" to the eighth grade.

It was about this time, while riding his bicycle on a typical jaunt across town, that he had what he calls his "epiphany."

"For the first time," Julian recalls, "I fully realized that it was up to me—not my parents and my teachers—to make my way in life. Instead of trying to please other people, I needed to set my own goals and try to achieve them." He was very much looking forward to the next chapter of his life: Sewanee.

3

The Sewanee Years: Mountain Top Experiences

I F JULIAN's Cullman years resembled Hollywood's film version of *Pleasantville, U.S.A.*, his time at Sewanee Military Academy corresponded more closely with the movie *Dead Poets Society*: an environment of rigid decorum, offset by a formidably non-conformist teacher who was happiest when jousting with the system.

Replace Robin Williams's character in *Dead Poet's Society* with a bearded, broad-shouldered coach and teacher named Bill Goldfinch, who encouraged his English students to look at the world around them from unconventional perspectives.

Julian says he fondly remembers Goldfinch's "anti-authoritarian rumblings," at the academically prestigious school, which "helped make life more relaxed and less military."

Julian's life at SMA began in early August of 1959, with twice-a-day football practices with the varsity team under a broiling sun. Still only twelve, but a stout 5'8" and 160 pounds, he was thrown into blocking drills with eighteen-year-old seniors—and in his "off" hours, an oppressive military routine as well. Any residual baby fat got chiseled away that summer, along with any lingering doubt that his boyhood was over.

Sewanee, founded in 1857, is the site of a liberal arts college that has been called "the Oxford of the South." Located along a mountain chain known as the Cumberland Plateau, the Tennessee forestland is reminiscent of the Swiss Alps in miniature. The air is thinner, but pure. Rising steadily up an incline between Chattanooga and Nashville, the campus is outwardly as peaceful and serene as a resort in the Great Smokies. But Sewanee's scenic environment belies the tough regimen that its parochial children, military cadets, and college students had to undergo.

Juniors and seniors at what is known today as The University of the South wear academic robes to classes, and must pass rigorous comprehensive exams in order to graduate. Sewanee's institutions are an unusual blend of Southern manners, British tradition, and Episcopal Church history. Latin, for example, is one of the most highly revered studies. Over the years, the university has produced twenty-two Rhodes Scholars.

Julian made the best of the opportunities there, winning the schools' Latin Medal two years in a row. He consistently made the Honor Roll, which required a 3.62 or higher average. He placed second and third in statewide math tournaments, and during his senior year missed being named valedictorian by a fraction of a grade point.

There were sixty-four cadets in his class. Freshmen at SMA were required to sign a strictly enforced Code of Honor, taking a military oath that they would not cheat on exams, and were bound to report seeing another cadet do so. Honor and integrity were the system's watchwords.

Unaccustomed to the thin air, Julian found that the mountainous environment made the physical regimen even tougher. He recalls his group bivouacking (camping out) in the snow, and taking long runs through the cold air—sometimes through clouds floating close to the ground.

The military drills and workouts took up much of a cadet's time, but somewhere between "Reveille" and "Taps" there were bugle calls known as "CQs" for "Called to Quarters," one-to-two hour study halls each night when the students were confined to their rooms for hitting the books as part of the college preparatory curriculum.

Julian remembers one semester during ninth grade when his class was studying Plato's classic *The Republic* at the same time that Julian Sr. was studying the same book in seminary, and it became the stuff of long father-son discussion. Even during summer vacation, Sewanee's students were required to take home long, mimeographed reading lists, which included biographies, memoirs, and fiction by writers from around the world.

And in all of this, time had to be carved out for athletics. In the eighth grade, his junior varsity football team went undefeated under Coach Bill Stewart, a University senior who years later retired from the Air Force and became a good friend of Julian's in Montgomery. Julian played football for Sewanee in the Mid-South Conference. From the ninth to the twelfth grades, as a pulling guard in the single-wing offense, and a linebacker on defense, Julian won four varsity letters. SMA's schedule included Notre Dame High School and McCallie, in Chattanooga; Battle Ground Academy and Montgomery Bell Academy in Nashville; Riverside Military Academy of Gainesville, Georgia; Asheville School and Christ School in North Carolina; Millersburg Military Institute of Kentucky; and Marion Military Institute in Alabama.

But the sport at which he most excelled was a one-on-one game: wrestling. He was captain of the team, wrestled alternatively in the 183-pound and heavyweight classes, while Bill Goldfinch was his coach and mentor. During the 1963-64 season, Sewanee went 8-2—with team captain Julian the top individual wrestler, undefeated in dual meets, and often demonstrating a knack for scoring quick pins (scoring one in only thirteen seconds).

As aficionados of the "true" sport like to point out, this wrestling is not the variety that people watch on Monday night TV, but the kind the public has traditionally gotten to see only when the Olympics roll around. "It's not just a question of strength," Julian says. "You have to outwit your opponent both physically and mentally." At Sewanee, he did double duty with his training— practicing with both the Academy and the University teams, followed by a seven-mile run around the mountain. As a result, he says, "by the time I got to Princeton, wrestling was a cake-walk."

Throughout, Julian's touchstone and inspiration was Goldfinch, whose students addressed him affectionately as "Coach" or "Captain."

"He had a real passion," Julian says, "not just for the sport, but for the youngsters, too." In addition to coaching wrestling, Goldfinch taught English from 1957 to 1967.

Another cadet at the time, Tom Taylor, remembers Goldfinch as being "a wonderful, if unorthodox teacher. He was always doing radical things to get our full attention, for the purpose of teaching us." For instance, Goldfinch lectured with his chair sitting *on* his teacher's desk, not behind it—not unlike Professor Keating in "Dead Poet's Society" who stood on his desktop to lecture.

Goldfinch's other great loves included Shakespeare and the Bible. He played performances of Shakespeare on vinyl LP albums, and often quoted from scripture—applying its ideas to areas not traditionally theological. He often led discussions about the deeper meanings of Jacob wrestling with the angel in Genesis 32, and he exhorted his charges to memorize, understand, and practice the principles contained in I Corinthians 13, often called the "Love Chapter" of the Bible. Julian referred to him as the "Agapé King," an honorary title based on the Greek word for "unselfish love" that's exalted in the chapter.

Goldfinch, for his part, still has a very high regard for Julian. "I admired his wrestling abilities," Goldfinch says now, "but I respected him even more as a Christian. He was a Christian knight and a Christian hero, who lived his testimony in a setting—a military school—that could be very rough on people."

"Academically, athletically, and otherwise, he proved himself." One of Coach's favorite memories is when Julian volunteered to give up his 183-pound class and move to heavyweight during a meet, to help the team. "There's no question in my mind that he came out of the Academy as a Christian gentleman," Goldfinch says. "I believe he was preserved for our time. He's clear-thinking, and he's honest to a fault."

With sports such as wrestling increasingly under the budget axe at many institutions as a result of what Julian calls "a misguided application" of a Title IX provision aimed at gender equity in college athletics, many major universities have dropped their wrestling programs. "Misguided" because, rather than raise money for female sports, many schools simply cut money spent on male sports teams.

Princeton came close. But between 1993 and 1996, Julian led a successful battle—with both public relations and legal action—against a decision by the university's administration to terminate the sport. Photos in the family album show Julian, his kids, and Princeton alums at his twenty-fifth reunion in 1993, carrying picket signs that say, "Save Princeton Wrestling!"

Notwithstanding the pressures of elsewhere, in April of 1999, headmaster Bill Wade of St. Andrews-Sewanee announced that "wrestling here is alive and well," during a ceremony to mark expansion of the school's gym. Julian remains close to his coach thirty-six years after graduation, and chaired a campaign in 1998-99 which raised $100,000 for an expanded wrestling room named in Goldfinch's honor.

SEWANEE in the 1950s and '60s had a strict dress code: cadets wore gray-and-blue uniforms at appropriate times, coat-and-tie at more social occasions. It was in keeping with the institution's image of tradition, protocol, and money. Sending one's son to Sewanee was an expensive proposition for residential students. But Julian, as a day student, escaped this financial burden during his first three years of schooling and had a priest's son's scholarship for his final two years.

While Julian's father attended the seminary at Sewanee, the large family lived in a tiny, two-bedroom brick house known as the "Alabama Cottage." Once they settled into their new home with all five kids in the summer of 1959, Julian Sr. and Eleanor realized that there was enough sleeping space to accommodate everyone—except themselves. As a result, they "made do" with a pullout sofa in the living room for the duration of his seminary training.

Julian remembers that the family gathered each night for devotionals, and when Julian Sr. studied Greek, the rest of the family learned along with him. "It was tight quarters," Julian says, "but a close family." After his father accepted a call to Montgomery's Episcopal Church of the Ascension in 1962, Julian stayed on at Sewanee as a boarder to complete his junior and senior years.

That summer of 1962, after the McPhillipses moved into their new home at 1329 S. McDonough Street, adjacent to the Church of the Ascension, Julian agonized over his future. Should he return, this time as a boarding student, to Sewanee Military Academy, where he was established in academics, sports, and leadership opportunities? Or should he live at home with his family and enroll in Sidney Lanier High School, a few blocks away? Lanier High at that time enjoyed a national academic reputation and had a state championship football team. Prayerfully, Julian sought God's will, but the answer was not clear. Finally, he sought pastoral guidance from his own father, who counseled his son that either choice could be God's will. What mattered most, the senior Julian said, was not which of the schools to attend, but the attitude and spirit taken to either place. The younger Julian still recalls the poignant moment. After that advice, he says, his tension disappeared and it became clear that he should return to Sewanee.

In the summers and holidays of 1962-64, Julian became well-acquainted with Alabama's capitol city. During Christmas vacation of 1963, he helped

Billy Livings coach Sidney Lanier High School's first-ever wrestling team. His social life was also active, dating or escorting to dances such Montgomery belles as Priscilla Crommelin, Betty Scott, and Melville Douglass, daughter of St. John's Episcopal Church rector Charles Douglass.

For Julian, Sewanee represented a continuation of his childhood faith. Each Sunday morning, the cadets would march in formation from Quintard Hall to All Saints' Chapel, the campus's Gothic-style cathedral, to the strains of "Onward Christian Soldiers."

Active in the Otey Parish youth group, young Julian became friends at this family Episcopal parish with Dr. C. Fitzsimmons Allison, a theology professor of Julian Sr.'s, who also became the Episcopal bishop of South Carolina. Sparked by correspondence and contacts over the years, the friendship continues to this day. A letter exchange in 1981 between Bishop Allison and Julian on the theology of salvation became the subject of seminary class discussion in subsequent years at St. Luke's Seminary in Sewanee.

His grades at Sewanee were exceptional: A's, with only a few B's, which were in ROTC. Keeping his shoes shined and brass polished at all times were not among his favorite activities, and his laxity in that regard once lowered his discipline grade to a D. (Fortunately, discipline grades didn't count in academic standing.) But the rigid structure was to a great extent counterbalanced by the natural beauty of the campus setting, as both he and his parents recall.

"The magnificence of the mountain," Julian's mother wrote in her memoirs, "moved us deeply and we were at peace with ourselves, truly believing God was involved in this decision. We felt about as close to Him that summer as we would feel for a long time."

Julian also remembers an extraordinary level of closeness and camaraderie among the school's cadets, many of whom come back to "The Mountain" every five years for a class reunion. Julian chaired the Class of '64 for the Alumni Weekend in 1999, (as he had for every five-year cycle reunion since 1979), making phone calls and sending letters to classmates inviting them to "Come to the mountain on April 23-25, to share, to ruminate, to regale, and to simply relax, smell the mountain laurel, and have a good time."

At the reunion there was no shortage of activities—golf tournaments, early mountain jogs, dances, parties, brunches, luncheons, buffet dinners, and servings of nostalgia sufficiently large that attendees could for a while imagine that the "golden age" of the late 1950s and early 1960s has not faded away.

Americans were in their glory days then, in many ways, with the calm and optimism following World War II and the name "Vietnam" just tiny letters on a globe.

Many cadets, like Julian, would eventually become lawyers. Others became doctors and accountants. One buddy even made a fortune in blue marlin fishing off the Florida Keys. But others had their lives changed by being sent to the other side of the world: Vietnam.

A number of Julian's Sewanee classmates served there, mainly by volunteering, and the cadets from the Class of '64 were fortunate to have none of its soldiers lose their lives in the war.

While theology was interesting and daily chapel attendence mandatory, the military environment of the school was the predominant influence. As cadet Tom Taylor comments, "A military school is not about 'playing war' . . . it's about generations of tradition, and following on. Our training had more to do with issues like Honor and Duty and Loyalty and Fidelity than with learning the 'art of war.'"

Alex Kitchens, from the Class of '64, became a marksmanship instructor for the Marine Corps at Parris Island, South Carolina, before serving as a sniper in Vietnam. While in Marine boot camp, he received the highest award possible, which he says "was all because of my training at SMA."

Classmate Bill Miller was a helicopter pilot in Vietnam. Tom Taylor was administrator at a training base in Memphis during the war. Tommy Bye, from an earlier class, became a Christian convert in Vietnam and is today an Episcopal priest in Texas. Joe Parker, SMA batallion commander Julian's freshman year and co-chair with Julian of the campaign to raise money for the wrestling room, was a Vietnam veteran who stayed in the Marines until retirement as a Colonel. Fellow wrestler Tommy McBee avoided further military involvement after graduating from F&M College in Pennsylvania and became a lawyer in nearby Winchester, Tennessee, down the mountain from Sewanee. He occasionally refers Alabama cases to Julian.

Julian was temporarily deferred from military service his senior year at Princeton because of his serious sports injuries (he still can't bend his right leg to the angle he can with his left), and the draft board never called him back for a second physical (as it was supposed to do in six months). He would later participate in anti-war demonstrations, and at Columbia debated publicly with the Law School dean about what sort of strike, and when, the student body should take in protest against America's involvement in the war.

"I have great admiration for the American soldiers who fought in the Vietnam War," says Julian. "My beef was not with those fellows who at great sacrifice were doing their patriotic duty. My complaint was with the presidents, Johnson and Nixon, and the top generals and cabinet officials who put us, and kept us, in the war. In the end both the doves and the hawks agreed that the war was against our national interests. Patriotism in a democratic society like America sometimes involves standing up to, and speaking out against, bad national policy. Growing up in the aftermath of World War II, which was glorified in the movies and on T.V., and while spending five years at Sewanee Military Academy, I always envisioned myself fighting in the military someday. But Vietnam changed all that."

After Julian's parents left the Sewanee seminary and his father became a minister in Montgomery, Julian Sr. and Eleanor were active in both the civil rights movement—once meeting Coretta Scott King and Martin Luther King, Jr., in Atlanta—and the peace movement, positions which were often very uncomfortable to sustain in a Southern community of that era.

"Mother and Dad had two things they were especially steadfast in," Julian says. "One was civil rights, and the other was opposition to the Vietnam War, and I agreed with them strongly on both subjects. In those days, if you were for civil rights and against the Vietnam War, you passed the litmus test for liberalism." Julian says their stances on both issues had more to do with theology than with politics.

But whether one volunteered for Vietnam, got drafted into it, burned one's draft card, or fled to Canada, it was an issue that caused deep divisions for the men of Julian's generation—division in families, friendships, communities, and most of all in one's own conscience. The decision of whether to go to Vietnam was more than Julian's younger brother David could handle. He sank into a spiraling clinical depression, and eventually took his own life.

Those years were a time when words like "authority," "loyalty," "duty," " honor, " and "tradition"—the exact values inculcated into the SMA cadet— were being questioned. There was a rebirth of popularity for J.D. Salinger's

1951 novel *The Catcher in the Rye*, which struck a chord with young people for its themes of modern anxiety and the desire and dissatisfaction of non-conformists concerning popular culture.

As president of SMA's "Cum Laude Society," Julian chaired a meeting in which "authority" was the topic of debate, and two eminarians spoke to the group on "juvenile delinquents and rebels against society."

In many ways, Julian's first years at Sewanee were a perfect cross-section of the era's Zeitgeist. But everything was about to change.

If there's a single day that marked the end of America's mid-century Golden Age, it was November 22, 1963, when President John F. Kennedy was assassinated in a Dallas, Texas, motorcade. Julian remembers being horrified to learn that students at some high schools, whose parents had strongly opposed Kennedy's election, actually cheered when the news was announced.

For his own part, young Julian sat down that afternoon and wrote a letter about his own reaction to the event. "I started writing about an hour after it happened," he remembers. "I was looking for some way to express myself, and wrote a letter home to my parents. A few days later, Dad called me and said that he and Mom were so touched by my letter that they wanted to submit it as a letter to the editor of the local paper."

One of Julian's proudest items in his scrapbook of that year is a now-yellowed clipping of the letter, as it appeared in the November 29, 1963, issue of the *Alabama Journal.*

> The whole corp of cadets was informed at lunchtime today that President Kennedy had been shot, along with the Governor of Texas. The silence and gloom that fell on the corps was halting. After lunch, everyone went to the Study Hall and from 1:00 to 2:30 we watched the reports on President Kennedy come in until it was announced that he had died. I was so moved emotionally that I found it hard to keep back the tears. After gaining my composure sometime later, I have had time to let something be absorbed which seemed at first like a fantastic unreality . . .

Though Kennedy had served in World War II, the torch he passed to "a new generation" on Inauguration Day was mainly to the nation's baby boomers, basically those born between 1946 and 1964, which included

Julian's classmates and friends. They and their peers would later be classified as the dreamers, the dedicated, the doers, the daredevils, the dodgers, or some combination of the above. Julian's letter continued,

> I hope this event [the assassination] will really tie our people together in a bond of unity, peace, and mutual respect as citizens and as human beings. This could serve to do our country some good, to make us strive for the high ideals for which President Kennedy stood. I think, hope, and believe that God will make something good come out of what, at the present, seems so terrible.

It was an idealism that Julian would carry in his heart for the rest of his life. He had learned it in Cullman, it was strengthened at Sewanee, and it was crystallized by Kennedy's inspirational life, tragic death, and enduring legacy.

But now some hard choices lay ahead of Julian: he had been accepted to several universities, including SMA's neighbor down the street, namely The University of the South, as well as Duke University in North Carolina. His final decision, influenced by Episcopal Bishop C. C. J. Carpenter of Alabama and his son Doug, also a priest, was to go to Princeton University in New Jersey. Faculty advisers looked at Julian's achievement test scores and recommended that his skills in mathematics best suited him for an engineering degree.

"What I really wanted was something more *verbal*," Julian recalls now. He chose to major in History instead, and hasn't regretted the decision. "The exciting thing about history," he says, "is that it helps an individual overcome the limitations of time and place; you can experience the lives of other people and other eras, without actually being there."

4

Princeton and Columbia

MCPHILLIPS enrolled as a freshman at Princeton University in the fall of 1964, and from the first his college years appeared to be off to a great start. He quickly made new friends—including, to his delight, several Alabamians—and was elected captain of the freshmen wrestling team. The turmoil of the civil rights struggle, and the beginning of the United States' ominous early involvement in Southeast Asia, seemed more than a world away.

The one big exception was what happened in September 1963. One Sunday morning Julian read, with stunned disbelief, the top story in the national news that day: Birmingham's Sixteenth Street Baptist Church had been bombed, killing four young black girls who were attending Sunday School.

"We were outraged, of course, all of us," he remembers, "as anybody would be, by such a tragedy. The images were still strong a year later upon our enrollment, and some students gave us a really hard time, those of us from the South. They kept saying how terrible it must be, and asking us how on earth could we stand to live in a place where people did things like that.

"Every chance they got, they reminded us that Birmingham ought to be called 'Bombingham.' Somebody even put in the yearbook that 'Julian McPhillips came from Birmingham, where people use bricks and bats instead of wrestling mats.'"

"Some of the other guys would get so tired of it they'd try to defend themselves a little, but I just didn't have the heart. It was a terrible blot on our history. What could I say? And for pretty much the whole time I was at Princeton, I couldn't imagine moving back to Alabama, going back to a place where such an abominable thing could happen. I was so morally offended, and

I was in love with the university, and for a long time I thought I'd just stay in New Jersey after I graduated.

"Most people who drive through New Jersey on the I-95 corridor just see the ugly parts, the factories and the smokestacks and the junkyards, but there's some really beautiful country up there, off of the beaten path. They don't call it the Garden State for nothing."

During the Christmas season of 1965, though, Julian's good fortunes took a downward turn. During a holiday wrestling tournament at the University of Virginia, he broke his leg. He made a remarkable comeback, wrestling again in four more matches starting only six weeks after the first break, and was undefeated in them all.

But in early March of 1966, only ten weeks after the original injury, he broke the leg a second time. The repeat of the pain and suffering was not his only worry, though. Doctors told him he should never wrestle, or play football, again.

"It was devastating, to say the least," Julian recalls. "For one thing, it showed me how much of my self-identity came from being an athlete. And now, they were telling me that this whole aspect of my life was virtually over."

It was one of the lowest points of his life, and not surprisingly brought him to his first—and only—bout with depression. Though he sank very low emotionally, to his great fortune the depression never evolved into the far more serious clinical form that would later claim his brother's life.

He credits two significant events that summer of 1966 with helping turn his emotional state around. He spent the summer break in Birmingham, working with the brand-new Anti-Poverty Program—chiefly with Head Start centers around Jefferson County, but also with the Neighborhood Youth Corps. His mentor was Paul Ware, principal of one of the area's black high schools.

(Julian's friendship with Ware would endure long past the summer. In 1978 Ware—although by then in a nursing home—enthusiastically telephoned his friends and professional contacts throughout the city, recruiting them to help in Julian's campaign for attorney general.)

"The summer of 1966 was really an eye-opener for me, as far as my social conscience was concerned," Julian recalls. "Working every day with young children and teenagers who were suffering—both financially, and in so many other ways—sensitized me to the magnitude of what they were going through. It certainly helped snap me out of dwelling on my own problems.

"Seeing those bright, sparkling faces of kids living in extreme poverty really 'lit my fuse,' I guess you could say. It was a spirit-changing, mind-opening, formative experience."

(Before the summer was over, Julian's own face gained more sparkle—helped greatly by the fact that a young woman active with Head Start become his first serious social interest.)

During his last two years at Princeton, Julian was also active with the "Princeton in Harlem Project," a program that brought junior high and high school students from Harlem to Princeton to see the campus and hopefully aim for higher education.

Each week, a faculty member made a presentation on his or her field, and a group discussion followed. One topic was "The Relationship of Rock-and-Roll to Church Music." Other subjects ranged from Pop Art to civil rights to former Princeton basketball star Bill Bradley, who was by then making waves with the New York Knicks.

The program also brought Princeton students into Harlem neighborhoods, tutoring and working with younger residents. By his senior year Julian had become chairman of the project, and it took up a great deal of his time. (Those contacts endured during the next three years, while Julian attended Columbia Law School in New York City's Morningside Heights neighborhood, just to the west end of Harlem.)

Somehow, he also found the time to stay in the top fourth of his class academically at Princeton (graduating *cum laude* in history), go undefeated in four years of Ivy League wrestling competition, be named All-American honorable mention by the *Amateur Wrestling News*, serve as a chapel deacon, and stay active in campus ministries.

Despite the load, Julian became involved in another effort during those last two Princeton years: raising money to help Hindu refugees fleeing from East Pakistan (known today as Bangladesh) who were flooding the state of West Bengal, India, of which Calcutta was state capital.

"It was poverty and suffering on a scale that I could never have imagined," Julian remembers. "At the train station in Calcutta, there was virtually no room to walk around because so many of the refugees were lying on the floor.

And outside, the streets and sidewalks were the same, covered with people who had no place whatsoever to go."

The Rev. Julian McPhillips, Sr., served as director of the American Peace Corps in India from 1966-69. Part of his contract called for his college-age children to receive transportation to the McPhillipses' home in Calcutta. Julian Jr., David, and Betsy, all in college, came home to India during the summers of '67 and '68. The first summer they made stops in Europe and the Middle East en route to India, where they spent five weeks. They came back home through the Orient. During this time, Julian and his brother David visited much of India, including West Bengal, Delhi, Bombay, the Taj Mahal, and Kashmir, and also got up to Nepal. The following summer, traveling by himself, Julian filled in gaps in those parts of India he had missed the preceding summer. "This greatly enhanced my Princeton education, giving it a real international flavor," said Julian.

Julian also spent much time in France during the summers of 1965 and 1967, greatly improving his ability to speak French. Armed with a McConnell Foundation grant from Princeton's Woodrow Wilson School of Public and International Affairs in 1967, Julian researched and later wrote his thesis on "The Role of the French Communist Party in the Resistance Movement Against the Nazis During World War II." He received firsthand accounts from a number of resistance fighters. Leading French historian Henri Michel helped guide Julian's work in Paris.

During his four years at Princeton, Julian found his career orientation gradually changing from following his father's footsteps as a member of the Episcopal Church priesthood, to a more public avenue of service.

A fellow native Alabamian at Princeton, namely history professor Sheldon Hackney, instructed Julian in "The Civil War and Reconstruction," "Populism and Progressivism in America," and "The History of the South." In 1965, Hackney and his Alabama-born-and-raised wife, Lucy Durr Hackney, invited Julian to their Princeton home, where he met Virginia Durr for the first time. "Virginia carried on about how my 1963 letter to the editor in the Montgomery newspaper, following JFK's assassination, was the subject of much Sunday School discussion."

"Princeton's motto was 'In the Nation's Service,'" Julian says, "and that was certainly the case. I was awed by the number of Princetonians, past and present, who had contributed to America's history and well-being. They ranged from the American presidents James Madison, Grover Cleveland, and Woodrow Wilson, to Albert Einstein, to F. Scott Fitzgerald, to Cold War statesman Dean Acheson and LBJ advisor Eric Goldman, also a pop historian. The list went on and on.

"My college roommate the last two years, Steve Pajcic of Jacksonville, Florida, became the Democratic nominee for governor of Florida in 1986, but was defeated in a close general election contest. Suitemates Bill Potter of California, Lew Retrum of Ohio, and Stanley Bynum of Alabama were all drawn to majors and theses involving public and international affairs, and all eventually attended law school. Princeton just had a way of inspiring its students into public service," Julian recalls. Good friend Fred Billings of Nashville broke the trend by going to medical school and today practices medicine in Baton Rouge.

But the Princetonian who perhaps influenced Julian most during his years at the university was fellow student Bill Bradley, a senior the year Julian became a freshman. By that time, Bradley was already a three-time, first team All-American, twice on the cover of *Sports Illustrated*, star of the 1964 Gold Medal Olympic team, winner of the 1965 Sullivan Award for the outstanding amateur athlete in America, and just named Rhodes Scholar at Oxford.

"I was absolutely in awe of him," Julian says. "One spring day in 1965 we were both leaving an organizational meeting of the Fellowship of Christian Athletes on campus, and we struck up a conversation. The next thing I knew, we'd been sitting on a bench talking non-stop for an hour and fifteen minutes. I was popping him with questions about his Christian faith, and he explained to me how his faith was the foundation of everything he was, and did, and hoped to be.

"From that point on, I did better at Princeton—academically, athletically, and spiritually—because of Bradley's example."

Columbia Law and the Vietnam War

Julian recalls his days at Columbia as some of the "most heady" of his life. The summer of 1968, before classes started, he was offered a job teaching Lebanese students at the International College of the American University of Beirut for the 1968-69 academic year. Julian initially accepted the offer, but with the draft board likely to call him up for a physical exam, he changed his direction at the end of the summer, accepting a late admission to Columbia Law. The day law school started, Julian was flying back across the Atlantic— torn by a desire to remain in what was then "a beautiful and peaceful jewel of the Mediterranean, in the intriguing Middle East."

Nevertheless, Julian plunged into his studies, helped coach the school's wrestling team, and served as a residence hall counselor for undergrads to reduce his law school expenses. He was on the school's International Law moot court team, served as editor of the *Columbia Journal of Transnational Law*, and, ignoring the doctor's earlier advice, twice won the Eastern A.A.U. heavyweight wrestling championship while competing for the New York Athletic Club.

But it was in the politics of Columbia Law School, during the spirited days of the Vietnam War protests of 1968-71, that Julian especially made his mark. He was president of the Law School Senate his last two years, and one day in early May of 1970 found himself catapulted into a debate with the dean of the law school, Michael Sovern, before an audience of some nine hundred students and faculty. The subject: whether students should strike in response to the U.S. invasion of Cambodia.

A majority of the students wanted to go on strike, in solidarity with some four hundred other colleges and universities across the U.S. The administration, not surprisingly, was opposed. Eventually, Julian and Dean Sovern worked out a compromise plan that allowed students three options: those who wanted to remain in class until after final exams could do so; those who wanted to strike could do so, with the sub-options of either taking their exams in the fall for letter grades, or taking the exams home for the summer and sending them back for pass/fail grades. Julian, and the majority of the students, chose the third option.

McPhillips's presidency of the Law School Senate automatically launched him into another leadership vehicle, the chairmanship of the Columbia Law School Coalition Against the War. In that capacity, he attended the two historic anti-war marches in Washington, D.C.—the first in November of 1969, the second in May of 1970, and both with over a million people reported present. His brothers David and Frank were also active in the movement. So were Julian's parents, following the lead of their sons.

"There was the smell of revolution in the air," Julian recalls. "Sideburns and long hair were pretty much standard, but I managed to avoid getting into drug use, in part because I was still so serious about my wrestling training."

Though Julian frequently debated the faculty in guest columns of the Columbia Law School student newspaper, and organized and spearheaded anti-war efforts, he somehow avoided any brushes with the law. To this day he's never been arrested—"not even on a misdemeanor charge," as he points out.

Ironically, the same cannot be said about his parents, who were both arrested during a D.C. demonstration in the spring of 1970 in Lafayette Park, directly across the street from the White House. At the time, they were conducting a prayer vigil as part of the Clergy and Laymen Concerned About Vietnam. They were in good company, including Dr. Benjamin Spock, a leading anti-war spokesman, whom they met behind bars. They were later released, and the charges dropped.

"Actually," the younger Julian laughs, "my name might still be on some FBI computer list, but if it's there it's because it's mixed up with my father's name, exactly the same as mine, which has been a frequent occurrence throughout our lives, especially since we also share the same birthday, November 13."

5

Transition Back To Alabama

D ESPITE his travels and his growing connections in New York City, the South kept exerting its subtle attraction on Julian. During law school he spent one summer in Richmond, Virginia, and another in New Orleans, which had been the home of his mother's family. "I liked them both, but it was in Richmond that I saw more potential," he remembers. "Virginia's a beautiful state, with a rich history and a lot of gorgeous countryside. It just seemed to me like a nice median ground between the Deep South of my upbringing and the Up East of my education."

Once more, his parents felt the same way. After the Peace Corps stint in India, they moved to Alexandria, Virginia, in 1969, where Julian Sr. commuted to his job in Washington as executive director of the Peace Corps from 1969-71. They liked it so much they planned to retire there. But fate had other plans.

In 1970, a different kind of tragedy shook the entire family to its foundations. Julian's brother David, suffering from manic depression, attempted to take his own life by carbon monoxide poisoning. Sheerly by chance, some friends returned to the house early and revived him—but at the cost of significant brain damage from which he would never fully recover. He spent nearly a year in the hospital.

Not long afterward, when the family's vegetable-canning plant in Cullman County fell on hard financial times, Julian Sr. was recruited to try to turn the business around. So the couple's decision to move back to Alabama was twofold: while Eleanor gave David the daily care he needed, helping him through the confusing welter of physicians, rehabilitation, and the sometimes difficult readjustment to living on his own, her husband would spend long hours at the plant trying to piece together the details of its money troubles and what would be required to get the operation back on its feet.

Julian resumed his law studies, still with an eye toward an international practice, and upon graduation from Columbia Law he was offered a job that any new law grad would give his wingtips for: the prestigious Wall Street firm of Davis Polk & Wardwell, that represented a roster of blue-chip corporations, and also had offices in London, Paris, and Hong Kong. The future looked secure, and for the next few years Julian worked hard and counted his blessings. He had an interesting job, was winning wrestling tournaments, and had met his wife-to-be—J. Leslie Burton, appropriately enough a young woman who was a world traveler herself. Of Scandinavian ancestry, she had grown up in Brazil where her father was a bank executive.

How Julian and Leslie met on March 30, 1973, as they've afterwards joked, was like finding a needle in a haystack. New York City, in those counter-culture days, was teeming with young divorcees and swinging singles. It was a place to have fun, but not necessarily to find marriage material.

A party on the East Side of Manhattan brought them together. Leslie, twenty-five, was invited by a Princeton classmate of Julian's he didn't know, namely Charlie McCrann. Julian, twenty-six, was invited by McCrann's roommate Bob Wise, a fellow Davis Polk associate attorney. Julian recalls he "almost didn't make the party, because I was in the middle of the Eastern AAU wrestling championships." The location of the tournament, however, at the New York Athletic Club (NYAC), on Central Park South, was not far away. With three quick pins in earlier rounds, Julian found the time and energy to walk over to the party that Friday evening.

"I knocked on the door," said Julian, "and there was this beautiful, tall, blonde with a radiant smile standing over in a corner. It took me no time to get over to her. We talked a lot about Brazil, which I had visited only two years earlier. I was greatly impressed. It was obvious she was someone special." Soon thereafter they started dating. Leslie met Julian after wrestling workouts at NYAC, or Julian would meet her at the dance studio, and dinner would follow. Although they came from different backgrounds, and had different interests and personalities, they shared many common values, including love of family. The attraction quickly grew.

One of the many things Julian and Leslie had in common was a competitive spirit, though it expressed itself in very different pursuits.

One weekend in April 1973, during their courtship, they had to be apart while Julian entered the National AAU Wrestling Tournament in Cleveland and Leslie participated in a national grand ballroom dance competition in Miami.

Julian lost. Leslie won. Leslie vividly remembers the late-night phone call afterward. At first she couldn't reach him but by the next day they exchanged their news: "That was the first time I knew, instinctively," said Leslie, "that our getting married was inevitable. It just felt like such a perfect fit." Julian adds, "While she was waltzing to victory, I was suffering ignominious defeat."

A couple of months later, Leslie met Eleanor McPhillips, her future mother-in-law, for the first time over the telephone. Two days earlier, Julian had arrived in Tahiti, via a Pan Am airliner, en route to New Zealand and Australia, when the international news reported that a Pan Am plane had crashed into the Pacific Ocean, just short of Tahiti, with everyone on board perishing. "It was a tearful, awkward introduction, as we compared schedules," recounts Leslie, finally grasping that Julian was not on that doomed flight. But he was on the very next Pan Am flight out of Tahiti. "I'll never forget," says Julian, "how we passengers, in a reversal of the usual role, comforted the sobbing stewardesses and pilots who had just lost their dear friends."

On December 28, 1973, after a visit with grandfather Julian B. McPhillips in Mobile, Leslie and Julian became engaged. They waited to announce it to their families that New Year's Eve, at a gathering in New Orleans just before the legendary 1973 Sugar Bowl game between Alabama and Notre Dame.

During the next six months, Leslie (of a non-denominational Protestant background) was first baptized and then confirmed as an Episcopalian. They received marriage counseling from two Episcopal priests, the Revs. Fitz Allison and Doug Carpenter, in addition to Julian's father. On June 22, 1974, they were married at an Episcopal church in Wellesley, Massachusetts, and celebrated afterward with a big party at the home of Leslie's parents in Weston.

A three-week honeymoon trip took them to Scandinavia, where they traced Leslie's ancestral Norwegian roots and met Julian's brother Frank in Finland. They also squeezed in a trip to nearby Russia, with expenses substantially reduced by the discounts Julian received from his second Wall Street job, as associate counsel at American Express Company, which he had begun in the summer of 1973.

Summer weekends of '72 and '73 were frequently spent in Quogue at the

Hamptons of Long island, enjoying the camaraderie of Princeton-Columbia friends Cliff and Judy Fenton, Tim and Ilia Smith, and Walter and Mimes Bliss, as well as a motley diversity of others, particularly Davis Polk suitemate John Siebold. The Fentons and Smiths got married just before the McPhillipses, and the Blisses not long afterwards. "We were falling like dominoes," Julian recalls with a grin.

Back home, Julian and Leslie settled into housekeeping and enjoying the bright lights, Broadway shows, and world-class museums of New York City. But Julian gradually realized that his dream job was not all it was cracked up to be.

"As fascinating as it all was," he says, "what it came down to at the end of the day was that I had helped rich people get a little richer. Not that there's anything wrong with that, but I was certain at a really gut level that it wasn't something I could spend my life doing."

New York City, they also agreed, was not the ideal place to raise a family. So in March of 1975 they left the Big Apple and headed home to Montgomery—taking the long way, with a tour of the African continent and a two-week visit to Brazil, to see Leslie's friends. There, in April, they received good news: Julian had passed the Alabama Bar exam he'd taken in February.

They returned to New York City just long enough to load a U-Haul trailer and attach it to Julian's red Chevy Vega. Then they drove to Montgomery, where Julian had accepted a job as assistant attorney general under populist activist Attorney General Bill Baxley, whom Julian considered "a great philosophical match."

Interlude

The Road to Montgomery

THE CRADLE of the Confederacy. The Birthplace of the Civil Rights Movement. Hometown to Hank Williams, Rosa Parks, Zelda Fitzgerald, and Nat King Cole.

If the "weight" of history were literal, the city of Montgomery, Alabama, would long ago have been pressed a good distance beneath the surface of the earth.

There are two ways to get from Cullman, Alabama, to Montgomery. The express route – otherwise known as Interstate 65 South – passes through Birmingham and is fairly uneventful for the first hour or so. The traffic is composed largely of hurtling eighteen-wheelers, doing their intricate ballet with RVs and automobiles though a stretch of putative seventy-mile-per-hour speed limit that is, as Shakespeare would say, "more honored in the breach than the observance." (A state ordinance gives lawmakers immunity from traffic violations while the legislature is in session.)

The shopping malls and fast food restaurants might be on any highway, anywhere in the country. Birmingham's southern corridor has seen an unprecedented explosion of growth in recent years. Suburban Hoover, home to the giant Galleria Mall and a metropolitan baseball stadium where the Birmingham Barons play teams with the names like the Chattanooga Lookouts and the Georgia Mudcats, has just become the state's fifth most populous city – behind Birmingham, Mobile, Montgomery, and Huntsville.

The phenomenon extends down into northern Shelby County, which was largely rural just ten or fifteen years ago but is now among the fastest-growing areas in the U.S. But the new pace is not to everyone's liking. Less than a week after an Atlanta gunman killed nine people and wounded thirteen in downtown office buildings during a rampage apparently set off by his stock-trading losses, the Shelby County town of Pelham made national headlines when a truck driver with no previous criminal record shot and killed three former associates, apparently over a dispute about changing his route schedule.

About fifty miles down I-65, though, the landforms begin changing dramatically. The hills and tall pines of the Appalachian foothills give way to Chilton County's rolling plains of farmland and fruit orchards. It's the state's peach-growing capital, a fact that the town of Clanton proudly announces to interstate traffic via its municipal water tower, a fifty-foot-high imitation of a ripe peach. Nearby are the Peach Tower Restaurant, Headley's Big Peach, and Peach Queen Campgrounds.

The lower half of the I-65 route to Montgomery also shows a burgeoning of religious sentiment. One large billboard – in red, white, and blue – displays the Bible verse John 3:16 "For God so loved the world, that he gave his only begotten Son, that whosoever believeth in him should not perish, but have everlasting life."

Just a bit farther on, a different billboard cuts to the chase. Alongside a tall red silhouette of a figure with horns and a scythe is the admonishment, "Go To Church Or The Devil Will Get You!"

But to get a sense of the region's place in history, it's better to take the scenic route – turning on the two-lane back road of Highway 82 just past Clanton. Here, it's easier to see the pace of an earlier time, as well as the strikingly dark soil that gives the agricultural area its traditional name: "the Black Belt." The fertile cotton lands of the Tombigbee-Alabama river basin, plus access to the great seaport at Mobile, drew farmers and investors in unprecedented numbers. But in the 1820s the Black Belt name had a grim double meaning: slaves outnumbered whites in the district, and the plantation economy expanded so rapidly that per capita wealth for whites in the 1830s averaged more than $700, a figure that America as a whole wouldn't attain until well after the Civil War.

With prosperity came influence and the struggle for political power. Some local historians wryly note that the state's eventual capital literally began in a state of bitter contention. A Georgia general named John Scott formed the Alabama Company and advertised plots of land on the river bluff in a new town he named (presumably liking the sound of "New York, New York,") Alabama, Alabama.

A Massachusetts lawyer, Andrew Dexter, bought another section of the bluff at seven dollars an acre, but became strapped for cash after making the down payment. Other Eastern investors came to his aid, and their company competed with Scott's by laying off lots in a neighboring town they named New Philadelphia. Settlers, though, preferred the name "Yankee Town."

A somewhat eccentric visionary with a checkered history, Dexter previously tried to develop a seven-story office center in Boston, which was to be billed as the tallest building in America. But the project fell through, leaving him more than a million dollars in debt. He had come to Alabama hoping to make a new start.

The prime spot of real estate in Dexter's holdings, though, was not for sale. He explained that he was reserving it for the state capitol – a plan that was the butt of much humor at the time, especially since Alabama was not even a state yet, and would not come to pass for thirty years while the capitol was first in three other cities. Meanwhile, the hillside lot served as prime grazing ground for local goats. To this day, Montgomery residents refer to the State Capitol complex as "Goat Hill." (Dexter would never live to see his dream vindicated; after again facing financial reverses he moved to Mobile, where he died of yellow fever in 1837.)

Scott's company reacted to Dexter's enterprise by blocking New Philadelphians' access to the riverfront, but Dexter's town still thrived by being the first settlement seen by the growing stream of Georgians traveling into the area from the east along the Federal Road. Scott retaliated by buying another piece of land upriver, alongside New Philadelphia, and naming it East Alabama. Both enterprises held their own for several years, but when Alabama officially gained statehood in 1819 Scott's group wanted to call a truce and merge the two towns with a new courthouse to be built on the dividing line.

The newly combined town was named in honor of Revolutionary War hero General Richard Montgomery – not to be confused with Major Lemuel Pernell Montgomery, killed at Horseshoe Bend, for whom Montgomery County had been named three years earlier by the Mississippi Territorial Legislature.

In 1820, a Boston newspaperman shipped his printing press by rail to Savannah, from which it was hauled overland to Montgomery, resulting in the city's first newspaper. The following year, the steamboat Harriet made the first journey to the city from the port of Mobile in sixty-five hours. A fledgling stagecoach line connecting the city with Milledgeville, Georgia, soon expanded into eight routes, and even skeptics had to agree that the boom times had begun.

Law and order would take a good bit longer. Between 1841 and 1843, in a county with fewer than three thousand white adult males, the Circuit Court saw eighty-nine trials for violent crimes, including nine murders and twenty assaults with intent. Some of the cultured members of the community relied on pistol duels to settle their disputes. These included the legendary political orator William L. Yancey. After the state added a section to its penal code forbidding duelists from holding public office, the Alabama legislature had to pass a special act in 1846 – the year the state capitol was moved to Montgomery – exempting Yancey, so that he could take office as a representative.

But as the violence flourished, so did churches. The original "Union Church" that housed all Christian denominations soon split off into Presbyterians, Methodists, and Baptists. Shortly afterward, Episcopalians organized St. John's Church and appointed the state's first bishop. The town's Catholics formed St. Peter's, the Jewish congregation built Temple Beth-Or, and for a short while a Universalist church held services.

Today, a drive to Montgomery along Highway 82 makes it plain that the proliferation of churches has never stopped. Austere buildings with names like Christ the Rock Church, One True Way Fellowship, and Full Gospel Tabernacle dot the roadside between fields, farms, and abandoned barns, bringing to mind author Flannery O'Connor's description of the South's "Christ-haunted" landscape.

And where there's religion, politics generally is not far behind. On this particular week, a forty-seven-year-old ex-Marine from Springville, Alabama, is traveling by bicycle across the state's back roads in protest of a proposed lottery measure that will go before the state's voters in the fall. A red-and-white sign on the back of Curtis Garrett's bike reads "Yes Lord, No Lottery" and he wears a T-shirt with the message, "Our Kids Need Love, Not Lottery Money."

"Yeah, I've had a few disparaging remarks hurled at me," he tells reporters. "But this is something that God has laid on my heart. And if getting God's message across means sticking me on a stupid bicycle, that's just the way it is. The basics of the Bible need to come back."

LESLIE liked Montgomery, and commented to Julian that its friendliness, tree-shaded old homes, and laid-back pace made it feel a lot like Brazil to her, particularly after the hectic New York scene – and it helped Julian see the familiar place in a new light. "I guess it reminded her of a banana republic," Julian jokingly observes.

Their first two weeks back, in April 1975, they stayed with the renowned Clifford and Virginia Durr, at their "Pea Level" home in nearby Wetumpka. In the evenings, Clifford would regale Leslie and Julian with his storehouse of Indian tales.

Both Durrs were native Alabamians, of old Southern families. He was a famous New Dealer, a former member of the Federal Communications Commission, and the only white lawyer in Montgomery who aided the early civil rights movement. She was the sister-in-law of Hugo Black, the friend and confidant of Eleanor Roosevelt, and one of the great voices of white Southern liberalism from the thirties to the nineties.

"Both of the Durrs were a great inspiration to me, professionally and personally," Julian says.

But a week after Julian and Leslie moved to their own place, Clifford died of a stroke. The extended circle of family and friends gathering for the funeral and related events included the young McPhillips twosome.

Virginia lived for twenty-four more years. She would become an intimate friend of the young McPhillips couple, often encouraging Julian to pursue civil rights cases and, on one occasion, to draft a memorial resolution honoring her late husband, which he did for the Young Lawyer's Section of the Alabama Bar Association in 1975. Virginia died in 1999, at age ninety-six.

"The thing I remember most about Virginia Durr," Julian says, "is her indomitable spirit and courage. She hated injustice, and practically nothing scared her. She was a wonderful inspiration and friend, not only to Leslie and me, but to three or four generations of other people. She richly deserved the accolades she received."

Virginia Durr was an especially notable example, but she was just one of a number of distinctive people who made Montgomery an interesting place for Leslie and Julian to put down their roots. Over the years, of course, Julian himself has joined the ranks of those characters who make Montgomery unique.

II.

The Practice of Law

6

The Young Assistant Attorney General

AS ASSISTANT attorney general, McPhillips soon found himself on the opposite side of the fence in the corporate equation: prosecuting cases that ranged from white-collar crime to corporate fraud to environmental issues. Increasingly, he was on the side of "the little guy," and he realized that being there filled a void he had felt for so long on Wall Street.

"Taking up for the underdog was something I just sort of gradually worked into," he says now. "I didn't start out with the clear idea that being a champion for the ordinary person on the street was the one thing God had put me on earth to do, but I did realize early on that standing up for the rights of the oppressed greatly appealed to me. And to a certain extent it's a part of the Christian creed. It's part of the Sermon on the Mount. It was just something ingrained in me, for as far back as I could remember, that basically we're put here to help other people. Like the scripture where it says, 'To whom much is given, much shall be required.' And Leslie and I were very fortunate. We'd been given a lot."

Public Interest Litigation

Julian hit the ground running in his new assignment.

In June 1975, he obtained a $125,000 judgment in Birmingham for Alabama consumers against several Florida companies engaged in fraud.

In September and December he tried two cases of securities fraud in his home county of Cullman, in which companies were charged with preying on elderly and ill-educated people. He obtained convictions in both, gaining much publicity in both Birmingham's and Cullman's newspapers. One case resulted in a seven-year sentence, the other in a year's sentence, and the victims of the fraudulent practices received restitution.

Also in September 1975, Julian obtained an injunction in Birmingham against an Alabama company fraudulently selling Caribbean vacation trips to Alabama residents. Principals of the company, whom McPhillips described in court as "rip-off artists," were later indicted and convicted.

That December, Julian brought a suit against Birmingham Trust National Bank on behalf of the Greater Birmingham Foundation, a charitable organization assisting churches, schools, and other charitable interests in the Birmingham area, charging that BTNB had breached its fiduciary duty in making poor investments. The case resulted in a win for the state and a $2 million judgment against BTNB. But the victory came with a price: later when Julian ran for attorney general, the chairman of the board of BTNB worked energetically against his candidacy.

Also in the last month of 1975, Julian teamed with Securities Commission director Tommy Krebs in obtaining a restraining order against Louisiana and Texas oil companies selling non-existent oil wells to Alabama investors. The settlement, again widely publicized, returned $600,000 to the defrauded plaintiffs.

In March 1976, McPhillips and Krebs teamed again to reach a settlement with an Alabama insurance company violating securities laws by selling worthless stock. The settlement returned more than $200,000 to the citizens defrauded.

That same July, McPhillips obtained a letter of agreement from a bank in south Alabama, refunding $60,000 to Alabama consumers it had overcharged for credit life insurance. That same month, Julian also took on a national hamburger franchise building a restaurant in Alabama, claiming it had unfairly been granted tax-exempt industrial bond status, in violation of the Wallace–Cater Act, designed years earlier to attract out-of-state industries to Alabama. It was not designed, Julian argued to the court, to allow pre-existing businesses tax-free bonds every time they wanted to expand, with taxpayers footing the bill. The bond issue was stopped.

Julian's next two legal battles took to the air. In July and August, the assistant attorney general initiated efforts leading to commencement of Montgomery–Mobile air service and increased Montgomery–New Orleans and Mobile–New Orleans air service. Prior to the addition, the lack of service had hampered commerce and travel. "Not only did the business community applaud the new services," Julian says, "but it was a great benefit for the public as well."

In August, Julian petitioned the Civil Aeronautics Board for an investigation of air traffic congestion at Atlanta's International Airport, alleging a threat to public health and safety, especially to Alabama residents. This was a pet peeve of Julian's boss, Bill Baxley, who regularly fumed over his wasted hours waiting in the Atlanta airport. Baxley and McPhillips sought a re-routing of traffic to other Southeastern airports, including some in Alabama.

Despite their energetic efforts, the attempt was stymied by what Julian recalls as "an enormous amount of bureaucratic red tape. The Civil Aeronautics Board made promises that better flight service was in the works for Birmingham, but Montgomery saw very little of the benefit."

The Ed Lowder Case

Perhaps the largest and most significant case during Julian's time as assistant attorney general involved the civil lawsuit by Baxley against one of the state's most powerful men: Ed Lowder, executive director of the Alabama Farm Bureau Insurance Companies and owner of many family businesses.

The case essentially charged Lowder with engaging in self-dealing and conflicts of interest by using his position at Alabama Farm Bureau to steer plum business opportunities and deals to himself and his own companies, rather than to the policyholder-based Farm Bureau companies.

Baxley chose Julian to handle the case. After considerable research, Julian drafted a lawsuit naming Baxley as a plaintiff on behalf of numerous Alabama citizens who were policyholders in the Farm Bureau Insurance Companies. A separate co-plaintiff, Douglas McCartha, president of the Elmore County Farm Bureau, and his wife Louise, brought a companion mutual policyholder's derivative lawsuit, which Julian also researched and drafted.

Baxley and McPhillips convinced attorney Sonny Hornsby (then fourteen years away from being elected the state's Chief Justice) to represent the McCarthas, but McPhillips recalls doing virtually all the legal work behind the scenes. "Afterwards," Julian says with a chuckle, "Sonny told me he appreciated 'all the help.'"

The central legal battle was over "standing," namely the right of Baxley, as attorney general, to bring the suit in the first place. Lowder and Farm Bureau brought out the big guns from the start—hiring not one, but four, of the capital's most powerful law firms: Hill, Hill, Carter, Franco and Cole; Rushton, Stakely, Johnston and Garrett; Smith, Bowman, Thaggard, Crook and Cullpepper; and Ball, Ball, Duke and Mathews.

Judge Eugene Carter, pushing ninety years old, was in his last year as Montgomery County Circuit Judge and was chosen to hear the case. McPhillips was assisted by local Montgomery attorney Bob Steiner, who made no bones about his dislike of Lowder. After much local and state publicity, Carter ruled in favor of Baxley, McCartha, and McPhillips.

"That one was really an adrenaline rush," Julian recalls. "I felt like David against Goliath. I think the Court's ruling surprised a lot of people."

After the victory, McPhillips was contacted by Lowder's defense lawyers, who wanted to work out a settlement. Eventually, by late 1976, a tentative settlement, favorable to the policyholders, was reached, and McPhillips presented it to Baxley, McCartha, and Hornsby. Six months passed and, much to Julian's frustration, by the time McPhillips left the office in June 1977, Baxley had still not approved the settlement. It wasn't finally approved until the end of 1977, and then on terms never revealed to McPhillips.

"I was very loyal to Baxley, and I never criticized him over the issue, either publicly or privately," Julian says now. "But the 'whys' and 'wherefores' are still totally puzzling to me. I guess the only person who knows all the details is Baxley himself. And maybe Sonny Hornsby."

Nonetheless, the case was a very heady experience for the young assistant attorney general. But Julian had not heard the last of Lowder.

IN ONLY two years and two months spent working for the Attorney General's office, Julian had obtained seven judgments or settlements totaling more than $3 million on behalf of Alabama citizens, as well as several criminal convictions. He also won three injunctions against pyramid schemes and other corrupt business practices on behalf of the state's consumers, without having to share a percentage of the take with the plaintiff's private lawyers.

These successes, and the publicity they generated, led some of the other assistants to encourage Julian, near the end of his tenure in the spring of 1977, to run for attorney general himself in 1978, which he did (Baxley was running for governor that year).

During the summer of 1978, after polls and endorsements showed Julian surging ahead in the attorney general's race, a local lawyer who had defended Lowder telephoned Julian, and said that Ed Lowder wanted to meet him.

"Naturally, I was a little hesitant," Julian recalls. "But I thought it would be the courteous thing to do, so I agreed." The two men met privately at Lowder's Farm Bureau office. Lowder was not long in laying his cards on the table.

"He told me he didn't think I was going to win," Julian says, "but he admitted I was doing pretty well in the polls, and said he thought I was going to have a bright future, and so on." Therefore, Lowder said, he wanted to make a contribution to his campaign of $2,500.

Regaining his composure, Julian told Lowder he appreciated the offer, and could certainly use the contribution ("That kind of money was not chicken feed, back in the 1970s," Julian interjects) but he felt it best to decline, because he was obligated by law to report it. When the public learned of the donation, McPhillips told Lowder, some might think that the former assistant attorney general had "sold out" the interests of Farm Bureau policyholders in the settlement with Lowder, in anticipation of financial support for his campaign.

Julian remembers Lowder's expression changing to one of amusement.

"Smart fellow," Lowder mumbled to McPhillips. "I was afraid you'd feel that way. That's why I've got this sack over here, just in case."

Lowder nodded toward a common, brown supermarket bag next to his desk. McPhillips looked into it, and saw that it was filled with cash. Exactly $2,500 worth, Lowder assured him.

"I thanked him again," Julian recalls, "but I told him I still had to refuse."

The look of amusement on Lowder's face was replaced with an incredulous frown.

"He looked at me like, 'What kind of naïve so-and-so *are* you?'" Julian says. "I'd obviously offended him. Apparently he wasn't accustomed to people turning down money. But I did what I had to do."

The two never crossed paths again. Several years later, Ed Lowder died.

Introduction to Governor Wallace

Any Alabamian over the age of forty knows first-hand that George Wallace dominated Alabama politics like no one else in its history—sometimes for bad, sometimes for good.

The first time McPhillips remembers hearing Wallace's name was in 1958, when Julian was in the sixth grade at elementary school in Cullman. The then-current governor, "Big Jim" Folsom, a towering political figure in his own right, was prevented by law from succeeding himself. Julian remembers the town being blanketed with Wallace campaign posters: in store windows, on utility poles, in residents' yards. Against a backdrop of rapidly worsening racial politics, John Patterson won the 1958 election, after which Wallace was famously quoted as saying he would never be "out-niggered again."

In 1962, Julian was only sixteen, but he remembers being "very embarrassed" by Wallace's strong segregationist stand during that governor's race, which he won (for the first of four times). "I think the fact that most people around the country believed George Wallace personified Alabama was the major factor in my doubting, during college and law school, whether I would ever come back to Alabama to live," Julian says.

But McPhillips did come home in 1975, and Wallace was physically—and to some extent politically—a shadow of his former self. Confined to a wheelchair after an assassination attempt while campaigning in a third-ticket presidential bid, he had also seemingly mellowed a great deal on the race issue.

Within a year, Julian would find himself on Wallace's side in a court case. When the legislature failed to pass a budget in 1976, Wallace attempted to extend the old one by executive edict. State Senator John Baker filed suit against Wallace, charging a violation of the "separation of powers" doctrine. Julian assisted Deputy Attorney General George Beck in Wallace's defense. Baker won the case. The budget was later passed in a special session.

Bringing Alabamians Back from the Ivy League

During the 1970s, with future statewide elected official Lucy Baxley greeting them while working for her then-husband, the office of Attorney General Bill Baxley became a re-entry point for many talented young lawyers returning to Alabama after Ivy League educations. Some have said recruiting these assistant attorneys general was one of Baxley's greatest accomplishments.

Baxley's contingent of Ivy Leaguers became known, sometimes humorously, as his "Brain Trust." Humorously or not, they were highly regarded and their dedication to civil rights, education, the environment, and consumer affairs helped reshape the state after Alabama's segregationist fifties and sixties.

At a going-away party for McPhillips in June 1977, Chief Assistant Attorney General Walter Turner proclaimed, "If I am ever in trouble, I'll tell you who I'm calling first. That's Julian McPhillips."

Besides Julian, future U.S. Magistrate Vanzetta Penn McPherson of Montgomery came from Columbia Law School, while U.S. District Judge Myron Thompson of Tuskegee came home from Yale College and Yale Law. Rick Middleton of Birmingham, future founder of the Southern Environmental Law Center, returned from Yale Law to practice environmental law. Bill Stephens of Huntsville, now deputy director of the Alabama State Retirement Systems, and Mobile attorney Hank Caddell, originally from Decatur, both returned to Alabama from Harvard Law School. Both made significant contributions as assistant attorneys general of the State of Alabama.

Other non-Ivy Leaguers during Julian's era who also made significant contributions to Alabama and the Attorney General's office included Gil Kendrick, Rosa Hamlett-Davis, Jock Smith, David Dunn III, Joe Marston, John Yung, and Carol Jean Smith. Hamlett-Davis and Carol Jean Smith remained at the AG's office for thirty plus years. Kendrick enjoyed a strong local practice before becoming counsel to the Alabama Bar Association. Jock Smith distinguished himself in plaintiff's civil work, and teamed up with Julian on several big cases. Dunn, three years behind Julian at Sewanee Military Academy, continues a strong international law career in Washington, D.C., following years in Paris, France. Yung had a stellar career with the Bar Association and has been retired for several years. Marston, a criminal appellate whiz, was employed as a staff attorney with McPhillips Shinbaum LLP from 2004–2005, and now does outside contract legal work for the firm.

7

Taking on Governors

G EORGE Wallace lost the 1976 lawsuit in which Julian helped represent him, but in the course of the case Julian learned enough about "separation of powers" as a cause of action to know that it was a powerful tool against holders of high office, and he would go on to use it in successful cases against Governors Fob James in 1981 and Guy Hunt in 1991.

Pruning Governor Wallace's Political Plum Tree

The next time Julian and Wallace went to court, Julian was in private practice and the two were on opposite sides. McPhillips represented Ruffin Blaylock, who was ousted as director of the Alabama Criminal Justice Information Center when Wallace began his fourth term on January 17, 1983. At a hearing in early March of that year, Julian got Blaylock reinstated with back pay.

The case gained a great deal of publicity around the state. Along with other cases in which Julian was involved at the time, it prompted Phillip Rawls of the Associated Press to write a syndicated column headlined "Julian McPhillips Likes Role, Not Name, of Public Watchdog." Soon, UPI columnist Bessie Ford wrote a similarly positive column titled "McPhillips Man to Watch in 1986."

Another effect of the publicity was that other Fob James appointees who had lost their jobs in the new Wallace administration came calling on Julian to represent them.

One was Gayle Parker, a Montgomery County license inspector, and another was Jim Pugh, an executive with the State Department of Conservation. Julian approached his friend and own personal attorney Bobby Segall to assist him on the Parker case, but Segall suggested to Julian it would be a good opportunity for him to work with Segall's associate attorney Dexter Hobbs, the oldest son of federal judge Truman Hobbs. Julian agreed.

After a hard-fought legal battle, Judge Myron Thompson in October 1984 issued a landmark opinion in favor of Gayle Parker, saying that Wallace had violated the First Amendment's "freedom of political association" clause. Mrs. Parker was ordered reinstated, with full back pay. Including attorney's fees, the verdict topped $100,000.

"We put a lot of energy and hard work into that case," Julian says, "and I give Dexter credit for carefully organizing it, getting the witnesses ready, and writing an excellent brief."

Wallace's choice for conservation commissioner, John "Toppy" Hodnett, quickly abolished top manager Jim Pugh's job in what was described as a cost-saving move. On August 31, after another tough fight by Julian in front of a federal court jury, Pugh was awarded $175,000. The jury ruled he had been wrongfully dismissed from his job for political reasons, and the court upheld the verdict.

At the time, Julian was quoted by the *Birmingham Post-Herald* as saying that the precedent-setting Parker ruling "is not only going to revolutionize the patronage system in Alabama, it's going to change politics. Henceforth, a new governor is not going to be able to dole out patronage to campaign workers in the counties the way it used to be done." McPhillips predicted the Parker and Pugh cases could affect hundreds of positions throughout county and state government that are traditionally appointed by the governor, adding that "these two First Amendment cases are going to be heard all over state government." And they were. "And they still are," says Mac McArthur, executive director of the Alabama State Employees Association in the year 2000, some sixteen years later.

In September 1986, Julian represented Charles James, an official of the Alabama Emergency Management Agency who contended he'd been fired from his job because of making negative comments about George Wallace. The jury agreed and awarded James $50,000 in damages.

With these four judicial wins under his belt—Ruffin Blaylock, Gayle Parker, Jim Pugh, and Charles James—McPhillips didn't endear himself to Alabama's legendary governor. But, state employees began knocking on Julian's door in great numbers.

Taking on Governor Fob James: Keeping Seniors at Work

Alabama history books owe governor Forrest Hood "Fob" James, Jr., a very special place. First elected as a Democrat in 1978, and again as a Republican in 1994, James is the only Alabamian elected governor from both major parties. In his first administration, James billed himself as a progressive, non-political, no-nonsense businessman. Opting not to seek re-election in 1982 and defeated in his 1986 and 1990 gubernatorial bids, Fob returned to his Republican roots and swept back into office in the 1994 Republican tidal wave that upset incumbent "Little Jim" Folsom and saw U.S. Senator Richard Shelby switch to the G.O.P.

Julian and Fob had developed a "very cordial relationship," by Julian's reckoning, when the two ran for state office in 1978. But as soon as James was elected Alabama's governor, Julian saw no problem in representing citizens in cases against the new administration.

The first opportunity presented itself in 1980, when a long-time employee of the Alabama Department of Pensions and Securities—Eulene Hawkins, then seventy-four years old—asked Julian for help. Governor James had just issued an executive order saying that, because the state was strapped for money, employees beyond the age of seventy could no longer work for state agencies or departments. The only exception was for employees in the "public health" sector.

Julian's research showed that Governor James's decision contravened a statute of the Code of Alabama which said that state employees, upon reaching the age of seventy, could continue to work for their agencies and departments, provided the department heads "needed their services," and the employees "furnished evidence of their physical and mental fitness."

Though the question was potentially a close judgment call, Julian filed a lawsuit on Mrs. Hawkins's behalf, maintaining that Governor James had violated the "separation of powers" doctrine of the Alabama Constitution by usurping legislative authority when he issued his executive edict relating to age and employment of state workers.

At the trial court level, Judge Randall Thomas considered the evidence and ruled against Mrs. Hawkins. Julian appealed to the Alabama Supreme Court, and argued before them Mrs. Hawkins's case, one of some forty cases he has pleaded before the Alabama Supreme Court in his career. The court—in a 5-3 opinion written by Justice Janie Shores—ruled in favor of Mrs. Hawkins.

The precedent-setting ruling, Julian says, "opened up the floodgates" for other state employees over the age of seventy to keep on working. Mrs. Hawkins, along with employees of other departments and agencies throughout the state, received a substantial amount of back pay. One of Julian's favorites of these employee/age cases was that of Mrs. Lillie McIntrye, who was seventy-five years old when Julian pursued her case in 1982, but, as he recalls, was "bubbling over with energy."

Mrs. Hawkins continued to work for the Department of Human Resources for many more years, eventually winning the National Social Worker of the Year Award, in large part for her efforts in this case. In her acceptance speech, she acknowledged that Julian's legal help had made the award possible. She lived a productive life until June 2000, when she died, at ninety-four, in her sleep.

Another client/beneficiary of Julian's legal work during Fob James's first administration was Ernest Patillo, of Tallassee, Alabama, who had sold the state thousands of small boxes of "Patillo's Corn Meal Mix" for promotion purposes. For some reason, Governor James refused payment for Patillo's corn meal mix. After haggling with the administration and getting nowhere, Patillo approached McPhillips about filing suit against the state, which he did in 1982.

Governor James "bristled" when his deposition was taken, Julian recalls, but in the end Patillo was paid in full for his corn meal mix.

Taking on Governor Guy Hunt: The 'Plane' Truth Revealed

They said it couldn't be done. But in 1986, Guy Hunt proved the experts (and a great many non-experts) wrong. He came out of nowhere on the political radar screen to be elected the first Republican governor of Alabama since the Reconstruction period following the Civil War—in other words, a little more than one hundred years.

Hunt, a native of rural Holly Pond, Alabama—just ten miles east of McPhillips's hometown of Cullman—was considered at best a novelty when he initially paid the $500 filing fee to run for the governor's office. Every election, candidates ranging from "Libertarian" to "Other" traditionally entered the race on principle. After a minor flurry of "human interest" or "local color" stories on their candidacy, they quickly became ciphers (i.e., single digits if not decimals of same) in straw polls.

Hunt was a farmer, an Army veteran who served in Korea, an ordained minister in the Primitive Baptist Church since 1958, and (as both state and national media could rarely resist pointing out) a part-time Amway salesman. What's more, he was running against the two men whom conventional wisdom judged most likely to lead the state into a new era after the unprecedented twenty-five-year reign of legendary Governor George Wallace.

Bill Baxley and Jere Beasley, both seasoned trial attorneys who had served as lieutenant governor during the years of the Wallace dynasty, were stymied in their 1978 efforts to secure a promotion—as were Charlie Graddick and Baxley (again) in 1986.

The day following the 1986 election, pundits around the state scrambled to put their own individual spins onto Guy Hunt's upset victory. Most of the reasons given for Hunt's win boiled down to one word: spite.

In the pressure of the 1986 campaign's final weeks, both Baxley and Graddick resorted to increasingly rancorous attacks on one another, transcending the political and becoming personal. Graddick won the 1986 Democratic primary, but apparently only with the aid of Republican "cross-over" voters, which the state Democratic Executive Committee challenged. Ultimately, Baxley was declared the Democratic nominee, but many Alabama voters were disgusted by the process. Guy Hunt was elected in what most observers saw as a protest vote.

In the beginning, all was well—if . . . different. Hunt announced that his goals would be to attract more industry, and more tourists, to the state—which rankled those who maintained that improving Alabama's schools should be the top priority of state government. Hunt's subsequent cabinet appointments were a powerful shot in the arm for the Republican party statewide, despite criticism that his choices were too male and too white to be representative of Alabama's diverse population.

Birmingham's most popular morning radio DJs, Courtney Haden and Greg Bass, whose topical humor included a daily parody of current events, announced: "This bulletin just in . . . in a surprise move, Governor Guy Hunt has appointed his wife Helen to be in charge of increasing minority participation during his term. Hunt's exact words were, 'If blacks want jobs in my administration, they can go to Helen Hunt for them' . . ."

Hunt's approval ratings were far from stellar, and the Democratic majority in the legislature managed to thwart the greater part of his agenda. One exception was the elaborate year-long tourism promotion known as "The Alabama Reunion," which critics charged was basically a one-year promotion of Guy Hunt.

But four years later, when Hunt's perceived blind-spot toward education led the Democrats to run the director of the Alabama Education Association, Paul Hubbert, Hunt was again victorious.

Soon after, though, things went steadily downhill for the history-making phenomenon from Holly Pond.

In the summer of 1991 a series of articles from the Associated Press brought to light that, for many of Hunt's weekend "preaching trips" of the past few years, he had traveled on state-owned aircraft at taxpayer expense, despite the fact that the congregations he visited gave him private donations for the sermons—or, as the governor preferred to phrase it, "love offerings."

In August, Julian agreed to bring a lawsuit against Hunt on behalf of Ralph Windom—a retired Army officer from Millbrook, Alabama—asking that the governor return to the taxpayers any money he had earned from the disputed outings. (Windom, coincidentally, is the father of Steve Windom, who was elected lieutenant governor of Alabama in 1998.)

Hunt countered that a private citizen had no right to bring a suit against a state office-holder over misspending. His attorneys cited a somewhat obscure 1935 U.S. Supreme Court precedent that only the governor and attorney general of a state have that power.

But McPhillips, at the hearing, told Judge Gene Reese, of the Circuit Court in Montgomery, "God help this state, and God help this republic, if a taxpayer doesn't have the standing to recover money illegally spent by an elected official." That argument eventually won out—Reese gave the go-ahead for the lawsuit to proceed, and also ordered the governor to turn over his personal tax returns to Windom and McPhillips.

Hunt's attorney appealed Reese's ruling to the state Supreme Court. They lost, in such a big way that the Associated Press story made headlines in the next day's *USA Today*. The court had ruled against Hunt, 8-0, on both the validity of the lawsuit and the tax-return question, saying that, "If a taxpayer does not launch an assault, it is not likely that there will be an attack from any other source, because the agency involved is usually in accord with the expenditure." In other words, a sort of fox-guarding-henhouse theory where state politicians were concerned.

Windom commented to reporters, "I felt all along that we were in the right. Hunt talks like being governor gives him some kind of imperial power."

Julian's response, which was chosen as the pull-out quote on the next day's *Montgomery Advertiser* editorial page, was, "I'm all for the Christian gospel being spread, but it should be spread on his time or the church's time, not the taxpayer's time."

Hunt, for his part, issued a statement saying that the ruling would leave all of Alabama's elected officials vulnerable to being sued by disgruntled constituents, that it was "a severe mistake" that would open "a Pandora's box." At the time, he couldn't have known how prophetic the prediction would be—at least, where his own political future was concerned.

Julian, when being interviewed by another reporter, insisted that he had no ill will toward Hunt personally: "It's just that if we don't draw the line on this, the next thing you know, taxpayers' money will be supporting a Buddhist ministry." Though the comment presumably left the state's Buddhists scratching their heads, it rankled the Hunt faithful even further.

In an interview soon after, the governor fired off: "Oh, I get sued by Julian about once a year, every six months. It's not surprising to me. This is just the same basic group of people who don't want prayer in the schools. The truth is, they don't want any semblance of religion in any place."

Not long after, Julian got a call at his office from a reporter asking for comment in response to Guy Hunt's charge that McPhillips was targeting Hunt's ministry because he, McPhillips, was an atheist.

"Actually," Julian told him, "there's somebody in my office right now who's probably more qualified to comment on that than I am. Would you like to talk to him?" Then he handed the phone across the desk to the rector of his church. The conversation—though lost to history—was reportedly very brief, as the Rev. Mark Tusken laid to rest any questions of Julian-as-atheist.

Initially, records showed that although Hunt had pocketed some $10,000 in offerings from the churches he visited, the actual cost of the state plane, fuel, and staff was in the $200,000 range. Julian assured reporters that looking at Hunt's tax returns—which the ruling obliged him to keep confidential—was "not going to open any Pandora's box." The opinion had a limited application, he said, and only in cases where public officials make money personally at taxpayer's expense. It would not affect officeholders who made bad decisions on spending tax dollars, as long as their own income doesn't benefit from their actions.

Not long afterward, a coal miner named John Tipton circulated a petition against the church-related trips and got five hundred signatures—the requirement set by the Alabama Ethics Commission for launching a special investigation. This made Hunt the first sitting governor to be targeted by an AEC inquiry since the commission was created in 1973. The agency had provided advisory opinions to both Governors George Wallace and Fob James, but made it clear that their findings were "intended only as guidance" to help the two men comply with the ethics law.

Julian's case was based instead on Article 1, Section 3, of the state Constitution: "No one shall be compelled by law to . . . pay taxes . . . for maintaining any minister or ministry." He announced he would seek an injunction to stop Hunt from using the planes for preaching trips, but the governor responded that this was unnecessary. He said he would no longer take any church trip on the state aircraft unless the Department of Public Safety first cleared it specifically with the Ethics Commission. In the meantime, the suit gave Hunt twenty days to produce tax returns, flight logs, and other documentation, and thirty days in which to repay any money that was due the state.

Hunt's lawyers appealed to the Supreme Court, who took up the case on May 12 of that year. Oral arguments on appeal cases are limited to one hour, and the court was expected to issue its ruling in a few months. On September 4, it did.

The Birmingham News headlined its coverage, "Governor Hunt Has Bad Day in Court." Some would have called that an understatement. The Supreme Court upheld the Circuit Court's ruling, giving Hunt ten days to supply the plaintiffs with copies of flight logs, state and federal tax returns since 1987, and "all correspondence between Guy Hunt and various churches at which he was preached since he has been governor." Windom's lawyers—McPhillips and partner Kenneth Shinbaum—also subpoenaed Hunt to appear at their offices two weeks later to answer detailed questions about the trips.

In an unrelated matter, Circuit Court Judge Joe Phelps rejected Hunt's plan to triple a state tax in order to pay for the disposal of hazardous waste in landfills.

The *Alabama Journal* applauded the plane-travel decision in its editorial pages, saying that,

> Keeping the issues straight in Governor Hunt's tangled legal affairs is vital to an informed understanding of this situation and why the situation is not the politically inspired plot he tries to label it. The legitimacy of the Windom suit should be beyond question now, in light of the state Supreme Court's decision . . .
>
> However, the constitutional issue on which the court ruled last week is not the same as the ethics law issue now being probed by a grand jury, even though both involve some of the same activities. Governor Hunt was paid for his preaching engagements, and it is these payments that have him in apparent conflict with the ethics law.
>
> The issue is not religious practice, as the governor would have Alabamians believe. Had he been paid for anything else, the ethics law issue would be the same. The fact that he was paid for preaching is irrelevant.

Keeping track of Hunt's "tangled legal affairs" was about to become even more difficult. Hunt filed a lawsuit claiming to be exempt from the state ethics law. A federal judge ruled against him, and Hunt appealed to the Eleventh U.S. Circuit Court of Appeals in Atlanta, which did likewise—leaving him only the resort of the U.S. Supreme Court.

Meanwhile, the ethics investigation led by Attorney General Jimmy Evans discovered that the governor's private lawyers had already billed the state for some $187,000. Hunt called a news conference to say that was only the beginning. The final tab would easily exceed $1 million, he predicted, and he said the taxpayers were rightly being required to pay because he was sued in his "official capacity," not as a private citizen. He closed with a plea to Evans to bring the widening ethics investigation to an end.

Julian went to court asking that Hunt stop billing taxpayers for the legal costs connected with his ethics case, and to repay any money that had already been spent. "Certainly the governor has the right to have the very best lawyers," he said. "But the governor should pay for them out of his own pocket."

When reporters at a statehouse news conference relayed Julian's comments to Hunt, and asked for his reaction, he laughed. "Then somebody hand me a hat," he quipped. "If I'm going to do this, I need some donations." And then added, "No, I have no response." A request to see the vouchers for Hunt's legal bills was turned down by the governor's office, with a spokesman saying they were "private communication between the lawyer and the client" and that analyzing their meeting times and the topics of their conversations could tip off the plaintiffs to the defense strategy.

On October 16, the *Advertiser's* headline read, "Attorneys Fees Reach $250,000 for Investigation of Governor." The story pointed out that the amount did not include time spent by state employees working on the case, which it agreed "show no signs of being near an end."

The governor's press secretary Terry Abbott called the fees "pretty amazing," especially since they started with the disputed amount of only $10,000 in church donations. With the governor fighting in court on three fronts, he was being represented by at least four members of the prestigious Birmingham law firm, Balch and Bingham, before adding to his team a prominent criminal defense attorney, George Beck of Montgomery. "Mr. Evans has repeatedly said the grand jury is on its own timetable," the article noted, "and there has been no indication the year-long probe of Governor Hunt is winding down."

By mid-October 1992, just when it seemed the governor's legal woes had reached a crescendo, he was hit with another McPhillips lawsuit. Butler County Commissioner Jimmy Crum, of Greenville, Alabama, approached Julian to represent him, on behalf of taxpayers, after reading a newspaper story saying Hunt used money from the state's Medicaid fund to make a "questionable" payment of some $67,000 to a Republican nominee for the Alabama Supreme Court—who also happened to be the former law partner of the governor's chief of staff.

The governor's press secretary called the transaction "legal and appropriate," since it was paid to Supreme Court candidate Mark Anderson for work he had done representing the State Health Planning and Development Agency (SHPDA), which supervises expansions of hospitals and other medical services with an eye toward controlling costs. Abbott said other governors had transferred Medicaid money in the past without it being questioned.

But the newest plaintiff wasn't appeased. "$67,000 may not seem like much to the State of Alabama," Crum told reporters. "But to *my* constituents, it's a huge amount of money."

In November 1994, nineteen months after Hunt left office, the State of Alabama, in a settlement agreement filed in the Circuit Court of Montgomery County, officially admitted that Governor Hunt wrongfully transferred Medicaid money to his Contingency Fund, whereupon the money was used to pay SHPDA expenses. Details of reimbursement were left to the attorneys for subsequent handling.

THOUGH the airplane case was the most visible, Julian had grappled with Hunt many other times.

In 1989, McPhillips represented two of Hunt's office employees who claimed they were fired without due cause: Bill Heatherly, a Cullman native who was cabinet-level director of the Alabama Department of Industrial Relations under George Wallace before being recruited by Hunt as an administrative assistant, and Glynnis Bates, another administrative assistant of Hunt's, who was fired after signing an affidavit of support for Heatherly's cause.

Hunt fired Heatherly on July 25, 1989. The reason, Heatherly said wryly at the time, being that he was "suspected of having Democratic sympathies." Heatherly said that he had "no particular political affiliation," and was not a registered member of either the Democrat or Republican Party.

Julian filed suit on Heatherly's behalf, claiming his First Amendment right to freedom of political association had been denied. Julian attempted to discuss settlement with Hunt, but was rejected.

As a result, U.S. District Judge Truman Hobbs heard the case and accepted Hunt's defense of "qualified immunity." Under that doctrine, if a constitutional law violation doesn't involve "a matter of clearly established law," no money damages can be recovered. The Eleventh Circuit Court of Appeals in Atlanta agreed with Judge Hobbs.

As for Ms. Bates's firing, however, Hobbs decided that qualified immunity was not involved and ruled in her favor. Alvin Prestwood, who had represented Hunt in both cases, appealed that ruling to the Eleventh Circuit. There, appellate judge J. L. Edmondson—a Reagan appointee whom Julian describes as "ultra-conservative"—reversed the ruling. At the oral argument stage, Edmondson told McPhillips that the only reasons he would have accepted for wrongful termination were if Hunt had told her to lie or refuse a subpoena.

The Bates loss at the appellate level was one of the most disappointing defeats of Julian's whole career, he says, particularly after the resounding win at the trial court level. "It was tough for me to accept that the First Amendment had been so badly 'watered down,'" Julian says, "that an employee could give an evidentiary affidavit, under oath, and get fired for it."

Judge Hobbs was riled as well, and called Julian, urging him to take the case to the U.S. Supreme Court. But McPhillips had been handling the case on a contingency basis from beginning to end, and neither he nor Bates could afford going to the highest and most expensive court in the land, where only one or two percent of the cases appealed ever get heard.

But up until the end of the Hunt administration, Julian continued to take cases of Hunt employees who believed they were wrongfully fired or mistreated. On May 11, 1991, Joyce St. John-Marcus was fired by Hunt from her job as director of the Alabama Office of Volunteerism, despite her high marks for service under Governors Fob James and George Wallace. St. John-Marcus alleged that Hunt fired her because she "wasn't a partisan-enough Republican."

The suit was ready for trial on June 4, 1991. But at the last minute, a settlement was reached. She was given another job in state government with the same pay and benefits, with her health insurance intact.

Meanwhile, the 1992 Alabama Supreme Court victory for Windom and McPhillips against Hunt in the airplane case was described by some capital observers as a "falling domino," sparking Attorney General Jimmy Evans's 1993 investigation and subsequent indictment and trial of Hunt on criminal ethics charges. On April 22, 1993, a Montgomery County jury returned a guilty verdict against Hunt, removing him from office and replacing him with then-Lieutenant Governor "Little Jim" Folsom.

As late as May 7, 1993, *The Birmingham News*, in a front-page story, quoted Julian as saying "The taxpayer's suit over Hunt's preaching flights shouldn't be delayed despite Hunt's conviction and the continuing probe into Hunt's administration."

In reaction, Hunt, now out of office, proclaimed that the taxpayer's suit violated his Fifth Amendment right against self- incrimination. After the trial court turned down this defense, Hunt appealed to the Alabama Supreme Court, going up for a second time in as many years. On July 1, 1994, in another 8-0 ruling in McPhillips's favor, the high court turned down Hunt's argument and allowed the plane trip suit to proceed again. Not long afterwards, the case settled, with Hunt reimbursing the state.

8

Attorney Wrestles Grinch

L IKE many, if not most, great imbroglios, the political pay-raise flap
had very modest beginnings. On December 14, 1982,
Montgomery's *Alabama Journal* carried a brief item headlined
"Graddick Says Officers, Judges Should Get Extra Payday This Year."

The article reported that "Alabama's constitutional officers and judges will
get an extra payday this year, thanks to an advisory opinion from Attorney
General Charles Graddick. The additional payday will cost the prorated state
General Fund about $1 million extra this year, according to Tom Braswell,
state comptroller. State judges, district attorneys, and constitutional officers,
including Graddick, will benefit from this opinion . . ."

"Graddick's Pay Challenged in Circuit Court by Montgomery Attorney
Julian McPhillips," the local headlines read, adding, "McPhillips contends
Graddick has been accepting pay increases while in office despite a constitutional prohibition against increasing the pay of officeholders during their term
of office." A picture of a smiling McPhillips accompanied the article.

A little less than twenty-four hours later, the *Montgomery Advertiser* ran at
the top of its editorial page a cartoon by staff artist Jim Palmer that depicted
Graddick with a huge sack of money slung over his shoulder, strewing dollar
bills as he fled a crowd of outraged citizens. The cartoon was titled "The
Grinch that Stole Christmas."

Alongside the piece, an editorial headlined "Ye Merrie Swill" was equally
caustic. It pointed out the irony that, the same day as the pay raise was
announced, Graddick's public relations office splashed a news release about
the great progress being made by the attorney general's special task force
created to prosecute welfare cheats. The release announced that no less than
146 indictments had been produced, naming food-stamp recipients and
welfare mothers who had swindled taxpayers out of some $315,000. The

amount, the *Advertiser* pointed out, was less than a third of what taxpayers would ante up for the Graddick-approved pay raise.

The greedy politicians, the editorial writer argued—with tongue lodged firmly in cheek—". . . surely should not be accused of the acquisitive fraud they seem to display. Perhaps they wish only to accumulate a little something for the holidays, to care for the poor, to light a candle of hope where they can in this winter of our unemployment. Then, far from being the super-welfare cheats they now appear on the surface, they doubtless plan in the softer light of springtime to pay it all back. With interest."

Not surprisingly, the Graddick camp issued a statement claiming that Julian's lawsuit was politically motivated because of his defeat at the polls by Graddick in 1978. But public opinion was so overwhelmingly on McPhillips's side that that charge sank almost as quickly as it had surfaced.

Still, pundits who expected the tempest in a Capitol teapot to soon blow over—much less their more cynical colleagues—could not have imagined that the controversy would still be swirling the following spring, having spawned an outpouring of opinion and debate from experts and private citizens alike, taxing their editorial page and talk-show creativity on topics ranging from political ethics to business math.

The math came in because numbers were Graddick's justification for the raise in the first place—which he said wasn't a raise at all, but a fluke of the calendar over which he had no control. The reasoning behind it would be recounted in dozens of articles, with varying degrees of clarity.

One of the most coherent came in early reporting by the *Alabama Journal*: "About once every ten years, there are twenty-seven bi-weekly paydays in the year instead of the usual twenty-six. For officials whose bi-weekly pay is not set by law, the state usually divides the annual salary by the number of pay periods.

"Merit system employees whose salaries are set at a specific bi-weekly amount are not affected by the opinion. Graddick's opinion authorizes division of the annual salaries by twenty-six pay periods, but directs the state to pay the resulting amount twenty-seven times."

Clearer, now? Most voters didn't think so. What was clear, Julian argued in court, was the constitutional provision that says the attorney general's salary cannot be "increased or diminished" during his current term of office. Graddick's attorney, Oakley Melton, took a totally different tack of maintaining that Graddick's "sovereign immunity" as state officeholder protected him from the lawsuit.

Further clouding the issue was the fact that, even before the controversial raises, a separate and somewhat obscure state law tying the attorney general's salary to that of state Supreme Court associate justices had substantially increased Graddick's pay twice—from $39,500 to $48,000 in 1980, and again to $58,000 in 1982. As a result, he had earned roughly $25,000 more than if his salary had stayed fixed at the same rate as when he ran for office.

The periodic adjustment of the judges' pay, which was not new, had taken place without fanfare the previous summer. What *was* new was that Graddick, unlike his predecessor, took his raise *immediately*, rather than waiting until his next term began.

Julian had sent a letter on August 2, 1982, pointing out the constitutional prohibition on changing the AG's pay in the middle of a term. The letter prompted then-Governor Fob James to ask the state Supreme Court for its opinion on the matter. In the meantime, Julian filed his lawsuit in Montgomery County Circuit Court. Circuit Judge Sam Taylor, on hearing that the Supreme Court advisory was pending, put the suit on hold for the interim.

But in the interim came Graddick's okay of the two weeks of extra pay because of a calendar quirk. In the weeks following, about fifty of the some 450 officials who stood to gain by the decision came forward one by one and announced they would not accept the extra payday. Secretary of State Don Siegelman–elected Alabama's governor in 1998—condemned the increase as "immoral."

The members of the Supreme Court, using the same logic as Judge Taylor , returned the question to his lap by saying they couldn't issue an advisory opinion about a matter that involved a pending lawsuit.

"The adversary system," the justices wrote, "permits all interested parties to have their 'day in court.' The very nature of the judicial process mandates that decisions be rendered only after all sides have presented their respective views."

The decision led the *Advertiser* to observe on its editorial page, " . . . So the answer now is within the bosom of the courts. The rest of us remain dependent on the kindness of others."

The *Journal* added its two cents in an editorial headlined "A Costly Opinion": "Attorney General Charles Graddick's advisory opinion which boosts his salary by $2,230 this fiscal year seems a greedy and unbecoming grab for more money. He ought to reconsider . . . This opinion, which seems to ask taxpayers to believe there are fifty-four weeks in the year and then pay for them, would be no less disappointing if the general fund bulged with cash. But with the state strapped for funds, the prospect of getting stuck for another million dollars in obviously unwarranted pay is particularly hard to take."

To the south of the capital, meanwhile, *The Dothan Eagle* weighed in with similar pronouncements: "Alabama Attorney General Charles Graddick may not be the most imaginative law enforcement officer the state has ever had, but his imagination is apparently endless when it comes to increasing his state salary . . . The case is a blatant example of wallowing in the public trough."

Over the Christmas holiday, Graddick apparently decided that some damage control was in order. He called a news conference for 10 a.m. on January 4, at which he stood in front of a chalkboard and attempted to do math demonstrating that the whole dust-up had been only a misunderstanding—one brought about by the state finance department, which had "misinterpreted" his original ruling.

The mistake had resulted in Graddick, individually, being wrongly paid exactly $640 during the calendar year 1982, his calculations showed, an amount he fully intended to pay back. And, Graddick added, if the finance department had so disliked his opinion to begin with, "they should have thrown it in the garbage can." In any event, the finance department could now fix their "mistake" and the whole matter would be settled.

Most of the state's news media—not to mention public opinion–failed to concur. "Our Constitution," the *Alabama Journal* commented, "hardly a well-composed document, appears uncharacteristically clear on the matter of salaries." The morning after Graddick's news conference, the paper ran an editorial cartoon showing him in front of the now-infamous chalkboard, with a piece of chalk in his right hand—while his left hand attempts to dislodge his foot, which is stuck solidly in his mouth.

The *Montgomery Advertiser* published a trenchant, one-paragraph letter from N. W. Gibson, of Troy, who opined, "Question: Has an attorney general for the State of Alabama ever been impeached? Of course, I suppose the answer is no. Certainly with today's trend he would rule in his own favor."

Another reader who advocated impeachment was Brian Moore of Montgomery, who concluded that "This whole sordid affair smells more and more like Graddickgate. At a time when the state general fund is in the red, Alabama is leading the nation in unemployment, and Graddick is prosecuting welfare mothers for stealing bread crumbs, the attorney general's gift to the state judges and himself stinks to high heaven."

Gibson's and Moore's how-to questions regarding impeachment soon drew a reply from Montgomerian Malcolm Brassell, who was quoted in the newspaper, saying that, "The Code of Alabama, Section 36-11-6, says that any five resident taxpayers, by posting a bond to cover all costs, may institute impeachment proceedings against any elected or appointed official.

"Everyone who believes this law could be carried out in Alabama will be standing on their heads in Court Square tomorrow at one o'clock."

As the appointed court date for the suit slowly approached, the Graddick story refused to budge. Or as *The Birmingham News* wrote in a headline, "Graddick Pay Issue Continues to Boil." *The Dothan Eagle*, in an editorial headlined "Mr. Graddick Strikes Again," pleaded for any court to decide the "touchy" issue, for better or worse, and be done with it: "Somebody has to make these rulings, whether there's a conflict of interest or not . . . The result may not be perfect, but it's the best the U.S. and Alabama can do, because there's no one else to whom to pass the buck."

The buck officially made its way to Judge Taylor's bench in late February. McPhillips argued before the judge that if an Alabama statute and the Alabama Constitution are at odds on a subject, as Graddick's attorney seemed to concede was the case with the pay-raise furor, the Constitution should take precedence. At least, McPhillips maintained, the pay raise should not have gone into effect until the attorney general's second term began on January 17.

But Melton, Graddick's attorney, argued that the first pay raise was technically not in violation of the Constitution, because the statute which made the raises possible was not *passed* during Graddick's actual term, but before he took office.

In the end, Montgomery County Circuit Judge Taylor sided with McPhillips, in what Julian called "a great victory for the people of Alabama."

"The Constitutional prohibition," the judge's ruling said, "is controlling and superior."

Judge Taylor didn't immediately rule on whether Graddick had to give the

$25,000 back. In fact, the judge agreed with Melton that the case "is considerably more complicated than it first appears," adding that his ruling was a "launching pad" to get the suit appealed to a higher court.

Afterwards, reporters described Julian as "jubilant" about the victory, saying that the ruling "just vindicates what I've said all along. The state Constitution was violated by the state's chief legal officer." McPhillips said he would wait seven days longer to see if Graddick would voluntarily return the excess pay. If that didn't happen, McPhillips said, he would go back and seek a court-ordered reimbursement by Graddick and an award of attorney's fees to himself. Because he had filed the suit in his own name, without paying himself, McPhillips declared he would also ask the judge to award him attorney's fees—which he would then donate to charity.

Even the distant *Pensacola* (Florida) *Journal* carried the story at the top of its front page the next morning. And newspaper editorial writers around Alabama, who had been calling for weeks for a swift resolution of the case, made it clear they weren't about to throw in the towel. The *Alabama Journal's* brief editorial response was headlined, simply enough, "Give it Back":

> Though Taylor's ruling did not legally require Graddick to reimburse the state a prompt and voluntary payment should be forthcoming. The raises Graddick unlawfully took were paid with public funds and Taylor should not hesitate to order the money returned if Graddick fails to do so on his own.
>
> There is not much to admire in our 1901 constitution, but the provision fixing salaries during terms of office is a good and prudent law. As Alabama's chief law enforcement official, Graddick should obey it, as he promised to do in taking the oath of office, and return the money at once.

The following week, when Graddick's attorney announced his decision to appeal the case to the state Supreme Court, the *Advertiser* responded with an editorial cartoon showing a man in a farmer's hat and patched overalls standing nervously in line, searching his pockets, before a banner that reads "Pay your Bills Here." There are four clerks at stations, labeled "Rent," "Utilities," "Food," and "Medical." The fifth station, labeled "Graddick Pay Raises and Legal Fees," is manned by the AG himself—energetically stuffing dollar bills into what appears to be a meat grinder.

It was about this time that Bessie Ford, a political columnist for United Press International, wrote her piece titled "McPhillips a Man to Watch in 1986." Ford began:

> Watch out for Julian McPhillips. Go ahead and ask—'Julian who?'
>
> McPhillips, 36, ran unsuccessfully for attorney general in 1978 and charged the election was stolen from him. Remember him now?
>
> Well, McPhillips has been tangling with the big boys, including Attorney General Charles Graddick, former Governor Fob James, and Governor George Wallace's family in the legal arena. So far, he is batting a thousand.
>
> McPhillips, a cocksure lawyer in Montgomery, admits the success he has had in representing sometimes controversial causes has him thinking about running for attorney general in 1986 . . .

The column drew Julian a note of congratulations from long-time supporter George McMillan, a former lieutenant governor and unsuccessful gubernatorial candidate, now perhaps better known as the creator of Birmingham's annual City Stages concert event. "Someday," McMillan closed, "please tell me how you managed to get Bessie Ford in your corner. I believe you are the first person I have ever known her to compliment."

Meanwhile, newspapers reported that the Graddick flap had already cost the state $7,250 in legal bills, and would likely cost another $3,000 if it were appealed to the Supreme Court.

This renewed the *Dothan Eagle's* outrage, in the form of an editorial headlined "Graddick Wolfs Down His Cake, Still Has It." On the Supreme Court appeal, the paper said, "There are no 'larger questions' here. There is just one base, low question of a constitutional officer letting his greed for money supercede the constitution he was sworn to uphold . . .

"Unfortunately, Mr. Graddick apparently will not be punished for this behavior by state officials or judges. Even the voters can't make him cough up that $30,000 cake. But they could make sure he never again holds a position of power in this state."

It appeared the case was drawing to a conclusion. But the durable controversy once again took a ninety-degree turn. Sam Taylor, the judge who had ruled Graddick's raises illegal and was due to rule on their possible repayment, was appointed to a different post, the Court of Criminal Appeals—leaving his successor, Judge Mark Kennedy, to take it from there.

Julian asked the Supreme Court to turn down the appeal because the case had not been fully settled in Circuit Court. But Kennedy acted to put the Circuit Court proceedings on hold until the Supreme Court weighed in with its opinion to hear the appeal or not.

Ultimately, in *McPhillips v. Graddick*, the Alabama Supreme Court upheld Judge Taylor's ruling that Graddick's in-term pay raise violated Alabama's Constitution. But, on a technicality, the Court stated that because an attorney general's opinion had been issued authorizing the pay raises, and because a state statute immunizes from liability state officials acting pursuant to the attorney general's opinion, Graddick didn't have to pay back the money. (No note was taken of the fact that the original opinion, written by assistant attorney general Jerry Weidler, said the in-term pay raises were improper, but Graddick exiled him to the Highway Department and found another assistant to write a more favorable opinion.)

Such is Alabama politics, at times. But after the pay affair, a friend of Julian's told him that an associate of Graddick's joked that the attorney general "shook in his boots" whenever Julian's name was mentioned.

Julian soon decided to give Graddick reason to shake again.

In 1984, another Graddick assistant, William North, wrote a letter—"in his private capacity," as Julian points out—to the editor of the *Montgomery Advertiser*, critical of capital punishment and its pending application to a particular death row inmate. Graddick reportedly hit the roof when he saw the letter, and immediately re-wrote North's most recent employee evaluation, lowering his score from the nineties to the fifties. North, claiming he was then harassed and ostracized by his colleagues, quit the job and immediately paid a visit to Julian.

Julian wrote a letter to Graddick, with no response. So he filed suit in federal court and braced for battle with the attorney general again.

But to Julian's surprise, Graddick responded with an "offer of judgment" to North, including a reasonable attorney's fee. Julian wanted to proceed, but left the ultimate decision to his client, who wanted to avoid lengthy litigation and took the settlement that was offered.

"I think it's ironic," Julian says now, "that in the space of two years I won two cases against Attorney General Graddick, one for violating the Alabama Constitution and the other for violating the U.S. Constitution, both of which he was sworn to uphold."

In North's case, Judge Truman Hobbs awarded an attorney's fee of $8,500. Though Julian got no money from the pay-raise case, the barrel of publicity it generated brought a record number of new clients flocking to his door. "In the long run," Julian says with a grin, "I think I came out of the pay raise case better financially than Graddick did."

And so things stood until the early 1990s. After completing two terms as attorney general and a brief stint as Montgomery district attorney, Graddick left to enter private practice. One day, it turned out that McPhillips and Graddick were to be representing clients on opposite sides of a small district court case. Julian says he knew the encounter would be difficult, so he decided to call Graddick before the court date and attempt to reconcile.

"I told him, on the phone, that the whole heart of the Christian faith was about forgiveness and reconciliation," Julian remembers, "and I asked him to forgive me for any hard feelings I'd caused. I heard a sigh of relief, and he asked me to forgive him, too. After that, I just let the bad feelings go. And I've felt better ever since."

9

Protecting the Environment

IN THE late 1970s and early 1980s, news about the natural environment—and organizations that were threatening it, and others that were trying to preserve it—took the forefront of America's headlines like never before. It wasn't surprising that much of Julian's case-work in that period took a slightly different fork in the stream, with emphasis on safeguarding natural resources that had been such a large part of his life, dating back to childhood summers at Lake Guntersville, vacations at Gulf Shores beaches, a family cottage on Lake Logan Martin, and a longtime love of boating and hiking.

Environmental foes were not long in rearing their heads. The first, ironically, was the federal government.

Julian's first environmental case came in March 1979, when McPhillips represented Walter Chandler, Sr., in a federal court suit against the Environmental Protection Agency for allowing radon needles to leak radiation into the environment. Though the EPA was aware of the practice, it had gone on unchallenged for several years.

In a court settlement, the EPA was forced to remove the harmful materials.

Julian's next battle began in April 1980, and took on the environmental Goliath known as Westinghouse Electric Corporation, which wanted to build a nuclear fuel-making plant on an eight hundred-acre site near Prattville on the Alabama River. Though the setting appeared remote when viewed from the ground, in truth it would only have been some six miles, as the crow flies, from populous Montgomery. And, according to a scientific expert from the University of Alabama, the plant was likely to leak and ooze radioactivity by water, air, and land, considerably raising the risk of cancer for those living nearby.

The role of "David" in the scenario was taken by an official-sounding organization known as the Safe Energy Alliance of Central Alabama (SEACA), which challenged Westinghouse in court. In actuality, the Safe Energy Alliance had been formed by Julian, Cathy Donaldson, and Jake and Randy Aronov.

Its membership of about fifteen generally met either at Julian's office or Donaldson's home. And though Aronov threw in a couple of thousand dollars toward the legal expense, the disparity of resources was still enormous. Still SEACA began getting its message out, in a big way.

In frequent front-page stories and appearances on TV news, McPhillips talked about the health hazards of the plant, saying that they would far outweigh any short-term economic benefits from its construction and staffing. Public sentiment appeared to be on SEACA's side, and soon McPhillips announced that he had prepared and filed a petition to intervene before the Nuclear Regulatory Commission, contesting Westinghouse's plans.

After a dedicated legal battle spanning fourteen months, Westinghouse officials finally announced on June 10, 1981, that plans to build the nuclear fuel plant near Prattville had been "indefinitely deferred," and that the company had withdrawn its license application with the Nuclear Regulatory Commission. In the next day's *Montgomery Advertiser* the headlines read "Westinghouse Drops Fuel Plant" and quoted Julian McPhillips, attorney for SEACA, as calling the decision "a victory for businessmen and persons who live in the area . . . I'm certain the actions of SEACA were instrumental in Westinghouse's decision, but I won't act like it's the only factor."

NOT LONG AFTERWARDS, in October 1980, Julian represented John and Mary Singleton in suing an EPA inspector, an Alabama Department of Agriculture inspector, and a landowner, where an insecticide spray was used, causing the Singletons serious health hazards. The case was later settled.

A year later, in October 1981, McPhillips was at it again, representing the group "Lowndes County Citizens to Fight Deadly Dumping," which involved taking on Browning-Ferris Corporation for depositing hazardous waste materials in its local landfill. To avoid litigation, BFC agreed to take the waste elsewhere.

As the years passed, environmental legal actions became ever more complex and specialized, and two of Julian's colleagues followed the call. Rick Middleton, a Yale law grad with whom Julian had worked at the Attorney General's office during the mid-1970s, moved to Charlottesville, Virginia, and formed the

Southern Environmental Law Center, which Julian helped support financially. And attorney Ray Vaughn, who was in Julian's and Leslie's youth group at the Church of the Ascension from 1975 to 1977, also started specializing in environmental cases, to Julian's delight. Julian and Leslie presently continue to support a number of pro-environment groups, including the Sierra Club and the Alabama Wildlife Federation.

Joe Turnham, an Auburn businessman, also deserves much credit, says Julian, for organizing support in the state legislature for environmental protection needs in Alabama.

Flash forward to 1995, when McPhillips once again found himself in the thick of an environmental battle—but this time, one with a political slant. Julian represented a friend, John Smith, a former director of the Alabama Department of Environmental Management. Smith was suing Governor Fob James and the Environmental Management Commission for wrongfully firing him—in retaliation, Smith claimed, for his part in an Environmental Protection Agency investigation that reflected poorly on Governor James. Unfortunately, for McPhillips and Smith, the case got moved to federal court where a judge more sympathetic to the governor issued procedural rulings that, in effect, deflected Smith's case.

That same week, oddly enough, Attorney General Jeff Sessions—good friend of Governor James, and coincidentally a just-announced candidate for the U.S. Senate—said he was issuing a criminal indictment of John Smith for supposed wrongdoings that had occurred almost six years earlier. Former attorney general Jimmy Evans had already investigated Smith in these incidents and decided that the charges were unfounded.

Julian, incensed that his friend had been indicted for what he considered purely political reasons, called a news conference which was carried by Birmingham and Montgomery TV stations that night, and newspapers the next day, blasting Sessions for the action. Sessions, in response, arranged for Governor James to call a news conference in reply, defending Sessions against McPhillips's claims. In the end, Smith was acquitted of all criminal charges, in a case which Circuit Judge Charles Price, later speaking to a lawyer's group, described as "an abuse of process."

The Smith environmental case, though it leaked no radon, nevertheless left a bad taste in the mouth of Julian and many other Montgomerians.

10

The Highway Department Class Action

IGHWAY engineering assistant Johnny Reynolds had had enough, he told Julian, after coming to consult with him in early 1985 about a work dispute, of being humiliated on the job just because he was black.

Among the many harassments inflicted upon him by his white co-workers was their putting a dead rat, pierced with a nail, on Reynolds's drafting table. His table was also once sprinkled with white powder, with the letters "KKK" written in it. White employees also repeatedly told Reynolds that if they saw him look at a white woman, they'd "pluck his eyes out." Reynolds also suffered at work from having his tires cut and acid poured on his car. His home had eggs thrown at it, and harassing telephone calls were a constant disruption.

They were hoping he'd get mad enough to quit, Reynolds said, but he was not going to oblige them.

Such racial incidents were definitely not the first to come to Julian's attention where the Highway Department was concerned in the mid-1980s. Its critics in state government had long condemned the Department as "the last bastion of racism" in state government, and also as a "hotbed of nepotism," with fathers, mothers, sons, daughters, uncles, and nephews working in various niches of the system.

"They made no bones about it," Julian recalls, shaking his head. "One long-time employee shrugged and said, 'We just look out for our own.'"

Julian and his friend, fellow attorney Gil Kendrick—who, like McPhillips, had served as an assistant attorney general in the Baxley years—decided to take on the challenge of looking out for everybody else, namely: Highway Department workers who were (a) not white, and (b) not blood kin of someone on the staff. They had their work cut out for them.

"Their 'good-ol'-boy' policy worked pretty well for whites," Julian says, "but very badly for blacks. There were few to be found in the Department at all, and the few blacks that were there were generally frowned upon."

Johnny Reynolds was referred to Julian in 1985 by local Montgomery black businessman Tom Wright, a mentor to many young blacks in that era.

When Judge Myron Thompson was named to hear the case, McPhillips and Kendrick considered it a good omen. The state's attorneys did not.

The suit was filed in April 1985, and it was not until July 1988 that McPhillips, Kendrick, and attorney Rick Harris plowed through the numbing stack of depositions and the massive other preparation involved. That month, they put before the court a detailed proposed settlement agreement: forty-seven pages worth. The injunctive relief called for by the agreement included paying $355,000 to black employees denied merit system jobs or promotions, and $145,000 for the plaintiff's counsel.

The agreement required court approval, and Judge Thompson took the document under advisement. It stayed under advisement for more than a year before Thompson, denying court approval, kicked the plan out in late 1989. But he did so for reasons the plaintiffs found encouraging: he said the provisions for the workers weren't strong enough.

Meanwhile, in 1989, as the litigation continued, the Highway Department moved Johnny Reynolds to Huntsville and assigned him to a non-existent road project and gave him a non-existent crew to help him. Since both existed only on paper, his "work" consisted of a Highway Department vehicle dropping Reynolds off alone in the morning at a remote roadside, and then picking him up when his shift was over. It was a continued infliction of emotional distress, which Reynolds believed was designed to get him to quit. With McPhillips's legal help, and occasional prayer with Julian over long distance telephone, Reynolds "hung in tight," and refused to quit.

After the first agreement was rejected, both sides went back to the drawing board. By mid-1992, a second settlement proposal was given to the court—this one containing lengthy "opt in" and "opt out" provisions. But in the meantime, Birmingham attorney Bob Wiggins was representing a group of more than eighty black Highway Department employees from Birmingham, Gadsden, and Tuscaloosa, who didn't like the terms of the plan and so objected to it.

Given those numbers, the Highway Department itself pulled out of the second agreement. It was back to the drawing board again for everybody concerned, but this time the board was vastly enlarged.

Complicating the situation for Julian further, his two top comrades-in-arms, Rick Harris and Gil Kendrick, had by this time moved on to other jobs: Harris to the State Health Department, and Kendrick to the State Bar Association. After much deliberation, McPhillips associated Wiggins to take over leadership of the case—along with his welcome legions of attorneys and clerks.

The case continued to grow beyond all expectations. Julian and co-counsel Gary Atchison remained active in the case and were paid attorneys fees through 1995, at which point they decided that Wiggins and crew were doing an excellent job and receiving ample favorable rulings from the court, and so they moved on to other projects.

As of 2000, the Johnny Reynolds case Julian set in motion fourteen years earlier was still ongoing in the court system. Julian is still on the court's list for receiving orders, and says he and Reynolds have remained the best of friends.

And, though lacking final resolution, Reynolds finds his lot today immensely better than when he endured the dead rats, KKK circles, car damage, and threats at home. He is now district engineer for the highway district based in Bullock County's Union Springs, Alabama.

Likewise, numerous safeguards and improvements benefitting minority employees have been instituted as a result of the Reynolds class action. Substantially more black employees have been recruited, hired and promoted than ever before. Additionally, grievance procedures with teeth have been installed and greater opportunities for minority employees have opened up. The other named plaintiffs with Reynolds from the 1988 era, a total of nineteen, have received from $300,000 to $900,000 as back pay damages, and all have been hired at a civil engineer manager position or higher.

Unfortunately for Johnny Reynolds, the continued pressure of pursing this case over fourteen years has taken its toll. He had three heart attacks in late 1999. After open heart surgery, he is now back on the job as district engineer, but he has yet to receive his own monetary damage award due to ongoing appeals.

Royce King No 'King for a Day'

Julian and Highway Department director Royce King had not seen the last of one another, by a long shot, following initial encounters. Having battled during the Reynolds race discrimination class action suit and the Byrne Stewart sexual harassment case, McPhillips and King squared off again in 1987, when Julian filed suit against King and Governor Guy Hunt on behalf of two black businessmen, George Young and Miles Robinson, charging race discrimination in the awarding of state contracts. After a hard-fought battle in front of a federal judge, the court ruled against the plaintiffs, but the Highway Department became more even-handed with minorities in its award of future contracts.

In 1991, as Hunt's second term began, King and McPhillips tangled yet another time. Julian represented a Tennessee highway contracting firm that had won the low bid on a Highway Department project in the Huntsville area, only to see the contract go to a Montgomery firm, at a cost of about $1.2 million more to taxpayers.

"King had disqualified the Tennessee firm on the flimsiest of grounds," Julian says now, "when it was well within his discretion to allow the contractor to cure the minor discrepancy. The successful bidder, local contractor Billy Newell, later bragged publicly about having given more than $30,000 to Hunt's last gubernatorial campaign."

At one point, hoping to avoid another court fight, Julian and his Tennessee client dropped in to see Royce King in his office. Seeing the Tennessean first, King gave the contractor a friendly greeting, but when he saw Julian accompanying him, "King turned ten shades of red," McPhillips recalls. "He went into a rage. He shouted at me, 'You might think you run this department, but you don't! You've probably got my office wired and bugged!'

"I started laughing," says Julian, "and then I realized he was serious, which made it all the funnier. But in a nutshell, you could say that our meeting was over before it started."

The following week, McPhillips filed suit against Hunt and King, making statewide headlines. But just before going to trial, a satisfactory settlement was reached for his Tennessee client.

SCLC Award

On December 3, 1999, in Anniston, the Alabama Chapter of the Southern Christian Leadership Conference awarded Julian McPhillips its "Man of Distinction Award" for "your undaunting commitment toward the ascertainment of a just and non-violent society . . ." Along with numerous African-American recipients, Julian was referred to as one of the "heroes and sheroes of the civil rights movement in the twentieth century." Martin Luther King, III, presented this award to McPhillips, the only Caucasian ever so honored by the SCLC.

Rev. John Alford, president of the Montgomery Chapter of the SCLC, who nominated McPhillips for the award, cited Julian's handling of the Reynolds class action suit against the Highway Department and numerous other race discrimination cases during the last twenty years. Alford also referred to Julian's successful efforts in 1986 in getting Montgomery's "South Africa law" struck down, and a 1993 suit Julian brought which resulted in the Montgomery City Council's repeal of an ordinance used to harass civil rights demonstrators. Alford also listed numerous police brutality cases Julian had handled over the years, and his standing up for disadvantaged and oppressed people in other situations.

Displayed proudly in McPhillips's office on South Perry Street is a frame of the SCLC award with a picture of Julian, Leslie, and Rev. Alford, with Martin Luther King, III, giving Julian the award.

A handwritten note from Alford says:

Julian, your drum major instinct for justice and truth is beyond measure. Keep the faith.

Your Brother,

John

Interlude

Near-Death Experiences in Underground Garages

Did I ever tell you about the two times I was almost killed? They were both in underground parking garages." This parenthetical remark by Julian is an illustration that casual conversations with him rarely proceed in a straight line.

While high-profile cases such as Julian handles can earn attorneys a growing conglomerate of enemies over the years of their careers, it's ironic that Julian's two close brushes with death both came accidentally.

In 1986, Julian and fellow attorney Gary Atchison were defending a Montgomery fireman in a termination review, in the mayor's office. When McPhillips arrived at City Hall, he found all the parking places on the street taken and, running tight for time, parked in the underground garage at the nearby Madison Hotel.

It had rained heavily the night before and Julian noticed that the underground lot was mostly flooded. Giving up on trying to keep his feet dry, he settled for walking in the spots where the water level appeared lowest. But a few yards later, stepping into an apparent shallow spot, his footing disappeared completely and he sank precipitously into what turned out to be an open manhole, whose cover a worker had apparently removed to help speed drainage but had neglected to mark with a barrier.

By instinct, Julian's arms shot outward and he found himself barely suspended at the manhole's rim, as the force of the water's suction exerted powerful pressure to pull him under from the neck down.

After he caught his breath and regained his bearings, he was able to gradually hoist himself from the maelstrom and to get one foot, then finally the other, on solid ground.

"It was absolutely terrifying," he recalls. "I have no doubt that if I had been much smaller physically, or maybe older and somewhat frail, it would have drowned me. I'd have ended up somewhere in the Alabama River."

Julian drove home and – before changing into dry clothes – called Atchison, told him what had happened, swore him to secrecy, and asked him to carry on the hearing until Julian could drive back downtown.

A short time later, he strolled into the hearing room as casually as he could manage, and was met by laughter from all sides. Atchison had caved in and explained Julian's delay. Which may have been, Julian reflects, sound legal strategy on Atchison's part. In any event, the review board was in a sufficiently good mood to quickly rule in favor of his and Atchison's client.

A medical checkup found that, except for some painfully bruised ribs, Julian was okay. The hotel offered him an official apology which, seeing as it was attached to a $1,000 check, he "graciously accepted."

That night, at a lawyers' party, the word of Julian's mishap had quickly spread before he arrived. Present at the party was Alabama Bar Association president Walter Byars, who chuckled, "McPhillips, I heard what happened. You're invincible, man!"

As it turned out, Byars's compliment was also prophetic. In 1993, Julian and Leslie were in Atlanta, where Julian was preparing for a Eleventh Circuit Court of Appeals argument on behalf of his client Marcia Edwards. The McPhillipses spent the night at the Peachtree Hotel, and once again parked in an underground garage. The next morning, Julian went down to get a book he had left in his car. As he was walking back up the ramp, out of nowhere came a red, ten-feet-long metal guard arm, which apparently had gotten stuck in the "up" position after the last car went through, and chose the exact moment of Julian's passage to come back down. Miraculously, the heavy pole just missed the top of Julian's head, instead scraping down the front of his face: knocking his glasses off, bloodying his nose, and toppling him onto his back, dazed, on the concrete.

After Julian recovered his composure, he realized how close he had come to death. If he had passed under the arm a split second later, the barrier could have cracked his skull like a hammer splitting a pecan.

At that moment, Julian recalls "thanking God the Father, Son, and Holy Spirit," and rushing back to the room to get at least partially cleaned up before the court session began.

On the way to the courtroom, he remembers debating with himself about whether to preface his remarks to the judges with a description of the accident. He finally decided against telling, not only because the story sounded so incredible, but because it also would have taken away valuable time from his client's argument.

"As it was," he says, "I guess the judges thought I had been in a fist fight."

Subsequently, the Peachtree Hotel also gave Julian a $1,000 apology.

"I wouldn't recommend it as a way to earn money," he says.

11

Other Historic Cases

R EPRESENTING the rights of minorities and other societal "underdogs" has been a running theme of Julian's legal cases, from the beginning.

Striking Down Montgomery's "South Africa Law"

In 1985, McPhillips represented Peruvian immigrant Jorge Carpio in a lawsuit against the Montgomery Police Department over the constitutionality of Montgomery's "failure to identify" ordinance, after Carpio charged that he was harassed and arrested by officers solely because he had no form of identification. Criminal charges were dropped after Carpio sued, and Carpio in turn voluntarily dismissed his suit. Although Carpio was satisfied with his confidential settlement, the ordinance remained intact.

But the topic of no I.D. was far from laid to rest. In 1986, Julian associated brand new lawyer Janie Baker Clarke to assist him in representing Michael Timmons, a black man who was roughed up and beaten by two Montgomery police officers when he failed to produce identification papers. McPhillips challenged Timmons's arrest under both the U.S. Constitution's Fourth Amendment "unlawful search and seizure" provisions, and the Fourteenth Amendment's due process clause.

"We argued in court that the 'failure to identify' ordinance, or 'vagrancy law,' as it was sometimes called," Julian says, "had become Montgomery's 'South Africa law,' resembling the one used in that part of the world to enforce apartheid at that time." One of Julian's most vivid memories is of a 1975 visit to South Africa during its apartheid years: "One night I woke up at about 3 a.m. and couldn't get back to sleep. I left my hotel and went for a walk, and found that the police with their paddy wagons were out everywhere, rounding

1870s photos of Julian's great-great-grandparents, Rose (1846-1889) and James McPhillips, Sr. (1833-1910). He was a Civil War veteran.

Left, Julian's great-great-great-grandfather, John Thomas Bocock (1773-1845), and his great-great grandfather, Henry Flood Bocock (1817-1892), of Appomatox County, Virginia, who witnessed Lee's surrender to Grant.

Left, maternal great-great grandfather Howard M. Poole (1840-1910), in his Civil War uniform.

Below, Julian's maternal great-great grandfather, the Rev. David Davidson Sanderson (1821-1891), was pastor of the First Presbyterian Church of Eutaw, Alabama, 1860-1891, and co-founder of Stillman College, Tuscaloosa.

Four McPhillips brothers: from left, John, Harry, Joe, and James, Jr., the sons of the first McPhillips in Alabama, James, Sr., an Irish immigrant who moved to Mobile in the 1850s. He was Julian's great-great-grandfather.

Great grandfather James McPhillips, Jr., standing in the center of the photo above, had three sons. The middle son, Julian Byrnes McPhillips, married Lilybelle McGowin (1898-1969), right. She was Julian's paternal grandmother.

Julian's maternal grandparents: Frank Dixon (1893-1938) and Stuart Sanderson Dixon Clay (1897-1987). Their only daughter is Julian's mother, Eleanor Dixon McPhillips.

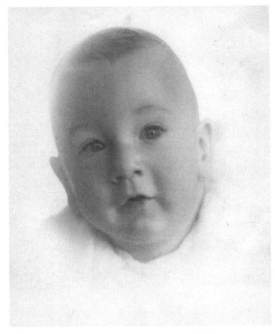

Julian at six months, 1947.

1950 on the McPhillips family slide in Cullman: (L-R) Sandy, Julian, David, and Betsy.

The McPhillips family on a 1955 visit to Eleanor's childhood home on Palmer Avenue in New Orleans. From left, David, Sandy, Julian Sr., Julian Jr., Frank, Eleanor, and Betsy.

Julian, age nine,
in his Pee Wee
football uniform.

Below, his 1955
Cullman County
Cub Scout pack —
top row, standing,
Tony Hancock, John
Knight, Julian,
Butch Reader, and
Keith Carter;
brother David is
second from left on
the bottom row.

Left, a Cullman pageant in 1951 included Sandy McPhillips, Julian, and Joyce Ponder.

Below, the 1959 Cullman County Little League All-Star Team — Julian (pitcher) third from left, top row; John Shaw (catcher) to Julian's left; Courtney McKoy, far right, top row; Keith Carter, far left, top row.

Julian attended Cullman's East Elementary School, 1953-1959.

Two views of Julian's childhood home in Cullman, 1948-1959.

Julian L. McPhillips, Sr., at his ordination into the Episcopal priesthood in 1962, with his three sons — Julian bearing the cross and Frank and David carrying flags.

Above, Charles "Bill" Goldfinch, wrestling coach and English teacher at Sewanee Military Academy. Left, Julian in his senior year as a cadet at SMA, 1963.

Above, Julian wrestling for Princeton against the University of Pennsylvania for the Ivy League Championship in 1967. (Julian won.)

Below, the Princeton freshman wrestling team, 1964-65. Julian, at center on the front row, was team captain; by his senior year, eight of the ten were still starters.

Julian L. McPhillips, Jr., as a Senior at Princeton University, 1967.

Below, the family picture at the marriage of Julian and Leslie, June 1974.

Julian and Leslie, June 1974.

The three Julians, 1977: father, Julian L. McPhillips, Sr.; son, Julian L. McPhillips, Jr.; and grandfather, Julian Byrnes McPhillips.

In July 1978, Julian's father, mother, and grandfather worked in his campaign for the office of Attorney General of Alabama.

Above, in 1980, after election as a Carter-pledged delegate to the Democratic convention, Julian met President Jimmy Carter and Roslyn Carter at the White House.

Left, Julian with law clerks Terri Sewell (left) and Farris Curry, 1983.

Julian's growing law practice in 1987: from left, partner Kenneth Shinbaum, attorney Gary Atchison, client Beth Kirkley, Julian, Lynelle Howard, and Carroll Puckett.

1991, the *Case of the Missing Doors v. the Congressman Bill Dickinson:* from left, standing, Kenneth Shinbaum, Lynelle Howard, William Gill, client Meri Amos, Julian, and Carroll Puckett; kneeling, Eric Schufford, Gibson Vance, and Allen Stoner.

Above, Julian has been friends with Bill Bradley since their days as
student athletes together at Princeton. Below, Leslie and Julian with new
friend Mahesh Chavda, international Christian evangelist, August 1989.

up black people whose only crime was that they didn't have identification papers on them."

In Montgomery, the I.D. law was repeatedly abused by police officers over the years to arrest people—usually poor and usually black—walking along the sidewalks or streets without identification papers.

The ordinance stated that a person was guilty of disorderly conduct if he loiters or wanders "from place to place without apparent reason or business" and "refuses to identify himself and account for his presence" when asked to do so by a police officer. Under the Montgomery law, those actions were termed illegal if surrounding circumstances were such that "public safety demands such identification."

In a landmark decision, the U.S. District court ruled in Timmons's favor on both grounds, effectively striking down the city's "South Africa law" and entitling the plaintiff to damages and attorney fees. In his written opinion, Judge Myron Thompson said that the ordinance's wording was imprecise and therefore unconstitutional under the due process clause of the Fourteenth Amendment.

Judge Thompson also agreed with McPhillips that the Montgomery police violated Timmons's rights under the Fourth Amendment to be free against unreasonable searches and seizures. In this instance, the judge ruled there was no probable cause to believe that Timmons had committed a crime. Hence, the search violated his rights.

Chest Hair Too Plentiful?

The case of Montgomery fireman Matthew Stalter gave new meaning to the phrase "get it off your chest."

In April 1990, Stalter was ordered by his lieutenant to either shave his chest hair, or wear a T-shirt under his uniform shirt while on duty.

Stalter, an independent-minded as well as hairy sort of guy, told the lieutenant, "The city didn't issue me a T-shirt, and chest hair is not facial hair."

The lieutenant didn't back down, and under pressure Stalter finally complied and shaved his upper chest. But nine days later, still peeved over the incident, he filed a grievance with the Fire Department.

That same day, Fire Department officials struck back by issuing a ruling saying Stalter had violated three articles of its rule book: "poor appearance," "neglect of duties," and "insubordination." The punishment, they determined, would be twenty-five consecutive night watches and a suspension of twenty-nine days without pay—incidentally, one day short of the minimum suspension required for an appeal to the city's personnel board.

By this time, Stalter was feeling both burned up and burned out. He found a lawyer: Julian. Their suit against the City of Montgomery on July 24, 1990, claimed that Fire Department officials had violated Stalter's constitutional rights by forcing him to shave his chest, had acted in a "mean-spirited" and "cruel-hearted" manner, and as a result owed Stalter damages.

"Enough is enough," Julian said in announcing the suit. "It's time to draw the line."

Department officials claimed the chest hair was a safety violation, and that, in ordering Stalter to shave, they were only acting in his best interests. But many people, both fire fighters and the general public, took Stalter's side in the matter.

Retired veteran fireman Pete Wethington told the *Montgomery Advertiser*, "Chest hair has absolutely nothing to do with a person's ability to fight fires." An editorial cartoon in the July 25 issue of the *Advertiser* showed Montgomery's fire chief sitting across the desk from Smokey the Bear, and holding a job application.

"I'm sorry, Smokey," the caption says, "but you can't be a Montgomery fire fighter unless you shave your chest."

Not only was Montgomery having a good laugh over the episode, but the national press got wind of it. The magazine *Woman's World* published a humorous feature about the lawsuit, with an "only in Alabama . . ." slant, and which quoted Julian.

When tempers had cooled, the case was settled by compromise. Most of the punishments against Stalter were dropped, in exchange for his pledge to keep a hairless neckline while on duty.

"It wasn't a total victory," Julian recalls, "but Matthew was grateful to me for standing up for him."

Matthew Stalter has since left the Fire Department.

"Policeman Poet" Spars with Mayor Folmar

The topics of police officers and poetry seem, on the surface, to be unlikely bedfellows. But in 1983 "The Case of the Policeman Poet" was a hard-fought battle that brought to a head Julian's continuing battle with Mayor Emory Folmar's administration over employment practices, particularly those of the Police Department.

"In the early 1980s," Julian says, "police officers, both white and black, began coming to me because of their frustration over the way Folmar was dominating the department. They said that officers with higher education were looked down upon, and that the mayor based rewards on cronyism, particularly those who served as his personal bodyguards."

In fact, by 1982 Folmar's police-related actions and rhetoric had gained so much attention that he was enough of a conservative political figure to win the Republican nomination for governor, to face none other than the legendary George Wallace.

"True, Folmar was trounced in the general election," Julian says, "but it was still clear that he was using the Police Department to further his political ambitions. The rewards were great, for those who jumped on his bandwagon and kissed his you know-what."

Most of Montgomery's past mayors had gotten along without full-time bodyguards, but when Folmar became mayor he had several police officers assigned to be his driver-bodyguards. One of Folmar's bodyguards was corporal John Wilson. A musician, Wilson served a dual role of playing and singing for the mayor's campaign appearances. When re-elected, Folmar promoted Wilson in one fell swoop from corporal to police chief.

Among the many police officers aggrieved over what they saw as rampant favoritism was corporal Steve Eiland. Eiland had had a distinguished career, winning a number of commendations for his outstanding investigative work, which in some cases unraveled crime scene evidence that no one else in the department had been able to figure out. Nonetheless, Eiland felt his good work was ignored at the highest levels of the administration, and that he was continually harassed over petty issues.

One way he worked off his frustration was by writing (some accounts say co-writing) a poem, which was later posted anonymously on the department's bulletin board and in the elevator. It read,

Emory 'Amin' is our ruling God;

We flinch when he blinks, we jump when he nods.

The Police Department adds zest to his day;

To our happiness?? Nay, our dismay!

He selects certain men to escort him around;

These are the true dullards, who I think must have found

They cannot function without Emory's advice.

They're no longer men, they've been transformed into mice.

(I think the word "rat" applies in some cases, especially for

those fond of wearing two faces.)

Down with the dictatorship!

Many officers were amused by the poem, but John Wilson was not among them. The mayor also took a dim view of this spontaneous act of creativity. When they discovered through the grapevine that Eiland was responsible, he was immediately fired.

Eiland's next step was to call on Julian, who in early 1983 filed two separate lawsuits against the Montgomery Police Department and Emory Folmar, both with Steve Eiland as plaintiff. One, which became known as "the poem case," claimed wrongful termination, a hostile working environment, and infringement of the corporal's right to free speech.

The second case addressed the city's promotional practices in general, and was a broad-scale challenge to what the suit called "political favoritism" and "arbitrary and capricious standards" of the police department's promotional practices. Because the suit charged a violation of the "due process" clause of the Fourteenth Amendment of the U.S. Constitution, Julian associated friend and constitutional law guru Alvin Prestwood.

Both cases crept slowly through the system—no surprise to Julian, who in the past had often charged the city with "foot-dragging" and "obstructionist discovery tactics." Finally, trial dates were set for April 1985: two weeks apart.

On the morning that the poem trial was to begin, a bomb threat was called in to the mayor's office. "Because the poem had questioned Folmar's need for bodyguard protection, the threat certainly appeared contrived," says Julian, who was trying the case with attorney Vanzetta Durant before a jury and U.S. District Judge Myron Thompson.

Specious or not, the bomb threat had done its work on the jurors, who promptly ruled for Mayor Folmar. Julian and Vanzetta appealed to the Eleventh Circuit U.S. Court of Appeals. "I had worked hard on the case," Julian recalls, "but Vanzetta wrote an excellent brief and argument, and I give her all the credit for the appellate court reversing the earlier verdict and rendering in favor of Steve Eiland."

The promotional practices case, ironically, suffered the opposite fate. Deemed a non-jury case, it was tried by Julian and Alvin Prestwood over a grinding week, with many witnesses both pro and con. Thompson ordered briefs and took the case under advisement in late April 1985.

At the time, no one could have predicted that the case would stay "under advisement" for three years and two months. But when the District Court finally ruled in June 1988, Thompson's opinion and judgment were strongly in favor of Steve Eiland. As Eiland, Julian, and Alvin cheered the ruling, the headline of the June 18 combined edition of the *Montgomery Advertiser* and *Alabama Journal* proclaimed, "Judge Rules City Coerced Policemen."

Judge Thompson was quoted as saying, "The evidence was convincing that the city and mayor knowingly created an atmosphere in which police officers felt they had to show open political support for the mayor, if they were to receive promotions. Because Folmar was so intimately involved in the department, the court is convinced that Folmar knew of the practice and acquiesced in it for his own personal benefit."

Julian told the newspaper that Thompson's description of police promotional practices was "damning . . . a landmark decision that's going to echo not only around the Montgomery Police Department but throughout other areas, as well." Still, he added, "Promotional practices have not yet improved one whit, and are based on who supports Folmar and Wilson politically."

Lawyers for the City of Montgomery appealed. To make a long story short, the Eleventh Circuit reversed the verdict in 1989 and rendered against Eiland on the promotional practices case. Their reason? The "retaliation theory," the court said, upon which Thompson had ruled in Eiland's favor, had never been raised in the initial pleadings and was therefore invalid.

The "Bully Boy" and the Case of the Missing Doors

Most people think of The Doors as a rock group. But for a U.S. Congressman, a Montgomery homeowner, and Julian McPhillips, "The Case of the

Missing Doors" was a big-time headache in 1991.

It all began when Montgomery resident Meri Amos, a widow, sold her prominent Woodley Road home to U.S. Congressman Bill Dickinson, who was soon to retire and return to Montgomery to live. The sale went smoothly. Some time later, Mrs. Amos returned to the house and picked up several wooden doors that had been in storage in the carport.

When Mrs. Dickinson discovered the removal, she went ballistic. Shortly, the congressman did also.

The next thing Mrs. Amos knew, she was being arrested for "felony theft of property." Highly upset and humiliated, she sought out Julian. It was exactly the kind of "underdog" case he could get his teeth into.

In a swift counterattack, he filed a civil suit against the Dickinsons and began taking depositions to learn the critical facts of both the civil and criminal cases. With the help of then-associate William Gill and paralegal Carroll Puckett, Julian began preparing for the criminal case.

With the help of one of Julian's friends in Washington, D.C., Dickinson was served with a subpoena—while Congress was in session, no less—and the local Circuit Court denied Dickinson's motion to quash. Dickinson and his wife both testified, and in Julian's opening and closing argument he described the congressman as a "bully boy."

"Both Dickinson and his wife came off looking pretty foolish to the jury," Julian recalls. In any event, the jury was quick to return a defense verdict for Mrs. Amos in the criminal case.

The civil suit was later settled out of court. The amount the Dickinsons paid was confidential. "Let's just say the terms were very satisfactory to Mrs. Amos," Julian says. "And I think Dickinson's reputation really got sullied in the process."

Teachers v. Administration: Julian Takes Sides, 100+ Times

In the twenty-two years since his race for Attorney General, Julian has represented more than one hundred faculty members at Auburn University, as well as many others from Auburn University at Montgomery, Tuskegee University, Huntingdon College, Troy State, the University of Alabama, and the University of Alabama at Birmingham.

Many of the cases involved age discrimination—as did the first such case, in December 1986, when McPhillips represented five older professors at Auburn who charged that young graduates from Texas A&M were being hired at the same salary it paid established faculty members who were not only distinguished in their fields, but had served the university faithfully for decades.

The five plaintiffs included Business School professors Milton Alexander, then sixty, and Charles Snow, fifty-five; Engineering professors Winfred Shaw, sixty-seven, and David Hall, fifty-one; and fifty-five-year-old Wallace Pedersoli, a professor of Veterinary Medicine.

Auburn assembled a powerful defense team from the Montgomery firm of Balch and Bingham, and Julian heard through the grapevine that some members of the university's administration were openly boasting that the plaintiffs' case was going to be "blown out of the water," come trial date.

The defense argued that Auburn was justified in paying "market rate" to attract the best young professors—despite the fact that Milton Alexander, for example, who had written textbooks currently in use by more than four hundred colleges nationally, was paid roughly the same.

Julian, along with then-associate Kenneth Shinbaum and partner Jim DeBardelaben, responded by methodically trying to punch holes in the defense's reasoning. They seem to have punched enough, since the jury came back in favor of all five professors, awarding substantial damages. The court also awarded attorney fees.

In the December 12, 1986, *Birmingham News*, McPhillips was quoted as saying the verdict was "truly historic . . . a landmark case with national significance and ramifications." Balch and Bingham appealed to the Eleventh Circuit U.S. Court of Appeals in Atlanta, which affirmed the original judgment. Julian recalls it being a "very proud day for us" in 1987 when the university paid the professors and their attorneys a substantial bundle of money. "It was a tremendous amount of hard work," Julian says, "but it was certainly a nice payday, and justice was served."

Soon after, another group of professors—all formerly from Auburn's Engineering Department, and including earlier plaintiff Winfred Shaw— asked Julian to represent them in a First Amendment case, charging their right to freedom of speech had been violated after they published and distributed a self-study critical of the department.

"Ever since the landmark U.S. Supreme Court decision of *Connick v. Myers* in 1984," Julian says, "the First Amendment's freedom of speech protections have been watered down across the nation. There's a very elaborate four-step process that you have to pass in order to have a chance of winning such a case."

Julian found the most formidable obstacle, though, to be Judge Truman Hobbs himself. He obtained a favorable jury verdict for only one of the professors and, to Julian's great chagrin, that professor decided to leave Auburn despite the successful verdict. When the defense brought that fact to the judge's attention, Hobbs granted a defense motion for a "judgment notwith-standing the verdict."

"In common parlance," Julian says, "that means Auburn won in spite of the fact that the jury ruled against them. But, it's all part of the rough-and-tumble of practicing law. It's hard enough to get a jury verdict, but even when you get it you run the risk of the court taking it away."

Another lawsuit against Auburn University involved Veterinary School students from Kentucky, David Nash and Donna Perry, who in 1985 insisted they were falsely accused by a professor of cheating on exams, and denied due process in challenging their expulsions. The U.S. District Court provided no relief. Julian appealed to the Eleventh Circuit in Atlanta, which affirmed the District Court's dismissal, citing that "great discretion" must be afforded university administrators, and very little due process is required.

In yet another case, in 1990, Conner Brothers Construction Company of Auburn claimed university officials wrongfully bypassed Conner's low bid on a new campus building, awarding the contract to another firm.

Julian represented Conner Brothers in Lee County Circuit Court in Opelika. The outcome was a favorable settlement for the construction firm against the Auburn University Foundation.

Shades of the Scottsboro Boys Trial

Most attorneys in private practice set a high value on the referrals they get from satisfied clients. In the incident Julian labels "Shades of the Scottsboro Boys," the infamous race trial of the 1930s, it was repeat business that brought him what he considers one of his most memorable cases.

First, a woman named Sheila Mitchell came to see Julian in 1981 about a legal problem. Shortly afterward, her brother Arnell Sloan sought out Julian for advice. Third was their sibling Charlotte Payne, a realtor in the town of Scottsboro. Payne had recently lost her small real estate office building to a fire of suspicious origin.

She believed it was no coincidence, Payne told Julian, that the fire came not long after she had shown a black couple a house in an almost exclusively white neighborhood. Adding insult to injury, when Payne filed a claim for the loss with her insurance company, Nationwide, it refused to pay. The reason given was that they suspected Payne of setting the fire herself, to collect the insurance money. In other words, her insurance company accused her of arson, even though the evidence was much too insufficient for criminal charges.

As is often the case in small towns, many professional people in Scottsboro wore multiple hats. The irony was that Payne's local Nationwide Insurance agent was also Scottsboro's police chief, who was reported to have friends who were members of the Ku Klux Klan, or were at least strong Klan sympathizers.

Julian filed a suit against Nationwide for both breach of contract and bad faith. In the trial that followed, one of the most compelling pieces of evidence that Payne was innocent of arson was that her most prized possession was lost in the fire: a desk that had formerly belonged to Franklin and Eleanor Roosevelt, which she had bought at an auction of items from FDR's Warm Springs, Georgia, estate.

When Julian was preparing the case, Payne was distraught that she had no way to authenticate the value of the desk. Later, she remembered that she had stored away, in her home, two black-and-white photographs she found in a desk of the drawer. The original photos showed the Roosevelts in the White House on their respective sixtieth birthdays.

The judge dismissed the bad-faith claim, but an all-white jury nonetheless returned a verdict for Payne on the breach-of-contract claim and awarded her $35,000 in damages, the appraised value of her office and the lost furniture.

"It was a real disappointment to both of us that the bad-faith claim was tossed out," Julian says now. "We appealed it to the Alabama Supreme Court, but the appeal was unsuccessful."

Payne, though, was so grateful for Julian's help throughout the ordeal that, in addition to paying the contingency fee, she gave Julian the original Roosevelt photographs. Today, the pictures are proudly framed on the wall of Julian's home office.

No Deal for Creel

In 1980, Brenda Fulmer and other policyholders of American Public Life Insurance Company came to see attorneys Tommy Gallion and Julian, claiming they were wrongfully switched as policyholders from their original insurance company to Assured Investors Life Insurance Company—the latter associated with state school board member Ron Creel who, the plaintiffs said, had badmouthed American Public Life Insurance Company, in an effort to get the plaintiffs to switch. The initial group of policyholders turned out to be representative of many others.

Michael Allred of Jackson, Mississippi—"a very sharp attorney," Julian says—came to Montgomery "to work with us on the case. He deserves a lot of credit for organizing it," according to McPhillips. Julian and Tommy were part of the team examining witnesses, and making opening and closing arguments.

The judge was Joe Phelps, and Assured Investors Life Insurance Company retained top Montgomery defense lawyer Maury Smith.

When the dust settled, the jury had returned a $1.3 million verdict for fraud and slander against Creel and his insurance company. (As part of the settlement, the verdict against Creel was later vacated.)

Local TV stations and the *Montgomery Advertiser* trumpeted the results: as of that date—June 1, 1981—the punitive damages award broke the former Montgomery County courthouse record.

On and Off Ballot

Considering Julian's success in electoral disputes—both at representing and challenging candidates—it was not surprising that in 1986 he found himself in the thick of another ballot controversy.

Lucius Amerson, famed as the first black elected sheriff of Macon County, decided to run for the state senate. His opponents joined to have Amerson disqualified from the ballot, for supposed deficiencies in his candidacy papers. Amerson cried "foul" and McPhillips and Kenneth Shinbaum went to work studying the fine-print legalities of the process and arguing that Amerson had "substantially complied" with the election laws in filing his papers.

The battle was fought before a subcommittee of the State Democratic

Executive Comitteee, who ruled in favor of McPhillips and Shinbaum and duly certified Amerson as a candidate.

IN 1987, McPhillips and Shinbaum went into the political arena again, representing client Peter Stenstrom in a suit seeking to invalidate Governor Guy Hunt's appointment of Brigadier General Ivan F. Smith to lead the Alabama National Guard. "As in cards and war," Julian says, "if you play a lot you can't win 'em all." Such was the case of Stenstrom. The Circuit Court ruled against him, and the Supreme Court affirmed.

IN 1994, a Birmingham man came to see Julian McPhillips asking for help in disqualifying a challenger to Jefferson County Commissioner Chris McNair in his commission district. Birmingham City Council President William Bell, the plaintiff claimed, had made his home in a different district for a number of years, but had recently moved into a downtown hotel to meet the residency requirement necessary for running against the incumbent.

"I had no personal axe to grind against Bell," Julian says now. "I'd never met the man. In fact, he was a friend of my brother Frank's. So I called Frank to tell him what was going on. He agreed that I had a job to do as a professional, and that it was nothing personal against him or his firm. We can't always be on the same side of a case."

Julian put the case into gear, and the citizen's challenge led to a hearing before a panel of the State Democratic Executive Committee in the Jefferson County Circuit Court, and later an appeal to the Court itself. McPhillips and Shinbaum prevailed—Bell was disqualified, and McNair re-elected commissioner.

"Today," Julian says, "I see it as a blessing in disguise for William that we got him disqualified. He got to be interim mayor for several months in Birmingham. On October 12, 1999, he led the mayor's race in Birmingham. I'm sure he liked that post better than being one of three Jefferson County Commissioners." (In the general election in November 1999, Bell lost to challenger Bernard Kincaid, the new mayor of Birmingham. Bell remained as president of the City Council.)

The Secretaries' Best Friend

In 1986, two state secretaries, Martha Hubbard of the Revenue Department and Hazel Weaver of the State Military Department, came to see Julian, claiming that the director of the Personnel Department was denying them extra pay they were due under a 1978 statute.

The statute specified that state-employed "clerk stenographer IIIs" should receive the top rate of pay—that of a "clerk IV"—if they had been "employed by the state for twenty years, while holding the position for ten years, provided the employee was at the top rate level of their current job for at least five years."

While most folks would need a good bit of time to untangle the concatenations of those requirements, Hubbard and Weaver were not among them. They had done their homework, and were convinced they qualified for the raises, though personnel director Dr. Halcyon Vance Ballard said otherwise.

McPhillips filed suit in Montgomery County Circuit Court, which ruled in favor of his clients. But defense lawyer Richard Gill said "not yet," by appealing to the Alabama Supreme Court.

As the May 28, 1987, edition of the *Montgomery Advertiser* reported the outcome, "State Workers Win Claim for Back Pay." In a 9-0 opinion, the justices ruled against Ballard and the Board, awarding Hubbard $20,000 in back pay and Weaver $12,000.

Julian was quoted as saying, "It was a big victory, not only for these two ladies, but for a class of people entitled to benefits. It's a victory for state employees because they took on the state personnel board. So many people lose, and leave it at that."

And the publicity was good for business. Though state employees had long come to the firm for help with employment disputes, the number began to increase significantly.

12

The Church Trial of the Century

B EING the son of a minister, and having an almost lifelong familiarity with the inner political workings of a Protestant church, Julian seemed the perfect choice to represent clients in a 1983 case that involved two prominent Methodist ministers in Montgomery.

But as it turned out, McPhillips had no idea what he was stepping into. The case that would come to be called "the church trial of the century" held more twists and turns than a soap opera, and would leave a bad taste in his mouth regarding spiritual bureaucrats that still hasn't been dispelled, almost twenty years later.

One Sunday in early 1983, a visiting young couple approached Julian after services at Christ the Redeemer Episcopal Church and introduced themselves. Both Methodists by upbringing, they told him, they had once been members of Montgomery's socially prestigious First United Methodist Church. They asked if they could meet with Julian the following week at his office.

When they did, Julian learned that the wife might be called to testify against her former pastor, the Rev. Thomas Lane Butts, whom she claimed had wrongfully seduced her. She was not alone. Later several other women and an irate ex-husband came forward and made similar claims.

As the case unfolded, it turned out that the case would not be heard in a traditional court, but rather in an ecclesiastical court convened by high officials of the national United Methodist Church. In the administrative stages, Butts, as the accused, was given the choice of having his trial take place privately, behind closed doors, or before the general public.

The pastor, claiming that the charges were untrue and politically motivated, responded that, since the charges were already public knowledge, he insisted on "defending his reputation" in a public trial.

In doing so, he set a precedent. In the past 106 years of the denomination's

106-year history, never before had a church trial gone public.

And the public was in for quite a show.

"I don't think any fiction writer or dramatist could have come up with such intrigue and incredible happenings," Julian says now. "To really do it justice, I think, will require somebody to write a book about it, one day."

Indeed, it was not the immorality charges by the women that had set the trial in motion, but rather a charge of "violating due process" filed against Butts by his associate pastor, the Rev. Al Norris. Several chapters of the odd story had already taken place before the court action came about.

As Norris would later testify, he knew that it had been commonplace, for years, for Butts to seduce parishioners—married or not—and that he (Norris) had sadly fallen under the pastor's "spell of promiscuity."

Things finally came to a head, Norris said, when Alabama National Guard Gen. Taylor Hardin—whose daughter claimed to have been seduced by Rev. Norris—came to Rev. Butts with the charge and asked him to take appropriate action.

The action Butts took, Norris later testified, was to get Norris "boozed up" one night at the church office and persuade him to turn in his credentials. In the light of day, Norris changed his mind and went to Butts, demanding to be reinstated. Butts refused.

Norris then turned the tables, pressing charges against Butts with church officials for violating his rights of due process. Meanwhile, the aggrieved women were continuing to press charges against Butts of "immorality," as the term was defined under church law.

One of the many ironic turns the story would take is that Norris would hire to represent him attorney Bobby Segall, close friend and associate of Julian's, who by then was also representing a married woman in the case, who had earlier come to Segall for representation.

But they would be playing under rules that were foreign to both attorneys: neither Segall, Julian, nor any of the other private counsel, could ask questions of witnesses, much less cross-examine them. Those tasks were delegated to United Methodist ministers, who were in turn assisted by their own attorneys, who happened to be prominent in the Methodist Church.

"I think the reason Butts made the trial public," Julian says in retrospect, "was that he hoped to 'scare away' the women making the accusations. But they didn't scare away. They all testified before a large audience that included reporters from the *Montgomery Advertiser* in the morning and the *Alabama Journal* in the afternoon, who were passing along all the scintillating details to their readers.

"The trial was definitely the talk of the town."

For Butts's part, he had a large number of supporters—mainly liberals, not just in the church but the whole community—who argued that the pastor was the victim of a massive "civil rights conspiracy" designed to get rid of him because of his liberal views on race relations.

In fact, during a break in the trial, Julian overheard a conversation between two elderly female parishioners in which one said, "Isn't it a shame, what they're doing to Dr. Butts? It's just like they crucified Jesus Christ."

Meanwhile, the more conservative element in the church and around the town believed that Butts was the victimizer, not the victim, and should be punished accordingly.

"Butts was a master manipulator of public opinion," Julian says. "A year later, I was speaking to a Unitarian Church gathering and one of the members told me, 'I've cheered for and supported you and Leslie over the years, and usually agreed with you, but there's one thing I can't understand. Why did you treat Thomas Butts that way?'

"I told him it was because I believed with all my heart that the women were telling the truth."

The revelations that came from the daily sessions of the trial often seemed more like bizarre soap opera than actual court testimony.

At one point, Norris testified that he and Butts had engaged in a *ménage a trois* with a young woman in the minister's office.

"I'd never even heard the term," Julian says, "much less knew what it meant."

At another session of the grueling two-week trial—which sometimes ran from 9 a.m. to 9 p.m. with only short breaks for meals—Butts admitted that he kept a loaded pistol in his desk drawer at all times. "He acted," says Julian, "like it was just a normal thing for a priest to do."

McPhillips and many other observers felt that the evidence against Butts had become overwhelming. And that was before the prosecutors brought to light a civil lawsuit against Butts in the early 1970s that charged numerous incidents of "questionable behavior." That case was handled by attorney Janie Shores, before she became a state Supreme Court justice, and since Butts's testimony under oath had been preserved by depositions, it was a matter of public record.

When the testimony was finished, the jury that was convened consisted—again by church law—of thirteen Methodist ministers, and no lay people.

Their verdict was a surprise to almost everyone. They found Butts "not guilty" on the immorality charge, but "guilty" of violating the due process rights of his assistant pastor Al Norris. As a result, Butts was stripped of his pastorship but not of his ordination, and was reassigned to another church in south Alabama.

"It was an absolutely incredible result," Julian says now. "The message the jury appeared to be sending was, 'You can do whatever you want to with members of the congregation, but when you mess with one of us ministers, you're asking for trouble.'"

"It's no wonder so many people get so cynical with the modern-day church. If behavior like Butts's can be condoned with a slap on the wrist, then many conscientious, previously committed Christians wonder why they should go to church at all."

About a year later, on appeal to another panel of Methodist ministers in Atlanta—with volumes of transcribed testimony several feet high—Butts's conviction on the due process charge was overturned.

13

Other Precedent-Setting, Notable Cases

ALTHOUGH most of Julian's legal practice has been in the Montgomery area, his high visibility during the attorney general's race and the wide coverage of his lawsuit against Alabama governors has led clients from all around the state to come calling for his services—resulting in numerous trials on his opponents turf, some of them in remote county seats.

Brothers McPhillips Smash Cherokee County Record

In 1983, a young businessman from Tuscumbia drove down to Montgomery to seek Julian's advice about a major bind he was in. Randy Rollison's company, Rollison Logging, had rented $348,000 worth of logging equipment to John Lloyd Ellis's Cherokee Land Company.

Ellis, Rollison told Julian, had put the equipment to hard use for three months, harvesting timber, but never making a rental payment. Finally Rollison was forced to repossess the equipment. He found it in "greatly depreciated condition," but still had not received a cent from Cherokee Land Company, despite repeated promises.

Julian filed a lawsuit on Rollison's behalf in northwest Alabama's Colbert County, but after two years of frustrating delays the case was transferred to Cherokee County. Ellis's family was the most prominent in the area, a fact which by this point was no surprise to Julian—he'd uncovered information that Ellis's firm had earlier dealt in exactly the same way with two other logging equipment companies in Georgia. The Georgia business owners said they'd be happy to testify at Rollison's trial, and they did.

Julian, feeling the need for "new energy and organizational skills" in going up against a powerful defendant on his and his prominent family's home turf, called his brother Frank, who agreed to help. The two brothers—Frank was thirty-one at the time, Julian thirty-nine—found the ante upped even further when Ellis retained his county's two best-known defense lawyers.

To make matters worse, the David-against-Goliath aspect of the matchup was heightened when Julian pulled a hamstring while water-skiing the weekend before the trial started in April 1986, and he came into the courtroom sore and limping badly.

The plaintiff's team was in serious need of a friendly face, and they found one—in the form of Cherokee County attorney Dean Buttram: Julian's county campaign coordinator for the 1978 attorney general's race, and today a federal judge. Buttram knew the political lay of the land and Julian acknowledges his crucial help during the jury selection phase for giving him and Frank a fighting chance to get Rollison's money back.

History, though, did not bode especially well in that regard. The County's all-time record for a monetary jury verdict was only $34,000.

The trial lasted a week, and when the time came for closing arguments Frank and Julian were sufficiently buoyed by their progress to ask the jury to award the plaintiffs an even $1 million—a request that, for several seconds, left the defense silently staring in disbelief.

The jury complied so quickly that Julian figures his side could have gotten even more if they'd asked for it. "Those jurors were really fired up about the way Rollison had been mistreated," he says.

The local judge eventually reduced the verdict to $200,000. Rollison was satisfied to take half and let Frank and Julian split the rest. The money was appreciated, Julian says, but both he and Frank greatly value the letters of thanks their client sent them afterward:

> Words cannot describe how delighted I am. It couldn't have been done without your personal touch. I've never met or had the pleasure of dealing with anyone as trustworthy, knowledgeable, or deserving as you. Thank you from the bottom of my heart

Beth Kirkley Versus the Mental Health Department

In late 1987, Beth Kirkley came to see Julian for advice. A staff member of the Tarwater Development Center—a Mental Health Department home near

Wetumpka for retarded adults—she said she had been harassed and retaliated against for assisting in an FBI probe and Justice Department prosecution that had proceeded from a co-worker being charged with homosexual abuse of some of the residents.

After she testified in the trial, Kirkley told Julian that the director and assistant director of Tarwater—Cathy Maddox and Jim Earnest, respectively—had suddenly instituted a dramatic and bizarre "reorganization" plan for the facility that in essence quadrupled the duties of the five habitation team leaders, of which Kirkley was one.

The administrators' aim, Kirkley said, was apparently to force the leaders to quit. Kirkley did, and three others followed suit, leaving only one of the original team. Julian and attorney Gary Atchison pleaded the case before Judge Myron Thompson and a seven-person jury.

"At first the judge told us in open court, outside the presence of the jury," Julian recalls, "that he had difficulty understanding the plaintiff's theory. But by the end of the case he understood it very well, and it became plain that defense strategy was obstructionist. The defense gave us a lot of difficulty, but it backfired. It just motivated me to work harder."

The two-week, hard-fought trial resulted in the jury awarding Kirkley a $650,000 verdict for violation of her First Amendment constitutional right to freedom of speech—$200,000 in compensatory damages, and $450,000 in punitive damages.

"It's a hard life, being a whistle-blower, sometimes," Julian reflects now. "Beth was a very tenacious lady, and it was very satisfying to help her get compensated for the eight months of work she missed and the intense mental anguish she suffered."

Tuskegee Mayor Ron Williams

When Julian ran for attorney general in 1978, Ron Williams of Macon County took a leadership role in campaigning for him. A year later Williams was especially glad he did, because Julian was in a position to return the favor.

Williams had been convicted on charges of attempting to bribe state senator Dudley Perry in a vote on the Macon County Dog Track in 1976. The Court of Criminal Appeals upheld the conviction, but McPhillips convinced Montgomery Circuit Judge Randy Thomas to reduce Williams's sentence to

a few daytime weekends at the Macon County Jail, so that Williams never had
to spend a night behind bars.

Over the next twenty years, Julian and Williams ran into one another
occasionally but didn't have frequent contact. In 1996, Williams proved his
astute political skills by unseating long-time mayor Johnny Ford, the first black
mayor of Tuskegee, when Ford ran for a fourth term. Williams campaigned on
a platform of "spiritual renewal," which had appealed not only to the voters,
but to Julian as well.

But by 1999, Williams's relationship with the Tuskegee City Council
("which had never been good," Julian interjects) reached a new low. The
council passed an ordinance stripping Williams of most of his powers, and
delegating them to a city manager who was yet to be named. Williams gave
Julian a call.

Williams was ready for war, but his ammunition was rapidly dwindling.
The council had fired city attorney Milton Davis after Davis informed them
they were acting illegally in regard to Williams. And the council refused to pay
many of the mayor's bills, claiming that Tuskegee was "floating in red ink,"
despite the fact that Williams had reduced the debt to one-tenth of what it had
been when he first took office.

With no money up front, and a questionable possibility of any down the
road, Julian and partner Kenneth Shinbaum headed to Tuskegee to see what
they could do.

When negotiations with the council broke down, Julian filed suit in Macon
County Circuit Court on Williams's behalf against the Tuskegee City Council
and four of its five members.

On August 26, 1999, Judge Howard Bryan signed a temporary restraining
order Julian had prepared in advance, putting the council's ordinance to strip
Williams's powers on hold. A hearing was set for September 7, but on a defense
motion the restraining order and hearing were continued until September 30.
Then, it was continued again, with the restraining order still in force, for an
indefinite length of time.

At the end of 1999, Williams's status as mayor seemed shaken but solid,
and he told Julian he believed the controversy had actually strengthened his
political support. He also thanked Julian for coming to his rescue one more
time.

In April 2000, the City Council opposition tried to reactivate the suit but McPhillips and Shinbaum managed to delay the proceedings as Mayor Ron Williams headed toward a re-election battle in late August 2000, with twelve opponents.

Taking on the Loan Sharks

In September 1984, a middle-aged black woman, Oreadus Davis, who was impoverished and suffering from diabetes, came to see Julian because she couldn't pay off her mortgage loan and the company had already started foreclosure. She'd soon be without a home.

Julian examined the loan papers Ms. Davis had signed a year earlier and found that the annual interest rate of 18 percent on the amount borrowed ($8,840) was certainly high, but not illegal. But as it turned out, the fine print showed a "non-refundable origination fee" of $4,160—almost half as much as the loan itself. When the fee was included as interest, Ms. Davis was in effect paying twenty-eight percent.

McPhillips filed suit in Montgomery County Circuit Court, asserting that the loan was "unenforceable because it is unconscionable," as well as a violation of Alabama statutory law. The suit alleged that the company, First American Mortgage, had suppressed information that would have made clear to Ms. Davis her total obligation under the loan, thereby inducing her signature by fraud. Due to the diabetes, her eyesight was so poor she couldn't read large print, much less fine print.

At the time she had borrowed the money from First American, she was five months behind on payments of $100 a month to another mortgage company. She was unable to pay because her only income was from food stamps and occasional money sent by her son.

On September 28, Julian obtained an injunction from Montgomery County Circuit Judge Randall Thomas, preventing First American Mortage Company from proceeding with its foreclosure. At the same time, Julian and his friend Bobby Segall filed a motion asking the court to declare Davis a class action representative against First American on behalf of other borrowers in various parts of Alabama with similar origination fees.

Families from around the state—including six from Macon County alone—flocked to see McPhillips and Segall, asking to be added as additional plaintiffs. Depositions began, but before the class action could be certified, aggressive attorneys for First American appealed the case to the Alabama Supreme Court and stalled the proceedings.

"After a while," Julian recalls, "it appeared to be in the best interests of all concerned to work out a settlement. In the meantime, the company had been selling off these questionable loans to other companies who were gullible enough to buy them. So one by one, other mortgage companies became defendants also."

First American's local attorneys seemed to be negotiating in good faith, but kept "dragging their feet and stringing things out," says Julian. The next thing the plaintiffs' attorneys knew, First American had declared bankruptcy and obtained a stay of all proceedings.

The company remained in bankruptcy for years. Over time, McPhillips and Shinbaum settled the remaining cases one by one. In most instances, the plaintiffs kept their homes, with their loans either wiped out or substantially reduced.

None of the three plaintiffs' attorneys, McPhillips, Segall, or Shinbaum, made a cent from the case.

But Julian considers priceless the account of their efforts published in a *Montgomery Advertiser* column on October 29, written by senior editor Joe McFadden. With the headline "Private Attorney General Does Well," McFadden proclaimed:

> Sir Julian of McPhillips has raised the Boy Scout oath to Nobel Prize level. Any little old lady hereabouts who doesn't want help across the street had jolly well better not go near the curb.
>
> What brought this to mind was a back-page story last week about six families in Macon County suing a mortgage company they claimed overcharged them on their house payments. Instead of the 18 percent interest they thought they were paying, the suit said extra one-time fees brought the interest to more than 35 percent in one example and brought the family near bankruptcy.
>
> Macon County has its share of well-known lawyers — Fred Gray, for instance — but to no one's surprise, the earnest fellow leading the low-paying charge turned out to be Julian McPhillips. It prompted us to check with the

offices of McPhillips and DeBardelaben in Montgomery to see if there really were as many of these public interest cases as they seem to be. The mortgage suit is the thirty-third in the past year. That's about one every eight working days . . .

After recounting many of Julian's major public interest cases, McFadden concluded:

> Attorney General Graddick appeared unbeatable and had no opposition for his second term in 1982, but the first campaign, in 1978, was much the opposite. He emerged then from a turbulent field of several lawyers including McPhillips.
>
> But Graddick was a man one could trust not to go out and generate unexpected social waves on his own. The resulting void left to a restless McPhillips the pick of virtually the entire crop of central Alabama's "public interest" cases. So he became what he described to one reporter as a "private attorney general."
>
> Those lovers of the status quo who embraced Graddick as one of their own six years ago have watched Sir Julian tilt at every windmill in sight and topple a surprising number of them. If he had won the election, he might not have had the time.
>
> Some must look back and wonder if things wouldn't have been more peaceable.

Dell Ellis v. the Coffee County Commissioners

The Coffee County voting fraud case took more twists and turns than an old-fashioned cliffhanger movie serial.

On September 26, 1988, Coy Dell Ellis and his wife Nancy received a letter from the Coffee County Board Of Registrars, informing them that their names had been purged from the county's voting lists, because they supposedly lived in neighboring Geneva County. The Ellises filed a civil appeal in Coffee County Circuit Court.

Two years later the appeal was still on hold after two mistrials, and in the meantime the Ellises and their daughter were criminally indicted for voting fraud. In early summer of 1990, they came to Montgomery and retained Julian to represent them in the appeal and to defend them against the voting fraud charge.

McPhillips and Shinbaum quickly filed motions to dismiss the criminal charges, and Circuit Judge Terry Butts just as quickly granted them. The state appealed the case to the Alabama Court of Criminal Appeals.

Finally, the Ellises's civil case went back to the Circuit Court on the week of December 3, 1990. The case lasted several days, with frequent interruptions.

Julian argued to the eight-woman, four-man jury that although a portion of the Ellises' land was in Geneva County, their actual homestead was more in Coffee County, as witnessed by the fact that the family had voted in Coffee for more than 150 years, ever since Coy Dell's great-great-grandfather had helped settle the county in the early 1800s.

The jury was charged on Thursday afternoon, and deliberated exactly twelve minutes before reinstating Coy Dell, Nancy, and their daughter as official voters in Coffee County.

The tradition, and the voting rights, apparently meant a great deal to the family: upon hearing the verdict, they were overwhelmed by emotion. Coy Dell told a reporter for the *Enterprise Ledger*, "It's hard for me to make a comment, right now. I've just been under such a strain. I can't tell you how proud we are to get this verdict."

Ellis also told the press that the machinations of the past two-and-a-half years had "scarred him for life," and praised Julian for helping them bring the nightmare to an end.

The next day, the *Montgomery Advertiser* reported that, "As a result of the testimony in this week's trial, Circuit Judge Terry Butts announced he will ask for an investigation by the District Attorney's office and the U.S. Department of Justice into possible civil rights violations." Butts—who several years later would be elected to the Alabama Supreme Court—added that he was "shocked, shocked, shocked, and stunned, stunned, stunned at some of the testimony I have heard."

Members of the Coffee County Commission, who had originated the voting fraud charges, were not happy. They would be far less so when Ellis and his wife proceeded to file suit against the members individually, as well as the Commission collectively, for violating their civil rights by depriving them of their right to vote.

The federal suit was assigned to U.S. District Court Judge Truman Hobbs of Montgomery, and the state dismissed its appeal of the criminal charges to the Alabama Court of Criminal Appeals.

Amidst depositions, summary judgment motions, and court hearings, Hobbs gave the Ellises victory number three by ruling that the family's constitutional rights had been violated.

They were on a roll. But not for long.

The defense appealed the case to the Eleventh Circuit Court of Appeals in Atlanta. Both sides of the case wrote meticulously detailed briefs. But the judge who heard the case was Julian's old nemesis, Judge J. L. Edmondson. In his opinion months later, Edmondson ruled in favor of the Coffee County commissioners.

"All I could think," Julian recalls, "was 'zapped again.'"

In Edmondson's view, the commissioner's actions and motives, whether right or wrong, were protected by a legislative immunity doctrine because the Coffee County commission had "acted as a legislative body" in removing the Ellis family from the voting rolls.

Coy Dell Ellis was so agitated by the ruling that he debated with McPhillips and Shinbaum the merits and costs of taking the case to the U.S. Supreme Court. Finally, the three reluctantly agreed that the slim chance of getting a review petition granted was not worth the large cost of pursuing it.

Though Julian still aches over the reversal on appeal, he takes comfort in the fact, he says, that "I don't think anybody in Coffee County will ever mess with the Ellises' voting rights again."

Coach Robert Fuller, Sidney Lanier High School

In May 1990, the position of head football coach became open at Montgomery's Sidney Lanier High School. Robert Fuller, assistant coach at the school for twelve years, applied for the position, but instead it went to John Maddaloni, from local Cloverdale Junior High.

Maddaloni is white. Fuller is black, as was some 90 percent of Lanier's football team. But never in its history, as of 1990, had the school had a black football coach.

Fuller came to see Julian, who took up his cause before the Montgomery County School Board. Julian and Fuller were on the verge of filing a complaint with the Equal Employment Opportunity Commission in Birmingham, when the School Board suddenly reversed itself and offered the job to Fuller.

Nine years later, Fuller is still head coach at Lanier—and in 1999 had a pretty good season.

Fighting Sexual Harassment: The Door Swings Both Ways

One of the most significant areas of Julian's work, through the years, has been cases of sexual harassment, and many cases were far from the traditional scenario.

In 1983, for instance, he represented two male nurses at Montgomery's Baptist Medical Center who, after losing their jobs, charged that the head nurse, a female, was overbearing and treated them differently than the female nurses—making inappropriate jibes, pinching their ears, and generally making them feel like second-class citizens. The hospital settled, and the men got their jobs back.

In 1983, McPhillips represented Fairelynn Morris, Forrestine Paige, and Dennis Lane, in pursuing sexual assault and negligence claims against Covington County Sheriff Glen Chambers and certain deputies, and settled on what Julian calls "favorable terms for the plaintiffs."

In 1984, Julian went to bat for Robert Edwards, a male prison guard at Julia Tutwiler Prison for Women, who claimed he had been demoted from shift commander to bus driver because of his gender. A hard-fought case in front of Judge Myron Thompson resulted in a court judgment in which Edwards got his old job back, plus damages and attorney's fees.

Most of the harassment cases, though, have more familiar story-lines, such as a 1993 incident in which three former employees of General Electric Corporation—the number one company of the *Fortune 500*—claimed they had lost their jobs because of sex and age discrimination. In November of that year, Julian represented the three in U.S. District Court in Dothan, Alabama. Four days of hearings resulted in a hung jury and a mistrial for the two women on their sex claims.

Attempts to settle the case with GE were unsuccessful, and eventually the case went back to U.S. District Judge Myron Thompson in May 1994—this time in non-jury form. Thompson's ruling would be two years in the making, but his opinion was a landmark, awarding plaintiffs Irene Hearn and Betty

Kendrick $325,000 in compensatory and punitive damages, in addition to back pay and attorney's fees. Altogether, the judgment came up just shy of $600,000.

Thompson is Julian's favorite judge. "I look on Judge Thompson with great admiration and respect," Julian says, "and it's not just because I've had so many precedent-setting cases with him. I think Judge Thompson simply interprets the law as it should be interpreted, with any given set of facts. But he also seems to be more sensitive to prejudice and injustice than any other judge I've known, and he does what he can do to right those wrongs."

In 1982, Julian brought suits on behalf of two rape victims in Dale County, which led to significant monetary settlements with the owners of the premises for their failure to provide adequate security. Rushton Stakely attorney Jim Upchurch defended both cases.

In 1986, Julian represented Korean immigrant Lee Grier in a sexual harassment lawsuit against Mr. G's Gourmet restaurant, after she was fired for her supposed difficulty in speaking English clearly. The jury decided against her. "I never claim to win them all," Julian adds.

In 1988, Julian represented Highway Department employee Hazel Chapman in a high-profile sexual harassment claim against the Department Deputy Director, Byrne Stewart. Amid considerable newspaper coverage, the case settled, to Ms. Chapman's satisfaction.

In 1988 Julian represented Department of Corrections employee Jeanie Kelley in a newsmaking sexual harassment suit against the Department's deputy commissioner Tom Allen. In a hard-fought courtroom battle, the plaintiff came up short.

A 1991 case pitted Julian's client Rita Wright against the director of the Glenn Ireland Mental Health Center after she claimed sexual harassment by a high-level male administrator. The defendants settled, and Julian had another happy client.

But increasingly, McPhillips's firm became known for its employment cases, which ranged from going to bat for state employees against constitutional rights violations, to representing private employees in cases of race, sex, age, ethnic origin, or religious discrimination. Later, with the passage of the Americans with Disabilities Act, cases of handicap discrimination became a part of the firm's portfolio. Many of the cases, Julian says, were settled quietly without attracting the attention of the public or the press.

Although most gender discrimination cases involve female plaintiffs, Julian occasionally represents male plaintiffs alleging sex discrimination. While a high majority of his race discrimination cases involve black plaintiffs, Julian has represented white plaintiffs claiming reverse discrimination because of their race. In one of the firm's cases currently pending in the 11th Circuit, U.S. Court of Appeals, a white male Serge Lecomte claims he was unlawfully discriminated against by his employer, due to a combination of his white race and male gender.

"There are definitely such cases out there," says Julian. "The fact that it exists for both sides validates the law, showing it's not just for blacks or females but for everybody."

In 1994, McPhillips and then-associate attorney Mary Goldthwaite, now a partner, found themselves in a newsmaking sexual harassment case against Ben McNeill and his company, United Service Stations. Appointed by the federal district court to represent plaintiff Kathleen Cronin after originally turning the case down, Julian credits Goldthwaite with building a winning case.

"I'll never forget the daggers in Mary's eyes when she started cross-examining McNeill," Julian says. The court found McNeill liable for sexual harassment and ordered the attorneys to agree on a figure for damages and attorneys fees, which they ultimately did out of court. A year later, coincidentally, defendant McNeill was elected to the Montgomery City Council.

In 1996, McPhillips again teamed with Goldthwaite in a sex discrimination case against the Covington County Sheriff's office on behalf of former deputy sheriffs Tamela Odom and Lanorah Martin, who claimed they had been discriminated against in non-promotion as well as belittled and harassed because of their female gender. Julian credits Goldthwaite again for a winning effort, and the case settled.

Perhaps the most atypical of Julian's sex discrimination cases came in 1997 when he represented a muscular fourteen-year-old girl—Brandi Houston of Russell County, Alabama, near the Georgia border—in a case charging she was deprived of an opportunity to play football, due to her female sex.

The media found the case a natural human interest story, particularly given the revelations that Brandi could bench-press more weight and do heavier squats than any boy on the team, and moreover had once in practice knocked out two male players she collided with.

Although Julian eventually had the coach agreeing to take Brandi back on the team, Brandi and her mother decided that Brandi would transfer to another school. Nonetheless, mother and daughter—who once appeared at McPhillips's office in her prom dress to show her feminine side—felt vindicated for having stood up to what they considered narrow male attitudes.

But for each high-profile case, human interest or otherwise, Julian says, there are many others settled without fanfare—some requiring only the filing of a charge with the Equal Employment Opportunity Commission's office in Birmingham.

"Why slug it out in court," he reasons, "when you can get the same result with far less time and energy spent?"

The Sunshine Lady

In twenty-two years of private legal practice based in Montgomery, McPhillips has handled a wide range of cases that don't fall under any easy category.

Take the Sunshine Lady. In 1986, the ninety-year-old Ms. Fannie Bingham, a distinguished alumna of Tuskegee University, insisted that she be allowed to sit in on a meeting of the University's board of trustees that its members had for some reason deemed "closed to the public."

Sit in, Ms. Bingham did, refusing the members' repeated pleas for her to leave. The standoff ended when two of the members lifted Ms. Bingham, chair and all, and deposited her in the hallway.

Eventually, with Julian's help, Ms. Bingham got her voice and presence satisfactorily respected before the Board.

The Tale of Two Julians

In 1988, McPhillips got great satisfaction from once again taking on his nemesis, the Alabama Farm Bureau. In a case he refers to as "The Tale of Two Julians," he represented—with the assistance of Bobby Segall and partner Richard Gill—a man named Julian Elgin in a class action derivative suit on behalf of policyholders, claiming that Alfa had illegally dipped into its $220 million surplus during a reorganization.

The finale didn't come until 1992, but the settlement was considerable: $18 million was awarded to Alfa policyholders, and McPhillips, Segall, and Gill split a $900,000 attorney's fee.

Challenging Mike Tyson

Another notable case in 1992, making national headlines, was Julian's representation of Miss Black Alabama, Pasha Oliver, in a claim that heavyweight boxing champion Mike Tyson had made "unwanted sexual advances" towards her at the Miss Black Teenage America pageant in Indianapolis. Oliver ended up becoming a key witness in Tyson's subsequent rape trial, which ended with his conviction and imprisonment. She later dropped her civil claim against Tyson.

Other Partner Heroics

Some of the firm's best cases, McPhillips says, have been those delegated by him to other firm attorneys. In 1986, partner Jim DeBardelaben represented Crawford Hunt, a former Elmore County road commissioner, in obtaining a $90,000 verdict against the Elmore County Commission for a wrongful termination that violated his U.S. Constitutional rights. And in 1991, partner Frank Hawthorne, Jr., and then-associate William Gill represented the widow of a deputy sheriff, Robert Rollinson, who died after completing a fight in a local "Bad Man Contest." The attorneys sued a chiropractor for wrongful death, after the chiropractor pronounced the deputy medically fit to participate in the fight, despite his obesity and very high blood pressure, and obtained a $200,000 jury verdict.

Julian says he's a great supporter and admirer of his legal staff, particularly law partners William Gill and Kenneth Shinbaum. Gill sued the FBI for wrongfully harassing Wayne O'Ferrell after the government falsely accused O'Ferrell in the bomb assassination of federal judge Bob Vance. After more than a hundred FBI agents harassed O'Ferrell in Enterprise, Alabama, for the better part of a year, O'Ferrell lost his wife, his health, and his business.

McPhillips and Shinbaum had earlier turned down O'Ferrell's case on immunity grounds, but O'Ferrell came back to Gill for another opinion. Gill was also from Enterprise—an added incentive to stand up for O'Ferrell—and decided to take his case, with his partners' approval. Gill won many critical battles, before finally being ruled against on immunity grounds by federal judge Harold Albritton in a non-jury trial. Gill has appealed the ruling to the Eleventh Circuit Court of Appeals, where it remains pending.

Gill also obtained the firm's biggest verdict, one for $8.2 million in Macon County in 1997, following a wrongful death of one family member and numerous serious injuries by others, as a result of faulty work done by a state highway contractor. After the local judge significantly reduced the verdict, Gill appealed it to the Supreme Court of Alabama, where, contrary to trends in other cases, much of the verdict was reinstated. McPhillips brought the case into the firm, but Julian says he couldn't have handled the case as well as William did.

On March 18, 1997, Shinbaum obtained a $3.5 million verdict in favor of Delores Carter, who lost part of her leg in a 1995 run-away bus accident. Her right leg was amputated below the knee and Ms. Carter incurred $350,000 in medical bills. Adding to the tragedy, the New York bus was only covered by $25,000 in insurance. "Kenneth thought of a creative way to bring in an additional $1 million in insurance by suing an insurance company," says Julian, but the U.S. District Court rejected his theory, and the Eleventh Circuit affirmed. "I give Kenneth tremendous credit, however, for his hard work. 'Under-insurance' and 'no insurance' are national tragedies for trauma-tized victims, as in this case," McPhillips added.

Jealous Husbands, Fingerprints, Alibis, and Murder Cases

Though criminal cases are not a large portion of McPhillips's practice, he's handled many sensational ones over the years. Five were murder trials before a jury—capital murder in three of those—and the outcomes were acquittals in all five.

The first case, in 1983, involved Arthurine Ringstaff, a middle-aged black woman from Montgomery, charged with two counts of capital murder. Another woman had pulled the trigger. Ms. Ringstaff said she hadn't killed anyone, but had merely and naively been at the scene when the younger woman did the shootings.

Ms. Ringstaff had two strikes against her: she was illiterate, and she had already signed a confession to the murders. Later, she said she confessed only because two Montgomery policemen had beaten her into submitting. She was also very poor, and had no way of raising an attorney's fee, and no bond is granted on capital murder cases.

Arthurine's four young adult children came to see Julian, who quoted them a much-reduced fee of $5,000 for taking on the complex defense, but all of Ms. Ringstaff's relatives combined could only raise $2,400. Julian said that amount was close enough, and went on to try the case without additional fees.

He wasn't comforted by the fact that the trial would pit him against what he considered the two best prosecutors in the Montgomery County district attorney's office at the time, Kenny Mendelson and Billy Addison. The only assistance Julian had was from a nineteen-year-old nephew David Pitre, a college freshman untrained in the law, who took notes.

The most crucial portion of the trial, Julian recalls, was the testimony of the two policemen, who allegedly coerced Ms. Ringstaff's confession. Under intense cross-examination, their accounts "seemed less and less to hold water," Julian says. Apparently the jury agreed, returning a not-guilty verdict on all counts of both cases.

The next case teamed Julian with his law partner Frank Hawthorne, Jr., himself a former deputy district attorney. In 1988, the two defended Dennis Heard, an employee of the State Department of Education charged with murder after stabbing a jealous husband who attacked Heard for supposedly trying to renew a relationship with the man's wife.

Heard testified that the man—who was much larger physically than Heard himself—had knocked on the front door of his apartment, and after being let in, began pounding Heard in the head with his fists. Heard said he scrambled to find a knife, and stabbed the man—fatally, as it turned out—in self-defense.

Julian was later informed by the prosecutor, deputy district attorney Randy James, that the D.A.'s office had never received so much pressure from a victim's family to prosecute the murder charge.

Complicating the situation, for both sides, was the fact that the husband had brought with him a loaded Magnum revolver, but had left it outside the door before coming in. Theoretically, the revelation of the gun could cut both ways. The prosecution could say that the victim's leaving it outside was, relatively speaking, an act of good will, while the defense could argue that the gun suggested the man had expected a violent outcome from the beginning.

McPhillips and Hawthorne presented Heard's cause to the jury as a classic self-defense case, and argued that "a man's home is his castle," etc. The jury agreed, and acquitted Heard on all counts.

Julian's two most recent murder trials both involved capital charges, and he was assisted in both by Bill Honey, an attorney and professor at Auburn University at Montgomery. In February 1994, client Richard Lee Steele was indicted for allegedly murdering eighty-five-year-old Charles Minch, who was found beaten to death in his Montgomery apartment.

Steele languished in jail for fifteen months before his trial, since again no bail was allowed in a capital murder case.

Julian's defense claimed that the only evidence against Steele was circumstantial, namely a palm-print found in a room adjacent to the crime scene. No other forensic evidence linked Steele to the crime, and there were other legitimate explanations to account for the palm print—indeed Steele had moved furniture into Minch's apartment shortly before the murder.

As the verdict was read—finding Steele innocent of all counts—he leaned across the counsel table in tears, giving Julian a bear-hug. "It was one of my greatest moments ever," Julian recalls, "I was about to say that it doesn't get much better than that, but in fact it did. The trial was the same week as daughter Rachel's high school graduation. My parents were visiting, as were Leslie's father and stepmother, and they were all present to hear my closing argument. It was just a great, great day."

Julian also treasures a note he received from Steele afterward, which is now displayed in a personal scrapbook: "Thank you," Steele wrote, "for going through the trial and tribulation of helping me lift a burden that was hard to bear. Glory from the Father in heaven through you to me."

THE SECOND case teaming McPhillips and Honey was in the defense of Alton Dandridge, a Montgomery man accused of murdering and robbing Riley Manning, Sr., in 1995. Dandridge's indictment was based on fingerprint evidence found in the victim's bathroom, which was supposedly made in blood. The prosecutor argued this was the victim's blood, but there was no evidence it was, given the destruction by the police of the DNA sample.

The defense team claimed that there were other plausible explanations for the prints. One was that Alton had done work in the bathroom only months before the murder. Another was that the prints weren't Alton's at all, but those of the victim's son, whose fingerprint pattern closely resembled Alton's. A co-defendant, David Sudduth, earlier confessed to the crime and initially said Dandridge had nothing to do with it. But when police offered Sudduth an incentive of no capital punishment if he would implicate Dandridge, he changed his story.

"The Montgomery County D.A.'s office was so eager to get a conviction in one of my cases that they over-reached," Julian says, "especially by injecting fear into an alibi witness, Dandridge's girlfriend." Though the woman testified at a preliminary hearing that she and Dandridge were elsewhere on the night of the murder, the girlfriend waffled about that point on the witness stand. She was told by a D.A. investigator that if she testified at trial that she and Dandridge were even together the night of the killing, then she, too, would be indicted for murder. "No wonder she hesitated to repeat the truth," says Julian. One of the jurors later told Julian that the inconsistency may well have altered the outcome of the case.

Strategically, Julian says, the D.A.'s office elected to try Dandridge first. Meanwhile, Sudduth played his role by refusing to testify, under advice of counsel, pleading the Fifth Amendment, thus denying the defense the right to bring out all of his prior statements that Dandridge had nothing to do with the crime. And when the defense team tried to elicit testimony from other witnesses to whom Sudduth had stated he acted alone, the court sustained the prosecution's hearsay objection.

"There were so many holes," Julian recalls regretfully. "The key pieces of fingerprint evidence were either damaged by time, or wrongfully unavailable. And jailhouse witness Jimmy Hill was a con artist with twenty-three previous felony convictions who, in return for a deal from the prosecution, had no problem fabricating the story that Dandridge had admitted to the killing."

At the end of the hard-fought trial, the jury once again stayed out for two days. When they came back, they acquitted Dandridge of both capital murder charges but found him guilty of a lesser degree of murder, based on the bloody fingerprints.

Since then, Dandridge's case has worked itself through a round of appeals, which have been affirmed by the state's appellate courts. As of this writing, Honey is representing Dandridge on a *habeus corpus* petition in federal court, challenging the trial court's refusal to allow the testimony of rebuttal witnesses to whom Sudduth confessed that he had acted alone. The petition also challenges the State's use of Jimmy Hill's perjured testimony and the State's withholding notice it had made a deal with Hill for his testimony.

McPhillips's firm and Brian Stephenson, executive director of the Alabama Equal Justice Institute, are providing research assistance to Honey and Dandridge on appeal.

The sum total of Julian's criminal defense cases has impressed upon him a number of ideas regarding the legal and penal systems.

Chief among them, he says, is the fact that, "While the vast majority of people in prison are criminals who fully deserve to be there, there's also a very disturbing number—even on Death Row—who are innocent and wrongfully convicted."

"The disparity of legal talent afforded to criminal defendants, particularly those who don't have any money, runs the gamut of zero to one hundred. As a basic comparison, when the average person goes to the average physician, the quality of care they receive, on a scale of one hundred, might be between thirty and seventy, or thirty and one hundred. On the other hand, there's much likelihood that criminal defendants will get a young attorney just out of law school, with very little experience. A few may be close to zero on the scale."

It's a serious problem, he says, that probably will not be solved in the near future. The cause is what Julian sees as a major weakness of America's current justice system: "Criminal defense work very rarely pays what it's worth except in cases of celebrities or well-heeled white collar criminals. But there's no feeling in the world like getting an innocent person acquitted of a capital murder charge. There's no other circumstance in life where a lawyer's adrenaline, focus, concentration, instinct—and, let's be honest, apprehension—are all so heightened, so concentrated. It's at those moments when I feel like I'm most truly doing God's work."

Enabling the Disabled

When the U.S. Congress passed the Americans with Disabilities Act in 1991, Julian became one of the first attorneys to make frequent use of the new federal law.

But first, he started at home. He had a wheelchair ramp built for the front entrance of the Scott and Zelda Fitzgerald Museum. The law firm also had its bathroom doors widened on the downstairs floor, making them handicap accessible. There's also a ramp and wide door facing the parking lot.

In April 1995, Julian filed suit on behalf of Ricky Hinders, a quadriplegic, against the Village East Shopping Center for refusing to build ramps at the entrance of their stores. A settlement required that the ramps be built, and that the defendant pay McPhillips, Shinbaum & Gill, L.L.P., a reasonable attorney's fee.

That November, McPhillips and Shinbaum represented Sarah Smelley of Moundville, a driver's license examiner, against the Alabama Department of Public Safety for its failing to make a "reasonable accommodation" for her disability, following two minor strokes that prevented her from climbing into big trucks to give commercial driver's license exams. The DPS had fired her in November 1992, but the slow wheels of the law ground on for three more years before Julian got her case before a federal court jury in November 1995.

That August, in fact, partner Kenneth Shinbaum had first tried the case on behalf of Ms. Smelley. Defense counsel for the Department of Public Safety was Bill McKnight, a former assistant attorney general under Bill Baxley and a friend of Julian's from the mid-1970s. The first trial ended in a hung jury. The court declared a mistrial and set a second trial date. Shinbaum then associated Julian to help.

The battle began again on Wednesday, November 9, and recessed on Friday, November 11, for Armistice Day. Julian argued that there were several reasonable accommodations the DPS could have made for Ms. Smelley, including a ramp or a hydraulic lift.

At one point in Julian's closing argument, he asked a rhetorical question and was surprised when two of the jurors answered him out loud: "Yes!" and "Of course."

"I remember looking at Kenneth and he was grinning," Julian says. "I was, too, because we knew that meant the jury was with us." The degree to which the jury was "with them" would soon become known. Judge Harold Albritton instructed the jury on the matter of damages. The issues of backpay, other benefits, and attorneys' fees were reserved for the Court. The maximum damages McPhillips and Shinbaum could ask for under the law were $300,000. They asked for the maximum.

As a result, they were surprised when the jury read its verdict: they wanted to give Ms. Smelley $325,000. Though the court would automatically clip the extra $25,000, by the time attorneys' fees, back pay, and benefits were awarded, the verdict was still worth almost $500,000.

Julian told a reporter for the *Birmingham News* that the trial had been about "a clear-cut, classic case of handicap discrimination."

The Department of Public Safety appealed to the Eleventh Circuit Court in Atlanta. But before the appeal was heard, McKnight, McPhillips, and Shinbaum settled the case on what Julian calls "a most satisfactory basis" for Ms. Smelley.

The Yom Kippur Massacre

Julian refers to it as "The Yom Kippur Massacre."

Alan Berkowitz had been hired by the Montgomery Humane Society in August 1998, only to be fired five weeks later—on September 30, Yom Kippur, the holiest day of the Jewish calendar.

It was not the first friction between Berkowitz and his employer. Earlier that month, a senior manager had signaled her displeasure to him for taking off for a different Jewish Holiday, Rosh Hashanah. Berkowitz became even more frustrated when he told them that Yom Kippur was coming up and got an unpleasant reaction from the Society's president.

Berkowitz spent all day September 30 worshipping at Montgomery's Temple Beth Or. When he came to work the next morning at the Humane Society, an executive committee member told him he was fired. When Berkowitz asked for a reason, he was told "cultural differences."

The expression struck a raw nerve with Berkowitz, because he says he had heard it used before as a negative "code word" toward Jews.

Berkowitz sought out Julian to represent him on his charge of religious discrimination. McPhillips had handled his share of discrimination cases over the years—race, sex, age and disability—but a Jew claiming racial and religious discrimination was a new one for him.

Julian, as usual, fired off a letter to the Humane Society's board members on October 9, 1998. When it was ignored for two weeks, he sent a second. When there was still no reply after two *more* weeks, McPhillips filed suit on behalf of Berkowitz in Montgomery's U.S. District Court.

On November 11, 1998, the headline of the *Montgomery Advertiser* read,

"Former Director Files Suit Against Humane Society." The publicity caused two Humane Society employees—one former, one active—to approach Julian voluntarily and offer evidence of anti-Semitic comments made by a Humane Society official who was a defendant in the case. Testifying under oath, one of the employees said the official referred to Berkowitz, behind his back, as "that old tightwad Jew" and "the Polish Nazi." The other employee testified that the same official openly admitted to him that Berkowitz was fired because he was Jewish.

In late July, the parties and their attorneys met in a mediation session with U.S. Magistrate Judge Vanzetta McPherson (formerly "Durant," of police poet Steve Eiland fame). Though the case didn't settle that day, Julian felt that "momentum" was created for later settlement. Two weeks later, both sides agreed on a confidential settlement, at which time Berkowitz proclaimed he was "vindicated."

The biggest surprise along the way, Julian says, is that Berkowitz felt his support during the ordeal by Montgomery's Jewish community was "luke-warm, at best" which bothered him considerably.

As Berkowitz put it, "If Jews today don't believe anti-Semitism is alive and well in our society, they're totally in denial."

In the fall of 1998, Julian and Leslie joined the Standard Club, the formerly all-Jewish country club in Montgomery that had opened up to Gentiles one year earlier. In the years since, the McPhillips have enjoyed the club facilities and fellow members.

A Gross Result

In terms of landmark cases, the most fruitful time of Julian's career so far was the mid-1980s. One of those cases—against Lowder Realty, on behalf of client Charles Gross, Jr.—established a new cause of action under Alabama law in the area known as "tortiously (wrongfully) interfering with a contract."

McPhillips filed suit in 1985 for realtor Gross, claiming that interference from Lowder had wrongfully denied Gross the opportunity to close a sale on a house.

At the time, the nearest cause of action recognized in Alabama was "intentional interference with business relations." Alabama was among a minority of states in the U.S. not recognizing this lawsuit basis.

Historically, the tort of interfering with business relations involved interference with one's trade, profession, or business—a broader right. The more limited suit basis of "interfering with a contract" related to the wrongful interference by a third party with an existing contract between two other parties. In the Gross case, the Supreme Court of Alabama noted that lower courts had sometimes failed to differentiate between the two actions.

The case drew on Julian's first year of experience right out of law school at the New York firm of Davis Polk & Wardwell, in 1971–72. In a huge case, Davis Polk defended U.S. Lines and its subsidiary Sea-Land Shipping Company against a competitor's suit, which maintained the companies had wrongfully interfered with an existing contract the smaller shipping company had. Julian's assignment was to research the law on "tortious interference with contractual relations."

In *Gross v. Lowder Realty,* Julian argued that the two causes of action were largely indistinguishable. The Supreme Court of Alabama agreed.

The lower Montgomery County Circuit Court had originally granted summary judgment against Gross, who had signed a contract to buy the house from a seller represented by Lowder, after an earlier would-be purchaser failed to consummate his contract within the time period required by the earlier contract. Notwithstanding, the house sellers, with Lowder's help, disregarded Gross's completed offer and sold the house to the earlier would-be purchaser, who had missed the important deadlines.

The Supreme Court of Alabama used the Gross suit to clarify the law and carve out the new cause of action.

In the fourteen years since, the 1986 case—officially known as *Gross v. Lowder Realty/Better Homes & Gardens*, 494 S.2d 590—has been cited numerous times in scholarly publications, law review articles, and Alabama courts at all levels.

Though the court's finding made new law with this additional cause of action, the Supreme Court of Alabama decided to apply the new precedent "prospectively," rather than retroactively—meaning that although the case has helped many victims of wrongful contract interference in the years since, it was not applied backward to Gross's complaint.

14

Challenging and Defending Police

I RONICALLY, it was police misconduct that launched Emory Folmar into the Montgomery mayor's office to begin with. In 1977, a local black man, Bernard Whitehurst, was shot by police—who were later charged with planting a gun next to the victim to make the shooting look like police self-defense. In the wake of the scandal Mayor Jim Robinson resigned—although he had nothing to do with the original wrongful actions—and City Council president Emory Folmar was elevated to mayor.

A gruff Korean War veteran, Folmar soon gained a reputation as a "no-holds barred," "take-no-prisoners" type of mayor.

"In Mayor Folmar's mind," says Julian, "you were either for him, or against him. There was no in-between. And in his early days, especially, he tolerated almost no opposition. His racial views were well known, and he got much, much political mileage out of doing battle in TV interviews with black political leader and city councilman Joe Reed."

"The Rambo Element"

One reflection of the atmosphere Folmar created—or at least tolerated—in the city's Police Department was an incident in 1983 known as the "Todd Road case." Armed white men, not in uniform, apparently broke into a black family's home on Todd Road on the outskirts of Montgomery. A wake was in progress at the time, but the armed intruders, later revealed as plainclothes police, apparently saw expensive cars with out-of-state tags outside a modest home in a black neighborhood, put two and two together and came up with five, an unfounded assumption of drug-dealing. Family members later testified that the men announced themselves as police officers only after the unexpectedly large crowd of people in the house overpowered and disarmed the intruders. In fact, some people inside the house apparently phoned the police for help. In the resulting melee, weapons were discharged and some of the police officers were seriously wounded. So also were some family members.

Even though the police had caused the incident, the out-of-town mourners were arrested and Mayor Folmar and his then police chief held a middle-of-the-night press conference tinged with racial code language and labeling the arrested family members as "animals." It turned out that the arrested persons were well-respected in their home town of Detroit and, obviously, no illegal activity had been going on at the wake.

The black leadership of Montgomery was up in arms. Local attorneys Solomon Seay and Vanzetta McPherson took the lead in filing the suit, while certain family members quietly consulted Julian in the background. This regrettable incident was an example of the climate of poor relations between the black community and the police that figured in a number of cases Julian handled during this period.

In another newsworthy police misconduct case, he represented widow Jessie Allen, whose husband committed suicide in the Montgomery City Jail while imprisoned for overdue traffic tickets. Julian's suit charged the city with negligence in not preventing the death, since it had ample notice of Allen's suicidal state, and the means were readily available for him to commit suicide, but the jailers apparently did nothing about it.

Julian presented the plaintiff's case in front of a jury, but Judge Phelps, who once represented the City of Montgomery and who denied the Plaintiff's motion for recusal, directed a verdict against Mrs. Allen, preventing a jury from deliberating on the evidence it heard. The case was not appealed because Mrs. Allen couldn't afford the transcript and other costs of an appeal, even though Julian was otherwise willing to donate his attorney time.

Police Misconduct and Negligence

Some of the Police Department cases were not about deliberate misconduct, but negligence. In May 1990, McPhillips and Shinbaum sued the Department after an officer's car hit and killed Brian Adams, who was riding a bicycle. A pre-trial settlement which McPhillips calls "substantial" was reached.

In January 1991, Julian represented Doug McLemore, a man shot by police officers on New Year's Eve. The case was later settled. A month later, he represented Rufus Nettles in a civil rights violation suit charging police brutality. That case settled as well.

In April 1992, Montgomery police officers—who were not in uniform and in an unmarked car—ran off the road a carload of black Prattville High School honor students en route to an academic competition at Auburn University. The policemen threw the teenagers to the ground, at gunpoint, and refused to let them move, even though one girl complained she was lying on an ant bed. One of the young men testified that one of the officers held a gun against his head, and cocked it.

The police said they were part of a drug squad, and were acting on a tip the students were transporting drugs. No drugs were found, and the anonymous tipster never materialized.

Julian filed a $100,000 civil claim on behalf of each student, and with the help of Shinbaum and associate counsel Bill Honey, reached "a good settlement" for each of the students.

In 1993, abortion protesters were the target of the police. Julian charged they were unfairly harassed and mistreated and filed a lawsuit. Just before McPhillips and partner William Gill could obtain a federal court order striking down the city's ordinances that applied to "sidewalk counselors" and civil rights demonstrators alike, Mayor Folmar made a motion to repel the ordinances, and the City Council passed the motion. Nonetheless, Judge Truman Hobbs, who had earlier ruled the ordinances violated the protesters' right to freedom of speech and due process, awarded Julian and William an attorney's fee of $15,000, which they used to put up two pro-life billboards.

Also in 1993, McPhillips's firm sued on behalf of a black Montgomery woman, Gloria Porter, who was accidentally shot by police in a cross-fire. That case also settled several years later. In January 1994, Julian represented minority female Litschucia Martin, who claimed she was wrongfully beaten by two plainclothes city police officers. Her case was also settled on a confidential basis.

It was September 1994, when officer Raymond DeJohn—later to become involved in the Reginald Jones case—first came to Julian's attention. DeJohn had shot Gary Frank Kelley, a white Montgomerian, twice while Kelley was driving on a city street. Actually DeJohn fired a total of twelve shots at Kelley's truck. While Kelley admitted to being intoxicated, the McPhillips firm argued that he presented no danger to DeJohn. Julian gave the case to his partner Allen Stoner, himself a former deputy district attorney.

After four false starts, only to have the case continued at the last moment each time, Stoner finally went to trial on the fifth time, but the Court issued a verdict in favor of DeJohn, primarily because Kelley was drunk.

Representing Police Officers — James McBryde, Brad Sims

In 1987 Julian often found himself representing young black police officers who said they'd been mistreated by the top brass. One of those officers was James McBryde, who claimed he'd been fired because of his race. In a court settlement, McBryde was given his job back.

In October 1989, McPhillips represented police officer Brad Sims, a young black man who said he'd been set up and wrongfully charged with drug trafficking. The true culprits, Sims said, were Chief John Wilson and another top police official.

Publicity on the cases ran for weeks and then months. McPhillips and partner Kenneth Shinbaum defended Sims against the criminal charges in a trial that began in December of that year. The jury—composed of seven whites and five blacks—was out only four hours, and came back with an 11-1 vote in Sims's favor.

Judge Joe Phelps "much too prematurely," (after only four hours) Julian says, declared a mistrial, denying Sims the complete acquittal he deserved.

They were back in court less than a month later. This time Montgomery deputy district attorney Ellen Brooks, trying the case again, in defiance of Julian's argument that legal precedents of the *Batson* case prevented her, nonetheless used all but one of her strikes to remove only black jurors. Brooks also quickly made a motion to have the jury sequestered, which Judge Phelps granted before Julian could respond. Phelps also denied a motion to suppress what Julian described as "illegal and tainted evidence."

This time Sims had an all-white jury, except for one older black lady whom Julian describes as "very passive and timid." The trial went all week again. Chief Wilson took the stand, in full dress uniform with ribbons, and denied that any conspiracy existed.

The jury was charged on Thursday evening, then sequestered at a local hotel, away from home. Their opinions were sharply divided, and Phelps gave increasingly strong-worded charges for them to resolve the case. Deliberations ran through Friday, then again on Saturday. On Sunday, with the jurors increasingly red-eyed and weary, Phelps told them he would not grant a second mistrial under any circumstances, and gave the so-called "dynamite charge."

"They were worn out, and they wanted to see their families," Julian says. "So they finally caved in and found Sims guilty."

McPhillips and Shinbaum immediately appealed to the Alabama Court of Criminal Appeals, which quickly reversed the verdict. In an opinion written by Judge Sam Taylor, the court found that Ellen Brooks had indeed violated *Batson* case restrictions against striking jurors for racial reasons, the fourth time she had done so in her career. The Criminal Appeals Court also ruled that Judge Phelps had wrongfully failed to suppress illegal evidence.

Under the circumstances, the Police Department decided not to try Brad Sims again. A settlement was reached on Sim's civil claims, and this earthquake of a case that shook the police department and the City was over—but according to observers, repercussions continued in the Department for years to come.

In May 1990, Julian represented black police sergeant Willie Davis claiming that promotional practices in the Department were racially biased. The claim was later settled.

Defending Law Enforcement

In Julian's legal career in Alabama from 1975-2000, he began by defending law enforcement officers in his capacity as assistant attorney general for Alabama. Even after he went into private practice, he frequently defended officers who claimed they were wrongfully terminated or disciplined.

In 1982 Julian helped restore the job of Highway Patrol officer Luther Joe Pritchett of Scottsboro, by a successful jury verdict in Montgomery County Circuit Court before Judge Phelps.

McPhillips has also defended a number of police chiefs in towns across the state including Lanett in Chambers County, Elba in Coffee County, and most recently and notably Police Chief Lem Dubose of Grove Hill, in Clarke County.

"It's very unfortunate that police chiefs and officers so frequently get caught up in small-town politics," Julian says. "And in many ways, Montgomery is a 'big small town.'"

Because McPhillips, Shinbaum & Gill, L.L.P., specializes in helping "underdogs and victims," many of their clients are victims of crime. Julian is a strong supporter of such organizations as "Mothers Against Drunk Driving," and "Victims of Crime and Leniency," having contributed significant financial help to both organizations.

"Crimes of violence, and white-collar crimes, are both serious problems in Alabama," he says, "and need to be addressed vigorously by law enforcement at all levels, with the support of ordinary citizens, to redress the damage criminals do to our society."

BUT NOT all of Julian's police stories take place in a courtroom. One Sunday morning in 1994, Julian was exceeding the speed limit on his way to church. A Montgomery traffic officer pulled him over and asked to see his license. Julian gave it to him, and admitted he knew he was speeding.

Moments later, Julian looked back to see the officer chuckling with his partner over whose driver's license they had.

"I thought, 'Oh boy, I'm in trouble now,'" Julian remembers. The officer came back to him, smiling, and said, "So *you're* Julian McPhillips?"

"Yes," Julian said, swallowing hard.

"You have no idea," the policeman said, "how much your name is talked about down at the Department. The top brass, they hate you, but the rest of us—we love you."

"He wouldn't even give me a warning ticket," Julian recalls. "he just told me to drive a little slower and keep up the good work. I was really touched."

In February 1997, Julian defended black Montgomery police officer Sean McGrady, who had been found guilty in Municipal Court of third-degree assault against a girlfriend. Julian appealed to Circuit Court, and worked out a settlement that involved McGrady moving to Atlanta, and taking a higher-paying job.

"Over the years," Julian says, "we've represented many other police officers in various negotiations with the top brass. But to this day, we still get two or three complaints a week about police brutality. It's impossible for us to handle all of them, so we have to weed them out, taking only the ones that are strongest cases on the issues of liability and damage."

Once, at a deposition in a police brutality case where Julian was representing a young black plaintiff from the Trenholm projects, a City of Montgomery defense lawyer challenged Julian: "You and your clients live in Disney World."

"Well," Julian replied, "it's a lot better than living in Emory World, like you do."

Julian also enjoys recalling the time when a stranger told him that McPhillips, Shinbaum & Gill, L.L.P., is the "only thing standing between local citizens and the brownshirt tactics of Folmar's police department."

Julian himself is a bit more charitable. "I believe with all my heart that the majority of police officers are good and decent people. But there's a certain 'Rambo' element that just won't go away, and it's composed mainly of young tough-guy types who are attracted to the department. The problem is that their bad behavior is not only encouraged, but rewarded, all the way up the mayor's office.

"At least, it used to be. Now, time will tell."

In November 1999, the political pundits were proven fallible when Mayor Folmar lost his re-election run for the first time in twenty years, to young attorney Bobby Bright, whom McPhillips considers a "breath of fresh air." Folmar's nemesis Joe Reed and four other city council incumbents were also defeated.

15

Not Doing It Alone

J ULIAN takes obvious pride in what he and his firm have achieved over the years, and relishes praise and compliments as much as the next person. But he's also quick to spread the credit around.

Leslie is at the top of his list: "We've been married for some twenty-six years now, and she's very dear to me. I can't imagine anyone else giving me more moral support, or being such a great mother to our three children.

"We pray together twice a day, every day. I pray by myself, at times throughout the day, and with clients or staff if they feel comfortable with it. If I'm running on empty, prayer energizes me. And if I need calming down, it calms me down."

He also has high praise for his parents, Eleanor and Julian Sr., for giving him "good values, a good education, and a good upbringing, which is worth far more than any amount of money. They never pushed me into anything. Instead, they motivated me in a quiet, inspirational sort of way."

Julian's attorney sibling Frank rates high on his list of credits as well. "Truth be told," Julian says, "Frank is probably the smartest of Mom and Dad's whole brood of five. He's a bond lawyer extraordinaire, and a partner in the premier law firm of Maynard, Cooper & Gale, P.C.

"Frank is the unsung hero of why I did so well in running for attorney general in 1978. And one of my fondest courtroom memories is the time in 1986 when he and I worked as a team to smash the Cherokee County courthouse record with a $1 million jury verdict."

Julian says he also owes a great deal to attorneys outside his firm for their help in building his practice.

At a very low spot in McPhillips's life and career—September 1978, when he abandoned his challenge of the attorney general election results—he received a phone call from Tommy Gallion, son of former Alabama attorney

175

general McDonald Gallion. "Tommy invited me to move into his office, have free rent for three months, and work with him on some cases. It was not only a generous offer, but a great encouragement at a time when I needed it the most."

The two attorneys practiced law closely together for the next four years. In March 1982, Julian bought Tommy's in-laws' three-story, 10,000-square-foot building at 516 South Perry Street (known as the "Perry High" building), where he's practiced now for some twenty-two years. When Gallion moved away in 1982, McPhillips brought in his first associate attorney, Jim DeBardelaben, and paralegal Carroll Puckett, and continued to work with Regina Barron, a secretary who began working for him in November 1978, while a high school student, at the age of sixteen.

"Regina is a real success story," Julian says. "She's Asian-American through her Japanese mother, and she left the firm in 1987 to complete college in just three years, went to law school for three more years, and worked on her own as an attorney for a year. She returned to the firm as a lawyer in 1994."

Today, Regina's most vivid memories of those early days include Leslie pitching in to help with office chores while the McPhillips toddlers played on the floor nearby, and "the monster project," a massive brief she had to type for the landmark Johnny Reynolds case against the Alabama Highway Department: "There were no computers, just typewriters and carbon paper, and erasures weren't allowed. Every copy had to be perfect," she says. "It felt like I was going to spend the rest of my life typing that one document."

Today she's an attorney with the firm, specializing in family law. "It's a very emotional field, but it's a very rewarding one," she says. "You can actually see the difference you're making in people's lives."

Carroll Puckett, a realtor, originally approached Julian for help with some serious legal and financial problems. Julian was working on another case that involved complicated real estate matters. The two collaborated, and the association gradually became permanent. "I refer to myself as one of 'Julian's strays,'" Puckett laughs now, in his Perry Street office. "I was in trouble, I came, and I stayed. Julian and I are at far ends of the pole politically, theologically, and in other ways," says Puckett, a conservative Republican and lay minister in the Church of Christ. "But somehow we're always able to put aside those differences and do what needs to be done."

Montgomery attorney Bobby Segall also gets strong praise from Julian: "I don't know what I would have done without Bobby," Julian says. "I call him 'Super Lawyer.' He's the best in Montgomery, and he's gotten me out of several scrapes, as well as helped me get better results in many of my cases."

One of those scrapes was a lawsuit challenging McPhillips's residency during the attorney general's race in 1978. Segall appealed the case to the Alabama Supreme Court and, on the Friday before the voting, won a positive ruling. "I ballyhooed that victory for all it was worth," Julian recalls, "saying that my opponents were resorting to desperate tactics to stop me. In retrospect, I think the case helped me more than it hurt me."

Several years later, with Julian's career rising quickly, he found himself on the receiving end of what he calls "professional jealousy and political rivalry," in the form of an anonymous complaint to the Montgomery Bar Association about public comments Julian had made while trying a case against South Central Bell Telephone Company and its Yellow Pages, on behalf of a local businessman who said his omission from the directory had been financially devastating.

"I'll never forget that day," Julian says. "It was just Bobby and me facing six lawyers of the County Bar Association's grievance committee. Bobby stared them down and told them, very calmly, that if they insisted on violating my First Amendment rights in the matter, they may as well just get out their pocketbooks and start writing me checks, then and there." The complaint was dropped, and Julian says he's "never been more proud of Bobby than I was at that moment."

About a year later, Julian found himself—for the only time—called before an Alabama Bar Association state grievance panel, being questioned about a charge that he had improperly solicited a client. "It was basically a misunderstanding," Julian says. "The client had asked me to call him regarding a case. And it wasn't the client who complained—it was the Montgomery County panel going by somebody else's word of mouth. What hurt me the most, though, was that the panel never even bothered to investigate the facts before pressing charges, and never asked me for my version of what happened before pressing charges."

With so much at stake, Julian again called on Bobby Segall to represent him—and also added to the team prominent attorney Sonny Hornsby, who would later be elected chief justice of the Alabama Supreme Court, and Alvin Prestwood, an expert witness on constitutional law.

"We all went to the Civic Center one rainy day in 1985," Julian recalls. "The state panel had four lawyers sitting on its side, facing the four of us and again, I didn't have to say a word. Bobby began in his usual aggressive way. Then Sonny came on strong, too. And after Alvin chimed in, the next thing I knew, the panel had granted a summary judgment in my favor."

Greatly relieved, Julian later got out his checkbook. "I paid the other attorneys well, but Bobby refused to let me pay him a cent. I was overwhelmed and speechless, which is a rarity for me. Bobby's not just a great attorney, but he's been an awesome friend as well."

Julian was conciliatory toward the Montgomery County panel afterward, forgiving each member personally for not checking out the charge beforehand, "and they haven't messed with me since," he says. (And in the years since, Julian himself has represented many attorneys before Bar Association grievance panels.)

"I've had two human angels looking out for me in the recent years, Bobby Segall, my own attorney, and Kenneth Shinbaum, my next law partner," says Julian. "I'd feel much less secure in this world without either one of them."

Segall, who first met Julian in 1975 when Julian was interviewing at the firm where Segall worked, remembers his first impression of Julian: "You could tell immediately he was a very bright young attorney. But I think what carried more weight with me was his interest in public service—representing average citizens who have problems with the establishment, when he could have taken other directions that were much more lucrative.

"He's very big on constitutional principles, equal justice for all. From the beginning he's been an advocate for black causes, and he doesn't hesitate to take on cases that might aggravate some of his friends. I enjoy helping him, when I can.

"In court, he's kind of a mixture of Southern gentleman and aggressive advocate for his client. Sometimes he can come across as a little formal at first. But his sincerity is never at issue, and he's very, very tenacious in pleading his client's cause."

As the practice grew, Jim DeBardelaben became Julian's first partner in 1983, and Frank Hawthorne, Jr., his second in 1985. McPhillips, DeBardelaben

& Hawthorne had begun making a name for itself when Kenneth Shinbaum came on board in 1986 as an associate attorney. Julian and Carroll Puckett first met Kenneth as an opposing attorney during a complicated land dispute in Prattville during the early 1980s, and both came away impressed by Shinbaum's knowledge of the fine points of real estate law.

In 1988 the firm hired William Gill, a young attorney one year out of Cumberland Law School where he was at the top of his class. While Gill was clerking for Chief Justice Bo Torbert, Julian says he and his colleagues came to respect William's "razor sharp mind, and he's developed into a powerhouse of a lawyer."

In 1990, DeBardelaben left the firm for personal reasons not related to his practice, and in 1993 Hawthorne accepted an offer to go into practice with his father, who was retiring from another firm. "We all remain good friends," Julian says.

Allen Stoner, a former Montgomery County deputy district attorney, served the firm for seven years before returning to his native north Alabama in 1998.

Since 1993 the firm has operated under the name of McPhillips, Shinbaum, and Gill. "Kenneth has been the unsung hero of the whole operation," Julian says. "He's also a walking encyclopedia of the law. He's always willing and able to help anyone in the firm, and me especially. Kenneth and William are the brains of the firm, for sure."

The firm's first female attorney, Mary Goldthwaite, brought her strong prosecutorial background, which she'd developed in four years with the Montgomery County D.A.'s office. Her ancestors, two pioneer Goldthwaite brothers, helped found Montgomery in the early 1800s.

"Nobody works harder or is more conscientious than Mary," Julian says. "We all love her."

Then there's Karen Sampson Rodgers, an African-American from west Alabama, "a hard-working, aggressive lawyer who's developed a real niche for employment cases—as has Kay Dickey, who became a lawyer at age fifty, a year after her son started practicing law in Birmingham. Kay had retired from twenty years of school teaching," Julian says.

Aaron Luck's legal background is far from typical. An Idaho native, ex-Marine, and former wrestling champion of Great Britain, the young attorney married an Alabama girl and decided to stay in Alabama. His practice includes personal injury cases, contract litigation, and criminal law—as does that of Jim Bodin, a native of Louisiana, who joined the firm in 1995. Both are in their early thirties and are, Julian says, "very smart, conscientious, and hardworking."

The attorney most recently hired by the firm was Joe Guillot, who, at forty-five, was a retired Air Force lieutenant colonel and, like Bodin, a Louisiana native. "Joe's quiet, but very thorough and very proficient," Julian says. "At his Air Force retirement party, his commanding general praised Joe's keen intellect, and I certainly concur."

Overall, McPhillips, Shinbaum & Gill has grown to twenty-six staffers, including Puckett's wife and son, both part-timers. Julian has high praise for Amy Strickland, his chief executive assistant, for keeping the office well organized and his schedule timely. Two other unsung heroes of the office, he says, are receptionist Page McKee and bookkeeper Pat Hornberger.

Also deserving of recognition, Julian says, are the firm's two so-called "runners," Les Faucette and Kaylon Jenkins, who travel the state serving subpoenas, locating witnesses, and delivering documents. "But they do a lot more as well," says McPhillips. "Les doubles as a computer troubleshooter, and Kaylon, an ordained minister with Faith Crusades Ministries, is a spiritual boost to me—praying with me, and for me, at strategic moments."

Law clerk Sim Pettway, Jr., besides being helpful in matters legal and political, is appreciated at the firm for his great sense of humor, according to Julian. "Sim and I enjoy a 'deep in the belly' laughter from time to time, which helps to ease the daily tension." Paralegals Heather Hutto, Latarsha Scott, Tricia Deep, Monette Marbury, Connie Butts, Leah Knight, and Patricia Williams round off what Julian describes as a highly talented legal support staff, as of mid-2000.

Julian claims he'd be remiss if he didn't give credit to Lynelle Howard, his chief secretary and paralegal from 1987 to 1996, for her invaluable help during that period of time. "She had an awesome memory and was both fast and accurate on the computer. Lynelle moved out to Durango, Colorado, in late 1996."

Gibson Vance and Edmond Naman were two law clerks in the early to mid-1990s who gave valuable support to the firm but have since moved on to other professional challenges.

Today, Julian says, "we work especially well together as a team. It's a hard working atmosphere, but it's relaxed and home-like. It's not like some of the formal offices with expensive antiques, where everybody's afraid to make noise and you can walk through the whole building with nobody speaking to you.

"In some ways we're like a family, and I think that shows through in the successful results we obtain for our clients."

In 1997, readers of the *Montgomery Advertiser* voted Julian "Best Attorney in Montgomery." The same year, a columnist in the *Montgomery Independent* referred to McPhillips, Shinbaum & Gill, L.L.P. as the best law firm in town.

"I'm honored, of course," Julian says, "but if I'd voted myself, I'd have first picked Bobby Segall, and then Jere Beasley, who's not only the architect of big judgments but also a tireless consumer advocate. Joe Espy, on the defense side, would be high up, too."

In the *Montgomery Independent* article, Julian is quoted as saying that his practice is made up of three parts: "the professional end, the business end, and the ministry." When the writer asks Julian what advice he'd give to upcoming young lawyers, his reply is: "Think of your career as a ministry, and the business side will take care of itself. And the more you have a heart for your client, the more you'll enjoy your practice."

16

21st Century: No Stopping Point

WHEN THE clock struck midnight on January 1, 2000, it marked a quarter century since Julian returned to Alabama to practice law. But when the holiday was over, it was business as usual—i.e., forward—for the ten attorneys and sixteen other staff members at McPhillips, Shinbaum & Gill.

One of the earliest suits of the new millennium carried echoes of the previous fall's upset mayoral race in Montgomery. A nineteen-year-old college student, Sam Caraway, charged that he was roughed up by police on August 26, 1999 as he was attempting to put up a roadway sign that said "Folmar Still a Bigot." The suit charged that the officers (referred to as "the thought police" by some of the mayor's critics) hit young Caraway and choked him into unconsciousness. "I thought I was going to die," he later said.

When Caraway regained consciousness, he found that he'd been charged with harassing the policemen, and he spent twelve hours on the floor of the Montgomery jail. Sam and his parents, Jackie and Mac, came to see Julian late Friday afternoon before Labor Day weekend.

The family wanted to go public with what had happened to Sam, and Julian's office responded by faxing notification to the news media of a press conference to be held at his office the following Tuesday.

Not surprisingly, Emory Folmar got wind of the plans and his son, Wilson, contacted the Caraways and told them all charges against Sam would be dismissed if Julian called off the news conference. At first, the Caraways rejected the proposal, but eventually gave in. The deal was struck and verified through three different letters from Julian to Emory, with Wilson acting as intermediary.

A date was set for the official dismissal of the charges, but was later postponed by the city. A second date was also postponed. Then a third, fourth, and fifth. After Mayor Folmar was defeated by Bobby Bright in November and left office, the charges against Sam Caraway remained pending.

By January 2000, the Caraways had had enough. They asked Julian to file a lawsuit on Sam's behalf against the arresting officers, for assault and battery, and against the City of Montgomery, Emory Folmar, and Wilson Folmar for breach of contract. (The suit sought no damages against the younger Folmar, because the Caraways believed Wilson had acted in good faith.) Julian also added a state constitutional free speech claim against the officers and the City for denying Sam's free speech right to put up the sign in the first place.

On March 23, Julian and the Caraways settled the case, agreeing to drop their civil actions against all the defendants in exchange for the City of Montgomery's dismissal of the criminal charges against Sam, and the City's payment to him of $12,000.

In another case beginning in January, McPhillips represented Montgomery firemen Cecil Thomas and Lee McBryde, who claimed they were threatened and coerced by their fire department supervisors to support Folmar in the mayor's race, against their will. McPhillips and the firemen visited Mayor Bright in December 1999, trying to resolve the case. In February 2000, McPhillips sent the City a copy of a proposed lawsuit, and offered the City a chance to resolve the case first. After three more months of receiving no response, McPhillips filed suit on May 3, 2000, on behalf of McBryde and Thomas. Julian was quoted in the next day's *Montgomery Advertiser*, as saying:

"It's a sad story that these two men have been subjected to such Mickey Mouse treatment from the fire department's top brass . . . We've tried to resolve this with the new administration and have gotten nowhere. Our patience has run out."

In March 2000, Julian also forwarded to the Mayor's office and City Council the complaints of three City of Montgomery maintenance department workers, William McCollum, Theodis Stokes, and Michael Fuller, who objected to being retaliated against by the top brass of their department, due to their supporting Bright against Folmar in the Mayor's race. The cases of the fire and maintenance department employees remained unresolved as of July 2000, despite considerable public interest in both sets of cases.

But the most notorious case of early 2000 was Julian's defense of a thirteen-year-old student at nearby Cloverdale Junior High School who was denied permission by a substitute teacher to go to the bathroom, when the student repeatedly begged to do so. The teacher instead told the young student he could urinate in a waste can.

"He asked permission three different times, saying he really had to go," Julian recalls. "But the only choice the male teacher left him was the waste can or his pants. He tried to shield himself as best he could with his coat, but he was still embarrassed and humiliated." To add insult to injury, the school's principal called the boy, Ryan Calhoun, into his office and gave him a five-day suspension over the incident. Ryan and his parents were referred by their landlord to Julian.

Interest in the case snowballed: from the lead story of the next day's *Montgomery Advertiser* and coverage from local NBC, CBS, and ABC affiliate TV stations, to an Associated Press item that was carried by papers nationwide. The next thing Julian knew, he was getting calls from talk show producers in New York City wanting comment on the case. A friend of Julian's in Wisconsin (John Siebold of Davis Polk days in New York) mailed him a clipping about the waste-can case that was carried in a Milwaukee newspaper.

Julian sent a letter to Montgomery County school superintendent Clinton Carter, and things began happening. Carter immediately lifted Ryan's suspension and instead suspended the teacher for five days. Juvenile authorities reacted by filing charges against the teacher for "contributing to the delinquency of a minor."

Julian sent a claim for damages to the school system office, alleging invasion of privacy and intentional infliction of emotional distress, but held off on filing a suit until he could further assess the damages and do some research on the defense of "discretionary immunity," which means that the school system is immune from liability if the situation required a reasonable judgment call on the part of the teacher. Julian insisted that, under the circumstances, there was no such protective discretion.

In late April, after transferring Ryan to another junior high school, and weary of the whole affair, the Calhoun family, feeling the teacher had been sufficiently disciplined by the school board, and following Julian's advice, decided to drop their civil claim and to support dismissal of the criminal charges.

In another case in the news in February 2000, Julian represented three clients opposing the proposed merger of historically black Trenholm Technical School, in a largely black neighborhood, with historically white Patterson Technical School, claiming that Trenholm's "minority identity and leadership" would be lost in the transition.

At a meeting of the State Board of Education, Julian argued the case on behalf of the Southern Christian Leadership Conference, the NAACP, and the Montgomery Improvement Association. The Rev. John Alford organized this coalition of interest groups and brought Julian in to represent them. As time progressed, more local Montgomery political leaders expressed concerns about the merger, and as of June 2000, the matter remained unresolved.

CHALLENGING arbitration again, this time in a consumer contract, Julian filed suit in federal court on April 6, 2000, on behalf of Stanley and Jennifer Young of Wetumpka. The Youngs sought a ruling that a binding arbitration clause in a home sales contract with Florida corporation Jim Walter Homes was unenforceable.

In coverage by Montgomery's NBC, CBS, and ABC television affiliates that night, Julian charged the contract allowed Jim Walter to sue the Youngs for anything, while the Youngs could not sue the Florida company for any reason.

"It's outrageous that an out-of-state corporation can come into Alabama, build and sell a defective home, and escape adverse consequence," said Julian. "What is especially bad is that, under the sales contract, the arbitration agreement denies Alabama citizens the reciprocal right to take Jim Walter Homes to court for negligence, breach of contract, or any other reason. Instead, Alabama citizens must pay exorbitant arbitration fees of thousands of dollars, which they cannot afford."

In this case, Jim Walter Homes built a house for a prior homeowner without installing a septic tank (or even applying to the Elmore County Health Department for a permit). Jim Walter subsequently foreclosed on the original homeowner, and without disclosing the absence of a septic tank to the Youngs (despite Jim Walter's alleged knowledge of the same), Jim Walter subsequently sold the house. When the Youngs discovered the problem, they demanded a septic tank be installed, but Jim Walter refused, passing the responsibility back to the Youngs. Unfortunately, the cost of the arbitration (win, lose, or draw) would be the same as cost of the septic tank, about $5,000 to $6,000. Even worse, the Youngs couldn't afford a telephone or the $150 courthouse filing fee, which McPhillips's office advanced.

McPhillips, Shinbaum & Gill challenged the binding arbitration clause as "unconscionable, prohibitively expensive, and therefore unenforceable."

"This could be a precedent-setting case determining the future of arbitration in Alabama, currently a hot-button subject," says Julian.

Jim Walter filed an expected motion to compel arbitration in late April, and the case remains pending in federal court, awaiting a ruling.

Julian has high praise for Rick McBride, Sr., of the Consumer Arbitration Steering Committee, trial lawyer Tom Edwards ("a rising star politically and professionally"), and "the tireless Jere Beasley, for leading the good fight to preserve the constitutional right to trial by jury for Alabama's citizens."

OF THE varied lawsuits Julian has handled over the years, police brutality cases have been among the most explosive, and none more so than one he became involved with in July 2000.

Samuel Day, a slightly built black man, was standing in line at a Montgomery convenience store behind a police officer, J. F. Dodd. Dodd, a white man, was off-duty but still wearing his police uniform. Dodd reportedly turned to Day and said, "You're too close." The ensuing exchange of words apparently ended with officer Dodd chasing Day from the store, after which multiple witnesses have testified that Dodd knocked Day down and beat him with a police baton, even after Day was handcuffed. Another officer arrived at the scene and administered more blows, witnesses said, and Day—a medically controlled schizophrenic—was reportedly left lying in a pool of blood with a fractured skull, a broken arm and wrist, and lacerations to his head and ear. He was subsequently hospitalized for an extended period.

Day, knowing of his mental condition, had given his sister Mamie Green power of attorney in 1991, and Ms. Green came to see Julian after her brother's beating. On July 17, 2000, at a news conference covered by the city's three TV stations and the *Montgomery Advertiser*, Julian joined Ms. Green, eye-witness Darron Jenkins, and Montgomery SCLC president John Alford in decrying the incident as "police brutality without justification." Julian announced the filing of a claim against the city, requesting the $100,000 statutory damage limit. Julian said, "With some fourteen police brutality charges since 1999 alone, the time has come for Montgomery to have a new police chief, since the current one is unable or unwilling to put a stop to this problem."

The three TV stations were back at McPhillips, Shinbaum & Gill the next morning for follow-up interviews, and the next day Julian and Rev. Alford were telephone guests on a talk show in Washington, D.C. Later that morning, state senator Charles Steele, Jr., president of the Alabama Chapter of the SCLC, held a news conference downtown in front of the Civil Rights Memorial calling for the resignation of police chief John Wilson and a march on City Hall.

Another of Julian's police brutality clients is Chiranji Lal Sharma, a local motel owner of East Indian descent. When Sharma called the police to help an injured stranger lying on the pavement outside his motel one night, Sharma says, the officers arrived and asked him to hand over his flashlight. When he failed to do so quickly enough, he has testified, the policemen knocked him to the ground, kicked him, hit him with his own flashlight, and told him he was lucky they had not shot him. Over the coming days, additional charges of police misconduct surfaced, at least two of them from injured civilians who are represented by former city police officers who have subsequently become attorneys. "I'm glad to have the help," said Julian.

Meanwhile, in early August, independently of the on-going legal actions, Rev. Alford and Steele protested police brutality with the staging of a sit-in demonstration outside the office of new Montgomery mayor Bobby Bright. The mayor fired police officer Dodd, but he turned down the protesters' demands to dismiss long-time police chief John Wilson and to create a citizen advisory panel to examine current and future brutality charges. "It's been very disappointing," said Julian, who tried to be a peacemaker in the negotiations, engaging in conversations with the SCLC, Bright, and the city's attorney in hopes of resolving the mounting crisis. After Steele and Alford were eventually forcibly removed from city hall and arrested, Julian filed motions to secure their release from jail.

As this was written, the police brutality cases and the charges against the protesters were awaiting resolution.

17

Perspective on Plaintiff's Work

BEING A plaintiff's attorney, Julian believes, is one of the more difficult paths a lawyer can choose. "Trying a case to a jury is like building a house," he says. "You have to be the architect, the engineer, the carpenter, the painter, the plumber, and the electrician, all at the same time. You build the house, and if any room of it isn't built well enough, the buyer—the jury—will reject it. But defending a civil case is like a wrecking crew tearing down a house. You just go in with a big hammer and start knocking away at everything. It's a whole lot easier."

Julian has won a defense verdict in fourteen of the fifteen civil cases he's defended before juries. In the lone exception, he got a $1,000 verdict in a sexual harassment case, where the defendant admitted improperly touching the plaintiff, who was seeking a six-to-seven figure result. "Most people would consider that a defense verdict," he says.

"But I've found it much more fun being a plaintiff's lawyer in civil cases. It's entrepreneurial. You get a piece of the action. You don't get paid unless you produce. You also get to initiate, as opposed to reacting, which is the usual defense strategy. It's especially challenging when the defendant has much greater resources, which is often the case. You learn to 'do more with less.'

"I think burnout or fatigue come not from just working too hard, but rather from working without joy in your heart, or without a passion for your client's cause. I have great respect for my defense lawyer friends, but I'm happy my lot in life has been a 'people's lawyer.' It has its occupational hazards, though. Nobody likes being stood up to, especially bullies."

BY THE YEAR 2000, McPhillips, Shinbaum & Gill, L.L.P., though often representing employees versus bosses and injured parties against corporate interests, had become a thriving business itself, whose interests sometimes were contrary to those of the Chamber of Commerce. Still, the McPhillips firm and the Fitzgerald Museum (with Julian as president) are both members of the Chamber. (Julian's father, Julian L. McPhillips, Sr., in the 1950s was president of the Cullman Chamber of Commerce and vice-president of Associated Industries of Alabama, the forerunner of the current Business Council of Alabama.)

One thing Julian shares with business and industry groups is the desire for business development in Alabama. For a brief period in 1995, Julian was the darling of the Montgomery Chamber of Commerce. Through Princeton wrestling connections, Julian knew Bob Feldmeier ('43) and Jake Feldmeier ('70), a father-son team whose juice canister business was headquartered in Syracuse, New York. The Feldmeiers wanted to expand south. Atlanta looked crowded, so Julian encouraged the Feldmeiers to come to Montgomery. With help from the Wallace-Cater Act and legal assistance from Frank McPhillips, the Feldmeiers used an industrial bond issue to build a plant in Montgomery with a goal of employing more than one hundred persons. The Feldmeiers have never regretted moving their Southern operations to Montgomery, now operated by Bob's grandson Colby Clark.

MCPHILLIPS SAYS he's found staying in good health, both physically and emotionally, to be crucial to his law practice over the years. Along with faith and family, he credits his regular exercise routine of almost forty years as a "healthful addiction."

"Exercising relaxes and refreshes me, and helps clear away tension," he says. "When I exercise, I sleep like a log at night." He runs two to three miles a day, generally in nearby Cloverdale Park, regardless of the weather, and finishes by lifting free weights on his back porch and doing stomach, back, and neck exercises. On weekends, when the weather is good, he diversifies his routine by doing lawn-mowing, or swimming and water-skiing at the family's cabin on Lake Martin. He also sets aside an annual trip for snow-skiing, golf, or tennis.

He's especially proud of his yearly showing in Montgomery's 8K "River Run" on Memorial Day weekend, where he always finishes in the top third among some one thousand runners. In May 2000 he took third place in the men's 50-54 division—"Despite weighing 230 pounds," he laughs.

THE MAJORITY of Julian's client contacts don't involve sensational or precedent-setting cases, but what he calls "the mundane stuff." A sizeable part of his work is gently discouraging potential clients whose cases he feels aren't economically feasible because the cost of winning would exceed whatever proceeds were recovered.

"We also try to help would-be plaintiffs evaluate various defenses," he says, "based in fact and on the law. One of our biggest frustrations is explaining to prospective clients the many immunities that now insulate public officials from liability for their wrongdoing. Add to that the problem of arbitration and its prohibitive costs, and the sum is that the plaintiff's practice is much more difficult today than it was ten or fifteen years ago."

Julian has also enjoyed counseling and advising clients, both anonymous and well-known, behind the scenes over the years. He says he particularly enjoyed working with two young black heroines of Selma's civil rights movement, Rachel West and Sheyann Webb-Christburg, who were portrayed in the book *Selma, Lord, Selma* by Birmingham author Frank Sikora, and which became a made-for-television movie in 1999.

At the movie's premiere, Julian was invited to participate in a broadcast panel on the event at Alabama State University, along with ASU president William Harris, civil rights attorney Fred Gray, and U.S. Magistrate Judge Vanzetta McPherson.

"It was strange, being called on to give the white point of view," he recalls, "after having represented the black view so often over the years.

But what I remember most was my eight-year-old son David's reaction to the movie. He asked me, in tears, 'Why did they have to treat black people so badly?' It was a hard question to answer, but I did the best I could.."

AMONG THE many occupational hazards of practicing law, Julian says, is that "for every person you make happy by representing them energetically in an adversarial situation, you make somebody on the other side unhappy with you. And nowadays, certain reactionary interests are trying to make it sound like trial lawyers are on a level with bank robbers. They don't mention the fact that if it weren't for lawyers taking cases of poor victims on a percentage basis, and risking the loss of countless billable hours and out-of-pocket costs, most of those victims could never afford the pursue civil justice. The costs of depositions and expert witness fees can get into the five figures. Or sometimes six figures, in cases such as medical malpractice."

Julian remembers the time that friend Ted Copeland, a cofounder of Christ the Redeemer Episcopal, told him, "You and Bobby Segall are the only two lawyers in town who could represent Che Guevara one day and William Buckley the next."

"I considered it a compliment," Julian says, "but sometimes that sort of thing can get you in trouble. A lawyer has an ethical duty, though, to represent his client as zealously as he or she can. I make no apologies for representing underdogs and standing up to bullies and more powerful interests.

"I just thank the Lord for equipping me for the task. I think life is made to be lived with enthusiasm and in relationship with the Lord, and that makes me better able to help people who are in need."

Julian and PeeWee Face Judge Reaves

"ALL RISE!" the bailiff says, in a loud clear voice. "The Municipal Court of Montgomery is now in session, his honor Judge Randolph Reaves presiding."

The judge, in black robe, strides in and sits down without looking at anyone. Above his head, the chrome letters "Montgomery Municipal Court" protrude from a wood-paneled wall.

As the audience in the packed courtroom is seated, Judge Reaves reads a prepared statement that appears, from his weary tone of voice, to be memorized. Among other things, it tells defendants that if found guilty in his court they can be sentenced to up to six months in jail and up to $500, except in the case of multiple offenses of driving under the influence which can carry fines of up to $10,000, as well as court costs that can range from $98 to $186.

And lest anybody misinterpret the foot-high chrome letters behind him, he tells the crowd that this is *not* a civil court, and then repeats the message: "This is *not* a civil court."

As the judge begins thumbing through the packed manila folder in front of him, it does not take a swami to know that His Honor is in a foul mood. He mutters to himself, and occasionally to a clerk nearby, about the events of his day so far, which include a Mobile attorney calling him just twenty minutes before court began, on a car phone – *a car phone* – asking a continuance for his client.

While the judge is sorting through his docket, his assistants go into a complex routine that a computer expert might call multi-tasking: loudly calling out the names of the defendants from an armload of folders, watching for someone in the crowd to stand or raise a hand, all while attorneys confer and jostle and their clients approach the bench, waiting for a look or nod from Reaves, and he begins dispensing justice.

"Decario Baldwin?" a man calls out loudly, holding aloft a folder, going down the list. "Thomas Sims?"

A young white man in his twenties, called to the bench earlier, begins explaining to the judge why he shouldn't have received a speeding ticket.

"Son," the judge responds, "this is three times you've been caught going too fast to somewhere or other. I think there's a pattern there, don't you? You need to slow it down . . ."

After the young man is informed of his fine and court costs, a lawyer for another client walks tentatively toward the bench and begins speaking to the judge.

But whatever he's asking, Reaves is not having it. "No way!" he thunders. "Ain't no way. I don't care, man, there is just *no way* we can let this slide. A record like that?" He holds up a piece of fanfold paper, which cascades to the bench and then starts toward the floor. "Charges, charges, charges, charges, charges," he says. "Let me give you some advice. Don't plead today, or he'll get six months. I guarantee it." As the attorney backs meekly away, the judge leans toward a young woman with a calendar and says, "Set it for a Thursday in August. But wait . . . not the 14th through the 19th, that's, uh, I mean . . . what else do you have?"

A middle-aged black man, whose name was called earlier, approaches the judge and speaks earnestly in a voice so low the judge twice has to tell him to speak up. At last an attorney standing nearby speaks for him. "He says it's not his ticket," the attorney tells the judge.

"It's got his name and address and license number on it, but it's not his ticket?" the judge says, wide-eyed. "That doesn't even make any sense. Look, take it up with the Circuit Court if you want to. But pay this fine, and don't be back down here, OK?" The man shrugs and walks slowly away.

One by one, young police officers have been easing into the

room from a side door, until more than a dozen fill the front row of folding chairs nearest the judge's bench. Some wear the standard blue uniform, others the camo pants and black T-shirts of the department's SWAT team. Many have either very short haircuts or shaved heads, and a number of them have the pumped physiques of body-builders.

"Reginald Jones?" a court clerk calls out. Julian and Reginald approach the bench, as does the city's attorney for the case.

Julian's law office demeanor and courtroom demeanor are polar opposites. On a typical day over at South Perry Street he's in constant motion, doing several things at once: fielding phone calls, reading memos, checking documents, juggling Post-It notes, bounding into associates' offices for brief mumbled conferences, eating a deli sandwich, responding to a receptionist's reminders on the intercom line, all while conversing in what often amounts to sign language – a grimace, a nod, a shrug, an "OK" made with thumb and finger – with various assistants who hold up calendars, file folders, or other pieces of paper for his judgment.

In court, however, when his case is called to the bench, he ambles in that direction with a look of mild surprise and guileless good will, as though having just overheard part of a conversation that interests him. And at the point when an opposing counsel begins objecting, finger-stabbing, arm-waving, and other histrionic body language (which today will be fairly often, over the next ten minutes of Jones's hearing), Julian responds with a facial expression of concern and empathetic embarrassment, in much the same way one would if a colleague were to, say, break wind in public.

The city attorney calls his witnesses. Two young white policemen step forward, both dressed alike: camo pants, black T-shirts with the word "Police" on the front, and bulletproof vests. They walk in step with military precision, then halt before the bench and smartly slap their hands together behind their backs, standing in perfect parade-rest posture. The attorney swears them in, and then asks the first officer, Corporal R. J. Steelman, to describe the events of January 11.

Steelman says he heard on the police radio that a marijuana sale was going on near the Trenholm Court project, and that he rushed over to aid in the arrest. Arriving at a side road off Bainbridge, he saw "three or four subjects, underneath a tree, wearing dark clothing." One of the subjects, he says, "who wound up being the defendant . . . walked over behind some steps on the end of one of the buildings there, and reached down like he placed something behind them."

"When their vehicle approached the subject, Steelman says, "I said to him, 'Come here,' at which time he took off running."

"And did the defendant ever stop at your instructions?" the attorney asks.

Steelman says no.

Julian is quick to object: "Your honor, he said he didn't say 'Stop,' just 'Come here.' So it's a misleading question."

The judge shrugs "Well, he's already answered it."

In the ensuing cross-examination, Julian elicits the information that no drugs were found in Reginald's possession, or in the area where the officer saw him suspiciously "reach down."

"So you found no drugs in the vicinity at that time?" Julian asks.

"No. We had such a large crowd after we took him into custody that we didn't have a chance to look."

"But he actually stopped running at some point, didn't he?"

"Yes. He was finally stopped. That's correct."

"So he ultimately ended up obeying you, didn't he? I mean, inasmuch as he stopped and surrendered?"

The judge interrupts. "He was chased and caught," he says, with a wry grin. "Sounds like to me that's kind of obeying by default."

A hearty laugh goes up from the seated police officers.

"He had his hands in the air, didn't he?" Julian says, unflustered. "That's what I'm trying to determine."

The city's attorney objects again. "Your honor, I've already . . ."

The judge speaks directly to Steelman. "You finally caught up to him?"

"Yes, sir."

"Okay, then," the judge says, and turns to Julian.

"And he didn't resist you at that point, did he? You-all ended up apprehending him after that."

"That's correct."

Steelman is dismissed, and the city attorney does his direct of Corporal Raymond DeJohn, which basically duplicates Steelman's testimony – except that DeJohn says he himself shouted "stop" at some point after Reginald began running.

Julian begins the cross.

"Corporal, when you say you were in uniform, you're saying that you were simply in the costume you have on today?"

A beat of silence.

"It's not a costume, sir," DeJohn says, with an expression of aggrieved innocence. "It's a uniform."

Subdued snickering from the row of policemen.

"I mean," Julian says, "the *clothing* you have on today."

"This is my uniform *every day*."

"Right. Right. But you had on nothing more to identify you than the black outfit?"

"I had on a vest that said 'Police' across the front of my chest. And I had a ball cap that said 'Police Strike Force.'"

"I understand," Julian says. "Now . . . when you jumped out, did you say, 'Hey, we're police! We're not the Klan!'?"

DeJohn looks dazed, "The *what*?"

"'We're not the Klan.' The Ku Klux Klan."

The City attorney looks to the ceiling. His objection, and the judge's sustaining of it, are drowned out by chuckles from the police section. The testimony that follows goes point by point over exactly when DeJohn shouted and exactly when Jones ran.

"But do you recall that at one point he actually stopped and threw his hands up and surrendered?"

"I never seen him throw his hands up."

"Well, isn't it a fact that you jumped back into your vehicle and actually ran over him?"

"Objection!"

"Sustained. Let's stick to the charge, here."

"Corporal DeJohn, isn't it a fact that he *did* surrender at some point, while you were still in your vehicle?"

"He did not surrender."

"He was apprehended ultimately, wasn't he?"

"Yes."

"And did you search the area after he was apprehended, to find out whether there was anything there . . . drugs, weapons, anything of that sort?"

"I did not."

"And isn't it a fact that you didn't charge him with failure to obey a police officer until sometime *after* that incident occurred?"

The judge intervenes. "Well, now," he says sourly, "It *had* to be after the incident. It sure couldn't have been *before.*"

Much laughter.

"Well," Julian says, "how many days afterward was it, that you charged him?"

"I charged . . . signed a warrant on him the next day because my supervisors told me to go ahead and go home. It was the end of the day."

"So you didn't sign a warrant on him that day?"

"The next day."

"And you had nothing else to charge him with, other than failure to obey a police officer, isn't that correct?"

"That's correct."

Julian indicates that his cross of DeJohn is over. It's Reginald's turn to testify.

After Reginald is sworn in, Julian walks him through a recap of January 11: having his car washed, starting to pay the man for it, and suddenly hearing the noise of the Suburban jumping the curb.

"We heard this big boom, as I was paying the car wash man. And both of us just looked . . ."

The judge interrupts. "Wait a minute. You said 'we heard.' I thought you were minding your business?"

"Yeah. I was talking to the car wash man. I was fixing to pay him.

But when we heard that, both of us looked up. And we seen a big truck come up on the curb, and when the door opened I just took off running."

"Why," Julian asks, "did you take off running?"

"Because I didn't know who that was," Reginald says. "It could have been . . . I had just been . . . been in an incident with them a few weeks earlier that I had got jumped on, and . . ."

"Objection, your honor. This is some other instance."

"But you know what I'm saying." Reginald follows up quickly. "It could have been a truck full of white folks just coming to jump on us. You see anything up in there."

The judge goes wide-eyed. "Have you seen things like that happen in the projects?"

"I seen it plenty of times," Reginald answers. Chuckles, from the row of policemen.

"Don't you hear everybody out there laughing at you?" the judge scolds him.

"I don't care," Reginald says. "I'm telling the truth. They wasn't there. I was there."

Julian establishes through Reginald's testimony, once more, that he didn't hear any commands from the police to halt.

The judge interrupts: "Whose car was this?"

"My car," Reginald says.

The judge looks incredulous again. "You mean you just ran off and left your car and didn't pay the car wash guy?"

This time it's Reginald who looks wide-eyed: "What, like I was gonna sit out there and get beat up for an old *car*?"

"So anyway," Julian puts in, "you took off running around the building?"

"Yes."

"And when you eventually came back around, were there policemen there to stop you?"

"Yes, I was surrounded."

"And did you throw your hands up?"

"Yes."

"And a few seconds later, did you get run over?"

"Objection," says the city's lawyer. "Leading and irrelevant."

"Sustained."

"And you never heard the police say anything before that?"

"Objection, your honor."

Julian beats the judge to the punch. "I think I'm about through." He gestures for the other attorney to cross-examine Reginald, if he desires. He does.

"Mr. Jones, are you saying that you didn't know that was a police vehicle?"

"No, I didn't."

The attorney picks up a police vest from a nearby bench, and flourishes it around the courtroom. "So you've never seen one of these before?"

"Yeah," Reginald says, with a slight edge of irony. "I've seen plenty of 'em."

"And do you know how to read, Mr. Jones?"

"Yeah."

"Can you read what is on this vest for me?"

"'Police.'"

"You don't have any problem reading it *today*, do you?"

"No."

"But you couldn't see it on *that* day?"

"I didn't pay no attention. He was in the truck."

"But now you don't have any trouble reading 'Police' on that vest?"

"Your honor, we object," said Julian. "Asked and answered. He stated he didn't see the vest because they were in the car. So it's a moot question."

"All right, all right. Move along."

"No further questions," says the city attorney.

"Mr. McPhillips?" the judge asks.

"Nothing more, your honor. Actually, we'd like to be able to contend, on this motion, to dismiss."

"Motion denied," the judge says, looking at the next case on the docket. "His testimony defies logic, to me. You'll just have to give it to Circuit Court. Fully denied, here. Two hundred dollars and court costs. And Mr. Jones, you also have unpaid tickets."

A quick conference between Julian and Reginald. "He says he's paid them, your honor," Julian tells the judge.

"Well, he ain't," the judge fires back. "Are you ready to do the time, Reggie?"

"No sir."

"Your honor, let us look into that," Julian says. "And with all due respect, we file notice of appeal on your other rulings."

"That's fine with me," the judge says with a tired smile. "But right now, y'all need to go fill out the forms and make this bond."

Waiting in line at the clerk's window in the lobby, Julian remarks to Reginald and Sim that it went about as well as he had expected. And the Police Department having packed the front rows with policemen, he says, was clearly an attempt to provide moral support for Steelman and DeJohn. "You saw the judge and the attorney do that one-two on us, to keep out the part about running him over?" he asks. Sim nods.

"Man," Reginald says, "that burned me up . . . that, 'Can you read?' business."

And, Sim has bad news for Julian. The expected two main witnesses are now questionable. Lump – "Car Wash" – and a black woman in the neighborhood had both said they'd be glad to testify. But now nobody can locate Lump, and apparently the woman is intimidated because her home was searched by police a few days earlier. It's possible that one, or both, might not show.

After the tickets are paid, the three men walk a couple of blocks through a parking lot to a former small clapboard residence that says BAIL BONDS on the front.

A fifty-ish man in a blue and white sports shirt gets up from his desk as they enter and extends a hand to shake. "Well, looky here!" he says. "We got your *high*-price brand of lawyers in, today. What do we owe this privilege to, Julian?"

"Hi, Sonny," Julian says. "Looks like we need a bond."

(**Sonny Goolsby**, like seemingly every third person one encounters in Montgomery, is a former client of Julian's.)

After sizing up the situation, and hearing a brief recap of the court outcome, Goolsby shakes his head. "I tell you what," he says, "there's not many lawyers willing to keep taking on things like this. I admire you for it. And I say that honestly."

Julian, though clearly pleased, slightly ducks his head and clears his throat, "Well, thank you, Sonny," he says. "I try."

III.

Politics, People and Causes

18

Joe Reed: Wearer of Four (Big) Hats

J OE REED. It's a familiar name in Alabama politics. A longtime member of Montgomery's City Council, Reed also has been the leader of the state's strongest black political organization, the Alabama Democratic Conference, since 1968.

And when Julian ran for Alabama attorney general in 1978, Julian naturally courted Reed—as well as other county ADC leaders throughout the state—for support in the campaign. Reed's personal allegiance, though, was to one of Julian's opponents, Senate president Joe Fine, with whom Reed had worked closely for a number of years in the Alabama legislature. Still, Julian received the statewide ADC endorsement, thanks to strong support from other leaders.

When Julian's runoff spot disappeared in late-changing vote totals, it was Reed who called on behalf of Fine, trying to persuade Julian to abandon his contemplated challenge of the election results.

"I'll always be grateful to state representatives Alvin Holmes and John Knight," Julian says, "as well as to Montgomery attorney Vanzetta Durant (now McPherson) for playing key roles in helping me secure the ADC endorsement.

"But I'm also grateful to Joe Reed for allowing the endorsement to happen, when he could have tried to muscle it away to his personal choice, Fine."

As a result, Julian recalls, it was with a "mixture of care, caution, and courtesy" that he found himself on opposite sides from Reed in three politically based cases over the next several years.

The first involved two independent candidates for the Alabama House of Representatives in 1983—Charles "Buddy" Spears and Percy King, both black. Neither man was overly fond of Joe Reed, whom they openly criticized for what they considered his political dominance of the black community. As a result, both candidates had determined to run the race on their own, without asking for ADC support.

But in the weeks that followed, Spears and King both discovered they had the same problem: neither had crossed all his "t's" or dotted all his "i's" on the candidacy papers they had filed with the Alabama Secretary of State and the Montgomery probate office. As a result, then-Secretary of State Don Siegelman—a friend of Reed's—complied with Reed's request to officially disqualify both candidacies on technical grounds.

Spears and King came straightaway to see Julian, who once again associated Bobby Segall on the case. They urged Circuit Court Judge Bill Gordon to rule that the independent candidates had "substantially complied" with the requirements, though admittedly they had not done it one hundred percent correctly.

Gordon accepted the arguments of McPhillips and Segall, and ruled that the candidates had the right to be on the ballot. (Many years later, the Spears and King case was cited as a legal precedent in the more celebrated Hooper-Hornsby case of 1996.)

As for Spears and King, the 1983 court ruling was hailed as a victory for justice and fairness—but a pyrrhic one, since both lost their races on election day. Many insiders maintained that the challenge and the ensuing legal case had cast a "cloud of uncertainty" over both candidacies, to their disadvantage.

At the same time, a much larger legal battle over political issues was brewing.

The 1982 winners of the state's Democratic primary found themselves suddenly disqualified *en masse* in 1983, as a result of a federal court reapportionment decision that affected every Senate and House district seat in Alabama.

The federal ruling was the beginning of that year's notorious "Handpicking Case," in which state Democratic leaders were charged with handpicking personally favored candidates, often in contradiction to the Primary results—such as State Senator Lowell Barron, who was snubbed from the official ballot by party leaders but subsequently won a write-in campaign. One newspaper editorial of the time described the situation as "an odorous smell hanging over all of Alabama." The blame was laid on a powerful clique within the party, said to be composed of Joe Reed, Paul Hubbert, Democratic Party Chairman

Jimmy Knight, and from time to time, one or more powerful trial lawyers around the state, such as Lanny Vines of Birmingham.

A number of the disqualified candidates approached Julian about filing suit on their behalf in federal court. The case was assigned to U.S. District Judge Truman Hobbs, who expressed his "anger and dismay" at the way the whole process had been handled by the Alabama Democratic Party. Named as defendants in the suit for injunctive relief were party chairman Knight and then-governor George Wallace. At that point, a favorable ruling for McPhillips's plaintiffs by Judge Hobbs appeared imminent.

Upon a motion by the defendants, though, the case was instead transferred to a three-judge federal panel. There, attorneys for Knight and the governor argued that political parties had a right to choose nominees in any way they wanted, under the First Amendment's "freedom of political association" clause.

Julian countered by arguing that the situation in Alabama was far from typical. Here, he said, the Democratic primary—in 1982—is "in effect, the whole ball game" because, with the Republican Party in the state so weak, winning the Democratic primary is virtually a lock on winning the general election—and therefore deserving of "due process" protection.

"To my great surprise," Julian recalls, "the panel of judges upheld the handpicking. Kind of ironic, like going in a circle, because the whole disqualification thing had been prompted by another federal court decision requiring reapportionment due to the race issue."

THEN THERE was the Carter Hill sidewalk matter. While not the stuff of major headlines, it once again found Julian and Joe Reed on opposite sides of the fence.

In 1984, Montgomery's Carter Hill Road, directly across from Alabama State University, had a wide, sturdy sidewalk along its northernmost side. The south side had none, and the homeowners who lived along the road liked it that way. A sidewalk not only would have cut into their rich, green lawns, but (they were later to argue) would give "vagrants, burglars, and other undesirables" easier access to their property.

Enter Joe Reed, who lived only two short blocks beyond the south side of Carter Hill.

Reed, as it turned out, championed a sidewalk, and for "his" side of Carter Hill, found federal grant money, and announced the impending construction as a "done deal." But then, the past came back to haunt him.

Enter neighborhood resident Charles "Buddy" Spears, the independent House candidate whom Reed had earlier gotten disqualified. Spears stated his opposition to the proposed sidewalk, and was soon followed by neighbor W. J. Williams, a Montgomery postman with four sons—two of whom, incidentally, Norbert and Damund Williams, would later become attorneys. Then came J. J. and Ola Martin, also homeowners on Carter Hill who didn't want their lawns invaded.

Enter Julian McPhillips, who at the time lived one long block down Dunbar Street—some one hundred yards farther from Carter Hill than did Reed. Spears, Williams, and the Martins sought out Julian to represent them in asking for a temporary restraining order against the sidewalk construction.

"It was strictly a neighborhood issue, not a racial issue," Julian recalls now. "The people who would be affected by the sidewalk all had pretty much the same ethnicity." Just before the construction was to begin, Julian filed suit in federal court asking for both a restraining order and an order blocking the federal funds to be spent on the sidewalk. After a hearing and the submission of briefs, Judge Robert Varner ruled in Julian's and the homeowners' favor, halting construction of the sidewalk.

"But if there's any single thing Joe Reed is known for," Julian says now, with a grin, "it's his persistence. If something he wants gets blocked in one direction, he just goes in another direction. And it certainly helps that he's worn four very big hats: ADC chairman, co-executive secretary of the Alabama Education Association, a Montgomery City Councilman, and chairman of the Board of Trustees of Alabama State University." In other words, a worthy adversary.

"People have debated who was the most powerful figure in Montgomery, Joe Reed or Mayor Folmar," Julian says. "In Montgomery it might have been a toss-up, but statewide the money was on Joe."

And in this instance, Reed rose to the challenge. If federal funding wasn't available, he quickly arranged for city funding to replace it. Julian again filed suit, but this time drew Circuit Judge Joe Phelps (who, Julian adds, "needed Reed's support for his own re-election"), and the result turned out differently.

One of Julian's favorite memories is of sparring with Reed, who was on the witness stand for cross-examination in Phelps's courtroom. "At one point," McPhillips says, "Joe blurted out, 'Julian, you're a much better lawyer than you are a politician.'" The compliment, backhanded as it was, is one Julian treasures until this day.

In the end, Phelps ruled in favor of Reed. Julian appealed to the Alabama Supreme Court, but with the same result. ("They're all subject to re-election also," Julian can't help pointing out.) The sidewalk construction went ahead.

IN OCTOBER 1998, Joe Reed and Julian teamed up to preserve Montgomery's historic Oak Park. Earlier Mayor Folmar, without consulting neighborhood residents, declared eleven acres of the park the location for a new school. Julian was enlisted by Oak Park residents to serve as their attorney and spokesman. Amidst much publicity, and with Reed's support, the opposition snow-balled. The Mayor declared it a "hot potato," and duly backed away from the park where F. Scott Fitzgerald courted Zelda.

Occasional City Council appearances by Julian for clients roughed up by police or otherwise mistreated by City departments occurred throughout the 1980s and '90s. Julian often found Reed the most sympathetic member of the council, reflecting a "conscience for the disadvantaged."

"I get along well with Joe," Julian says. "And I certainly respect him. Joe Reed stood up to Folmar, on behalf of people oppressed by the city, when nobody else would."

In November 1999, after twenty-two years on the City Council, Reed was upset in his bid for re-election. He nonetheless retained great statewide influence as Alabama entered the 21st century.

In June 2000, he was elected chairman of the Alabama delegation to the Democratic National Convention in Los Angeles, the first black chairman ever of an Alabama delegation or of a Southern delegation. As his wife Molly joked the morning after his election, "it's a fifth big hat."

19

History Worth Preserving

A HISTORY buff by nature, and a history major by training at Princeton, Julian easily took to incorporating into his career a number of efforts to preserve Alabama's history.

Early in his professional life—August 1981, shortly after he and Leslie moved to their current home on Felder Avenue—Julian took legal action to save an early 1900s home directly across the street, at the corner of Felder and Park avenues. Like the McPhillipses' home, 842 Felder bordered on a small triangular park named in honor of Scott and Zelda Fitzgerald, former inhabitants of the house diagonally across the park on an acre-and- a-half lot at 919 Felder. A much larger park, Cloverdale, is just a hundred yards further down the street.

A retired Air Force couple, Lt. Col. Les Thompson and his wife Hannah, decided the location was an ideal site for the construction of four condominiums—or would be, after demolishing the house on 842 Felder.

Many residents of Old Cloverdale, Leslie and Julian among them, saw things differently. With neighbors Bob and Delores Bogard as co-plaintiffs, the McPhillipses filed suit in Montgomery Circuit Court. Another set of neighbors filed a separate, related, suit.

"It looked like the litigation was about to start rocking and rolling," Julian recalls, but at the last minute a compromise was hammered out. None other than Ms. Scottie Fitzgerald Smith, Scott and Zelda's only child, stepped in to buy the house as part of a settlement recouping the Thompsons their money, until a suitable alternative buyer could be found. But before the tempest in the teapot simmered down, Julian's on-site TV interviews and quotes in the newspapers became a fixture in the daily media.

In 1983, another prominent citizen of Old Cloverdale approached Julian about saving her home. Gladys Crenshaw, a widow, lived in an attractive old stone house just across from the Montgomery County Club. The house and the property had been bought by two developers, and the house was scheduled for demolition to make way for fashionable condos.

Mrs. Crenshaw phoned Julian at home, just hours before he was due to leave for a trial in Scottsboro. Julian called law partner Jim DeBardelaben to cover for him. As DeBardelaben would later recall, he was standing in the courtroom seeking a temporary restraining order when Mrs. Crenshaw, beset by the stress of the events, summarily fainted and hit the floor. "What to do? This was one they didn't teach in law school," DeBardelaben remembers.

Mrs. Crenshaw was revived, the case was postponed, and when Julian returned from Scottsboro he was able to work out a settlement with opposing counsel Richard Gill that allowed Mrs. Crenshaw to keep her home in return for giving up some adjacent land.

In late 1986, Julian and Leslie returned to the ramparts against another proposed condo development in their own historic neighborhood. Local real estate agent Martha Cassels called on Julian to help save the house and acreage at 919 Felder, where Scott & Zelda Fitzgerald had once lived.

The property was just two houses down from the McPhillipses, and Julian freely acknowledges that his motives "were not a hundred percent altruistic." A competing developer was primed to tear down the 8,500-square-foot house and subdivide its eight city lots into spaces for twenty town homes—with an estimated cool profit of $1 million—despite objections that it would seriously erode the historic character of the neighborhood.

This time, the alternate buyers for the property turned out to be Julian and Leslie. But credit for saving the house, he says, goes not only to realtor Martha Cassels but also to the preservation-minded Mobile attorney Jack Miller, who sold the Fitzgerald house to them instead of the condo developer.

In the coming months Julian and Leslie put considerable time and resources into the house—restoring it architecturally, as well as removing the thick bamboo that had taken over the side yard and replacing it with lush green grass that emphasized the impressive landscape.

Leslie and Julian's own home (two houses west at 831 Felder) has also undergone extensive renovation. Upon buying it in January 1981 they had every floor, wall, and ceiling restored to its original condition. The house is historic in its own right, as the former home of Mildred Keller Tyson, sister of the famous Helen Keller, who frequently visited Mildred there between the early 1920s and 1960. Today, hanging beside Julian and Leslie's front door is a photograph of Helen and Mildred sitting on the house's front porch in 1955.

The McPhillipses' other historic preservation activities include the Civil War Trust, the National Trust for Historic Preservation, the Alabama Historical Association, the Montgomery County Historical Society, Landmarks Society, and other non-profit groups.

"Historic preservation, especially as we enter the New Millennium, is extremely important," says Julian. "People need to know and appreciate their roots, to understand the connectedness we share between one generation and another. It takes roots to develop wings. If we don't understand history, as the old cliché goes, we're doomed to repeat its mistakes. Once a historical house or building is torn down, it's gone forever. With both sides of my family in Alabama before it was a state and in America before it was a country, I want to preserve history as much as possible."

Saving Literary History: The Fitzgerald Museum

Once Julian and Leslie owned the house at 919 Felder, they began quietly planning for another form of preservation, this time to keep alive the memory of the famous former residents of the house, Zelda and F. Scott Fitzgerald.

Zelda was a Montgomery native. She, Scott, and their only child, Scottie, had lived at 919 Felder from October 1931 to April 1932. In the house, Scott worked on his novel *Tender is the Night*, and Zelda began writing her novel, *Save Me the Waltz*.

"We had always admired Fitzgerald's work," Julian says, "and the fact that he went to Princeton was another connection for me. And Zelda was not only a talented author in her own right, but also a very good painter, with a sort of Picasso flair. She's also recognized as one of the originators of the 'flapper' persona."

Julian and Leslie attended the First International F. Scott Fitzgerald Conference at Princeton University in September 1996, the centennial of Scott's birthday, and began developing a network with Fitzgerald scholars and fans worldwide. Starting ten years earlier, piece by piece, whenever they could spare the time, Julian and Leslie began seeking out Fitzgerald books, letters, paintings, and other mementoes. They organized a board of directors that for thirty months had monthly meetings to plan and generate ideas. In May 1989, the Scott and Zelda Fitzgerald Museum—the only museum in the world devoted exclusively to the lives and work of the Fitzgeralds—officially opened to the public.

But not without a struggle. Ironically, when news spread about the plans for the house, a few neighborhood residents argued that the traffic drawn by a museum would endanger the quiet, peaceful atmosphere of their shady, little-traveled street.

Though Julian first was assured by the City of Montgomery that no variance was needed for a museum, nonetheless after a successful grand opening party, the City Board of Adjustment voted 3-2 to deny the museum a variance. Julian, with Bobby Segall representing him, filed suit the next day and the case was assigned to Judge Charles Price's court. A young law clerk, Brent Newton, son of the Museum's first executive director, Wesley Newton, wrote the brief on the Museum's behalf. Later, however, Julian and Bobby negotiated conditions that pacified the aggrieved homeowners. The conditions included low-profile signage in keeping with the neighborhood feel—a dignified stone marker, set a distance from the street. The two main opponents were also invited to join the Museum's Board of Directors.

In the years since, thousands of visitors from around the world have made pilgrimages to the Fitzgeralds' former home.

FOR A writer, the prospect of spending the night in Scott and Zelda's bedroom is no small thrill. From the street, the house looks like a nice — if unremarkable — brown-frame structure with a multi-hued brick base. It's one of many in a quiet neighborhood of old trees, just a few minutes from the State Capitol Building.

For Zelda, moving to 919 Felder was an exciting homecoming. The daughter of a local judge and an illustrious Montgomery family, she had been for years, by many accounts, the most popular young socialite in town—and was rarely without a horde of male admirers in tow.

That changed only when a young soldier from Minnesota, Francis Scott Key Fitzgerald—in fact, a distant relative of *the* Francis Scott Key—managed to cut her away from the herd and propose marriage. Despite wartime, he assured her, he was a writer on the way up. The engagement was rough sledding at times, but eventually they were married.

His prediction proved to be more true than either of them could have then imagined. When publishing giant Random House announced in 1998 its list of "The 100 Most Important Books of the Century," chosen by a panel of distinguished scholars, Fitzgerald was one of a precious few who has more than one entry in the list. His novel *The Great Gatsby* ranks at number two, and *Tender is the Night* is a little further down.

Fitzgerald is credited as being the coiner of, and the spokesman for, what is now known as "The Jazz Age." This pre-television era was the heyday of the high-circulation, high-paying magazines such as the *Saturday Evening Post, Collier's, Redbook, Esquire,* and *McCall's,* all of which openly competed for his short stories. Life was good. For the most part.

What history tends to gloss over is that—as is true of many other now-classic American writers—Fitzgerald, in his entire lifetime, never had a national best-selling novel. *This Side of Paradise* sold only about 50,000 copies in his lifetime and earned only some $15,000 in royalties. No small change, particularly for that era, but a drop in the bucket when viewed from the expenses of his and Zelda's international lifestyle.

Most of his income came from short stories published in magazines, the most popular of which brought him an average of about $4,000 each. Both *The Great Gatsby* and *Tender is the Night* were major financial failures, earning him total royalties (in 1929) of $31.77.

One of Fitzgerald's most-quoted lines is, "Show me a hero, and I'll write you a tragedy." Not only was it prescient of America's "culture of celebrity" in our own generation, but it ironically applied to his and his wife's lives as well. His was devastated by alcoholism, Zelda's by recurring mental illness. He died young from a heart attack, Zelda from a freak fire at the mental hospital where she was committed.

At 919 Felder Avenue, you can see the good years. Photos, love letters, party invitations, portraits. A galley proof from Zelda's *Save Me the Waltz* is framed on one wall, and Zelda's European and American art scenes abound. The collection of paper dolls she hand-colored as gifts for her nieces is a favorite of visitors to the museum.

Inscriptions by F. Scott to Zelda's father, "The Judge," appear on period books. A video entitled "Scott and Zelda: Their Montgomery Connections" is screened for visitors in a side room. With darkness coming on, a visitor can plug his laptop computer into the museum's phone line, listen to a softly falling rain, and doves calling from underneath the eaves of the house, and search the Internet for information about Scott & Zelda's lives and works. There are dozens upon dozens of sites, around the world.

Why such a fuss, over "ordinary" people? As scholar Matthew Bruccoli puts it, "Literature is what lasts. Literary history demonstrates that critical reception is an inaccurate forecast of permanent merit. The writings that turn out to be literature are frequently ignored or savaged at the time of their initial publication. But genius eventually compels its just recognition."

Or, as one Internet site proclaims on its opening banner, "The legend lives on."

On December 22, 1999, Julian and Leslie donated the museum house at 919 Felder Avenue to the Scott & Zelda Fitzgerald Museum Association, a non-profit corporation. Board member Wesley Newton said that the gift would "greatly strengthen the longevity prospects of the Museum," and member Janie Wall said the Museum's landscaping project was moving forward as well. Julian and Leslie have as their long-term goal to establish a literary colony at the site.

On July 22, 2000, the Fitzgerald Museum celebrated the centennial of Zelda's birth, with granddaughter Bobby Lanahan headlining the tribute. From June 27 to July 4, 2000, the McPhillipses represented the Fitzgerald Museum at the Fifth International F. Scott Fitzgerald Conference in Nice, France.

20

J. L. Chestnut and Selma

FEW INDIVIDUALS who were active in the legendary civil rights struggle in Selma, Alabama, are held in as high esteem as attorney J. L. Chestnut, Jr. He and his renowned law partners, Hank and Rose Sanders, have spent much of their careers battling the city's powers-that-be in seeking justice for their clients.

In 1990, journalist Julia Cass interviewed Chestnut in depth and produced a 423-page biography, *Black in Selma: The Uncommon Life of J.L. Chestnut, Jr.* (Farrar, Straus & Giroux; New York). In one section, Cass summed up her subject's influence this way:

> Chestnut was born in Selma in 1930. He grew up in the era of segregation, when most black people, including his parents, made accommodations to what seemed to be an unchangeable situation . . .
>
> When the civil rights organizations came to Selma in the middle 1960s to launch a voting rights movement, Chestnut represented demonstrators in court . . . He was there beside the Edmund Pettus Bridge when state troopers and local white men attacked the civil rights marchers on "Bloody Sunday," March 7, 1965, an event that led to the passage of the Voting Rights Act, a turning point for black America and for Chestnut personally . . .
>
> Since then, Chestnut has been a leader in the longer march, the process of turning the possibilities opened up in 1965 into real grass roots change . . .

Julian knew Chestnut's history well and had the good fortune not only to develop a friendship with the attorney in the late 1970s but later to work alongside Chestnut in trying some cases—an opportunity that Julian acknowledges as some of the most gratifying work of his career.

During the thick of the 1977-78 Alabama attorney general's race, Julian and his campaign manager brother Frank became friendly with Chestnut and his Sanders partners, with the three attorneys enthusiastically throwing their support to Julian in that race. (Later Julian returned the compliment by hosting a fundraiser for Hank Sanders in his first successful race for the state senate.)

During the 1980s, Julian himself did frequent battle in Selma's courts, on behalf of black policemen and other city employees who charged discrimination and mistreatment. As in Montgomery, *a la* Emory Folmar, McPhillips faced a colorful—and well-entrenched—power structure, including Selma Mayor Joe Smitherman and his attorney Henry Pitts.

In the mid-1980s, Julian and J. L. first teamed up on a difficult case involving allegations of child abuse at one of Selma's most venerable institutions, the Methodist Children's Home. After a hard-fought battle, McPhillips and Chestnut split the closing jury arguments. Julian remembers being in awe of both Chestnut's poise and rhetorical flourishes—"and learning from them, as well," he says. The case ended in a mistrial.

In January 1986, Julian represented Dallas County Judge Dick Norton in what he calls a "politically inspired" complaint filed with the Alabama Judicial Inquiry Commission. Norton had become unpopular, Julian says, because he didn't engage in the "almost country-club closeness" some other judges did with the local bar association. Norton had a reputation for holding lawyers accountable, and ruffled the feathers of some prominent attorneys who had difficulty making court dates.

Chestnut advised Julian in the background, and McPhillips ultimately succeeded in getting the charges against Norton dismissed.

In early April 1988, high school basketball coach A. A. Sewell was about to be fired by Superintendent of Education Norward Roussell, an educator recently arrived from New Orleans, who had become head of the Selma's predominantly black school system. Encouraged by his wife, Nancy Sewell, a future Selma city councilwoman, Sewell retained McPhillips to represent him. As Al Benn, the *Montgomery Advertiser* columnist for Selma, wrote on June 12, 1988:

> Quicker than anybody could say "Julian McPhillips," a letter was written
> to Roussell by Montgomery's well-known activist lawyer, telling him he'd be

sued if anything bad happened to Sewell's contract . . . The contracts will be extended — proving that where there's a will, and a Julian McPhillips, there's a way to retain a job.

In early January 1990, Julian was back in Selma again--this time defending Dr. Norward Roussell, who had apparently decided it was better to have Julian as an ally than a foe. Roussell was a forceful personality, with strong opinions on solving the school system's problems, and his ideas didn't sit well with Selma's majority-white school board. Few observers were surprised when Roussell ended up being fired by the board.

As Al Benn reported in the January 7, 1990, edition of the *Montgomery Advertiser*:

> Refusal by the board's six whites to extend the contract sparked resignations of the panel's five black members, a student boycott, and withdrawal of funds by blacks from banks with school board connections.

With McPhillips's help, Roussell appealed to the school board. McPhillips told the Board "you have an historic opportunity to bring together different factions of this community by retaining Dr. Roussell." Meeting behind closed doors with Mayor Smitherman and board chairman Carl Barker, Julian quietly received advice from J. L. about how to help Roussell.

The *Montgomery Advertiser* and *Birmingham News* had field days reporting on the Roussell case, and press coverage catapulted into a national story. A *Newsweek* magazine photographer quoted Mayor Smitherman, a supposedly reformed segregationist, as saying Roussell was an "overpaid nigger from New Orleans." Smitherman denied the comment.

Ultimately, a settlement was worked out, but not long afterwards, Roussell moved to Tuskegee, which is as far east of Montgomery as Selma is west (about fifty miles), as the new superintendent for the Macon County School Board.

By the mid-1990s, Julian and J. L. Chestnut were teamed up again, this time in Lowndes County Circuit Court on behalf of Susan Barganier in a lawsuit for malicious prosecution against Bill's Dollar Store. The case was tried before a jury in Hayneville. Defending the case were veteran Montgomery attorney Bobby Black and his associate Bill McGowin, a fourth cousin, once removed, of Julian's. At one point, Black and Chestnut were exchanging barbs, when a spectator was heard to mumble "two grumpy old men." The resulting laughter helped break the tension. The case was settled confidentially, but satisfactorily for the plaintiff and her counsel, Julian says, moments before the jury deliberations began.

In the late 1990s, Julian and J. L. worked together again, this time on behalf of Alabama black farmers discriminated against because of their race. J. L. was counsel for a class action, but Julian had several farmers as clients who were class members.

The farmers eventually received a proposed settlement. Some of them accepted it and withdrew their claim; others, however, challenged it, saying the settlement was not enough. The case remains ongoing.

"I have the utmost admiration for J. L." said McPhillips. "He is a tireless lawyer, a very eloquent advocate for his clients, and he has a great heart for people. He is also a friend and an inspiration." Having once been humorously described in Selma as the "white J. L. Chestnut," Julian's quick reply was that there was no higher compliment.

Interviewed at his Selma office in April 2000, Chestnut chuckled with satisfaction in his rich, weathered voice when told of the high regard in which Julian holds him, as both a mentor and a friend.

"We do make a good team," Chestnut says. "Julian's courtroom style, I would describe as . . . I suppose, 'passionately objective.' The jury senses that he not only has his facts straight, but that he genuinely believes in the point he's making. As for me, jurors have told me they see in me somebody who's 'been there, done that.' I've been around the block a whole lot of times. And when you put those two personalities together, it generally makes an impression."

As for the source of Chestnut's well-known, regal rhetorical flourishes—particularly in closing arguments—he credits black ministers. "Learning to do a closing argument is basically a process of trial and error," Chestnut says, "and learning from other lawyers.

"But I remember a conversation I had once with Martin Luther King in which I told him that I didn't believe he could have come anywhere close to achieving the many things he did, had he not been a black, Southern Baptist preacher.

"That familiar sing-song style in the voice is a comfort blanket to virtually all black Southerners and to a great many white ones. They grow up hearing it in the pulpit every Sunday, every Wednesday night, and they identify with it. And even those who are not totally put at ease by the style, it certainly helps their comfort zone with what's being said. So, there's a lot of the black Southern Baptist preacher in me."

But when the subject turns to the current civil rights atmosphere and the growing shortage of young civil rights attorneys, Chestnut's words are a lot less encouraging.

"The picture is bleak," he says. "No doubt about it. It's a very difficult field, with the mood of the country now so far to the right of center. For years now, some two-thirds of federal judges have been appointed by either Reagan or Bush. That makes a civil rights case a very hard row to plow.

" "When I started out, forty years ago, virtually every black lawyer *was* a civil rights lawyer, and we were supported by the NAACP Legal Defense and Education Fund. Today, a young lawyer probably couldn't make it on his own specializing in civil rights cases. In the old days, we used to run to the federal courts for help. Nowadays, we run *from* them."

"But something else that bears mentioning about Julian," Chestnut adds, "is that most black people around the state have either heard or read about him. He has a reputation for taking on the kinds of cases that very few white lawyers in Alabama would take on. He'd just as soon stand up to the governor of the state, or to General Motors Corporation, or whoever.

"That willingness to repeatedly stand up for the underdog gives Julian a great deal of credibility in certain communities around the state, I think, both black and white. You mention the name 'Julian McPhillips,' and you get a raised eyebrow. I mean that in a positive kind of way.

"Except, now, if you mention it over at the Selma Country Club." The rich laughter again. "There, you get a different kind of raised eyebrow. But that's all right, too."

21

The Political Instinct

WHILE JULIAN'S political instincts are rooted in Cullman of the 1950s, watered in the early 1960s by John F. Kennedy and the assassination that ended Camelot, and sharpened during the mid '60s at Princeton, it wasn't until his Columbia Law School days, from 1968-71, when the Vietnam War was challenging traditional notions of religion, justice, and country that Julian found himself, for the first time ever, elected to class office. He served during his last two years as president of the Columbia Student Senate.

It was a convergence of the right place and the right time that brought the latent politician in him to the forefront: he found that his Southern upbringing gave him an advantage in relating to other people, and his blend of radical sympathies and conservative manners played extremely well on Columbia's campus in Manhattan's Upper West Side.

Julian threw himself into the experience, and got his first rush of "leadership adrenaline" during a movement called the "Soap Box Conspiracy." Standing on a box in the law school foyer, he and other students argued for a 50-50 student/faculty senate to make all law school decisions.

The school's faculty members either ignored the initiative or viewed it with disdain, prompting Julian to write a heated column for the school newspaper headlined: "Faculty Arrogance Frustrates Students." It didn't get quite the result he hoped for, though. The next day, while riding on an elevator, Julian got his comeuppance from a professor in four succinct words: "Student Arrogance Frustrates Faculty."

The pinnacle experience of those years, according to Julian, was his debating Dean Michael Sovern (later president of Columbia University) over the law school's proper response to the U.S. invasion of Cambodia. Speaking before some nine hundred students and faculty members, Julian urged the school to join four hundred other colleges and universities around the country in "striking to protest an abominable and immoral war."

Likewise, the chairmanship of the law school's Coalition Against the War gave Julian his first experience in political organization. Observed Walter Bliss, Princeton '66, who knew Julian both in college and at Columbia Law and appreciated his leadership skills as a student senate president: "Julian has a genuine charisma, and a good sense of humor. He was good at motivating law students into more constructive channels in opposing the war."

A natural outgrowth of that was his subsequent involvement in the 1972 George McGovern campaign. The Democratic challenger was a very popular figure on college and university campuses at the time. In 1972, when Julian worked as a first-year associate attorney on Wall Street, he found himself chairing "New York City Taxicab Drivers for McGovern."

"It was a wonderful experience," Julian recalls. "I met some terrific people, from a very wide range of ages and ethnic backgrounds. My co-chair was a middle-aged Italian immigrant named Frank Melfi, and we developed a long-lasting friendship."

Julian wasn't the only member of his family whose path intersected McGovern's campaign. Back in Alabama, Julian Sr. and Eleanor McPhillips had just returned from the political cauldron of Washington, D.C., where the Peace Corps community had strong anti-war sympathies.

Hubert Humphrey and Edmund Muskie were front-runners for the Democratic ticket in 1971, with McGovern barely registering in the polls. But the McPhillipses' phone rang one day, and Eleanor talked with a McGovern worker in Washington wanting someone to serve as their Alabama campaign chair. Before he had time to fully consider it, Julian Sr. found himself opening a copy of the *Birmingham News* with an article announcing his chairmanship of the McGovern campaign in Alabama.

Some of Julian Sr.'s friends had shaken their heads in puzzlement and dismay when he left a prosperous family business to enter seminary. Some were puzzled and dismayed again when his 1964-66 sermons at St. Luke's Episcopal Church in Birmingham (then the largest congregation of the Alabama diocese) proclaimed that the Christian gospel required treating all people as brothers regardless of race, and others were surprised yet again when Julian Sr. resigned the rectorship of St. Luke's to join the Peace Corps. But these friends really thought the older Julian had gone beyond the pale when he became Alabama head of the McGovern campaign.

In one of Alabama history's interesting footnotes, Julian Sr. gave future governor Don Siegelman his first political job in 1972, selecting Siegelman— who had just returned to Alabama after studying at Oxford—to assist him as McGovern's state campaign coordinator. It was on a visit home to Birmingham that year that Julian Jr. and Don first met.

The following year, when Julian gathered with the three McPhillips generations on vacation at Point Clear, Alabama, he remembers feeling a very strong pull to move back to the state—particularly when he was offered opportunities at prestigious law firms in Mobile and Birmingham. But his relationship with girlfriend Leslie Burton in New York was fast blossoming, so Julian passed up the Alabama offers and returned to the Big Apple and a job with American Express Company.

But two years later, with the glamour of New York fading, and Leslie, now his wife, urging that they return to Alabama, Julian could resist the pull no longer. With the help of a door opened by Princeton alumnus Jim White ('64), Julian accepted a job as assistant attorney general, and quickly involved himself in prosecuting white-collar crimes, as well as counseling state officials in the banking, insurance, and securities departments.

In 1975, Julian was excited by the unorthodox, surging presidential candidacy of Georgia peanut farmer Jimmy Carter, and he became involved in Carter's campaign. A favorite photo on his wall shows Julian a few years later shaking hands with President Carter at the White House.

Meanwhile, cogs were turning in Alabama politics. Julian's boss, the popular Bill Baxley, could not succeed himself as attorney general and had announced a campaign for the governor's office. After two years of handling well-publicized cases as an assistant attorney general, Julian had achieved remarkably high name recognition around the state. At age thirty, he began to consider seeking his first public office.

Elective office had many appeals to Julian. He liked meeting and working with people from all walks of life. He saw the attorney's general's office as a way to practice his legal profession while making a significant contribution to his home state. He had seen in the examples of politicians he admired how the public stage gave opportunities for leadership on important social issues, and of course at the other extreme he had seen the examples of demagoguery by politicians who tarnished Alabama's image. He had enjoyed as an assistant AG the role of defender of the poor and powerless against those who would take advantage of them. And, he believes now, he was also subconsciously searching for a positive outlet to help overcome his grief from his brother David's suicide the year before.

In June 1977, after twenty-six months as an assistant attorney general, Julian resigned and opened his first private law practice, in an office across the street from Montgomery's Central YMCA. A couple of weeks later in Cullman, Julian called a press conference and announced from the steps of his boyhood home that he was "exploring" a campaign for attorney general and, if he could develop enough support, he would declare in the fall.

That summer, he practiced a little law. But his main focus was traveling around the state, laying the groundwork of a campaign. The odds against him were significant. He was the youngest of an eventual nine candidates, one of only two who had never run for office before, and he would be facing off against the original front-runner, state senate president Joe Fine of Russellville, who reportedly already had a campaign fund of a million dollars. Other strong contenders were state senator Dudley Perry of Tuskegee, state representative Douglas Johnstone of Mobile, and three district attorneys: Bill Benton of Phenix City, Bob "Hawkeye" Morrow of Selma, and Charlie Graddick of Mobile. Two other assistant attorneys general, Ray Acton and Bill Stephens, rounded out the field.

To say that Julian ran his campaign on a shoe-string is an understatement. He's particularly proud of the fact that due to the generosity of his family and friends, he never incurred the expense of a motel room during the year-long odyssey on the road. "My grandfather was in Mobile, my parents were in Pell City, my widowed sister-in-law, Sue, was in Birmingham, and my uncle Warren, my campaign chairman, lived in Cullman. Our home was in Montgomery. That covered most of the state."

Cutting expenses helped, but by election day Julian had raised only $100,000 and had spent $140,000, with the deficit covered by a personal loan from his parents. His expenses were dwarfed by those of front-runner Fine, and by the spending of Charlie Graddick—a lifelong Republican who, with strong

Republican financial support, switched parties in time to run in the 1978 Democratic primary, which at the time was basically the only political ballgame in the state.

The race heated up very early. In October 1977, one of Julian's cousins sent him a copy of a campaign letter from Graddick soliciting campaign contributions. What made the routine solicitation big news was that it was printed on district attorney stationery and carried postage from the district attorney's postage meter, which Julian saw as an improper use of public funds.

So he called a news conference in Graddick's hometown of Mobile, where he told the press, "I like to call an ace an ace and a spade a spade, and the time has come to call the hand of Charlie Graddick. I call for the resignation of Mobile's district attorney, if he continues to use the assets and resources of his public office to run for attorney general."

Graddick, who received the news at his office two blocks away, was far from a happy camper. While Julian returned home to be with Leslie for the birth of their first child, Rachel, Graddick called his own press conference. In it, he accused McPhillips of cutting a line from the bottom of his solicitation letter that read "Paid for by Charles A. Graddick" before circulating it to the press.

The next day, Julian heard from his Mobile campaign team that the newspaper headlines there read, "Graddick Claims McPhillips Lied." Julian was outraged, particularly since he still had the original letter in hand, which bore no such line. He returned to Mobile with the original letter, to refute Graddick's accusation. Though Graddick's charges had been local front-page news, Julian's counter-charge was buried on a back page. At the time, he had no way of knowing that the *Mobile Press-Register* reporter who wrote the article about his reply would join Graddick's attorney general staff as soon as the campaign was over.

"It was a rough introduction to politics, but it was definitely educational," Julian says now. Though sparks between McPhillips and Graddick would fly again on a couple of occasions during the race, Graddick never called another news conference to make charges against Julian. That role went to three other candidates: Morrow, Acton, and Stephens.

This happened late in the campaign, in August before the September 1978 primary, and it happened only after Julian had won the endorsements of the conservative *Birmingham News,* and the more liberal—and black—Alabama

Democratic Conference, back to back, a day apart. Suddenly, Julian looked like the probable candidate to be in a run-off with front-runner Joe Fine, who had been sullied by various disclosures during the summer.

The conventional wisdom among Fine's eight opponents was that whoever made it a run-off with the State Senate president would defeat Fine in the run-off.

Ray Acton—at fifty-five the oldest candidate, a former mayor of Homewood and a veteran assistant attorney general—fired the first volley, saying that Julian had "misrepresented the amount of time he worked in the attorney general's office. He says he worked there *several* years, but the truth is he only worked there two years, two months, and (so many) days . . ."

Julian shrugged and grinned. "If that's the worst thing my opponents can say about me," he told the reporters who called him for a response, "I'm not worried."

Next to attack was "Hawkeye" Morrow, Selma district attorney, who said in a stump speech, "Julian McPhillips is nothing but a wealthy, northeastern establishment liberal, just like the Kennedys." This charge drew another shrug and grin from Julian, who told reporters, "I wish that were true. I could sure use some of the Kennedys' money for this campaign."

The third attack, ironically, came from the candidate whose background and biography were most like Julian's: a former assistant attorney general, an Ivy League law school grad (Harvard), who had worked on Wall Street before returning to Alabama. Bill Stephens challenged Julian's residency eligibility for running.

Having anticipated this possibility, Julian had in 1977 obtained an opinion from Democratic party chairman Bob Vance, prepared by party executive director Don Siegelman, that "McPhillips has met Alabama's 'five years next preceding the election' residency requirement" because he maintained draft board registration, church membership, and other incidents of residency at his parents' home in Alabama, even while he was outside the state.

Moreover, the Demos' opinion said, the residency law itself violated the U.S. Constitution, and as a result was unenforceable.

These assurances cut no ice with Stephens, who hammered away through other venues. He encouraged a private citizen to file a residency complaint with the party, but the State Democratic Committee tossed out the challenge without even asking Julian to appear at a hearing.

In the end, Stephens's proxy challenger filed suit against Julian in Madison County Circuit Court, which happened to coincide with a Stephens news conference again hammering home the residency issue.

A copy of the lawsuit was served on Julian at a Huntsville political rally. He soon discovered that he wasn't the only individual who possessed a copy. Stephens's camp had mailed one to every probate judge in all of the state's sixty-seven counties, along with a letter saying McPhillips shouldn't be on the ballot.

"With the statewide publicity," Julian says now, "Stephens was obviously trying to do politically what he couldn't do legally." Moreover, Julian found that Madison County Circuit Judge Tom Younger wouldn't set a hearing on the suit until after the election, which would leave a cloud hanging over his candidacy on election day.

It was a hard blow. "For fifteen months," Julian says, "I had worked harder than any other candidate in the race. And now, at nearly the last minute, all that work was about to be undone."

But three heroes emerged to save the day. Huntsville attorney Bob Ford, Julian's Madison County coordinator, filed a petition for a writ of mandamus with the Alabama Supreme Court, and attorneys Bobby Segall and Truman Hobbs Sr. convinced the Supreme Court to rule in Julian's favor, allowing him to continue in the race. Julian's campaign spread the news personally to all sixty-seven probate judges, and the candidate was "ecstatically grateful" to Segall, who argued the case to the Alabama Supreme Court, for pulling a very big one out of the fire.

Eventually, the negative campaigning of his opponents began to boomerang. Julian capitalized on the free publicity he received in refuting all the charges, eventually becoming a favorite of the state's press to an extent no one could have predicted: he received some eighty-five percent of endorsements by Alabama newspapers. Julian also received the endorsement of every black political group in the state, including the heavyweight ADC.

Considering the large percentage of black voters and of educated professional white voters in Birmingham and Montgomery, it's not surprising that, of the nine attorney general candidates, Julian finished first in both cities.

Julian credits many others with the successful results of the campaign, especially his parents and the "Mom and Pop Machine" recreational vehicle they drove all over the state for the campaign, his wife Leslie, brother Frank, and baby daughter Rachel. He also had "excellent county leaders, many of whom graduated on to greater glories," says Julian, including Calhoun County chairman Doug Ghee, a two-term state senator from Anniston, Macon County chairman Ron Williams, mayor of Tuskegee, Myron Thompson of Houston County and Dean Buttram of Cherokee County, both now federal judges, and Bill Rhea of Etowah County, state circuit court judge. Attorneys John Harris, Lauderdale County coordinator, and Mark Wilkerson, West Alabama coordinator, established law practices in Florence and Montgomery respectively. Nineteen-year-old Ken Mullinax of Anniston, who had his first political job as Julian's driver, later became chief of staff to Congressman Earl Hilliard, and today has a public relations business in Birmingham.

Election Night

On Tuesday, September 5, 1978, the night of the election, Julian, his family, and close campaign supporters gathered at Montgomery's Governor's House Hotel to watch the returns come in.

The early news wasn't encouraging. Graddick had just wrapped up a three-week "get tough on crime" blitz in the state's media, and it was paying off: Graddick catapulted over both front-runners—McPhillips and Joe Fine—and, when the night was over, led with some 170,000 votes. But Julian had also stormed back in the totals, to take second place with approximately 130,000, and Fine was third with approximately 125,000.

Though these were unofficial tallies by the Associated Press and UPI, more than 95 percent of the vote was in, and Julian slept secure in the knowledge that he had a run-off position—and a tremendous amount of work ahead of him in coming weeks.

The next morning, McPhillips wasted no time campaigning hard—challenging Graddick to debates, and adding tongue-in-cheek that, if debates were out, he would also accept a wrestling match. Julian's brother Frank, his campaign manager, had to return to law school at the University of Virginia, and Jefferson County coordinator Nelson Head came to Montgomery to take over leadership of the state campaign.

But three days after the election, on late Friday afternoon, a telephone call brought Julian the shock of his life: the official tabulation showed that his approximate 5,000-vote lead over Joe Fine had somehow evaporated into a near 6,000-vote deficit.

A close look at the results was unsettling. In Randolph County, for instance, Julian had lost *exactly* five hundred votes in the final count. And in five other counties—Pike, Houston, Covington, Talledega, and Mobile—various vote amounts were lost by Julian, or had accrued to Fine, and in some cases both.

To Julian, it looked suspiciously like someone had manipulated the vote totals. He cried "foul" in the press, saying that the outcome "stunk to high heaven." The following Monday he filed a challenge of the results, a story that made front-page in newspapers around the state. In the meantime, there would informally be three candidates in the run-off, while officials determined which two would square off in the final race.

THE NEWS from the voting precincts was not good. In all the counties where the vote totals had changed, the voting machines had been erased over the weekend — before Julian's challenge was filed — to get ready for the coming run-off. There was no way to authenticate Julian's totals.

Supporters rallied to Julian's side, including former governor "Big Jim" Folsom, who told the press that voting machines made it far easier to steal votes than the old paper ballots of his day.

"The circumstantial evidence was compelling," Julian reflects, "that my run-off position had been stolen. But how, and by whom, was impossible to say." Besides the problem of the machines' early erasure, a new run-off election would require the challenger to put up a $200,000 bond as security. McPhillips (with a negative net worth at the end of the campaign) knew the cupboard was bare and, after consulting with his father, realized the only practical course was to drop the vote challenge—which he did, one week after initiating it.

'You'd Better Watch Out'

Of the many memorable quotes from former Alabama governor George Wallace, one came during his third-party bid for the U.S. presidency, when his vote total in one state dropped significantly in the final count. "I don't even know what 'recapitulation' means," Wallace told reporters. "But if anybody ever tells you they're gonna do it to you, you'd better watch out."

The grim humor was appropriate for Julian's situation as well. In the days to come, he would find that voter fraud was more prevalent and widespread than most people realized. He was interviewed by National Public Radio for a documentary on the subject, a program that would subsequently win first place in a national competition of news reporting.

Julian decided he and Leslie needed a change of scenery in the worst way. They picked Cancun, Mexico, as the place to lick their wounds, leaving Rachel in the care of Julian's parents. "We were down there a week," Julian says, "and I slept through most of it."

He came back to Montgomery "revitalized, though not recovered," and moved his office several blocks down Perry Street to practice law closely with Tommy Gallion. There, he found that the election ordeal had at least one silver lining: the attorney general's race had greatly enhanced his name recognition locally and statewide, and new clients eagerly sought him out. By the end of his first year of practice after the campaign, Julian found himself out of debt and earning in the low six figures.

Though politics had left a bad taste in his mouth, it was still apparently in his genes. As Jimmy Carter prepared for re-election in 1980, the State Democratic Executive Committee elected Julian a Carter delegate—over several state senators and other prominent Democrats—to represent Alabama at the Democratic National Convention in New York that year.

As a delegate, Julian found himself very much in demand. Ted Kennedy tried to woo Julian and other delegates away from the Carter camp, and President Carter invited Julian and Leslie for dinner with him and Rosalynn at the White House. Surprisingly, McPhillips found himself called even more frequently by representatives of independent candidate Lyndon LaRouche. At a White House dinner for Southern Carter delegates, Julian was accosted by yet another LaRouche supporter, who was disguised as a newspaper reporter complete with media credentials. Though Julian had to admire the LaRouche camp's ingenuity, he also had to wonder about the effectiveness of White House security.

At the Democratic National Convention in New York, Julian mingled with national Democrats—including U.S. Senator Bill Bradley of New Jersey, with whom he resumed his college friendship. Returning to Montgomery,

Julian was invited by the local NBC affiliate to represent Carter in a live debate, broadcast statewide, with Mayor Emory Folmar, who represented President Reagan.

Julian remembers the debate as "lively." At one point, Julian emphasized the return of clean, honest government to the White House in the aftermath of Watergate, and said the re-election of Carter, a fellow Southerner, would ensure that we had a president with "a heart for all Americans."

Leading up to the 1982 Attorney General's race, there were many overtures wanting Julian to take on Charles Graddick one-on-one. But several factors led to his decision not to run that year: Leslie had just given birth to their second daughter, Grace; his bustling law practice was providing him with an income roughly five times the Attorney General's salary; and he found that taking on private cases for "underdog" clients fed his appetite for public service. He did stay active in Democratic political circles, attending the party's mini-convention in Memphis, where he met a number of upcoming and major players, including a young Arkansas governor named Bill Clinton.

Every four-year election cycle since—1986, 1990, 1994, and 1998—the possibility of Julian's candidacy was a source of speculation by the state's media and local politicos as a candidate for either attorney general, lieutenant governor, governor, or U.S. Senator, but in each case he declined, saying that the "time wasn't right." In 1986 Don Siegelman approached Julian and said he was thinking about running for attorney general if Julian wasn't going to. Julian thanked Siegelman for the courtesy, and urged him to run (which Siegelman did, successfully).

During the election years, though choosing to sit on the sidelines himself, McPhillips supported Democratic candidates for governor and other state and local offices, particularly in the judiciary. "My law practice was just going too well," he reflects now. "We were flourishing financially, and I was getting a lot of personal satisfaction from the cases I was handling. And I also hated to give up my private time with my family, close involvement in church work, and other interests—traveling, hiking, boating. Life was just too good."

"Alabama twice missed great opportunities in 1990 and 1994 to elect Paul Hubbert as a progressive New South governor," said Julian. "Bill Baxley in 1978 and 1986 and George McMillan in 1982 or 1986 could have been great governors also. Fortunately, with the 1998 election of Don Siegelman as governor, Alabama is finally making the progressive strides forward it should have made sooner."

THE CLOSEST Julian came to running for public office again was in early 1998, when the clock was ticking down to filing day but nobody had stepped forward to oppose Republican U.S. Senator Richard Shelby, a two-term incumbent. Returning in January from a ski trip in France, Julian was amazed that Shelby still had no opponent. State Party Chairman Joe Turnham and other key Democrats urged him to run, and Julian's interest soared. Ed Kahalley, Sr., of Mobile got a group of fifty Bay area Democrats together in early March 1998, all of whom urged Julian to take on Shelby. At one point, syndicated political columnist Bob Ingram wrote a piece in the *Montgomery Advertiser* and other state papers about the intriguing possibility of Julian's candidacy.

But after two months of considering the possibility, Julian ("gut-wrenchingly," as he recalls) decided not to run, though most likely he could have done so uncontested for the Democratic nomination. His considerations were Shelby's high ratings in opinion polls (mid-60s positive, high teens negative), the Republican's $6 million campaign war chest, and President Clinton's low point in the "Monica-gate" scandal, which threatened to rub off on Democratic candidates nationwide.

Even more decisive—and disheartening—was the fact that many of the top Democrats in Alabama, especially those with money to support a candidate, were still tied to Shelby, whom they twice helped elect as a Democrat before Shelby switched parties in 1994. "They felt they had an investment in Shelby, which they needed to keep up," Julian says.

The clincher was a phone call in mid-March from his mother. Earlier his parents had encouraged him to oppose Shelby. But in this phone call, his mother—in the early stages of Alzheimer's at age seventy-eight—said she'd "worry herself to death" every day that he was in Washington. Though she later couldn't remember making the call, Julian was deeply affected by it at a critical time: "As I prayed about it," he recalls, "it seemed more and more that God had spoken to me through my mother."

Two weeks before the cut-off date for filing, Julian announced he wouldn't make the race. Instead, he said, he and his family would be traveling to South

America that summer to visit missionaries—a three-week trip as a member of the board of trustees of the South American Missionary Society. The itinerary included Chile, Bolivia, and Peru.

By the end of the year though, politics was calling him again. His friend of thirty-four years, Bill Bradley, was sounding more and more favorable about a 2000 presidential run. On December 1, 1998, Bradley called Julian to say that in a few days he would be announcing "an exploratory candidacy" and asked Julian to chair his campaign efforts in Alabama.

"I was overjoyed to have the opportunity," McPhillips says, "especially since I had strongly urged him to run for president in 1988, 1992, and 1996, and was disappointed each time he declined."

Julian hit the ground running, and on January 2, 1999, Alabama became the first state in America to qualify Bradley for matching federal funds, by raising the necessary $5,000 in contributions of $250 or less. Getting Bradley to Alabama in person turned out to be a more difficult task, with forty-nine other states wanting his attention—and most with primaries much earlier than Alabama's June date. But finally, after much communication, McPhillips and the Bradley staff worked out a May 4, 1999 visit for the candidate.

22

Bill Bradley for President

I N THE spring of 1999, the face of Bill Bradley looked out from supermarket aisles at millions of Americans, from the cover of *Time* magazine. His expression managed at the same time to be confident, canny, skeptical, serious, and "with the help of a touch of dramatic lighting on the part of the photographer" appeared to know more than he was telling.

How did the Princeton alumnus, basketball star, and U.S. Senator come from nowhere to being, for a long bright moment, a major presidential contender? Largely because of events such as a breakfast reception this past May 1999, at Julian's and Leslie's home.

Bradley's Trip to Montgomery

It's a bright, clear day, and by 7:30 a.m. several dozen people are milling comfortably throughout the big living room and dining room. The main table is spread with egg soufflés, biscuits, fresh fruit, frosty pitchers of orange juice, and urns of coffee. The faint scent of bacon frying heralds a replacement tray of it from the kitchen soon. Vases of fresh lilies and carnations and greenery fill the sunlit windows.

The visitors are mostly young, dressed in business clothes, and many of them sport the fresh-minted, red-white-and-blue "Bradley for President" buttons they were given at the door by the welcoming volunteers.

The star of the show and his small entourage arrived at the house from the airport a little after midnight, and are now in their upstairs quarters showering and dressing, preparing for a very long day. While Leslie is supervising the food preparations, Julian works the waiting crowd with enthusiasm.

"Well, General!" he says as he shakes the hand of an elderly man. "I almost didn't recognize you without your uniform. It's been a long time. How in the world are you doing?"

In the den, just of the two big rooms, young David lies on a couch watching "Rugrat" on a wide screen TV, periodicaly glancing over his shoulder to detect any tell-tale movement of the crowd that would suggest Bradley's arrivl.

On the living room coffee table, alongside a copy of Bradley's latest book, *Values of the Game*, is a large stack of photocopies of recent articles about Bradley's upstart candidacy, including *USA Today* and *The New York Times*.

"It's exhilarating to believe that this is a chance to lead," the *Times* pece quotes him as saying at a fundraiser in his home state of New Jersey. "I'm going to be guided by convictions, not polls. I'm not going to hog the spotlight What I *am* going to do is try to call attention to the actions of millions of Americns out there every day who shine, in hopes that people can see the America that I have seen."

In *USA Today*, reporter Jill Lawrence observes in an analytical piece that "Eleven years afterconsidering a presidential run ad deeming himself not ready, the former Democratic senator and Hall of Fame professional basketball player is starting what he calls his journey. His timing appears curious, to say the least. Vice President Gore appears to have a lock on the Democratic presidential nomination, and several prominent would-be challengers are taking a pass."

"But Bradley, fifty-five, says his inner voice told him to go for it, told him that he was at the top of his game and that he 'matched the moment.'"

"So here he is on the trail, a six-foot-five gentle giant, slipping in and out of roles as coach, author, interviewer, college professor, and Sunday School teacher. Once in a while, usually under questioning, he even sounds like a presidential contender.

"He is so soft-spoken that a loud laugh can drown out his punch lines. He once lined up a baby-sitter for a key adviser. He sent an aide one cold Iowa night to ask a reporter whether she had forgotten her coat."

"The realization dawns: This is what it would be like if Mr. Rogers ran for president . . ."

Finally, a buzz of conversation crosses the room to the effect that Bradley is on his way down, and the crowd steadily migrates toward the wide staircase of the foyer that will apparently be his podium. David follows them, where he stands raptly at the edge with a basketball under his arm, destined for autographing before the candidate gets away.

Bradley walks down smiling, shaking hands with those nearest him, as the flashguns of cameras resemble a miniature fireworks display. Julian, after greeting Bradley, walks midway up the staircase and waits for silence to begin his brief welcome to the crowd and his introduction of the candidate.

As Julian walks down to floor level and Bradley goes up the steps to take his place, Bradley quips to the crowd: "You can tell a born politician, like Julian. Always first to take the highest ground."

The crowd laughs appreciatively and the ice—if there *were* any—is instantly broken.

Bradley starts with a story, a related one. When his basketball team won the Olympic gold metal at Tokyo in 1964, they were greeted on their return at a White House reception hosted by Lyndon Johnson. As the photographers lined up the players and the president for photographs, Bradley found himself crowded elbow-to-elbow with Johnson, over whom he towered.

"I was nineteen years old, and here I was at the White House, and I was so nervous my palms were dripping sweat. And at just that moment, President Johnson leans over toward me and whispers, 'Son, if you could move a little farther down the line, I'd be tremendously grateful."

Widespread, easy laughter. Then, Bradley's expression turns serious.

"The decision to run for president is one that I've looked at before, in 1988 and 1992," he says, speaking without notes, "and for various reasons I chose not to enter the race at those times.

"But now, I'm convinced that we're at a point in history when my abilities match the moment, and that it's time for me to step forward. We live in a country with tremendous potential, but a time of unprecedented chaos in our country's leadership."

"What too often gets lost in that chaos is our story. Our internal narrative of where we, as a nation, are going, and why, in a time of such chaos, what's the only thing a person has to fall back on? *Principles . . .*"

He lets the word hang in the silence a moment, and repeats:

"Principles. The only true bedrock of a government is its principles. Not slogans, not inflexible posturing, not politics-as-usual, but principles. They're the compass that keeps a person, and a country, moving in the right direction.

"Sure, you're pushed off the track, sometimes. It's human nature. It's inevitable. But your principles are what get you back on the path.

"I've been on the road for some thirty years now—as a basketball player, a senator, a writer, a speaker, a businessman—and I've gotten a sense of who the American people really are. I've heard so many people's personal stories over those years, and the one continuous thread in all of them is that we're good people. There's so much true goodness, in most of us, and it's far too often overlooked.

"Then why are so many of us lonely, fearful, isolated? It's because we feel we've been left out of the process. And that's something I aim to change. My campaign is about empowering individuals.

"It's going to be a long, hard race. But I'm enjoying it tremendously. It's only eleven months till the primary, and it'll be the first one-on-one in history, so I think we'll see a very different pacing.

"I ask for your support, and I appreciate you coming out today."

After a round of handshaking, introductions, and more photographs, Julian and Bradley's aides help gradually steer him toward the front door. Waiting there is eight-year-old David McPhillips, his basketball held hopefully up to Bill Bradley, along with a black Magic Marker. Bradley kneels to sign the ball as more flashguns fire. He shakes David's hand and talks briefly with him, amid scattered applause, until his aides and the door's bright square of morning sunshine claim him for their own.

Bradley, his aides, and Julian stride quickly across the lawn and toward a waiting van. First they've got two more Montgomery stops, a news conference at the Alabama Education Association and a meeting with ministers at the AME Zion Church in west Montgomery. Then they're bound for Birmingham, where the candidate will make five more public appearances, including speaking to a Birmingham Kiwanis club luncheon and a town-hall style meeting at a black Baptist church. He'll meet Mayor Richard Arrington, followed by a meet-and-greet at the Alabama Sports Hall of Fame, where large portraits of Bear Bryant, Jesse Lewis, and other legends loom on the walls beyond his small podium. He'll finish with a Mountain Brook fundraising reception at the home of investment banker Jim White and his wife Marjorie before calling it a day.

Urging Bradley to Run

When Bradley graduated from Princeton, became a Rhodes Scholar at

Oxford, and went on to play for the New York Knicks, he and Julian were out of touch for those years. They weren't reunited until 1980, at the Democratic National Convention in New York. Julian was an elected delegate from Alabama, and Bradley from New Jersey. Both, not surprisingly, were pledged to Jimmy Carter.

"We had a chance at the convention to renew our friendship," Julian says, "and we've been in touch ever since."

In October 1987, columnist Starr Smith wrote in the *Montgomery Independent* of Julian's enthusiasm for Bradley:

> . . . Three years ahead of McPhillips at Princeton was a tall, lean Missouri boy named Bill Bradley, a basketball player of considerable note. Being an All-American wrestler himself, McPhillips and Bradley had a lot in common and the two jocks became good friends. They still are . . .
>
> Although Bradley is a non-candidate at this time, the Washington Post reports that he stole the show from the seven announced candidates at a recent fundraiser in Washington, D.C. Julian and his wife Leslie visited Bradley at his office two weeks ago.

Upon returning to Montgomery in the spring of 1987, McPhillips wrote his friend, "I am appealing to you to run for president; not because of your eminent electability but because of a duty you have to the world. You have been uniquely endowed with talents and abilities sorely needed at this time in our history . . ."

Bradley's response, though, was again to decline:

> Dear Julian:
>
> I am deeply flattered by your recent letter and your expression of confidence in me. I want to be totally truthful with you. I'm running for re-election to the Senate in 1990 and that is the only election I am thinking about right now.
>
> I would welcome your support for that effort and for my legislative initiatives. I recognize the important challenges that confront our nation, and I want to be a part of developing positive responses to them.

Julian repeatedly encouraged Bradley in the next two election cycles but to no avail. However, in an April 15, 1998, letter to Bradley, Julian was characteristically tenacious:

> As you know, I very energetically tried to encourage you to run for president in 1988 and again in 1992, as did many others across the country. If you should make the "big run" in the year 2000 . . . I believe you can beat Al Gore and anyone else who may run for the Democratic nomination. I believe you would be the strongest candidate, with the broadest base, against the Republicans.

In the letter of reply that follows, Bradley's signature looks much like the one that will appear on campaign buttons, T-shirts, lapel pins, bumper stickers, and other promotional objects in November of 1999—the same month that his first television spots will run, and some eleven months after he was contacted by Julian, asking him to be Bradley campaign chairman for Alabama.

Time marches on

Bright autumn leaves are falling outside the windows of the McPhillipses' den, and the same wide-screen TV that bore the faces of the Rug Rats while Bill Bradley was in Montgomery now displays instead the smiling face of Bill Bradley, being interviewed on network television, as Julian and Leslie watch with some friends.

"Bill Bradley has been a public figure," 20/20 host Ed Bradley is saying, "since he became an all-American basketball star at Princeton, won an Olympic gold medal, a Rhodes Scholarship to Oxford, and won two NBA championships with the New York Knicks, not to mention three terms in the U.S. Senate. Yet through it all, he has been deeply ambivalent about his celebrity. He's an intensely private person, who bristles when asked about his religious beliefs or even his favorite books or movies. So, why would Bill Bradley subject himself to the scrutiny of a presidential campaign, with the endless poking and prodding from the media, his opponents, and the people he hopes to convince to vote for him?"

"That's a question people always ask," the candidate replies. 'Why are you willing to do this?' And the answer is because I think that if I do it, there will be millions of Americans who'll have a better life. And that's the only reason. Believe me, that's the *only* reason to make this run."

"What Bill Bradley wants to do for the country," the host's voice says, over more campaign footage, "seems to be catching on. Only a few months ago, he was a long shot for the Democratic nomination. But now polls in several keys states show that Bradley is neck and neck with, in some places even beating, his opponent Vice President Al Gore. In response, the vice president has turned his campaign upside down, moving his campaign headquarters from Washington to Nashville, firing key advisors, and drastically altering his style and strategy. Al Gore says he's now the underdog."

When the scene cuts back to the studio, Bill Bradley is laughing.

"I take it *you* don't think Al Gore's the underdog?" the interviewer says.

"Well," Bradley replies, "I think that's what a lot of politicians like to say, but let's face the facts: He's got the support of the president of the United States, he's got the support of the Democratic National Committee, he arrives in Air Force Two, and he's fifteen points ahead in the national polls. I would say that we're running against entrenched power. And we are."

"You're taking a big political risk," the interviewer says, "by making race relations the centerpiece of your presidential campaign. The national polls show that the vast majority of voters, both minority and white, say that race is 'way down' on the list of issues that matter to most of them. Race is not an issue that sells well in this country."

"That's not why I'm doing it," Bradley answers. "I'm doing it because that's who I am."

And he follows up with a statement which, almost word for word, drew applause and head-nods during his meeting with black community leaders in the Baptist church in Birmingham, back in the spring:

> It is still the thing that reaches the deepest part of my being. So you know, when Ronald Reagan was president and you wanted to please the boss, what you did was talk about lower taxes, higher defense spending, and fighting the Communists.
>
> If *I'm* president and you want to please the boss, you're going to have to

show how your life, and your department, and your experience is promoting racial understanding. That's what *I'm* going to value.

The host turns to the camera. "This week, Bill Bradley will go one-on-one with Al Gore, in their first presidential debate. Gore is known as a formidable debater, but at 6'5" tall, Bradley may have history on his side. We looked at the presidential elections of the last few generations. And usually, the tall guy wins."

Bradley laughs. "Hey, that's a good omen. Maybe we ought to use that as the slogan for the campaign, 'The tall guy always wins.'"

Fade to black.

Responding to Colson's Fusillade

Charles "Chuck" Colson, White House aide who served prison time for his involvement in the events of Watergate, developed a renewed interest in Christianity in the 1970s, and afterwards created a new career for himself as a prison minister, social commentator, and defender of the fundamentalist, right-wing branch of the faith.

So far, so good.

But in the October 5 edition of Colson's national newsletter *BreakPoint*, his musings on the interrelationship of religion and politics in the U.S. got on Julian's "fighting side," to say the least.

For starters, Colson's cover story was titled "Denying Christ: Has Bradley Lost His Faith?"

And, Colson's assessment of the candidate went downhill from there, charging that Bradley "has renounced his Christian beliefs, and his actions are a warning of the perils of political expediency . . .

"Politicians in general are afraid to talk about tough moral issues. Since I believe that a person once saved is always saved, I have to conclude that either Bradley was not truthful in his earlier testimony, or that this is purely a political move—that deep down, Bill Bradley *does* know the truth. But is there anything scarier than someone who knows the truth and yet publicly denies it? One trembles for the state of his soul . . ."

Julian trembled, as well, upon reading this missive—not over Bill Bradley's soul, but rather in trying to hold his indignation in check while composing a coherent letter of response.

Julian's letter to Colson began:

Dear Mr. Colson:

Your recent column questioning Bill Bradley's faith was a partisan and erroneous shot, of which you should be ashamed, especially if you knew the real Bill Bradley.

When Bradley called me on December 1, 1998, asking me to head up his campaign in Alabama, I was delighted to do so since I had been encouraging him to run during the 1980s and 1990s.

At that time, I asked Bradley if he remembered our long conversation on that campus bench at Princeton in 1965. He said he did, to which I asked "Is your Christian faith as strong now as it was, back then?" Bradley's reply was that "my faith is much stronger; it is just that I don't wear it on my shirt-sleeve." Indeed, I understand and respect that response . . .

In brief, my view is that Bill Bradley practices what he preaches. As St. Francis of Assisi once said, "at all times preach the Gospel, and only when necessary use words." Bill Bradley's plan for health insurance for the forty-five million who are uninsured, his plans to help eliminate child poverty, and his programs to help spread America's prosperity to those left out of it, all fall under the nature of "being your brother's keeper," which is a true Christian ethic.

In Bill Bradley's life and work, and in the programs he espouses, in my opinion he comes far closer to living up to the highest ideals of Jesus's Sermon on the Mount than does any other candidate running for president. I am also quite comfortable, as an evangelical Christian, supporting Bill Bradley for president.

I urge you, in a spirit of Christian fairness and humility, to publish this reply.

The reply clock is still ticking.

The Alabama Campaign

Meanwhile, back at the McPhillips law office in Montgomery from

December 1998 through March 2000, the Bradley campaign in Alabama was humming.

More than three hundred Alabamians contributed to Bill Bradley's campaign for president. Upon Julian's urging, many top Alabama politicians got on board, including state senators Charles Steele of Tuscaloosa, Sundra Escott-Russell and E. B. McClain of Birmingham, and state representatives John Rogers and Oliver Robinson of Birmingham and Joseph Mitchell of Mobile. All became good friends of Julian's during the campaign.

Superdelegate and DNC member Natalie Davis of Birmingham became a co-chairman with Julian, as did Anniston attorney Cleo Thomas and the Rev. John Alford, president of the Montgomery SCLC chapter. Birmingham attorneys Ralph Yielding and Frank McPhillips and businesswoman Barbara McElroy spearheaded successful fundraising efforts in the Birmingham business and legal communities, while Montgomery lawyers Jock Smith and Corky Hawthorne and veteran political leader Dot Moore provided great leadership for the campaign. A "Youth for Bradley" campaign was stirred by Broderick Griffin, president of the College Democrats of Alabama and aided by Grant Moon and Sim Pettway. Many key business executives, lawyers, ministers, doctors, professionals, and average working people from around Alabama also supported the Bradley effort.

The momentum and polls were so favorable for Bradley from October through December 1999 that it appeared he had a realistic shot at toppling Gore. But the new year brought renewed reports of Bradley's untimely heart fibrillations, McCain's New Hampshire surge in popularity with independent voters, and Gore's revitalized campaign. Bradley's balloon soon deflated.

"If we had duplicated elsewhere the energy and organization Julian brought to our Alabama campaign, we might have had a better result," said Ed Turlington, Bradley's deputy national campaign manager.

On March 9, 2000, two days after the Super Tuesday primaries, Bill Bradley withdrew, conceding to vice-president Al Gore.

And Bradley's heart is still ticking.

June 6, 2000

Although disappointed by the premature ending to Bradley's campaign, Julian was pleased with the response of Alabamians to his effort.

After Bradley's withdrawal, Julian and Leslie qualified with the Alabama Democratic Party as candidates to be Gore-pledged delegates to the 2000 Democratic National Convention. Julian was one of sixteen male candidates and Leslie one of nineteen females vying for the two delegate slots of each gender from the Second Congressional District, which stretches across southeast Alabama from Montgomery to Dothan.

Julian failed to receive endorsements from the ADC and from New South, both of which picked black candidates. Still, he and Leslie ran a modestly budgeted campaign the final week before the election, with newspaper ads and ten-second TV spots bearing the slogan "The Lovable Couple."

"It was amazing," said Leslie, "what a spontaneous response we got to the 'Lovable Couple' ad, for so little money. Everywhere we went, people we knew and people we didn't know lit up with a smile and said, 'Oh, there's the Lovable Couple.'"

Even Judge Lynn Clardy Bright, in a speech to the Montgomery Bar Association, looked out at Julian with a wink and informed the audience that she and her husband, Mayor Bobby Bright, were a lovable couple, too.

"It showed me," said Julian, "how a short but positive message can reverberate quickly. The smiling, affectionate picture also helped."

On election day, June 6, Julian led Montgomery County's vote total with 2,421, ahead of the nearest challenger's 1,659. In the Second District as a whole, he came in second with 9,065 votes, ensuring him a spot in the delegation. Leslie, in her political debut, finished third among female candidates in Montgomery. But she didn't seem disappointed by the loss.

"Actually, it suits me fine," she commented. "I'm going to Los Angeles anyhow, and this way I'll get to spend more time sight-seeing with David and Grace."

In Los Angeles from August 13-19, in addition to attending the convention together, the McPhillips family visited the Universal Studios Park, Hollywood, the Getty Museum, and Disneyland, and the kids went surfing at Malibu Beach. By chance, both the Alabama and North Carolina delegations were sharing the same Hilton Hotel. Ed Turlington was a member of North Carolina's delegation and early on bumped into Julian and Leslie in the elevator and invited them to a Bill Bradley breakfast speech to the North Carolina delegation. The McPhillipses attended, and a grand reunion of

Julian, Leslie, and Grace, with Bradley, Turlington, and a few other key supporters ensued after the breakfast. Julian urged Bradley to remain active in public service and politics, reminding him how much he still has to offer America.

*JULIAN'S TRIP AS A MEMBER of the Alabama delegation to the 2000 Democratic National Convention did more than reunite him with his friend Bill Bradley and many others in the political arena. He came home from Los Angeles, he says, with renewed enthusiasm for the political process and the need for everyone to be involved. Typically, he clutched in his hands his own laundry list of analyses of some of the key issues facing his state and nation, and he said he was ready to do his part in addressing them. As we shall see in Part V of this revised edition, he set out to do so with a vigorous campaign for the U.S. Senate.

23

Ron Mays and the Arbitration Albatross

F EW SUBJECTS raise Julian McPhillips's ire as quickly as that of binding arbitration, which is being touted in some corners as a better alternative to traditional litigation.

His experience with the method has been otherwise, and he cites the case of plaintiff Ron Mays as the "best" bad example of arbitration in action.

In 1995, Mays—a successful salesman of copying machines for Lanier Business Products, and second cousin once removed of baseball great Willie Mays—came to Julian, claiming that new managers who had recently come in from Florida and New Jersey were encouraging an atmosphere of blatant racial discrimination and harassment at the *Fortune* Top 200 company.

It was a stark contrast to Mays's first year of employment, under native Alabama management, when he far exceeded his sales quotas and was rewarded with plaques, honors, and a trip to the Caribbean. In some months, Mays sold more copiers than the office's other twelve employees—all of whom were white—combined.

To say that the new managers got off on the wrong foot with Mays was an understatement. From the beginning, he said, they referred to him as "blue gum" and "the brotherman," and made monkey-like sounds behind Mays's back. Once, they invited him to go on a hunting trip with the other salesmen, joking that "you can be the target." To Mays, it wasn't funny.

Julian prepared a charge of discrimination and filed it with the Equal Employment Opportunity Commission, and sent a copy of the charge to Lanier with a letter suggesting the parties attempt to settle early on.

Lanier reacted by taking away much of Mays's geographical sales territory.

McPhillips responded by filing a "retaliation" charge with the EEOC, to which Lanier responded by treating Mays in such a "cold and hostile manner" that his sales declined. In June 1996, the company fired him, supposedly for non-performance.

As the case unfolded, Julian and law partner Kenneth Shinbaum learned that, unbeknownst to Mays, when he first came to work for Lanier in 1994, the employment agreement he signed contained a "mandatory arbitration" provision.

Shinbaum, after doing some research, concluded that their prospects looked bleak. He told Julian and Mays that, even if they contested the arbitration clause in court under then-existing laws, they would eventually lose in the Eleventh Circuit, after perhaps as much as two years of fighting the issue.

Reluctantly, Mays, McPhillips, and associate attorney Karen Sampson proceeded to arbitration and hoped for the best.

Their hopes were dashed pretty quickly. To begin arbitration, Mays had to pay the American Arbitration Association a filing fee of $3,600. (In federal court, the filing fee would have been only $150). Moreover, the daily bill of $2,000 for the arbitrators was split between Mays and Lanier. The prospect of paying $1,000 a day out-of-pocket was understandably daunting to Mays, but he was assured that the case would probably be finished in two days.

Instead, the Atlanta attorney representing the company stretched the trial into nine days, four of which he kept Mays on the witness stand, cross-examining him about matters that had happened fifteen years earlier.

"I objected and objected and objected," Julian recalls, "but the arbitrator's only reply was 'We'll give it the weight we think it deserves.' And the arbitrator didn't prohibit irrelevant questions or handle evidentiary matters the way a federal judge would have. It was obviously in the arbitrator's financial interest to keep the proceedings going."

By the time the hearing ended, Mays owed the American Arbitration Association $12,600. Then, the Atlanta attorney requested briefs based on transcripts of the hearing. The arbitrator complied, at a cost to Mays of an additional $8,500. By the time travel expenses for out-of-state witnesses and other discovery costs were added, Mays ended up owing some $23,000—win, lose, or draw.

For Julian and Karen Sampson, the only bright spot was that several of Mays's white co-workers confirmed the racist remarks and disparate treatment he claimed to receive from the new management. "We definitely expected to win," Julian says. But when the arbitrator rendered his verdict on September 1, 1997, he ruled against Mays on all of the issues.

"To borrow a phase from auto accident cases," Julian says, "we were 'knocked, shocked, bruised, and contused.' It was absolutely incomprehensible."

Mays, no stranger to the school of hard knocks, didn't take the affront sitting down. Actually, though, he *did* sit down—at his computer, where he spent countless hours on the Internet researching Lanier's relationship with the AAA. He was stunned to find that Lanier paid the Association a $10,000 initiation fee, plus thousands of dollars a year in subsequent fees—none of which had been disclosed to the plaintiff's side before the arbitration began.

"You can imagine the hue and cry that would be raised," Julian says, "if one side in a court case paid the judge money and the other side didn't. And even more so, if the Judge and the paying side kept it a secret from the non-paying side. It's totally ridiculous."

McPhillips and Sampson quickly filed a motion to set aside the arbitration award. Another lawsuit against Lanier, under another race discrimination theory, was hurriedly filed just before the two-year statute of limitations expired.

Lanier responded with denials of any wrongdoing, criticized Mays as being a bad sport for not accepting the arbitrator's decision, and filed a motion for summary judgment.

The conflicting motions of Mays and Lanier were deemed submitted to the U.S. District Court in December 1997. As of two and a half years later, the motions remain pending, with no decision released.

Julian estimates that between himself, Sampson, and two other lawyers in the firm, they put some 750 uncompensated hours into the case. And because Mays couldn't bear all the expenses himself, McPhillips and his firm "ate" some $7,000 of the court reporter's tab.

In September 1997, Mays also sued AAA and left them with an unpaid bill, though he'd already paid plenty earlier on, before the arbitrators' decision was released. He adamantly refuses to pay any more.

And so it stands.

"To say the whole thing has left a bitter taste in our mouths is an understatement," Julian says. "It's made me a fierce opponent of arbitration, whether it be in the setting of employment, consumer contracts, or insurance agreements.

"What it does is make 'double victims' out of consumers who have been defrauded—first they're victimized by the wrongdoing, and then victimized again by the arbitration process itself."

The possibility of strong legislation or a constitutional amendment at the state level, on the matter, doesn't look promising. Julian says, "What we've seen is the Alabama Supreme Court making law with egregiously anti-consumer and pro-big business decisions." Many of the justices, he adds, were elected with big business support.

"What we need is action in the federal arena, to outlaw binding arbitration—especially when it's imposed by a powerful party on a powerless party, as a condition to getting a job, buying a car, or having insurance coverage. What we need is strong legislation, and a U.S. president sensitive to the needs of working people, who won't veto it."

Many people, Julian says, confuse "arbitration" with "mediation," though the two are totally different. Mediation is non-binding, and Julian believes it's often helpful to both sides, because, even if the case eventually goes to court, those involved have a much clearer idea, going in, as to what all of their options are.

"Mediation is totally a voluntary matter, and that's the way it should be," he say. "But the right to a trial by jury is one of the most precious constitutional rights we have. And if we expect to keep this a free country, it's a right that's going to have to be preserved."

For the present, motorists can easily read Julian's position on the matter via the back bumpers of his and Leslie's vehicles: bold red, white, and black bumper stickers that trumpet ARBITRATION: A LICENSE TO STEAL.

24

Favorite Causes:
Church, Schools, Athletics, Missions

JULIAN's early-ingrained activism has found many outlets over the years, but most cluster around three main causes: education, sports, and church work, including the church's mission outreach.

Christ the Redeemer Episcopal Church

The title of the church retreat was "Curcillo No. 7," held at Camp McDowell in north Alabama in November 1979, and Julian's and Leslie's attendance proved a watershed event in their lives. The retreat was part of a "Renewal Movement" within the Episcopal church, which emphasized a much more enthusiastic—and less structured and sedate—approach to worship, including contemporary "praise music," and "a bolder sharing of one's witness."

As a result, Julian, Leslie, and other Montgomery-area Episcopalians were inspired, in November 1980, to form a new church based on the Renewal model. On January 7, 1981, it was officially named "Christ the Redeemer," a compromise between "Christ the King" and "Our Redeemer," and Julian and Leslie both took roles in its leadership. Both were on the vestry during Christ the Redeemer's first year, and one of the two have served on the vestry in every year since. Each has also served as senior warden at various times, and Leslie especially cherishes the time when members of the congregation referred to her as "the Angel of Mercy." Both Julian and Leslie had a leadership role in expanding the new sanctuary that was consecrated on Palm Sunday 1993.

From 1986 to 1994, Julian and Leslie enjoyed an especially close relationship with their second rector and his wife, Mark and Vicki Tusken. During those years, Julian says Christ the Redeemer was the fastest growing Episcopal

Church in the diocese of Alabama, by far.

In May 1999, Christ the Redeemer's third rector, Coleman Tyler and his family, left to do missionary work from a ship sailing to South America, Africa, and Eastern Europe. Leslie took over as senior warden, leading the church in what she describes as "a challenging time."

"We both feel like Christ the Redeemer is something we helped give birth to, and have helped raise," says Julian. "We think it has a great future. The healing ministry has been a real love and joy of ours. And we're forever in the church's debt, as it's been a wonderful place to raise our children, impacting them positively in so many ways."

When their daughter Rachel was a junior and senior in high school, Julian says, she and several of her friends (usually including Ann Mantooth, Darcy Johnson, Lisa Newman, and Sarah Thompson), could often be found at Christ the Redeemer singing spirituals, while friend Summer Whatley played the piano with gusto.

Daughter Grace took the leadership in her youth group in organizing mission trips to Central America during the summers of 1997 and 1998.

"Most Sundays, I get so high spiritually at Christ the Redeemer that it re-energizes me and renews me for the rest of the week," says Julian. "I can't overstate how much the church has meant to me and our family over the years. It's helped me develop a real 'love affair relationship' with our Lord, and that relationship doesn't just make a difference; it makes all the difference."

Princeton

When Julian and Leslie moved back to Montgomery in 1975, seven years after his graduation from Princeton, Julian was named Alumni Schools' committeeman for central Alabama, charged with recruiting Alabama high school students to attend Princeton. In the succeeding twenty-five years, he's recruited more than one hundred of them—many of whom say they would not have applied without Julian's influence.

The recruits included student athletes Farris Curry, Steve Stearns, and David Sawyer, all of Jefferson Davis High School in Montgomery, and Ed Bell and Rick McBride, Jr., of Montgomery Academy. Female recruits included academic standouts Barbara McElroy, Betsy Thaggard, Shannon Holliday, Terri Sewell, Susan Price, and others. Stearns is now Julian's stockbroker.

But in March 1993, Julian's devotion to Princeton became badly strained when the University's administration made a surprise announcement that it was closing down the sport of wrestling on the campus—"Lock, stock, and barrel," as Julian puts it. "They hadn't even consulted with anybody in the wrestling program beforehand: students, coaches, alumni. Nobody."

The day Julian found out, he settled in for a battle to make the administrators change their minds about the decision. The battle included drafting a lawsuit which he brought with him to his twenty-fifth reunion in June 1993. He hoped it would be unnecessary by then, but his hopes were dashed when a trustee subcommittee voted to uphold the original decision.

The lawsuit came out of Julian's briefcase, and unfiled copies were officially served on Princeton's president, vice-president, and athletic director just hours before a trustee meeting on the morning of June 7. When the trustees met, they backed off from the original plan and substituted a new one: to preserve varsity wrestling for a three-year "transitional period," after which they would institute club wrestling instead.

But during that time, Julian called a foul on the administration for stacking the deck against varsity wrestling, claiming that they "choked the program" by not admitting good wrestling prospects who were also top scholars. The program survived, Julian says, "but just barely." He and other alumni kept up their lobbying pressure, though, helped by their financial support for the program. In 1996, trustees voted to "continue varsity wrestling indefinitely," and Julian received congratulations from Clay McEldowney, Class of 1969 and president of the Friends of Princeton Wrestling, who credited Julian's 1993 lawsuit with turning the tide for Princeton wrestling's future.

St. James

Princeton isn't the only school benefitting from Julian's love of wrestling. In 1997, he launched a wrestling team at Montgomery's St. James School, which all three McPhillips children have attended. (Rachel and Grace both graduated from St. James before attending Elon College in North Carolina. As this book was published, David was beginning his fourth grade year.)

In 1997–98, Julian and Leslie gave $200,000 to triple the size of the school's original field house, now named "McPhillips Field House," in honor of Grace, Rachel, and David. Julian and Leslie have also financially assisted three other area high school wrestling teams, Robert E. Lee, Prattville, and Wetumpka. In addition, they've provided scholarships for minority students at St. James to help maintain diversity in the student body, and financially assisted the school's theater program while Grace was active in it.

St. Andrews — Sewanee

Julian's love of wrestling and his loyalty to his successor secondary school, St. Andrews-Sewanee, were both served when he chaired the campaign to raise $100,000 to renovate the wrestling facilities at the school. Contributing a good part of it himself, Julian was present in April 1999 for the dedication of wrestling room in honor of his beloved wrestling coach Bill Goldfinch.

Julian attended the predecessor school, Sewanee Military Academy from 1959 to 1964, years he thought would never end. SMA at the time, he says, was run like "West Point in the old days." The anti-military attitudes surrounding the Vietnam War cost SMA its cadet status by the late 1960s, and the school also became co-educational about the same time. As such, the new Sewanee Academy was no longer very different from its nearby rival St. Andrews. In 1977, Sewanee Academy merged with St. Andrews and a sister school St. Marys. The successor school's name since then has been St. Andrews-Sewanee. The new school assiduously courts the alumni of all three schools.

Elon College

Julian says that he and Leslie are feeling very much at home at Elon College, near Burlington, N.C., from which Rachel graduated and Grace is now attending. To show their appreciation, Julian and Leslie have made gifts to the college's new library and football stadium. "Elon is such a refreshing place to go to college," says Julian. "The students seem to be wholesome, genuine, and glad to be there. I think it's one of the best education bargains in America, and one of the best-kept secrets in the Southeast. Both our daughters have thrived there." Julian and Leslie have been members of the college's Parents Council since Rachel's freshman year in 1995 (she graduated with honors in 1999 and is now teaching at an elementary school in the Birmingham area) and are beginning their sixth straight year on the Council. Grace, now beginning her sophomore year, is (as was Rachel) on the Dean's List.

David Dixon McPhillips Memorial Scholarship

Julian and brother David Dixon McPhillips, twenty months younger, were very close. They shared a bedroom from 1948–1962, frequently talking one another to sleep as they exchanged hopes, dreams, and confidences. David's untimely death in 1976 is a wound Julian still feels.

In the early 1980s, in honor of his late brother, Julian began funding memorial scholarships, based on "Good Citizenship and Academic Excellence," at two of the schools David had attended in the mid-1960s: Montgomery's Sidney Lanier High, and Indian Springs School in Helena. The presentations of the awards each May, he says, are "satisfying, and very emotional, events." In the meantime, Julian and Leslie have contributed to launch the Loveless Academic Magnet Program (LAMP), a highly respected Montgomery public school program intended to challenge the brightest high school students.

Lake Martin and Gulf Shores

Since the early 1980s, Julian, Leslie, Rachel and Grace, joined by David in 1990, have frequently vacationed and relaxed at Lake Martin, thirty miles north of Montgomery, and at Gulf Shores Plantation, three and a half hours south. These times together have been wonderful rest and relaxation, re-energizing the family, and building bonds between its members. "We have a storehouse of wonderful memories in both places," says Leslie, " and we continue to be Lake and Beach people every chance we get."

"I can't wait to jump the waves on skis," says Julian, who was still doing that at age fifty-three in the summer of 2000. "Also mowing the lawn by the water is exceedingly therapeutic. I can feel myself unwinding. It restores my batteries."

Missionaries, Lions, and Columbians

In February 1994, Julian became a member of the Board of Trustees of the South American Missionary Society (SAMS), and he and Leslie spent a week in Honduras getting acquainted with the country's natives and missionaries. In the years since, he's become a member of the SAMS executive committee.

Julian says he's been inspired by the example of the group's executive director, the Rev. Tom Prichard, an active staff, and more than fifty SAMS missionaries who are working throughout Latin America.

In the summer of 1998, after Julian decided against a run for the U.S. Senate, he and his family traveled to South America to experience the Society's work first-hand and to support the organization's missionaries in Chile, Peru, and Bolivia. "It was really a time of faith-building for us," Julian recalls. "We got to pray and sing with South Americans in different languages. And when we had prayer gatherings, there were some astounding healings."

Although Julian isn't an ordained minister like his father, he's a vocal advocate of what he calls "the priesthood of all believers." "I think the ministry model is also very relevant to the practice of law," Julian says. "Sometimes the lay ministry offers greater opportunitues to reach people at their deepest spiritual and emotional levels in the workaday world."

Included in the workaday world is Julian's twenty-five years of membership in the Montgomery Lions Club. Over the years he's served variously as program chairman, a member of the board of directors, and helped organize the club's "Youth to Europe" committee.

"Dinner rolls no longer sail through the air like they did in the early days," he says. "But our camaraderie and humor encourage us for the approaching weekend."

One of the club's main projects is the annual Blue-Gray football game on Christmas Day. Julian's and Leslie's tickets to each game, and their invitations to the preceding dance, are preserved in their growing series of scrapbooks that fill most of a wall of shelves in their living room.

Finally, of all the academic experiences Julian had, none was more exhilarating than his three years at Columbia Law School in New York from 1968-1971.

While Julian has been more active as an alumus with his undergraduate alma mater, Princeton, he nonetheless contributes annually to Columbia Law School and returns for every five-year cycle reunion. He still stays in touch with some of his professors and fellow students.

Interlude

PeeWee's Case, Revisited

B Y THE end of August 1999, Julian is sure he's being stonewalled by the city's attorneys. His repeated re quests for discovery – in particular, a copy of Reginald's arrest report – have dragged on and on without compliance, for one excuse or another. He fires off a heated letter, and on September 9 finally gets what he's after.

Corporal DeJohn's typed, single-page report – officially stamped "Defendant's Exhibit 1" (when offered by the defense as evidence in open Court) – is headlined "Accident in Trenholm Court." Its preamble recounts that DeJohn and Steelman were patrolling the area when they got a radio message from another unit that "two black male subjects" had jumped out of their car when officers approached. Inside the car, the officers "located a quantity of marijuana that was packaged to sale." DeJohn and Steelman drove toward Trenholm to look for the fleeing suspects. The report continues,

> As we entered the housing area, Corporal Steelman observed a B/M standing in the 500 Blk of N. Union Circle. When the B/M observed our vehicle enter the housing area, he placed some unknown object down by the steps. We then made our way to the 500 Blk to interview the subject. As we brought our vehicle to a stop, the B/M took off running west-bound . . .

There follows a detailed description of which officers on foot approached from which directions, and the route the suspect took in order to evade them. DeJohn goes on,

This writer, used vehicle #2133 (1993 GMC Suburban) to go over the
curb to get closer to where Cpl. Steelman was attempting to take the subject
into custody. The B/M ran to my vehicle and began to run alongside of the
vehicle at the front quarter panel. The B/M had his left hand on the edge of the
hood on the right side. The B/M was looking over his shoulder at this writer
as I ordered him to stop.

I immediately began to apply the brakes. I could feel the brakes not
"grabbing" and began to slide. I then tried to turn my vehicle away from the
B/M. The B/M continued to step out in front, at which time he was struck by
the front right side of the vehicle. Also at this time, the vehicle struck a small
tree that was in the 500 Blk of N. Union Circle. At this time, I got out of the
vehicle to check on the subject. The B/M's first words he stated was, "That's
right, M — — F — — — , I'll get you, I'm going to sue you, bitch."

Paramedics and the Accident Investigations Unit were called to the scene.
Paramedics advised that his injuries were very minor but he was transported to
Baptist Hospital E.R.

**Steelman's report, (also offered as evidence in court) while much
shorter, is very similar, ending with:**

" . . . the subject was running toward me being chased by Cpl. Simmons.
I stopped and the defendant dodged me and continued running. The subject
then ran alongside Cpl. R.D. DeJohn's Suburban vehicle which jumped the
curb and was on the dirt area. At this time the subject tried to run around in
the front of DeJohn's vehicle and was struck by the vehicle. The Suburban slid
and hit a small tree.

**About this same time, Reginald's case took another strange
turn. He went outside one evening and found his car had been
stolen. He called and reported the theft to police. The two officers
who came to investigate apparently recognized Reginald from the
DeJohn case and, he says, they proceeded to harass him. "We know
who you are," he reported one officer as saying, "and you're not
going to get a dime out of the city."**

At a later Circuit Court hearing before Judge Tracey McCooey, on a motion filed by Julian to prevent continued harassment, the Circuit Court denied Reginald any relief. In open court, the Judge expressed her confidence that Montgomery police officers would do nothing to harm Mr. Jones.

IV.

Faith and Family

25

Signs, Wonders, and Miracles

FOR THE past decade, behind the scenes of politics and Julian's high-profile legal cases, a quieter force has come to play an increasingly significant role in his and Leslie's lives: charismatic worship and spiritual healings.

"It's not something we try to publicize, and it's not something we try to hide," Julian says. "It's just a part of who we are."

Though Julian remembers, while growing up, a number of cases of dramatic healings in his father's ministry, he thought them "just a result of Dad's being close to the Lord." But his and Leslie's first in-person encounter with a large-scale healing ministry was on their visit to Prague, capital of what is now the Czech Republic, in the spring of 1989. Though Mahesh Chavda's crusade had already moved on, the town was still a-buzz with accounts of massive healings in his audiences—ranging from the terminally ill, to people with long-term disabilities such as lameness, blindness, and deafness.

Afterwards, back home in Montgomery, they sought out information about Chavda's ministry—including his upcoming crusades in the U.S., one of which was scheduled in August at a black charismatic church in Atlanta.

"Mahesh preached that the healing came entirely from God," Julian remembers, "through the Holy Spirit. But he taught that there were barriers to the flow of such healing. The biggest barrier was 'doubt or unbelief,' and the next biggest was 'unforgiveness'—that is, if you don't forgive someone who's wronged you, it can block the flow of God's healing power in your own life.

"Forgiveness and healing are very closely linked, Mahesh said. And to the extent that a human being reflects God's compassion, and receives the anointing of the Holy Spirit, he or she can become a conduit for the flow of God's touch."

Both Julian and Leslie went forward to the altar for prayer after Chavda's message, with varying degrees of hesitancy. To their surprise, when Mahesh laid hands on them, each fell backwards on the carpet in a trancelike state of expanded consciousness that charismatic believers sometimes call being "slain in the Spirit," or "under the power of the Spirit."

It wasn't the couple's first encounter with the concept of spiritual healing. In February 1989, before their trip to Prague, healing evangelist Darlene Sizemore had preached at Christ the Redeemer Episcopal Church. Though they found her message of interest, Julian says, nothing unusual in the physical realm occurred during that visit.

"Maybe she was just warming up," Julian says. "Because when Darlene came back in September of that same year, about a month after we had met Mahesh, there were many dramatic healings when she laid hands on people. Folks were being slain in the Spirit, right and left. Some of the healings were physical, but many were emotional, having to do with personal relationships. A woman who hadn't spoken to her mother in years quickly reconciled. A divorced couple came back together.

"And there was a seventeen-year-old girl, who'd been badly injured in an automobile accident the year before and was still suffering chronic pain, and suddenly she was pain-free. The people who were there, that night, took notice. *Big* notice. Especially the other kids."

The next summer, Julian, Leslie, and five other members of Christ the Redeemer, including their friend and rector Mark Tusken, attended the "World Conference on Evangelism and the Holy Spirit" in Indianapolis. The conference drew some 25,000 "charismatically inclined" Christians from a broad range of denominations. About half of the participants were Roman Catholic, and Episcopalians were a one-tenth minority; the Montgomery group were the only Episcopalians from Alabama attending.

There, they met evangelist John Wimber, founder of California-based Vineyard Ministries. Wimber arranged a gathering of some five thousand people in a designated "Non-Denominational Room." After a message, he encouraged others in the room to lay hands on people nearby for prayer and healing of various physical ailments. Standing nearest Julian and Leslie was a Latvian immigrant who had been deaf in one ear for a number of years. The McPhillipses laid hands on him and prayed for him, and "the next thing we knew," Julian says, "he was jumping for joy. His hearing had returned. His nephew, a Catholic priest standing adjacent to his uncle, confirmed for us that the Latvian immigrant had long been deaf in that ear.

"I guess you could say Leslie and I were 'amazed, but not surprised,'" Julian says. "Miracles were happening all over."

At another session, Julian and Mark Tusken were set up as a team in the Episcopal Room to administer communion and lay hands on people during prayer. "The first seven people we prayed for just fell over under the power of the Spirit," Julian remembers. "They never introduced themselves to us by name, and we never knew the details of what had happened, but Mark and I agreed that the Holy Spirit was unquestionably in the room."

Julian recalls two dramatic healings much closer to home, in the fall of 1991. One morning in September, his receptionist, Pam Billingsley, was sobbing and clearly distraught. Her father, who was only forty-two years old, had just been told that he had advanced cancer in three different organs, and the doctors were predicting he didn't have long to live.

Soon after, when Julian's parents came to Montgomery for a Sunday visit, "I asked my father if he'd go with me to Baptist Hospital to see Scott Billingsley, and he agreed.

"When we got there, Scott was very humble and very grim. But he managed a weak smile and told us that he was ready to go home to be with the Lord, but that he was still praying God would spare him some more time with his children." Julian Jr. and Julian Sr. asked if they could pray for him. "We laid hands on Scott and prayed as earnestly as we knew how for God to heal him," the younger Julian remembers. "Suddenly there was this spine-tingling sensation, and we all knew—Scott included—that the Holy Spirit was all over us."

By Monday, Billingsley was feeling much better. A subsequent series of tests, Julian says, could not find the multiple cancers that had been diagnosed earlier. Scott was discharged from the hospital, and within a week was back at work. A year later, he led his daughter Pam down the aisle to marry Blake Trammer, an investigator with the Montgomery County District Attorney's office. Nine years later, Scott Billingsley is still cancer-free.

The next dramatic healing was of Julian himself. Earlier in 1991, he had developed serious bursitis in his right heel, the same ankle in which he'd torn several ligaments when he broke his leg wrestling some twenty-five years earlier. His podiatrist, Dr. Allen Stern, twice X-rayed the foot. Both times, the news wasn't good, confirming an advanced case of bursitis. Surgery would be risky and painful. Likewise for cortisone shots. The only other option, Stern said, was to wrap the injury in an Ace bandage and learn to live with it.

Julian chose Option Three, and though he asked various members of the congregation to pray for him, the foot gradually worsened—substantially hampering his daily running program, and threatening to stop it altogether.

One day in October 1991, a new client came to Julian—Norman Williams, a black minister in his early forties, who said he had been mistreated by Montgomery police while taking a church youth group to the State Fair. (The police said they thought Williams was a gang member because he wore a leather jacket with an L.A. Kings emblem and a knitted cap pulled low on his forehead.)

"It was a time of 'galloping gang-ophobia,' to coin a phrase," Julian recalls. "The police thought gangs were everywhere." The fact that the police incident occurred during a church outing was especially ironic in Rev. Williams's case. As Julian would later learn, Williams, a Montgomery native who had moved to Los Angeles and drifted into the drug culture, had a dramatic conversion story of his own. During a visit back to Montgomery because of his mother's illness, he had had a vision. "I knew that if I went back to my old ways I would die," Norman remembers. "The Lord spoke to me and told me he had plans for me: a ministry of healing and prophecy."

When the police at the fairgrounds ordered Williams to take off his cap, he refused. "I told them I'd just gotten over the flu, and it was freezing out there. There was no reason for me to take off my cap." While the young people in his group looked on, the officers roughed Norman up and took him to jail, where he was charged with disorderly conduct and resisting arrest.

"I remember how much it meant to our family," Julian says, "when people would give my dad a 'minister's discount.' So I represent ministers at a special discount—in general, little or no charge."

While Williams's criminal defense was being prepared, and Julian's bursitis kept worsening, one day he asked Norman ("I'm not quite sure why," Julian says) exactly what kind of minister he was. Williams handed him a card that read "Living Waters Pentecostal Church: Ministry of Prophecy and Healing."

"I believe in spiritual healing, too," Julian told Norman. "Would you mind praying for my foot?"

Williams recounts the event with clear relish, laughing and clapping his hands. "I knew he was serious," Norman says, "because he took off his shoe and sock, right there at his desk, and went to rolling up his britches leg. There wasn't anything proud about him, amen."

With a firm grip on Julian's foot, Norman began to pray. "I immediately felt heat all over my right foot," Julian says. "And the heat continued throughout the day, even after Norman had left. That night, my foot was ninety-nine percent better. And by the next morning, it was one hundred percent."

He says there's been no recurrence since. "Praise the Lord," Julian says. "The credit and glory all go to God, but the healing was a big spiritual boost not just for me, but for Norman, as well."

Norman Williams was later acquitted of the misdemeanor charges in Municipal Court.

In 1993, Julian and Leslie decided it was time to bring Mahesh Chavda to Montgomery. They assembled a steering committee, which included Norman Williams, Montgomery County Jail chaplain Tom Bridges, local minister Carmen Falcione, Montgomery physician Teresa Allen (who often prays with her patients and has a sign in her office stating "Jesus, name above all names") Rev. Clifford Terrell of Gospel Tabernacle Church, Rev. John Alford of Mt. Gillard Baptist Church, Methodist minister Dick Johns, Prattville AME Zion minister R. L. Robinson, Andalusia printer George Payne, and sisters Elon Steinberg and Meg Crawford. Four members of Christ the Redeemer also had leadership roles: Col. Joe Guillot, retired Col. Doug Cairns, Ann O'Ferrell, and Kay Dickey. Organizational sessions were combined with prayer meetings beginning that summer of '93 at the McPhillipses' home. By the coming February 1994, with Julian and Leslie donating the majority of the organizational and promotional costs, with help from George Payne, Julian felt that the local terrain had been "softened and prayed over thoroughly."

Some three thousand people attended Mahesh's 1994 weekend sessions. "Montgomery," Julian says, "had never seen anything like it. People all around were being slain in the Spirit and healed. Rev. Alford went out under the power and had a substantial healing of his heart, on which he'd previously had surgery." Rev. Forrest Mobley and his wife Nancy brought their daughter Allison and their blind one-year-old granddaughter Alie. Young mother

Allison and baby Alie "fell back under the power," Julian says, and were caught and gently laid on the floor by their grandparents. An ophthalmologist later determined that young Alie would not only be able to read, but could read fine print. Six years later, Alie was the best reader in her first-grade class.

"It was amazing," says Julian. "People with scoliosis, broken bones, cancers, and depression, were healed. Jim Sexson, a State Capitol policeman suffering from kidney dysfunction, came forward for prayer. Over a six-month period, Sexson's kidneys went from totally non-functional, with dialysis required every two hours, to one hundred percent functional. They performed surgery to remove his catheter, which was then unnecessary, and Sexson went back to work."

Chavda referred to the healings as "power evangelism," and said that he was only the tool for "imparting the anointing"—"anointing" being a biblical term for spiritual gifts or presence of the Holy Spirit. "He made it clear you didn't have to be a superstar to pray for, and see, healings," Julian says. "Average, ordinary people like us could do it. And we were all eager to receive the anointing and pray to help others."

Not long after Mahesh's visit, Julian had a chance to try the "gifts" Mahesh had imparted. Aaron Luck, a young law clerk at the firm, came into Julian's office and asked if he could go home because of a seious migraine headache—a problem he'd had sporadically since childhood, but which lately was recurring every couple of weeks.

"I had no problem with him going home," Julian recalls, "but I asked in a low-key way if he would mind me praying for him, and Aaron was willing. I placed my hand on his head and said a short prayer, invoking the name of God the Father, the Son, and the Holy Spirit to heal Aaron's headache."

Afterward, Aaron opened his eyes and grinned. "What did you do?" he said.

"I didn't do anything," Julian beamed, "but apparently God did." Luck, who became an associate attorney with the firm in 1997, has not had a return of the migraines in the six years since.

Luck remembers when the headaches first began in elementary school. He would know one was on the way, as he once told his mother, when the chalkboard "wouldn't line up straight."

"It's like my eyesight would break into strips, like glass or a mirror," he explains, "and the strips would slide out of alignment, leaving straight edges looking jagged. The medicine would help, but nothing ever got rid of them until Julian laid his hand on me. I haven't had another headache since that day. It's something I have no rational explanation for."

Other healings began to occur. Julian's partner William Gill was experiencing severe pain as a result of a lifting injury. "William and I prayed together, and the next day he said his back was ninety percent better, and the severe pain had vastly subsided." Then, law clerk Jim Bodin's wife, Mary, went into the hospital for a non-elective hysterectomy. But she suffered from a severe viral infection that wouldn't break, which delayed the much-needed surgery. Julian and two law clerks, Kay Dickey and Angela Key, went with Jim to Baptist Hospital and prayed for Mary. The infection soon disappeared. Mary had the surgery, and Julian is now trying to help the couple find an adoptive baby. Jim and Kay later became attorneys with the firm, and remain so as of mid-2000, when this book went to press.

Various other healings have occurred in the firm—of employees, says Julian, and occasionally of clients. Julian prayed by long-distance phone with long-time client Johnny Reynolds, then in Huntsville, who was suffering an excruciating migraine headache pain. Johnny reported immediate, instant relief. Till this day, he chuckles in recounting the incident. "It was better than going to the doctor," he says.

Mahesh Chavda came back to Montgomery in February 1996, this time with his wife and ministry partner Bonnie. Again, the healings were reported to be widespread.

Julian recalls: "Two women at Christ the Redeemer were released from deep emotional bondages. A young investment banker with cancer went into remission, a Nashville businessman regained his hearing, and people were released from arthritis and depression. At one of the sessions at the Governor's House Hotel, a lady who had been blind for years began to see. And at the opening night services at Gospel Tabernacle, Lynette Poulos, a young woman with a painful TMJ condition, was called by Mahesh to come to the altar for prayer for her problem, and the disorder was immediately healed. Those were exciting times. Again, after Mahesh left, Tom Bridges, Cliff Terrell, and I started organizing periodic healing services at Gospel Tabernacle Church in downtown Montgomery. The anointing was still strong, and spirits were touched and bodies healed."

The dramatic events were not without their lighter moments. Three days after Mahesh's 1996 visit, Julian was at Christ the Redeemer for Ash Wednesday services, after a fever of 102 degrees had broken not long before. There, he saw member Kelly O'Ferrell on crutches. She had tripped over a kneeler on the floor, after leaving the altar where Mahesh prayed for her, and X-rays the next day showed she had broken her ankle.

Julian shook his head at the irony of it, and repeated to her one of his favorite quotes about spiritual matters: "Kelly, you know 'God don't leave no spilt milk.' Would you come to the altar and let me pray for you?" She accepted. Julian felt no particular "flow of the Spirit" as he had on other occasions, and was still suffering the after-effects of the fever. But Kelly later reported feeling heat throughout her ankle at the time Julian prayed. Still on crutches, Kelly thanked him, but otherwise didn't comment, and went home.

The next morning, Kelly recalls, she woke to find the pain and swelling in her foot gone. She went back to the doctor, who X-rayed the foot again, and this time it showed no fracture. She then called Julian, and many others, to tell what happened, and also gave her testimony about the incident at Christ the Redeemer.

A banker friend of Julian and Leslie, Andy Hardin, who lived just down the street and had served several years as a member of the board of the Scott and Zelda Fitzgerald Museum, was diagnosed with colon cancer. Julian had urged Andy to come to "Mahesh II," as the 1996 conference was later dubbed, but Hardin opted for conventional medical treatment. After surgery and radiation, his cancer was apparently gone. But in September he experienced severe abdominal pain. A medical exam showed that the cancer had metastasized and spread, leaving eight deep cancerous lesions in his liver. Doctors gave him only weeks to live.

In October, Julian received a call from Dr. Rodney Dorand, a fellow member of the Fitzgerald board and a friend of both his and Hardin's. In an emotional tone of voice, Dr. Dorand told Julian he worried that Andy wouldn't make it back alive from the Johns Hopkins Hospital in Baltimore, one of several facilities where Hardin had received treatment. Adding to his grief was the fact that Andy had a young wife in her twenties, a Finnish immigrant, and two sons aged six months and two years. Dorand asked Julian if he had any ideas, and suggested that Julian pray for Hardin.

Andy, deeply despondent and grasping for straws, accepted Julian's invitation to come to services at Christ the Redeemer the next day, a Sunday, to receive special prayers for healing. When the service was over, Julian, Kay Dickey, and Ann O'Ferrell (Kelly's mother) joined Andy and his wife Sone in a side prayer room, off the main sanctuary. "We all felt it," Julian recalls. "That spine-tingling sensation when you know something is happening." Sure enough, Julian received a call from Andy the following week saying his local physician could find no trace of the various cancers.

The Montgomery doctor urged Andy to return to the M. D. Anderson Cancer Clinic in Houston, where he had been treated earlier, to have more tests done. Doctors there confirmed the cancer was gone, Julian says, and couldn't believe the healthy-looking Hardin was the same patient they'd treated months before. The only rational explanation they could give was that the earlier tests "must have been flawed."

Though overjoyed at his remission, Andy was troubled by a recurring question: Why had the healing worked for him, but not for many other patients? "The only thing I could tell him," Julian says, "is that questions like that are in God's realm, not ours. Of course, not everybody who's prayed for is healed. But there are times, in the late twentieth century, when people reach out through prayer and faith to figuratively 'touch the hem of Jesus's garment,' as the scripture recounts, and receive a miraculous healing.

"Mahesh's reply to the same question is that 'only God is God.' And I've come to believe that the ultimate 'healing' is when we leave this life and move into God's realm of knowledge and wisdom, which are infinitely greater than ours."

In 1997, attorney Aaron Luck was suffering from the second of three ailments that Julian and his co-workers prayed for. Luck, a former wrestling champion of Great Britain and no stranger to injuries, developed a herniated disc in his back that would require surgery. Julian, Kay Dickey, and Karen Sampson prayed with Aaron at the office. By the next day the pain was substantially gone and the surgery became unnecessary.

Two years later, in 1999, after suffering spells of weakness, Aaron went to the doctor for tests, which showed adult-onset diabetes. This time Aaron asked Julian if he could come to Christ the Redeemer that Sunday. He came and Ann O'Ferrell and Kay Dickey (referred to by Julian as his "sisters-in-the-Lord") joined Julian in praying for him. "The Holy Spirit was on us," Julian says. "More tests, days later, showed that Aaron did have diabetes, but he would be able to control it with exercise and diet, rather than requiring insulin injections, as had first been diagnosed.

"Aaron sometimes jokes that, 'At this firm, you don't need health insurance. You just get somebody to pray for you.'"

In recent years, Julian has had more experiences with the healing of migraine headaches. After Luck's migraines went away, Julian prayed with four people in a row, including a client's wife, Inez Berkowitz, and two handymen, Jimmy Lowery and Robert Ammons. Lowery came to Julian's home on Christmas Eve, 1997, for prayer. Like many others, Jimmy reports no recurrence of the migraines since then.

Julian's scrapbook continues to fill with personal notes from acquaintances, and even strangers, reporting successful healings.

One such note is from Joe Poole, a Montgomery attorney who was suffering from multiple myeloma, or cancer of the bone marrow, in October 1998. Poole was not getting much response from traditional chemotherapy, and asked Julian to come to his home and pray for him.

Poole reported that he "felt God's presence" when Julian placed hands on him and prayed, and that two weeks later some sixty percent of his myeloma cells were destroyed, even though his medication had been reduced by half. A few weeks later, the level of destroyed cells raised to eighty percent.

Poole's vastly improved health allowed him to engage in ministry work in state prisons. A year later, his myeloma cells began increasing again, and he again invited Julian out to lay hands on him and pray. And again, within a month, eighty percent of the malignant cells were destroyed.

In his December 1999, letter of gratitude, Joe wrote Julian that "God is truly working in many ways through you."

Also in the fall of 1999, Julian received a letter on the letterhead of Long Leaf Lumber Company, Inc., of Chatom, Alabama. A woman named Susan Wilcox Turner reported that, "Early this spring, I met you and your prayer group on Palm Sunday, after the service (at Christ the Redeemer Episcopal Church), when you prayed for me. I was a frightened woman who was about to begin testing to see whether or not I had breast cancer. I am happy to tell you now that it was pronounced benign several weeks later."

The letter continues, "I apologize for taking so long to write this thank-you letter to you, but it is sometimes hard for me to discuss issues of faith. But I must tell you that as scared as I was that day while you and others were praying for me, I felt a numbing, cold sensation run through my body to the lump of tissue. I do not know whether or not it was a cancer that was cured at that moment, but I do know that I felt a sense of peace that I had not felt, and an astonishment that something so powerful, so out of my control, had just happened to me.

"I have barely been able to talk to even my husband about this, so amazing it seemed at that moment . . . I pray for all of you who took me in, a stranger, and prayed for my healing. You were the hands and eyes and heart of our Savior that day, and I pray that God's blessings will follow you always. Thank you."

"THE GIFT IS CERTAINLY NOT something I advertise," Julian says. "I'm reticent to talk about it too much because I certainly don't want anybody to think I'm taking credit for it. But I feel moved to share some of the episodes as a testimony of faith, to encourage people.

"I try to be very careful and sensitive to suggest prayer only in cases when the need is great, and when the person seems to be receptive. I tell him or her that the prayer approach might be unorthodox, but it's certainly not unprofessional—especially when good results follow. In fact, I believe that many legal problems, like many health problems, have a spiritual base. Getting to the spiritual 'root' can often ease a situation in more ways than one."

Partner William Gill, Julian says, also credits prayer with his clients as a major factor in a recent good outcome in a case. Occasionally, Julian's secretary and receptionist receive calls from strangers who want to see Julian, not for legal representation, but for prayer.

Mahesh Chavda visited Montgomery for a third time in February 1999, and dramatic healings again resulted, Julian says, including two people who "stood in" at the prayer line for loved ones with cancer who were too ill to attend. One woman in her early fifties asked for prayer for her mother's leukemia. That weekend, up in Birmingham, her mother's leukemia count dropped drastically. A college student from Auburn stood in for his girlfriend in New Jersey who had a brain tumor, and afterwards the tumor shrank significantly.

"One of the many rewarding things about 'Mahesh III,'" Julian says, "is that in addition to people involved in organizing earlier conferences, many new people participated, such as attorney Corky Hawthorne and Morning Apperson of Prattville. They all played a leadership role in making the 'Healing the Nations' conference a success."

Again, Julian covered the conference's organizational and promotional expenses. "But whenever Mahesh comes to town," he says, "for some reason our firm's revenues always go up. I don't consider it a coincidence, but rather a 'God-incidence.' It's all about stewardship. When you give to God, God always gives back to you, even more than you gave."

Julian has never claimed one hundred percent success in prayers for healing, and he has never kept a count. "It's not mine to claim," he says. "'Only God is God,' and to Him be all the glory, credit, and praise. Sometimes the greatest healing, reflecting divine wisdom, is when God calls us home, to 'greater life,' beyond the grave, in that realm we traditionally call heaven. God's healing power is not something you can just 'turn on and off,' like a water faucet. But often I am amazed, humbled, and overwhelmed to experience God's dramatic touch, suddenly healing people of cancer, diabetes, bulging discs, migraine headaches, and the like."

Although evangelical and charismatic-leaning, Julian stresses that he's also ecumenical, believing that "we must emphasize the central nuggets of truth in all Christian denominations, minimize our differences, and maintain a healthy respect for other world religions, as a necessary foundation to spreading the Christian gospel.

"To a certain extent the Christian faith is like a cake, and all the denominations have simply decorated it with different types of icing. Unfortunately, sometimes the icing of cultural differences obscures the more important central truths.

"I'm often dismayed with the 'political correctness' and 'spiritual correctness' doctrines, found equally on both the left and right of political and religious thought," says Julian, "We need far greater respect and tolerance in this world, allowing for a healthy diversity of opinion. To do otherwise is pharisitical, judgmental, and setting yourself up for a great big fall. "

26

Unborn Children, Mahesh, and David

IN THE center of an otherwise empty courtroom, members of a television crew make final adjustments to their cameras and lighting before signaling the director, who stands to one side with clipboard and headphones, that the equipment is ready and they're standing by. He raises a hand in the air with his pointing finger extended.

And three, the director says, *and two, and* . . .

When the hand drops, a young female reporter walks slowly from off-camera into the blaze of lights that reflect from the dark oak and polished brass of the judge's bench.

"It's a new strategy in the attempt to stop abortion," the reporter says into the lens. "Get the fetus a lawyer. That's what Montgomery County Circuit Judge Mark Anderson did."

"It happened in July [1998]. A seventeen-year-old girl appeared in court asking for permission to have an abortion. She had to do so because she wanted it without her parents' consent. Judge Anderson appointed an attorney to represent the girl. But in a surprising move, he also named a lawyer to represent the *fetus*."

"Montgomery attorney Julian McPhillips has tried, on behalf of his unborn 'client,' to block the abortion. The judge's action has drawn fire from supporters of abortion rights. Michele Wilson is the coordinator of Alabamians for Choice . . ."

At the public television studio, a technician cues up the video of the prerecorded interview, and the scene on the monitor shifts to the face of a woman sitting in a paneled office, her name superimposed at the bottom of the screen.

"I think it would really be a mess," says Wilson, who is a Ph.D. and a sociology professor at a state university. "It would certainly employ a lot of attorneys, but I think that we're really getting into the idea that *potential* life can have more rights than an individual who is presently living and breathing, and trying to go about living her life. I think that it's probably an unforeseen precedent in terms of legal history, and I think that it's probably not a *good* precedent . . ."

ON A SATURDAY afternoon of the following spring, with a warm mist of rain falling, McPhillips pulls his car off the busy Montgomery thoroughfare into the edge of a retail parking lot and lowers his driver-side window. "This is one of two we've done, over the years," he says, pointing to the billboard above. "The message changes from time to time, but the theme is the same."

In stark black-and-white, the sign features a drawing of a fetus inside the uterus, alongside the text, "Before I formed thee in the womb, I knew thee . . . (Jeremiah 1:5)" A telephone number for Sav-a-Life is listed below. (The other billboard reads, "Abortion Stops a Beating Heart: Please consider the Alternatives, Including Adoption." The same telephone number appears).

"The people at Sav-A-Life tell us they've had a very good response, that a number of women have come in because of the billboard and changed their minds and not had an abortion," he says. "We help support Sav-A-Life as well." The organization, which has its local headquarters in a residential building nearby, provides counseling for pregnant girls and women who are considering an abortion. The counselors' purpose is to urge them instead to put their babies up for adoption, and they pave the way with referrals to adoption agencies.

Though many people in the city were surprised when Judge Anderson appointed an advocate for an anonymous teenager's unborn baby—an event that made national headlines—nobody who knew McPhillips was surprised at the judge's choice of attorney. He's possibly the area's most high-visibility figure in the pro-life arena, with a successful record of defending anti-abortion protesters who are arrested outside city clinics—ironically, under the same ordinances that have been used in the past against civil rights demonstrators. McPhillips has also sued abortion clinics and off-duty police officers for mistreatment of sidewalk "counselors."

"BUT OTHER people," the TV reporter continues, "argue that a fetus, though unseen by the naked eye, deserves legal protection."

"John Eidsmoe, a law professor at Jones School of Law in Montgomery, considers himself pro-life . . ."

Eidsmoe, an affable-looking man with short gray hair, is saying: "I think all of the evidence, to me, indicates that an unborn child is a living human being. The fact is, the child has a heartbeat that can even be heard on an electrocardiogram within four to five weeks after its conception, brain waves within a short time after that, and a DNA and RNA which, from the moment of conception, are distinct from the mother and father—clearly, its own genetic makeup. All of these things, particularly when taken together, indicate to me that the unborn child is, in fact, a living human being."

The TV reporter returns to the screen. "Judge Anderson's decision to appoint an attorney for the fetus," she says, "was the first of its kind in Alabama, and possibly the first in the country. He based his decision on a civil procedure rule allowing judges to appoint guardians for children or others considered incompetent.

"Known as Rule '17-C,' it also says, 'When the interest of an infant unborn or unconceived is before the court, the court may appoint a guardian *ad litem* . . . meaning, 'under the law' . . . of such interests."

"Experts say this portion of the rule is rarely used. And in doing so, supporters of abortion rights accuse Judge Anderson of forsaking sound legal judgment, instead using his own beliefs about abortion for making his decision—in other words, judicial activism."

The screen dissolves to video footage of Anderson, on the bench in his black robe, wearing a serious expression and writing notes on a legal pad.

The scene is replaced by Dr. Wilson speaking again:

"He was going beyond what the law in Alabama has generally been interpreted as being," she says, "and I think most judges have certainly not seen a problem with this in the past. But this judge went out of his way . . ."

"But John Eidsmoe," says the reporter's voice-over, "counters that the *real* judicial activism came when the U.S. Supreme Court effectively legalized abortion in the landmark 1973 case of *Roe v. Wade* . . ."

"What Justice Blackmon says in *Roe v. Wade*," Eidsmoe argues, "is that the right to choose your 'lifestyle' includes the right to decide whether or not to have an abortion. You see, I think *that's* judicial activism in the *extreme*.

"But I'd also add that there is really nothing in Judge Anderson's ruling that would directly contradict that. Nothing in *Roe v. Wade* says that the unborn child cannot have any legal rights that the state wants to establish, and nothing in Roe v. Wade says that Judge Anderson could not appoint a guardian *ad litem* to represent whatever legal rights that unborn child may have."

THOUGH McPhillips's anti-abortion stand is a strong — and at times, emotional — one, his viewpoint didn't come in some road-to-Damascus-type of experience, but instead gradually over more than a decade.

"I was just out of law school when *Roe v. Wade* was handed down," he says, "and there was such a turmoil of events going on in public life at that time . . . the war in Vietnam, the civil rights movement, all kinds of dramatic and historic social changes . . . that I didn't give a great deal of thought to the Supreme Court's decision, one way or another."

But as anyone in America who has paid at least passing attention to the daily news in the years since is aware, the landmark decision didn't settle the issue. To the contrary, it gradually polarized the moral and political debate over abortion into, arguably, the most strident and divisive of the nation's current social issues.

Even the central figure in the case has, herself, switched sides. Known originally in the lawsuit as "Jane Roe" (a female variant of "John Doe") for protection of her privacy, Norma McCorvey came forward publicly, after the victory, to serve as symbol of the pro-choice movement. In 1980—the same year that her case was the subject of a television movie—the Texas native wrote an autobiography titled *I am Roe: My Life, Roe v. Wade, and Freedom of Choice*. (Despite the tremendous publicity the case has drawn over the years, relatively few people know that McCorvey never had the abortion that she sought. At age twenty-one, in her third pregnancy, she gave birth to a girl, who was given up for adoption).

In *I am Roe*, she tells the story of a nightmarish childhood and adolescence. A ninth-grade dropout, she suffered physical and emotional abuse as a child, was raped as a teenager, spent time in a Gainesville, Texas, reform school, married an abusive husband at age sixteen, and endured long periods of alcohol and drug abuse. Her first child was raised by McCorvey's mother, her second by the child's father, and the couple who adopted her infant agreed that McCorvey would never have contact with her again. Her jobs were nearly all the dead-end variety, including bar-tending and working as a carnival barker.

But in 1995, at the age of forty-eight, McCorvey made a 180-degree turn. She was working at a Dallas women's clinic when the anti-abortion group called Operation Rescue moved its offices next door, and she often shouted insults at protesters picketing the clinic. Despite the edgy situation, she gradually became acquainted with the group's director, the Rev. Phillip Benham, who was also an evangelical minister. He introduced her to other staff members of Operation Rescue, and eventually talked her into attending church with them. That night she converted to Christianity, and shortly afterward Benham baptized her in the swimming pool of a private home in Dallas. The ceremony was filmed and widely shown on national television. She accepted a job as a computer operator at Operation Rescue, and often speaks publicly on the issue of abortion.

In the years since, Benham has compared her influence to that of Harriet Beecher Stowe, whose novel *Uncle Tom's Cabin* brought higher visibility to the question of slavery.

In retrospect, the lead attorney in McCorvey's case, Sarah Weddington, says she should have picked a different plaintiff, one who was more representative of the "average women" who seeks an abortion. But in the larger view, Weddington reflects, "Nobody ever said, 'I believe what Norman McCorvey said,' or 'I believe what Sarah Weddington said.' Abortion is something people make up their own minds about."

As did Julian. He says that by paying attention to news coverage on the subject—including evidence given by a range of experts in the field of medicine, ethics, philosophy, law, and theology—he came to side more and more with the "anti" camp. But it wasn't until the 1980s that the issue of abortion became more for him than a matter of conscience, and one that would forever alter the lives of himself and his family.

His and Leslie's first daughter, Rachel, was born in 1977. Grace followed in 1981, when Leslie was thirty-three years old and Julian thirty-four. "Leslie and I are both family-oriented people," he says, "and we knew that we wanted to have more children." In 1985, they were excited when Leslie became pregnant again. But after about three months, she suffered a miscarriage. In 1987, the same thing happened again, and with each advancing year their hope of having another child seemed less and less likely.

They consulted specialists and sought solace from their friends and their church community. During that time, both Julian and Leslie had separate experiences they felt were divinely inspired. Leslie, on a routine drive from Birmingham to Montgomery, received a "strong confirmation" that they would have a third child, and that it would be a boy. Julian, during a morning jog through their neighborhood, had a remarkably similar experience ("which I firmly believe was from the Holy Spirit," he says) but with the added element that the child's name should be David—the name of both a favorite uncle from New Orleans and of Julian's younger brother, who had taken his own life.

But a year passed, and then two, and nothing changed. It was during a trip to Eastern Europe in May 1989, when Julian and Leslie visited Prague, capital of what is now the Czech Republic, that they first heard of Mahesh Chavda. They learned by word of mouth that a Christian evangelist who had visited the city just weeks earlier had an international faith-healing ministry. Each night of Chavda's crusade in the former communist capital, many extremely ill people had reportedly experienced miraculous healings. Such an occasion was all the more remarkable because the Czechoslovakian government at the time officially frowned on public religious events.

At the time, Julian and Leslie had no idea what a pivotal role Chavda would come to play in their lives.

MAHESH CHAVDA had come to the Christian ministry by a highly unlikely route. Born in Kenya in 1946, of Hindu parents from India, Mahesh came to Texas in 1964 for college and later became an American citizen. In his memoir *Only Love Can Make a Miracle*, Chavda tells of his childhood in Mombasa, Kenya, where his father was a civil servant in the British colonial government.

Though it was uncommon for a boy of his age, Mahesh spent a great deal of time in the local Hindu temple: bowing before the sacred images, burning incense, and asking questions of the priests. "Yet the more deeply I delved into Hinduism," Mahesh writes, "the more I found its truth to be like smoke: something that seemed to be there until I reached out and tried to lay hold of it. When I did, it simply disappeared. It was interesting intellectually. But there seemed to be no *reality* to it."

As a teenager, Mahesh excelled at studying English in school—so much so, in fact, that he began to think and dream in English rather than his native *Gujarati* dialect. "As awkward as it was, in family situations," he recalls, "my 'second language' had become my first." About that time, a female Baptist missionary from Texas came through the neighborhood inviting children to an afternoon reading of Bible stories.

His family tradition obliged him to be polite, and Mahesh felt respect for someone committed enough to her religion to give up the comforts of home and move to a foreign country, but at first he wasn't buying her message. "The gods of Hinduism had lost their meaning for me," he says, "and I had no wish to trouble myself over this God of the West." Upon leaving, the woman gave him a copy of the New Testament and asked him to read it.

Mahesh did, and described it as a tremendously moving spiritual experience. "All my life," he writes, "I had understood truth to be something abstract and impersonal. Now, it came home to me that the truth could be a person, a person named Jesus." But he also felt "torn in two," at the prospect of being the first person in the eight hundred years of his family's lineage to renounce Hinduism. He finally made up his mind to put the gift Bible away and never open it again.

But that same night, Mahesh recounts, his life was forever changed by what he believes to be a supernatural vision. He remembers sitting at his desk and suddenly feeling his head fall forward and hit the desk's surface. Mahesh found himself in a semi-conscious state that would last almost until daylight. Recalls Chavda,

> I found myself to be walking on a street or pathway that appeared to be made of gold, but gold like none I had ever seen before. You could almost see through it. Years later I would read that when scientists purify gold with atomic particles, it becomes translucent. That's what the gold on this pathway looked like: thoroughly purified.
>
> Along both sides of the path was luxurious grass, like a thick blanket you could lie down on and fall asleep. There were trees and flowers of every size and description, and the quality of their colors was unlike anything I had seen . . . it was as though they provided their own color from within. The light wasn't reflecting off of them, but pulsating from inside them, an absolutely pure light

. . . I became aware that I was hearing music . . . as though the grandest symphony and the most splendid choir was performing, though I could not distinguish particular instruments or voices. It was glorious. I felt my whole being dancing in keeping with the music, as though every one of my senses was perfectly harmonized with it . . .

I was somehow part of the splendor, of the harmony, of the perfection. I didn't just experience joy and love and purity and harmony, I somehow became part of them, and they became part of me, I felt that I was home. This was where I was supposed to be. This was why I had been created.

Chavda describes coming upon a river that "seemed to be alive. Then I realized that the water actually *was* life itself. It was literally a river of life." At that point he was approached by "a brilliant white light," adding . . .

I had never seen a depiction of Jesus, as those who grow up in the West see artistic interpretations. On the natural plane, I had no idea what he looked like. Yet there was not a trace of doubt in my mind that the man now walking toward me was him.

On the one hand he looked like a normal human being. Average height. Average build. He was wearing an ordinary-looking robe, not unlike those I had seen so often on the Arab men in Mombasa. And yet . . . I was almost blinded by the light that was streaming forth from him. It was bright and pure and alive, as if it contained the fullness of heavenly glory. I could hardly look at him . . . As he came closer to me I could see that he was smiling. It was the same kind of smile you see on the face of a mother or father when they picked up their little baby, a smile of utter love and delight. Like a moth flying into the flame, I felt as though I was going to be instantaneously consumed by his love.

As I stood gazing into his eyes he stretched out his hand and placed it on my shoulder and said, simply, "My little brother."

At that instant, Mahesh says he awoke to hear roosters crowing. A few weeks later, he was baptized in the Indian Ocean by one of the American missionaries, at a spot in the Old Mombasa harbor where he had played often as a child.

With high school at an end, Mahesh told the missionaries he had always wanted to go to college, possibly in England. They urged him to consider a Bible college, and before long arranged for Mahesh to receive a full scholarship at Wayland Bible College in Plainview, Texas, just south of Amarillo, a town with a population of about fifteen thousand. A local Baptist church took up a collection for his ticket to the U.S., and in January 1964, with seven American dollars in his pocket, he said good-bye to his family and got on a jet.

BACK HOME in Montgomery after their Prague trip, Julian and Leslie learned more about Chavda and his ministry. The following August 1989, when they found out he was scheduled to hold services at a black charismatic church in nearby Atlanta, they made plans to go. At the climax of the service they came forward to ask for healing of Leslie's reproductive system.

At the service, both Julian and Leslie experienced for the first time the phenomenon the church calls "being overcome by the power of the Holy Spirit," also known as "being slain in the Spirit."

Initially, Julian says, he was more amenable to the idea of spiritual healing than Leslie was, since Julian knew that his father, an Episcopal priest, had often prayed for ill parishioners—some of them cancer victims—and in many cases saw sudden and unexplained healings.

Julian and Leslie report similar experiences when Mahesh first laid hands on them that night in Atlanta. "We had the sensation that we were floating upwards," Julian recalls, "though of course we were falling backwards into the arms of the 'catchers' and being gently eased to the floor.

"But what impressed me most about Mahesh's ministry was its size and scope. Even though he's always quick to deny credit for his abilities, saying it belongs to the Father, Son, and Holy Spirit, his ministry was Biblical, and apostolic, in its dimensions, with masses of people being healed at the same occasion. The man just has an awesome faith, combined with great humility and compassion."

Julian and Leslie returned home. After several months passed with no immediate changes in Leslie's reproductive system, they began consulting by phone with Mahesh, whom they considered "a new friend," about other possibilities, including adoption. Mahesh prayed with them by phone, and suggested relevant scriptures for Julian and Leslie to read together and meditate upon.

Mahesh also made a prophecy. He told them that he saw an adopted son in their future. But then, he surprised them by predicting that Leslie, by then almost forty-three, would conceive another child as well. Afterward the family—including Grace and Rachel, then ages nine and twelve—decided they should actively pursue adoption. And the new baby, they decided, should ideally be a boy.

That March of 1990, Julian and Leslie learned of an adoption possibility, but sonogram tests showed a ninety percent chance the infant was a girl, and so they passed on that option.

Two months later, Julian was sitting at his office desk talking with friend and senior legal assistant Carroll Puckett about how much praying Leslie and he had been doing over having an adopted son. "As soon as the sentence was out of my mouth," Julian recalls, "the phone rang. It was a lady—a total stranger—asking me if I knew anything about private adoptions."

"She told me she had a friend out of state," Julian says, "who was almost four months pregnant and the couple was coming to Montgomery in two days to have an abortion. The woman who was calling wanted to know if I would meet with the couple and discuss the possibility of a private adoption as an alternative for them to consider." Since Julian had just spent several months studying all he could find on the subject, he readily agreed.

Before he hung up the phone, Julian asked the woman how she'd been referred to him. "I just looked in the Yellow Pages, and somehow my finger landed on your name," she said. There was nothing in the Yellow Pages ad about Julian's firm that mentioned adoption services, he says. His name was just one of hundreds she could have picked from.

That weekend, when Julian met with the young couple, he had run in a five-mile race earlier that morning and "definitely looked older than my forty-four years," he recalls. As a result, "Nobody at the meeting acted like I might be the prospective father. And because the couple told me they wanted to know nothing about the adoptive parents, there was no conflict of interest."

Julian says now, "I believe the Holy Spirit was involved in it, from beginning to end," adding that he was not surprised at how quickly the couple decided not to have the abortion, agreeing instead to a private adoption. Julian told them about another Alabama attorney who specialized in private adoptions and could take care of all the legal procedures.

Before the couple returned to their out-of-state home, the mother-to-be visited a top sonogram expert in Montgomery—the same physician who had declared the previous potential adoptee a girl. The result: the second baby was also to be a girl. Downcast at the possibility of having once again come so close, Julian and Leslie tried hard to look cheerful at their daughters' school dance recital that night.

The next week, the mother of the first child the McPhillipses had considered adopting gave birth: a healthy baby boy. The fact that this contradicted the doctor's first prediction was, ironically, more bad news. Strictly by the law of averages, the odds were against a respected physician guessing wrongly. In fact, the physician's wife often told friends that her husband "never missed." As with lightning striking twice, the chances of the doctor making a wrong guess two times in a row seemed very remote indeed. Julian and Leslie were back to square one.

But a new possibility emerged. Sue Staff, the widow of Julian's brother David, who by then lived in Birmingham with her second husband, Mike, had expressed a strong interest in adopting a girl. So, Julian and Leslie entered into an agreement with Sue and Mike. If the child were born a girl, it would go to the Staffs; if a boy, to the McPhillipses.

That summer, Julian and Leslie went on vacation to the Holy Land, while Sue and Mike made preparations for their new daughter. Julian and Leslie offered prayers for their future son at a number of holy sites, including the cave-like enclosure beneath a Bethlehem church said to be the birthplace of Jesus; the underground site at an ancient Nazareth convert said to be his boyhood home; and the tomb at the Church of the Holy Sepulcher in Jerusalem where Jesus is said to have lain following the crucifixion.

Back in Montgomery late one afternoon in the fall, Julian got a call from the adoption attorney. "Julian, are you sitting down?" the attorney asked him, and Julian remembers that the hairs on his neck raised.

"You've got a baby boy," the attorney said. "I can deliver him to your house about 1:30 tomorrow afternoon." That night, the family chose the name "David Larson McPhillips"—Larson being the maiden name of Leslie's mother, who had died in 1984.

"WHAT THE judge did," Wilson is saying on the video monitor, "was to intervene in order to get on paper, and into the minds of people, the idea that the embryo could have a guardian *ad litem*. And I think that his agenda was to get that into circulation within the legal community."

"One case, by itself, doesn't do anything. But if that idea were to take off . . . well, that's what the problem is going to be."

The camera returns to the female reporter: "For a short time," she says, "the fetus had a voice in Alabama's court. Anderson heard arguments on whether the girl was mature enough to decide, on her own, to have the abortion. He ruled she was. The case went to the Alabama Court of Civil Appeals, and to the Alabama Supreme Court, which upheld that decision—the girl could, legally, have the abortion. But the issue over whether a fetus had rights will almost certainly linger. In Montgomery, I'm Mary Ellen Cheatham, *For the Record*."

Back at the studio, the screen cuts to the male anchor seated at a news desk.

"Joining us this evening are Montgomery attorney Beverly Howard . . . she represents the seventeen-year-old in the case . . . and Julian McPhillips. He's also from Montgomery, and was the lawyer appointed to represent the unborn. Mr. McPhillips, where does this case go from here?"

A wider camera shot shows the two attorneys seated across from the anchor's desk.

"Well, we have a good ways to go," McPhillips tells him. "We can go to the U.S. Supreme Court. I'm not sure that we need to, because with the opinion of the Alabama Supreme Court, the four judges in the minority are the only ones who ruled one way or the other on the issue of appointing a guardian *ad litem*. And they all said that a guardian *could* be appointed, upholding Judge Mark Anderson's decision. The majority of four didn't address that issue, one way or the other.

"We're also looking at some legislative changes that will help get a guardian in there, for the unborn child. But the case law, as it now exists, is very permissive and lenient, in terms of what a minor female must show in order for a judge to find that she's mature enough to make the decision on her own without her parents' consent. And I think that's what Judge Anderson went on. I didn't raise that issue on either of my appeals . . . although the Supreme Court raised it on its own, and said they thought she was mature enough."

"But the court was otherwise sharply divided . . . there was a 4-1-4 opinion; the 'majority' of four was no greater than the 'minority' of four. There was one swing vote who concurred in the result, but not in the opinion. So it's left this area of the law very unclear. But I think that, at least for the foreseeable future, judges in juvenile courts can appoint guardians *ad litem*, like myself. And I would hope that, secondarily, the young female who heard the evidence and the issues . . . we can't really get into the specifics because of confidentiality statutes . . . would maybe on her own decide now that having an abortion is not the right thing to do.

"So at least I think we've made some advances in terms of raising public awareness about how it's not 'just' a fetus, it's not just an 'it,' it's not just a 'neuter,' it's a *real person* in there—ticking away, as John Eidsmoe says, with a heart and brain waves."

The host turns toward Ms. Howard: "Do you think this decision by the state's Supreme Court clears up any of the issues?"

"I think the U.S. Supreme Court has already addressed the issue in several cases, the latest case being *Planned Parenthood v. Casey* in 1992. The Supreme Court of the U.S. said that a third party has *no* right in a case where a female is seeking an abortion to terminate her pregnancy. And they include in there the father of the child, the parents of the girl, and the fetus itself."

"Much of this case," the host says, "was sealed because your client is a minor. Still, what kind of impact has it had, with all the attention that's been placed on her?"

"Obviously," Howard says, "she's very embarrassed and humiliated by the court procedure itself, at this point. When we explained to her the process, at no time prior to the day of the hearing did we know that an attorney was going to be appointed to represent the fetus. But in that short time, I did the best I could to get her prepared for it."

The host asks, "Did she go ahead and have the abortion?"

"After the Supreme Court came out with the ruling, I informed her of what her options were, but at this point I can't tell you what she has done, based on confidentiality."

The host turns to Julian: "Mr. McPhillips, why should a fetus—who can't live outside the womb—have more rights than a grown woman?"

It's a question Julian has obviously addressed before:

"Well, you know, a baby born after nine months can't live outside the womb either, on its own. His own, or her own. I say 'his or her' because babies arc half boys and half girls; it's not just a female issue. What I'm saying is that an unborn child is at stake, here. A heart that's beating at four weeks, brain waves that are very strong at six to seven weeks. At eight weeks you've got all the organs in place, and the rate of maturation is terrific.

"What really galls me is the cruel irony that there are people out there who are trying to save the whales and save the field mice but who are not in favor of saving the children. And this is what we have here—a real, live person, a *being*, inside the mother's womb. And so I think out of respect for human life, if you have a conflict between a woman's right to privacy and the right of a person to live . . . if there's a conflict between the constitutional rights to life and privacy, I say the right to life should be greater."

"Basically," Howard says, "I think this case came about because the judge assigned to hear it is well-known as an opponent of abortion—as is Mr. McPhillips, who is a member of 'Attorneys for Life'—and not necessarily because he believes that's the law. In fact, the Supreme Court said in their 5-4 opinion that our legislature could *not* confer upon the fetus a right to appeal, because of *Roe v. Wade*. Under the Fourteenth Amendment, the woman has a right to terminate her pregnancy. And that is *her* sole right, not anyone else's.

"What's happening is that people who oppose abortion are using this as a *forum* to get to people—or to girls—that they normally wouldn't even be able to speak to outside of a clinic. In the courtroom they're able to get within two feet of them, and a girl—in this case a minor girl—is ordered to answer the questions asked. And some of them, I think, are highly inappropriate for a judicial setting."

"Mr. McPhillips," the host asks, "why do you think *you* were chosen, out of all the lawyers in Montgomery, to represent this case?"

"First," Julian says, "if I might respectfully disagree with Ms. Howard's statement earlier that the opinion was 5-4. It's really 4-1-4. But . . . why was I selected? I think it's known, by some people at least, that I have a heart for unborn children, and I'm proud of that. My law firm and I have handled some cases that resulted in statutes, ordinances of the City of Montgomery, being struck down that were used to harass sidewalk counselors—and I might also add, to harass civil rights demonstrators . . .

"So . . . I mean, I have a heart for unborn children just as I do for other underdogs and victims I represent in my law practice. In fact, I say there's no greater underdog, or victim, in life . . . and I emphasize the words 'in life' . . . than a baby who's about to be killed in his or her mother's own womb. It's just consistent with my overall philosophy and clientele. I'm just proud to be able to do what I can."

WHEN THE adoption attorney drove up to the McPhillipses' house with the new baby boy, a small neighborhood welcoming committee was already on hand. To Julian, that occasion is mostly a blur of tears and laughter, except for the clear memory of first lifting David from the car seat: "He was so peaceful, not crying at all," Julian recalls, "and I remember thinking he was the most beautiful baby I could imagine, especially to be less than twenty-four hours old.

"I savored holding him for a moment, and I thanked God, and then I handed him to Leslie. She looked at him for a long time, and then she pointed out to me that he had the same dimple, and the same basic hairline, that I did. And all this time the girls were just jumping up and down.

"I was almost forty-four that day, and Leslie was almost forty-three. We've both been blessed with good health, thus far. Of course, I know I'll be sixty-three at David's high school graduation, and presumably sixty-seven when he finishes college. People who don't know us often assume I'm his grandfather, but I don't mind. It's a challenge, trying to keep up with him and maintain a youthful frame of mind."

Two months later, Sue and Mike Staff got their own miracle: a baby girl, whom they adopted and named Rebecca.

David, at the age of six months, was baptized by his grandfather, the Rev. Julian L. McPhillips, Sr., with the Rev. Mark Tusken assisting. From the very first, Julian and Leslie recall, David seemed to have a distinct knack for one of the family's favorite activities: traveling. Before he was a year old he'd been to New Orleans and San Francisco for weddings, and had made a two-week vacation trip across Alaska and through the Inland Passage.

At thirteen months, he watched his first Yale-Princeton football game and spoke his first complete sentence, in the same day. It was, "I want my mommy." (Princeton won, 22-16.)

It wasn't much longer before what Julian refers to, only half smiling, as "the signs and wonders" began. Some were humorous, some not.

When Christ the Redeemer Church had the dedication for a building expansion in 1993, Bishop Bob Miller came down from Birmingham to preside over the ceremony. As communion was being served, Julian was kneeling at the altar rail, holding David, then two years old, and the bishop laid his hand on the boy's head to bless him. David suddenly looked up and smiled. "Jesus loves me!" he said, with a volume and clarity that could be heard several rows back. The bishop, after regaining his composure, replied with delight, "Yes, he does!"

Several months later, Leslie and David were riding in the family's van down Vaughn Road, which passes the church. Suddenly without preamble, David said matter-of-factly, "Jesus saves me." That night, Leslie told Julian about the incident.

"I was obviously moved," Julian remembers. "That evening before bedtime, I reminded him about what he had said, and asked, 'David, where did you come up with those words?'

"David said, 'I don't know, Daddy, but you helped save me too.' I was obviously taken back, since neither Leslie nor I, nor anybody else, had ever told David that he was saved from an abortion. He was too young—not even three, yet—to know what one was."

Julian waited a week before broaching the subject again: "Just to make sure it wasn't some kind of fluke, or that my ears weren't playing tricks on me, I asked the question again. David's spontaneous reply was exactly the same: 'I don't know, Daddy, but you helped save me too."

"To Leslie and me," Julian says, "this confirmed that the Holy Spirit was speaking to us through David." That was when they came up with the idea of sponsoring the billboards, the family paying for them, but in the name of Christ the Redeemer Episcopal Church. One was at Interstate 85 and Decatur Street, another on Southern Boulevard near Baptist Medical Center, in the vicinity of an abortion clinic.

Looking back on the whole experience with their adopted son David, including the initial phone call just one second after sharing with his colleague how much Leslie and he had been praying, "Combined with all the subsequent events," Julian says, "it's been to me like Moses's 'burning bush' experience.

"Even from an early age, David was praying for sick people. About the age of four, he was asking me so many questions about God and Jesus and the Holy

Spirit that I joked to Leslie one night that I was going to have to go to seminary so I could answer David's questions."

Speaking of the Princeton connection, David would later get involved—at his father's twenty-fifth class reunion there in June 1993—in the battle to "Save Princeton Wrestling." One of Julian's favorite pictures in the family's shelves of albums is of David standing beside a large sign painted with the slogan. The supporters prevailed, and wrestling at Princeton was subsequently saved.

"MR. MCPHILLIPS," the host says, "Judge Anderson used a civil procedure rule dealing with the appointment of guardians for 'children and the unborn.' What can you tell us about that rule?"

"Well," Julian answers, "Rule 17-C of the Alabama Rules of Civil Procedure specifically allows for the appointment of a guardian *ad litem* to represent an unborn child. The rule *doesn't* say that it has to be only for property or inheritance purposes. What *I* say, and what I think Judge Anderson was saying, is 'What's more important to an unborn child, life or property?' Without life, you can't have property. But if a property interest is a legitimate interest to protect—and the rule even allows for a guardian *ad litem* for an *unconceived* child . . . then what is more important, life or property? So there's nothing that limits it or prevents it being used for that purpose. And four of the judges found that it was perfectly all right, that it was correct. I think they were intellectually correct, and morally courageous, in making the decision."

"And of course, I feel that he used the wrong rule," Howard says. "We were in the *juvenile* court, and I feel like the juvenile rules of procedure should apply there. The Alabama Rules of Civil Procedure say that a specific court rule applies to the court that you're in—say, criminal court or circuit court. But juvenile court is different. There's a specific rule that says an attorney can only be appointed to represent a minor *person*, and a fetus is not classified as a person . . ."

"But if I might add," Julian says, "Rule One of the Alabama Rules of Civil Procedure says that these rules, including 17-C, apply in any case which can be appealed to either the Court of Civil Appeals or the Alabama Supreme Court. The juvenile court rules allow for the appealing to *both* those courts. So we say, therefore, the rules apply—including 17-C."

Julian in 1995 with Betty Kendrick (left), and Irene Hearns after the U.S. District Court's $595,000 verdict against General Electric Company for sexual harassment.

After a 1995 acquittal in a capital murder trial: From left, the defendant's mother, Queenie Steele; Julian; defendant Richard Lee Steele; co-counsel Bill Honey; and Mr. Steele, Richard's father.

With client Sarah Smelley and husband, seated, and law partner Kenneth Shinbaum after federal jury returned verdict of $325,000 in 1996 handicap discrimination case against Alabama Department of Public Safety.

The attorneys and staff of the law firm of McPhillips, Shinbaum and Gill, photographed in November 1999 — From left, seated: Kay Dickey, Aaron Luck, Mary Goldthwaite, Kenneth Shinbaum, Julian McPhillips, Joe Guillot, William Gill, Regina Barron, Jim Bodin, and Karen Sampson Rodgers. Standing: Tricia Deep, Patricia Williams, Amy Strickland, Monette Marbury, Page McKee, Les Faucette, Heather Hutto, Kaylon Jenkins, Betty Puckett, Carroll Puckett, Sim Pettway, Paul Puckett, Pat Hornberger, Latarsha Scott, and Connie Butts.

Bobby Segall, Julian's friend and personal attorney, visiting in the McPhillips Shinbaum & Gill law library, July 2000.

Julian's recent case of Reggie "Pee Wee" Jones typifies the work he has done over the years against police misconduct. Above, a crowd has formed as Reggie is being put on stretcher by paramedics after being run over by Montgomery police. Below, Reggie, January 1999, after being run over.

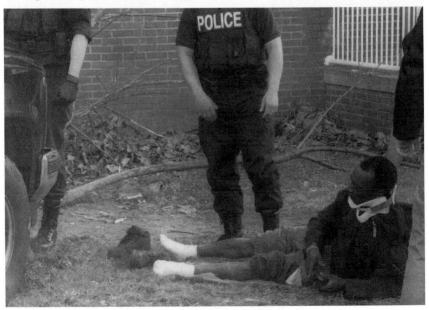

McPhillips Takes 'Hard Look' At Senate Race Against Shelby

BOB INGRAM

February 1998 syndicated column by Bob Ingram published in the *Montgomery Advertiser* indicates continued interest in Julian's political future.

He may be using me just to get a little ink, but I have been used before.

Montgomery attorney Julian McPhillips, whose high-profile cases have earned him more television time than a lot of on-air TV personalities, tells me he is taking a long hard look at running for the U.S. Senate in the Democratic Primary.

He is the first Democrat or Republican to even hint at challenging incumbent Sen. Richard Shelby, the Democrat-turned-Republican with the huge ($5.7 million) war chest. That fact alone, in my mind, warrants a column on this "considering" candidate. Besides, he gives good quotes.

"**EVERYBODY LOOKS** at Shelby like he is an 800-pound gorilla who can't be beat," McPhillips said. "I am not persuaded of that at all. For that reason, I am giving very serious consideration to making the race."

It is obvious McPhillips has already done a lot of homework. He is already fine-tuning his campaign speech.

"When he left the party that had done so much for him he turned his back on the people who elected him — the working people, small business," McPhillips said. "Now he has been captured by big banks, big business and big bucks."

An alliterative phrase like that will make a dandy soundbite on the 6 o'clock news.

"When he deserted the Democratic Party in 1994 he embraced the GOP agenda, which included term limits," McPhillips contin-

ued, warming to the task. "He may be for term limits for others, but not for himself. He has been inside the beltway for 20 years, but has shown no interest in leaving. In fact he is now running for another six-year term."

McPhillips said that Shelby's frequent disputes with the White House — the "acrimonious relationship," he called it — was hurting Alabama.

"We have already lost some jobs in Huntsville and we could see some federal jobs lost in Montgomery," he warned. "You have to believe that some of those cutbacks would not have been made if Shelby had a better relationship with the White House."

McPhillips says he knows there is no way he can match the campaign funds Shelby already has in hand.

"I could never match him dollar for dollar in the campaign. He is one of the best in Washington at raising money," he said. "But I think I can use that against him."

McPhillips said he had been encouraged by other major Democrats in the state to make the race.

He specifically mentioned Joe Turnham, chairman of the Alabama Democratic Party, who also aspires to go to Washington in 1999 as a congressman.

"I have talked to Joe several times and he is most encouraging," McPhillips said.

Should McPhillips cut the cord and jump into the race, it will not be his first venture into the political arena.

In 1978 he sought the Democratic nomination for attorney general. He came within a handful of votes of making the runoff in an election eventually won by Charlie Graddick.

"It is now 20 years later. I am 51 instead of 31. I have been very blessed in that my health is good and I have had a very successful law practice," he said. "I thought I had put behind me any desire for public service, but the desire is still there. If ever I am going to do it, it would seem now is the best time."

IS MCPHILLIPS REALLY serious about taking on the 800-pound gorilla?

"I would say that it is more likely I will run than I won't," he replied. Whatever, he promised he would make his decision one way or the other by mid-March.

If he doesn't run, Julian will have played me like a piano as others have played me before.

Ingram is a veteran political reporter who served as finance director during the Albert Brewer administration. Write him at: The Advertiser, Box 1000, Montgomery, AL 36101-1000.

With Bill Bradley and friends in Montgomery, May 1999: from left, Rev. Clifford Terrell, Johnnie Carr, Julian, Rev. Calvin McTier, Bradley, Zecozy Williams, Jock Smith, Frances Smiley, and Rev. John Alford.

Above, Julian, as Alabama chairman of the Bradley Presidential Campaign, in May 1999 with Bradley and local SCLC President Rev. John Alford at the historic King Memorial Dexter Avenue Baptist Church.

Right, the 35th reunion of the Sewanee Military Academy class of 1964, April 1999.

Julian receives the Southern Christian Leadership Conference's Award of Distinction in Anniston, Alabama, from Martin Luther King, III, December 1999.

Mayor Ron Williams of Tuskegee and Julian, April 2000.

One of the most powerful influences in Julian's spiritual life has been the healing evangelist Mahesh Chavda, pictured above preaching in Montgomery in February 1999. Below, Chavda prays at that service for healing; the people lying down have been overcome by the experience and lowered to the floor by the "catchers" standing behind them.

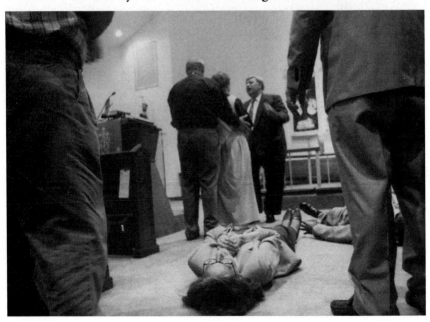

Above, the world's only Scott and Zelda Fitzgerald Museum, organized by Julian and Leslie, is two houses down from the McPhillips home.

Left, the celebrated Jazz Age couple. They lived in the house above from 1931 to April 1932.

Left, Julian and Leslie's first two children, in 1983: Rachel, five years old, and Grace, two years old.

Below, Leslie, Grace, and Rachel with golden retriever and ten newborn pups in October 1986.

Son David, two days old, sleeps on Julian's stomach, October 1990.

November 1990. The McPhillips family, November 1990: Julian, David (one month old), Leslie, Grace (nine), and Rachel (thirteen).

August 1995, Jerusalem. Rachel, David, and Grace with commemorative plaque that dedicated the fruit garden at St. George's College in honor of Rev. and Mrs. Julian McPhillips, Sr., on their fiftieth Anniversary, November 4, 1991.

June 1993, at Julian, Jr.'s 25th Princeton class reunion (saving Princeton's wrestling was big issue). From left: Leslie, Grace, Rachel, David, Eleanor, Julian, Sr., Julian, Jr.

Right, the home since 1981 of Julian and Leslie McPhillips, at 831 Felder Avenue, Montgomery.

Left, the McPhillips home was previously owned by Mildred Keller Tyson, who was frequently visited there by her famous sister, Helen Keller (left), as in this 1955 photo which hangs inside the front door.

Julian Jr. with siblings Betsy, Frank, and Sandy in 1998.

Left, in September 1998, Julian took son David, center, and great-nephew Patrick Anthon, to the St. Louis Cardinals game where Mark McGuire hit his record-breaking 67th and 68th homers.

Below, Julian and David helped land this 12-foot, 786-pound blue marlin, in July 1997 in Hawaii.

Below, in June-July, 1999, for their 25th Wedding Anniversary, Julian and Leslie and their children took a cruise around Norway; from left, Leslie, David, Grace, Rachel, and Julian.

December 1999, the McPhillips family at the Blue-Gray Colonels Ball in Montgomery. From left, Rachel, Grace, David, Leslie, and Julian.

Julian and Leslie ran this ad in Alabama's Second Congressional District as part of their campaign to be elected delegates to the 2000 Democratic National Convention.

On Tuesday, June 6, Vote for the
Lovable Couple!

Leslie & Julian **McPhillips**

for Female & Male
DELEGATES
to the DEMOCRATIC
NATIONAL CONVENTION
from Alabama's 2nd
Congressional District

Paid for by J.L. McPhillips, P.O. Box 64, Montgomery, AL 36101

Rachel McPhillips in graduation gown from Elon College; Grace McPhillips in graduation gown from St. James School, with brother David — May 1999.

Brothers Frank and Julian McPhillips, with their parents, got their families together to ring in the new century at 12:01 a.m., January 1, 2000. From left, Dixon, Alex, Jamie, Louise, Eleanor, Frank, Julian Sr., Julian Jr., Leslie, David, Rachel, and Grace.

"How significant would you say the ruling is, that Judge Anderson made in appointing you?"

"Very significant. To my knowledge it's never been done in Alabama, and perhaps not in the country. So it's a big first step toward recognizing the life interest of the unborn child. I must say, here, something in me just . . . *recoils* every time I hear it referred to as a fetus, because that reduces it to an 'it.' It's not just a blob of flesh. It's a real, live, heart-beating, brain-waves-pumping . . . in fact, if an adult in a *coma* had a brain wave that strong, you couldn't legally remove him from a life support system. So it's a real life interest, and I think it's very significant in terms of the future of this area of the law, in the U.S."

"Ms. Howard, do you think rulings such as this will succeed in the future, that more will come up and that one will succeed eventually?"

"I don't think so, because I believe most of the judges will follow the law as it is, and not try to make law from the bench."

"Mr. McPhillips, do you see the guardian issue resurfacing in Alabama?"

"I think it could. And I might add that there's another interest at stake here, too, and that's the interest of the parents of the minor. What's happened here is an interference with a parent's right to conduct the behavior of their own minor children. That's a due-process right that's really been stepped on, the government interfering through this statute.

"I think there ought to be three guardian *ad litems* appointed, really: one for the minor female seeking the abortion, one for the unborn child, and a third for the *parents* of the minor seeking the abortion, because they have an interest at stake. Back when Roe v. Wade was passed we didn't have AIDS disease. Today, it's rampant. And somebody who's going to get pregnant could easily be exposing themselves to AIDS or other illnesses out there. I think the parents of the minor need to know . . . they have a legitimate interest. So I think we'll be seeing a lot of changes in this law."

"Very quickly, before we leave," says the host, "do you see this case being used in other states in the future, or something similar happening in other states?"

"Very much so," says Julian. "In fact, I've gotten calls from many other states and many other lawyers about this, and I think it will be the wave of the future. Because again, the unborn child needs to have somebody standing up for them. Without it, there's no adversarial interest . . . the minor female can just walk in and say whatever she wants to and, boom, she's got the abortion."

The host apparently loses his place for a moment, forgetting that Howard has already answered the question.

"Ms. Howard?"

With a look of extreme weariness, she says once more, "I don't think so."

Defending Demonstrators: Fighting for the Pro-Life Cause

For a number of years, McPhillips, Shinbaum & Gill, L.L.P. has represented—at no charge—"sidewalk counselors" who claim to have been harassed by city police outside local abortion clinics.

One of them was Tom Blackerby, a Mongomery pro-life activist, who approached the firm in May 1993, seeking help after he and two other demonstrators—Kevin O'Connor and Jean Reaves—were charged under two city ordinances that forbade "engaging in boisterous conduct" (Section 34-6) and "illegally spacing participants" (Section 34-7). The latter ordinance said that no more than six people at a time could demonstrate outside a business, and moreover required them to stay at least ten feet apart.

McPhillips and partner William Gill filed suit in federal court against the City to invalidate these ordinances as applied to their clients and other sidewalk counselors. In response, City attorneys recommended to Mayor Folmar and the City Council that the ordinances be repealed.

After both sides filed summary judgment motions, U.S. District Judge Truman Hobbs issued a memorandum opinion outlining the history of the case and concluded that the repeal of the ordinance was in direct response to the lawsuit and therefore the city owed the firm attorneys' fees. Eventually a settlement was reached with the city's lawyers to pay Julian and William Gill some $15,000—which the two subsequently donated to pay for pro-life billboards around town.

IT WASN'T long until the issue flared again. This time the client was not Tom Blackerby, but his wife, Mary Jim, who alleged harassment by the police. On January 24, 1995, she was passing out literature and speaking to women coming into the Beacon Women's Center when police officer C. L. Newman told her she had to move because she was obstructing traffic. When she vehemently denied it, Newman arrested her and took her to city jail, whereupon she was fingerprinted, photographed, and charged with obstructing traffic and disorderly conduct.

Mrs. Blackerby claimed in a subsequent lawsuit that in the process of being handcuffed and transported to the jail, her wrists were bruised and her arms painfully twisted behind her back. At the Municipal Court trial on April 28, Julian presented her case before Judge Randolph Reaves and asked for a directed verdict, which Reaves granted, finding the woman not guilty.

After winning Mrs. Blackerby's criminal case in the city court, Julian and his partner Kenneth Shinbaum drew up a lawsuit charging the Summit Women's Center of Montgomery, and its officers and directors, Robert and Rita Lipton, with "malicious prosecution" and "abuse of process." (Officer Newman was originally named, but later dismissed by the court.)

After a great deal of legal maneuvering, the case was settled in late 1997. "Mrs. Blackerby felt vindicated," Julian says, "and she's not been harassed once by police officers since then, even though she continues her regular counseling efforts at abortion clinics.

"People like Tom and Mary Jim Blackerby, Deborah Giles, and many others have passed out thousands of pieces of literature over the years. They're unsung heroes in the movement. They can never be certain, of course, how many unborn lives they've saved, but undoubtedly there are a number of them. Even one life saved is an enormous accomplishment, for everyone saved is a real person, a real life, who otherwise would have been aborted."

Interlude

Dry Bones and Living Water

THERE'S sunlight everywhere, fragments of pure color from the high stained glass windows dazzling the eye – ricocheting off the rich purple of the choir robes, the glossy oak of the pulpit, the microphones and the polished guitars and the metal of the drum-set as the choir sings heartily, the audience clapping in unison.

"Praise the Lord, I'm here to have *church* this morning," a man shouts into the pulpit microphone. "How about you-all?"

He's answered by enthusiastic *amens* and *hallelujahs*.

It's a February Sunday morning in 1999 at the Gospel Tabernacle Church of God in Christ, on the northeast corner of Montgomery's Perry and High Streets, less than a hundred yards from Julian's office. Though the church is traditionally black, its full pews this morning look like a miniature United Nations: a variegated mix of races and ages, from the elderly to teenagers to couples with toddlers.

On the podium sit Julian, Mahesh Chavda and his wife Bonnie, church pastor Clifford Terrell, and a couple of deacons. As the choir ends its song, the pastor takes the pulpit. After making some routine announcements, he asks Julian to come up and introduce Mahesh and Bonnie. "It's been such a blessing to have Brother Julian with us, over the years," the pastor says as Julian is coming to the podium, and adds, "I believe we're even teaching him a little bit of rhythm, don't you?" Julian beams and ducks his head slightly as the audience laughs and applauds.

Julian strides to the podium, invokes the name of God the

Father, Son, and Holy Spirit, and thanks the audience for being present on such a "blessed occasion."

"It's a honor and a privilege," he said, "for me to introduce the 'dynamic duo' of Bonnie and Mahesh. Unlike another duo, Bonnie and Clyde . . ."

Laughter from the congregation.

". . . these folks have devoted their lives to the Lord. Mahesh has the most highly anointed ministry I know of, anywhere. Some people call him a modern-day prophet, and a modern-day apostle. And Bonnie's right up there with him, having soaked up the Spirit by osmosis, one would think, by living and working so closely with him."

More laughter.

"I think the secret, the key, to Mahesh's anointing is that he's so very humble. He gives Jesus as Lord all the credit and glory for the amazing miracles of healing and conversion that continue to flow from his ministry. And he has a heart of compassion and love for those who are hurting or are in need.

"As many of you know, Leslie and I first heard about Mahesh in Prague, Czechoslovakia, ten years ago, and met him in Atlanta soon thereafter. We've been blessed ever since, and have developed a new appreciation of the power of God's love to heal, redeem, and save lives and souls. And as some of you also know, when we first met Mahesh, Leslie was suffering miscarriages and infertility. Mahesh prayed for Leslie, she went down under the power of the Holy Spirit, and a year later we had a healthy, beautiful baby son, through a special gift from the Lord."

Applause.

"I'm very honored to introduce Mahesh Chavda . . ."

Mahesh takes the pulpit, to applause and *amens* from the audience. He says briefly how glad he and Bonnie are, to be back at the Gospel Tabernacle for the third time now, following appearances in 1994 and 1996.

Then Mahesh says, "I'd like you to turn with me, this morning, to the Book of Ezekiel, Chapter 37, beginning with the first verse . . ."

The mere mention of the scriptural citation stirs the crowd. There are scattered hand-claps. In the pew behind me, an elderly black woman turns to her companion and says heartily, "Dry bones! Oh, yes, Lord . . ."

"Praise Jesus!" her friend says, "Yes, yes, yes. Come on, now. You can *preach* it, Brother Mahesh . . ."

"These are the words of the prophet Ezekiel," Mahesh prefaces his reading of the scripture: 'The hand of the Lord was upon me, and carried me out in the spirit of the Lord, and set me down in the midst of a valley which was full of bones, and caused me to pass them by, round and about: and behold, there were very many in the open valley; and lo, they were very dry . . .'"

"Yes, Lord," someone in the congregation whispers loudly. "Dry, dry . . ."

"And he said unto me," Mahesh continues, "Son of man, can these bones live? And I answered, O Lord God, thou knowest . . ."

"He knows they can," another audience member says softly.

"'Again he said unto me,'" Mahesh reads, "'Prophesy upon these bones, and say unto them, O ye dry bones, hear the word of the Lord! Thus saith the Lord God unto these bones: Behold, I will cause breath to enter into you, and you shall live; and I will lay sinews upon you, and will bring flesh upon you, and cover you with skin, and put breath in you, and ye shall live; and ye shall know that I am the Lord . . .'"

"Hallelujah!" someone shouts. "He can bring 'em alive!" A number of people raise their hands in the air, swaying softly, their eyes shut. Some twirl bright-colored flags made of a silky fabric. Others wave streamers of gleaming mylar attached to wooden sticks like cheerleaders' pom-poms.

"And what did Ezekiel do? He did what God told him to. Continuing with the seventh verse: 'So I prophesied as I was commanded: and as I prophesied, there was a noise, and behold a shaking, and the bones came together, bone to bone. And when I beheld, lo, the sinews and the flesh came upon them, and the skin covered them above, but there was no breath in them.

"'Then he said unto me, Prophesy unto the wind, prophesy, son of man, and say to the wind, Thus saith the Lord God; Come from the four winds, O breathe upon these slain, that they might live. So I prophesied as he commanded me, and the breath came into them, and they lived, and stood upon their feet, an exceeding great army . . .'"

He pauses and shuts the Bible, looking out at the crowd. "An exceeding great army," he repeats. "All from dry bones."

"Oh, hallelujah," someone in the audience says and begins to moan, very low, some gospel tune.

And we find ourselves today, Mahesh tells us, once again living a dry land. Spiritually dry. A dry, dry land. But we're also living in the latter days, he says, and God, in His word, has promised us relief. Mahesh opens his Bible again and asks the congregation to please turn with him to the New Testament, the seventh chapter of the Book of John.

"Oh, yes," says the elderly woman behind me. "The water, the *living* water. Oh, praise the Lord . . ."

"Beginning with verse 37," Mahesh says, "we read, 'In the last day, that great day of our feast, Jesus stood and cried, saying, If any man thirst, let him come unto me, and drink . . .'"

"Yes, yes," a man's voice from somewhere interjects. "Let 'em come, let 'em come . . ."

"'He that believeth on me, as the scripture hath said, out of his belly shall flow rivers of living water.' Just picture that," Mahesh says. "Get an image of that, in your mind, for a moment. Not just *water*. Not just *living* water. Not just a river of living water. But *rivers*! Rivers. Rivers, plural!"

Around the sanctuary more hands are raised, more streamers fly. "Oh, hallelujah . . ." a young woman says.

"Just picture it. Out of the *belly*, out of the very *center* of our being! Rivers!"

"Living water!" someone shouts.

"Rivers of living water," Mahesh says softly. "That's what the Holy Spirit brings us, if we call on him . . ."

As the sermon concludes, Mahesh comes down off the platform for the laying on of hands, prayers of healing. Already there are people standing in the aisle, in line: young and old, all ethnic groups, all styles of clothing, one elderly woman in a wheelchair. The choir assembles again in their corner, and begins singing. A small group of assistants, mostly athletic-looking young men, come forward to stand facing Mahesh, flanked one to either side of the person who has come for prayer.

First is a blonde-haired young woman, in a peasant blouse and long, flowered skirt. Mahesh puts his hand lightly on her shoulder and leans forward to hold a brief whispered conversation with her about what her needs are. Finally, he nods, with an expression of both reverence and intense concentration, and places the palms of his hands against the woman's forehead. He shuts his eyes tightly, almost as if in pain, and his lips move as he prays in a low murmur. Two of the young men, in some synchronized choreography of memory, advance gently toward the woman from behind, placing their hands *almost* against her upper arms and back, millimeters away from touching her, their feet braced at an angle that will allow them to bear her whole weight.

Within seconds, they do: her body goes limp, with the slightest imaginable backward thrust, not produced by Mahesh's hands – which he has, by now, withdrawn – but by her own muscular momentum. The two young men (who are informally known in the charismatic movement as "catchers"), in a seamless motion, lower her to the sanctuary carpet where she lies unmoving, apparently unconscious – or at least, in a different state of consciousness.

The next person in line for prayer is a middle-aged black man. The same process is repeated. As the man falls backward, he is lowered to the floor, where he lies, arms outstretched, as if asleep. Mahesh moves on to the next person in line . . . and the next . . . and the next . . .

The choir sings on, a slow and peaceful tune. Some of the people in the prayer line are softly laughing, some are crying. Sunlight and sparkling colors are everywhere, dancing like dust motes. I'm watching the strange ceremony as if in a trance, trying to take in every detail without the aid of the familiar ink pen and reporter's notebook in my coat pocket. Any real-time words regarding these happenings are beyond me, I'm thinking, and must be sought later, if at all.

Suddenly I'm roused from my reverie by the gentle grip of a hand on my forearm. I look up and see Julian, who is smiling in a manner that can only be called radiant. He leans down to speak in my ear, above the noise of the choir and scattered hallelujahs and shuffling footsteps: "You're welcome to come up, if you'd like," he says. "Don't feel any pressure, of course, I just thought I'd mention it." For an instant, in my confusion, I imagine he has been reading my mind. Coming forward was exactly what I'd been thinking about.

"I tell you, it's like a magnum jolt," Julian says, with the unfettered enthusiasm of a young boy describing a baseball play. "There's nothing in the world like it." For some reason, this brings to my mind the Bible verse in which Jesus likens the kingdom of heaven to "becoming as a child."

At this point I'm very torn.

I grew up in a rural, fundamentalist Missionary Baptist church, and over the years our family sometimes attended revival services held in Pentecostal churches that practice faith-healing and "speaking in tongues." The Baptists I knew responded to Pentecostals with a strange mixture of reverence and fear. I remember watching with fascination on our first, black-and-white television set the weekly services of Oral Roberts.

In more than twenty years of working as a journalist, I had occasion to interview, and spend time with, a number of charismatic evangelists from around the country. I came away from these experiences knowing two things, for certain. First, the field – as does every field – has its share of charlatans and opportunists. And second, I have friends whose sincerity I would stake my life on who have had encounters with the "Holy Spirit" that are inexplicable to scientific and rational thought.

In retrospect, my reasons for not going forward to accept

Mahesh's laying on of hands seem disappointingly trite. Since childhood I've had a tremendous fear of being singled out in a crowd. And, I was reared with the almost universally Southern belief that hurting someone's feelings, for any reason, is one of the worst offenses a person can commit.

What if Mahesh laid his hands on me and nothing happened? I couldn't take the risk of hurting his – or Julian's – feelings.

"I think I'll pass," I say to Julian.

For the rest of the service, and the day, I feel an unseemly sense of regret.

The Laying on of Hands

On the outskirts of Charlotte, North Carolina, Julian slows the car to pass across a railroad track, in what looks to be mainly a district of warehouses. The track is one of the markers on our map, and from here it's supposedly only a few blocks and a couple more turns to the All Nations Church, headquarters of Mahesh Chavda's international ministry.

The day is a sparkling blue Saturday in mid-April, sunshine so bright it makes your eyes wince. There are two passengers in Julian's car: myself and Damion Heersink, a personable young pre-med student at Emory who is also the boyfriend of Julian's daughter Grace.

The only thing the three of us have in common is that we've come here for healing, and – speaking for myself, at least – have put on hold, for the day, any fears, hesitations, expectations, and doubts.

Julian has come because his recurring back problem has returned, an inflamed sciatic nerve that causes him a good deal of pain, not only in walking, but especially while sitting in the same position for long periods of time. For that reason, we're sharing the driving duties and making regular stops to stretch our legs.

Damion's medical problems are much more complicated, and of longer standing. At the age of eleven, he became infected – apparently after eating contaminated ground beef at a Boy Scout function – with a rare form of E-coll bacteria that reproduced in his bloodstream and, one by one, attacked all his major organs, several times threatening his life. The after-effects, today, include ongoing intestinal pain.

We turn into the asphalt parking lot of a small, strip-shaped office center from which can be seen the steady stream of traffic on nearby Interstate 40. The center is mainly two-story buildings of glass and cement, similarly constructed, with small signs on the front to indicate their function: a distributor of office-machine parts, an insurance company, an attorney, a CPA.

Other than the fact that the offices are nearly all closed for the weekend, there's nothing to distinguish them from a neighboring building across the way except that it, with the small sign "All Nations Church," is teeming with cars and people. The automobiles and RVs have license plates from Georgia, Tennessee, Kentucky, and a few from Maryland, D.C., and points even more distant.

The people who mill in and out of the building are not your typical church crowd. From elders in wheelchairs to toddlers in arms, they're nearly all casually dressed – more reminiscent of a crowd at an outdoor festival or a family reunion than some somber religious observance. They come and go in small groups, talking and laughing, enjoying snacks and soft drinks and styrofoam cups of coffee: teenagers in faded blue jeans and hiking shorts; middle-aged people wearing sweatsuits, jogging suits, coveralls, or long flowered skirts; a variety of ethnic clothing, from an East Indian woman in traditional head-wrap to a Native American man with a buckskin jacket and a feather in the headband of his sleek black hair. From inside the building come the sounds of music and clapping.

As we enter the vestibule, young ushers in business clothing welcome us and shake our hands. While Julian goes off to locate the particular assistant of Mahesh's who knows that we're coming, and Damion opts for a restroom, I wander into the main sanctuary and stand against a back wall, getting my bearings.

On the small spotlighted stage, in addition to scattered microphones, and musicians and singers on stools, is a six-foot-tall image of a flowing blue river, made of papier-mâché and blue paint and sequins. The theme of this weekend's conference is the same as Mahesh's topic at the church in Montgomery, two months before: "Rivers of Living Water."

The singing has begun to subside, and someone introduced as Brother Mickey is taking the pulpit, to the applause of the crowd of several hundred in the auditorium's folding chairs. In the front row I see Mahesh and Bonnie Chavda, sitting alongside three people Brother Mickey introduces as his son, his daughter, and his wife, who is also his partner in Seagate Ministries of Jackson, Mississippi.

Half of the evangelist's face is badly scarred by burns, and he's missing most of the fingers of one hand. But he's upbeat, funny, and in almost constant motion, with the easy rhythms of a stand-up comic, as the audience shouts encouragement and agreement. (I learn later from a brochure that Mickey Robinson narrowly escaped death in a plane crash, while skydiving, in the 1970s. He spent five years in treatment and rehabilitation, underwent more than seventy-five surgeries, and eventually recovered from blindness and paralysis through methods his physicians can't explain in medical terms.)

Right now he's reading from the Book of Revelation, a section about the church being "the bride of Christ."

"Husbands, love your wives just as Christ also loved the church and gave himself for her that he might sanctify and cleanse her, with the washing of water by the revealed word. That he might present her to himself a glorious church, not having spot or wrinkle or any such thing, but that she should be wholly without blemish.

"So husbands ought to love their own wives as their own bodies. He who loves his wife loves himself. No one ever hated his own flesh, but nourishes and cherishes it just as the Lord does the church. For we are members of his body, of his flesh, and of his bones. For this reason a man shall leave his father and mother and be joined to his wife, and the two shall become one flesh."

He closes his Bible and is silent for several moments, walking across the stage, appearing deep in thought. "I wonder,' Brother Mickey says suddenly, "How is the Lord going to straighten out this mess that's supposed to be the church today? Do you ever wonder about that? How is he going to take a church that's got so many problems – of immaturity, and pride, and enmity – and make it without a spot or blemish? It's a great mystery, about Christ and the church. The reason it's able to happen is because Jesus loves us. It's the love of Jesus. It's the love of Jesus . . ."

There is applause, shouts of "Yes!" and "Hallelujah!"

"Because he loves us, he's going to wash us, cleanse us, nourish us. Because he cherishes us a lot more than I do my own wife." He steps off the platform and walks to the chair in the front row where his wife sits, and rests his hand on her shoulders for a moment. "I tell you," Brother Mickey says, "I've had some revelations, about the love of Christ, through this mystery of the bride. He's going to present us, with himself, before the Father: clean, victorious, strong, full of love. So don't listen to the accusers of the brethren, talking their gloom and doom. No. You sit at this table and receive whatever God is serving, for he wants to nourish you . . . with . . . *himself!*"

More applause, shouts of "Amen!" Some in the audience raise their arms into the air, others sit silently weeping, their eyes closed.

"But when he comes, he's going to come for a lot more than what we have now. There's a revival taking place in America. Listen, some of you may have been hurt, wounded, misled, misunderstood." Some of the people who are weeping nod to themselves.

"I want you to understand that it's *all* about the love of Jesus. And when you understand how *much* He loves you, you're going to fall in love with Jesus. Yes. You're going to fall in love with this person Jesus, and after that, all of the rest of it just comes. Don't think you're going to *work* your way up, don't think you're going to educate your way up. He . . . just . . . *loves* . . . you. He has the power in his spirit. We've made Him too small in our society. Mahesh said it the first night, when he said we've not allowed God to be big enough in our lives.

"We sing about 'magnifying the Lord,' but let me tell you this: you are not going to make *Him* any bigger. What happens is, when you can realize who He is and how much He loves you, He gets bigger in you. His revelation of Himself, in you, takes up all the spaces where the weirdness, and the hurt, and the shame are. Then you're 'magnifying' God, by getting filled up with the *love* of God."

He stops, and points toward a dark-haired young woman near the edge of the stage. "I'm going to ask Kelly, if she can come up and sing 'Be Magnified.'" The woman goes to a stool on the stage, where she is joined by a man with an acoustic guitar.

"And when you listen to this song," Brother Mickey says, as the soft guitar chords begin, "I want you to make it like a prayer, just allow the Holy Spirit to minister to you . . ."

"'Be magnified . . .'" the woman sings, eyes closed, in a voice whose timbre is reminiscent of a young Judy Collins, "'Be magnified . . .'"

A few people begin kneeling at the altar, praying aloud, and I'm so focused on the soothing mixture of voices and music that I'm startled when a hand lightly touches my arm.

It's Julian, with Damion. Mahesh has sent word he'll meet us at the back of the auditorium in about five minutes.

Of all the scenarios I've envisioned for my first "laying on of hands," this one's not even close. Not wanting to be the center of attention, I had hoped for the ceremony to take place in Mahesh's private office, or perhaps even the living room or den of his home. But now I see how impractical that would be. Julian, Damion, and I stand about an arm's length apart, with two young men behind us who will be our catchers. Even before Mahesh arrives, the five of us take up more space than most offices or rooms would allow for.

I had also, incongruously, expected silence. But between the vocalist's amplified rendition of "Be Magnified," the guitarist accompanying, now an electronic keyboard joining in, and many people in the audience singing along, silence is in short supply. Moreover, through the swinging glass doors of the foyer, to our left, are a steady stream of people entering and leaving, greeting one another, hugging. The afternoon sun on the glass and the lawn outside is dazzling, and each time a door swings open it lets in the squeals and laughter of children gone outside for a breather – throwing a football back and forth, playing tag.

Suddenly Mahesh is in front of us. Wearing a coat and tie, he's much shorter than he appears onstage. He gives us all a friendly smile, glances to see that the men who will catch us are in place and ready. Whether Mahesh judges the three of us by eye contact, or on his own instinct, he rightly decides that Damion and myself are novices at this, and chooses to begin with Julian.

With the serious, questioning mien of a physician, he puts his hand on Julian's shoulder and begins a whispered conversation. After a moment, I see Julian motion toward his vertebrae, his hips. Mahesh nods, and leans to press those areas lightly with his hands, frowning slightly as if testing the consistency of some force or energy that can't be seen with the naked eye.

Finally, Mahesh straightens up and, with his eyes shut and speaking quietly to himself, presses his hands gently, but firmly, against Julian's forehead.

In less than a second, Mahesh withdraws his hand and Julian slumps backwards as if unconscious; the two men take the weight of his arm and shoulder on either side and lower him softly to the carpet.

He proceeds with Damion next. The same whispered conversation, the same exploratory touch, the same clasping of the forehead, the same gentle falling, backward into the catchers' arms.

When Mahesh finally stands facing me, I realize that I am curiously free of the nervousness and hesitation I had expected to feel, free of any concern over what I should do, or not do, upon feeling his hands against my forehead. The dazzling light and the outside laughter and the music seem to become different facets of some singular, peaceful force, beyond categories of vision, hearing, touch, but encompassing them all in some newer, joined, way of perception.

For no evident reason, I am not even apprehensive about the

fact that I have not thought, until this moment, what I would say to him, though I knew he was waiting now for me to speak. I have a flickering, incongruous vision of myself as a young child, being led up to Santa Claus, and it makes me smile. What to ask for? How to boil it all down for a man with so many needs with which to contend?

"I have arthritis," I hear myself say to him. "Pretty bad." Technically, I've inherited the early onset of severe osteoarthritis, which forced my mother to retire from her office job when she was only two years older than I am now.

Mahesh reaches for both my hands and squeezes them gently. "And worst in the hands," he says, nodding, "Yes?"

"Yes," I tell him. "Much."

"And other?"

Other. Where to start? At the time, I'm less than two years off a debilitating bout of clinical depression – my second, but the first to require hospitalization. That was shortly followed by a surprising, and devastating, divorce. Throw in some financial reversals, several trashed dreams, and so many other comparatively minor slings and arrows that the afflictions all begin to blur into one another. I've made great strides, in the interim, with much help from friends. More progress than I could have hoped for. Most days, lately, life seems like a good place to be.

"Depression," I tell Mahesh. He nods "And . . ." I go on, "just emotional healing in general, I guess." He nods very seriously, places his palms against my forehead, shuts his eyes tightly, and begins the soft, inward mumbling. By instinct I close my eyes as well.

What happens a few seconds later bears no resemblance to any of my prior expectations.

I recall the Rev. Clifford Terrell, pastor of the Montgomery church where Mahesh preached in February, telling me that his experience with the laying on of hands is almost never the same twice. "Sometimes I'm slain in the Spirit," he says. "Sometimes I just feel a great peace. It's like I feel the full presence, the full extent, of the Lord's divineness. Sometimes I just stand there, and know that my inner self is in direct contact with the Almighty God. Such an intense relationship. But don't ever forget, Mahesh is just an instrument God has chosen. His hands are just a conduit for God."

At a rational level, I was prepared for one of two things to happen: either nothing at all, or a jolt of almost electrical force from Mahesh's hands propelling me backwards, as I had seen happen to so many people in Mahesh's service.

What I received was neither.

The only metaphor that comes to mind, however imperfect, is feeling like someone whose hands are grasping the end of a rope, suspended from some great height, afraid to look down and see the actual depth of the abyss into which I must eventually weaken and fall.

But when I gather my courage and look below, I see with unthinkable relief that I am not suspended over an abyss at all, but rather am only a few feet above a warm, inviting crystal-clear lake on a cloudless day.

I let go. I fall. The water is exactly the warmth of my skin, and the floating more effortless than I've ever experienced in real life. There is no gravity, and no pain.

This lake, I realize, with my eyes still closed, is the carpet of the bright foyer onto which I've just been lowered, the catchers' hands so seamless in operation that I felt independent of them, could not distinguish between their motion and my own.

I'm fully conscious, fully aware of the same commotion around me. It's just that I have no desire at all to open my eyes, to let anything intrude on this warm, floating sense of peace.

The late poet, James Dickey, used to say that one of the greatest experiences in his life was a recurring dream he had, one which he referred to as "The Swimming Hole Dream." In it, he's walking through an unfamiliar stretch of woods, fearing he's lost, when he hears from a distance the sounds of splashing and laughter. Continuing towards the sound, he comes into a clearing and sees a beautiful, sunsplashed swimming hole. Moreover, in the pool of water is everyone he's ever loved. They see him, and call out to him invitingly, "Come on in, Jim. We've been waiting for you. We love you, Jim."

That feels like what I've found, on a spring afternoon on a carpeted floor in an office complex three blocks from a railroad track on the outskirts of Charlotte, North Carolina.

Whether I've been "in the Spirit," or whatever place this is, for ten minutes or an hour, I can't discern. I do know that the song has ended, and that at one point the vibrations of its notes seemed to be rippling the warm surface I'm floating on. And I hear, with unnatural clarity, Brother Mickey continuing his sermon, this time with – to me, at least – a new tenderness in his voice.

"And I tell you something else," he's saying, in the tone of someone confiding to a friend. "The Lord is not coming back for some scared, anorexic, withered, freaked-out church. It's the season of the bride and the bridegroom, and all these preachers who are prophesying the wrath of God described in this book. The wrath is intended for the enemies of God. For those who are trying to corrupt the church.

"It says in the Book of Daniel, Chapter 7, that judgment has been passed in favor of the saints of the most high God. Hear that? Not 'will be passed' but '*has* been passed.' Judgment may come up on the earth, but it's not going to come on you, because you're hidden with Christ in God.

"Listen, when somebody like me can walk out of absolutely hopeless adversity, that's God glorifying himself. I can stand here and testify about what God does 'impossibly.' I'm telling you, there's divine protection, divine provision, divine love, divine joy. It if weren't for signs and wonders, I would not be here."

There are shouts of "Glory!" and "Praise Him!" from around the auditorium.

"You're not blind for five-and-a-half years and have your eye opened and not know you're a recipient of God's divine love. You're not paralyzed in both legs, crippled like I was, and the doctors saying you're never going to walk again . . . and, in one second, have complete restoration of a nerve-damaged leg, and throw your leg brace across the room. The doctors were mystified. I want you to know, two months ago Barbara and I went snow skiing in Tahoe, and I went downhill as fast as these ol' paralyzed legs would go." The room erupts in shouts and applause.

"And if anybody out there is wondering, I was healed more than twenty-five years ago. And no, I don't think it was 'emotional,' and no, I don't think it's going to 'wear off.'"

When an even louder round of shouting, applause, laughter crescendos and dies down and he speaks again, his voice is more subdued.

"When you get lost in worship, that's when you realize that God loves you, simply loves you, and that it's not based on what you did last week, or last month. It's based on a personal revelation that God loves you right where you're at, and that you're clothed and protected by his love. Not by these 'works of the flesh' that some people talk about. Flesh is flesh, no matter how fancy you wear it. You're clothed and protected because you come to know that God loves you and that he's forgiven you, that he's cast your sins in the sea of forgetfulness.

"You know, in the original Greek, not the translation, the metaphor used in that verse is that God 'takes your sins and places them between his shoulder blades.' See? Try and take a look. See if you can see the middle of your shoulder blades. Do you know what that means? It means that God can't even remember the bad things you've done! And yet we've got church people reminding you, every chance you get, just how crummy you are. Huh? Well, that's not the work of God and it's sure not prophetic. And those folks are selling a whole lot of books to a whole lot of people who are being led astray.

"You are the righteousness of God, because you abide in Christ Jesus. And for goodness sake, don't come out of him into some religious person's trap who says, 'you've got to live up to my expectations.' No way. If you just abide in Jesus, you're not going to get any more righteous than that."

"Hallelujahs" and "Amens" ring out.

"Understand, we're not talking about some theory of God. We're not talking about somebody's experience about God. We're talking about people on the earth presently *encountering* the living God. See the difference, as opposed to believing in some historical thing that happened way, way back? We're *experiencing* the presence of God, and we're being led by that presence."

Soft guitar chords begin, then notes from a keyboard, and a man and woman singing, very low, a song I'm not familiar with. Brother Mickey is wrapping up his talk.

"It's not some emotional or mental gymnastics," he's saying. "It's about allowing the Holy Spirit to come into your life. Think of it! A glorious bride, luminously awaiting and adoring this man Christ Jesus. How does that transformation take place? Simply by expo- sure to God's glory, and being transformed by the message of his love."

Then Brother Mickey is silent, and the singers' voices expand to take his place.

I gradually open my eyes, and it takes a few seconds for the diagonal, ochre-colored stripes of sunlight on the ceiling to come into focus. I turn my head to the left and see Damion and Julian lying exactly in the postures they fell in, their breathing shallow and regular as if they're contentedly sleeping.

I roll onto my stomach, rise to my elbows, take deep breaths, and glance around. People in the audience continue to come and go, stopping in the aisles to hug or visit with one another, stepping carefully around the spot where the three of us are stretched out on the floor. From the direction of the glass doors I see a flash of color: a toddler is running past with a bright yellow helium balloon, her head thrown back in exhilaration.

I stand up, initially a little dizzy as if getting my land legs back. For some reason I'm drawn to wander outside. My sense of peace follows me. My perceptions seem oddly heightened, as if the world around me were an enhanced 3-D movie with digital surround- sound.

The monotonous truck traffic on nearby Interstate 40 now seems to have a pre-ordained flow, like a dance or a symphony, that was invisible to me before. Likewise, the familiar movements of two young boys tossing a football on the wide lawn seem fascinating and touched by a supernatural grace, the outward mechanics of the actions illuminated from within their shapes by some overarching continuity, an infinitely larger pattern continuous as a concept of physics that propelled not only my childhood but those of generations long dead.

I lie down in the middle of the brilliant, clipped green lawn and clasp my hands behind my head, the sun warm on my face in the cool, sparkling air. Directly above me, a mile or more, a single shred of white cloud in the formless blue undergoes a slow-motion metamorphosis, obedient to the changing winds at that keen level of atmosphere.

It's not until some indefinite span of time later, when I stand up and dust my clothes free of grass clippings in preparation for going back inside the church, that I realize that I am, and have been since I got up from the carpet, free of any pain in my bones or joints for the first time in almost twenty years.

I have a fleeting urge to join the boys tossing the football, but then decide that a stranger of my age might intimidate them, or – worse, in our day and age – have the friendliness of his intentions misunderstood. As if in synchronization with my thoughts, though the boys are still a good fifty feet away and appear oblivious to me, they scatter as if on cue into a larger group of children and the football is laid aside for other pursuits.

Back in the building, I see Julian walking around in the bright foyer, looking for me. I wave and head toward him.

"Well," Julian says to me, beaming, "What did you think?"

All I can do is smile and shake my head in wonder. My non-answer seems to please him.

We go to round up Damion, in preparation for the long drive home.

When I talk to Julian the next evening, a Sunday, I find out that he and Damion have both enjoyed a virtually pain-free day. Myself? he asks. I tell him, non-committally, that I'm still mulling over the whole experience, which I am.

Not until he reads this chapter does he discover that my inexplicable relief continued unabated for the next day and a little of the next, before the pain gradually reinstated itself in my life, and that on that first evening I slept more deeply, and with pleasanter dreams, than any other night in my memory.

*When this book went to press in 2000, MAHESH and BONNIE CHAVDA were continuing to conduct healing conferences, around the United States as well as in England, Switzerland, Germany, Korea, and Taiwan. In one wave of the apparent miracles, members of the congregations who said they were healed reported flecks of gold dust inexplicably adhering to their skin. As for Julian . . . the physical problems for which he visited Mahesh Chavda the previous spring, he says, have shown "one hundred percent relief." Julian acknowledged Mahesh's role as instrument, but gives the credit to "God the Father, Son, and Holy Spirit." He also thanked Dr. Teresa Allen for her alternative medicine treatments, which had strengthened his lower back to the point that he was, in the summer of 2000, again water-skiing with abandon.

27

The Foundation of Family

FRIENDS of Julian and Leslie refer to the large, furnished room in the couple's basement as the "Newly Divorced Lawyers' Apartment," and with good reason. Several colleagues, of both genders, have sought refuge there in search of some stability during the breakup of their marriages.

Julian credits two factors for the durability of his and Leslie's union, which has lasted more than twenty-six years: the role models of his parents and other ancestors, and what Julian refers to as the couple's "triangular relationship with the Lord." Julian didn't originate the concept, but heard it preached by the Rev. Julian McPhillips, Sr., at all of his children's and grandchildren's wedding ceremonies from 1963 through 1998, and reinforced by both him and Eleanor in practice.

"For Leslie and me, the foundation has been praying together, twice a day, every day. There's no way you can stay mad or ill-tempered with one another when you pray together. The Holy Spirit simply won't allow it."

It was a practice the couple began even before their engagement in 1973, and they've kept it up during what Julian and Leslie consider two of the most important milestones in their "walk with the Lord": helping to co-found Christ the Redeemer Episcopal Church in 1980, and developing their close friendship with evangelists Mahesh and Bonnie Chavda in the years since 1989.

In fact, Leslie says, daughter Rachel's life literally started at conception with "a very special prayer," when the couple decided on a night in December 1976 that it was time to start their family. And they couldn't be happier with the result, Julian says: "Everybody who knows Rachel remarks on how guileless and gentle she is. She just has such a sweet, cheerful countenance, that you can see God's spirit reflected in her actions, without having to be spoken. She's a lot like Leslie, in that way. Both of our girls just sparkle, but with very different personalities—Rachel in a quieter way, and Grace, more outgoing, never meets a stranger. Also strong-willed, you might say."

He breaks into a laugh. "At times, in fact, a little too much like myself for comfort."

But then, Grace was born into a whirlwind of sorts. The date was January 8, 1981, and her arrival was the family's third momentous occasion in less than twenty-four hours. The first was their signing a contract on January 7 on the home at 831 Felder Avenue in Old Cloverdale, where they still live nineteen years later. The second was an evening meeting of the new church's founders at which they settled officially on the name "Christ the Redeemer." In very short order, Leslie went into labor and Julian rushed her to Montgomery's Baptist Hospital where she gave birth to Grace at 5:30 a.m.

Thanks to their Lamaze training, Julian was able to be at the delivery table for Grace, as he was for Rachel. "I still remember the moments I first picked them up," he says. "Both times I was rejoicing with all my heart, and giving the Lord all the credit."

Dozens of artifacts of all three offsprings' early childhoods reside in frames or scrapbooks throughout Julian's home and office, and he's not at all averse to showing them off. Portraits of all three by the renowned Marguerite Edwards decorate the wall of the staircase by the home's front door.

When Grace was seven years old, she spent part of a day with Julian at the office. Before they left for home, Grace borrowed a sticky-note from an associate and wrote a message on it for her father: "Dads Are Great." Though it's faded substantially in the twelve years since, the note still sits in a tiny frame on Julian's desk.

But some of the best moments are undocumented, except in memory. "Grace was about three years old the first time we let her spend the night at a friend's house," Julian recalls. "The next day she told me, 'Daddy, a strange thing happened over there.'

"I said, 'Oh? What was that?' And Grace answered, 'They didn't say their prayers at bedtime, but I said mine anyway.'"

Not long after, the family was vacationing on the Alabama coast at Gulf Shores Plantation when Julian heard Grace call out his name on the beach. He looked up and saw her just above him on a somewhat tall sand dune, nervously poised to jump into his arms. As he braced himself to catch her, she turned and gave a quick nod toward the setting sun and said, "God, help me." She jumped, and it was a solid catch. "That," Julian says "is what I call a sermon in action."

Julian also recalls that Rachel, with a baby smile on her face, was the best campaigner in the family during the 1978 attorney general's race. She also crawled all over his law office floor while Leslie served as his first secretary for the two months immediately after the election.

Julian participated actively with both daughters in a softball league (sponsoring five straight "McPhillips Law" teams from 1990-94), at St. James School and in other family activities, including bedtime prayers.

Some of the foursome's best bonding adventures were extended travel, Julian recalls. Rachel and Grace went with their parents to England, Scotland, and Wales during the summer of 1985, and to Portugal, Spain, and Morocco in the summer of 1988. In 1987, Leslie, Julian, and Grace took a river raft and camping trip in Idaho. Meanwhile, Rachel, Julian Sr., and Eleanor opted for a scenic riverboat cruise down the Mississippi. Julian Jr. and Grace—only six at the time—frequently shot down the rapids of the Salmon River together, in a specially reinforced kayak, called a "funyak." An avid swimmer, Grace also decided to brave a jump into the river from a forty-foot cliff, a scene captured in a photograph as she was halfway down.

But the memories of those golden years are also mixed with Rachel and Grace sharing their parents' pain over a series of miscarriages while attempting to add a much-wanted third child to the family: in 1985, 1987, and again in 1993. (Mahesh was correct in his 1989 prophecy about Leslie conceiving again.)

"When David came to us in 1990," Julian says, "just a day old, Rachel and Grace immediately became his 'Mothers Number Two and Three.' It's been a mutually beneficial "symbiotic relationship" that's been fun to watch. The girls developed maternal instincts and abilities, while David's personality and intellectual growth have surely been enhanced by the time and attention his two older sisters have given him."

And like Rachel and Grace—and for that matter, Julian and Leslie during their own childhoods—David took to world travel like a fish to water, even before his first birthday, and has visited Europe, the Mediterranean, and North and South America in the years since. A highlight on July 4, 1997, was teaming with his father in Hawaii to land a twelve-foot, eight hundred-pound blue marlin.

As David has grown, Julian says that some of his favorite times with him have been wrestling together, jumping on the trampoline, coaching his baseball team, and camping on Cub Scout outings. "We read Bible stories and pray together at night," Julian says. "Bedtime is when I have some of the greatest conversations with him, even when he was at a very early age."

On a family trip to North Carolina in 1995, Rachel discovered Elon College as her college choice. She reported such a positive experience there, graduating in 1999 with honors, that younger sister Grace followed in her footsteps, entering Elon in the fall of 1999. Grace is a musical theater major, and landed the lead female role in the independent movie *Jared's Noose* (scheduled for filming the second half of the summer of 2000, but later delayed due to financial concerns).

Meanwhile, in the 1999-2000 academic year, Rachel taught special education students at the Cherokee Bend Elementary School in Mountain Brook. She landed a fifth grade teaching job at the Chalkville Elementary School in Jefferson County for the 2000-2001 academic year.

GARY ATCHISON, a friend and colleague of Julian's who spent time in the basement apartment in 1986 during a painful divorce, says: "Julian has accomplished a lot professionally, and fought some tough battles for causes he believes in. But I think his greatest accomplishment is the relationship he enjoys with his wife and children.

"He practices what he preaches, and that's not always the case, especially in these challenging times for families."

(Atchison's breakup with ex-wife Helen Moore had a happy ending, by the way: the couple's daughter Nancy, a friend and contemporary of Grace's, became an overnight movie star, starting with *The Long Walk Home*. Young Nancy was cast as little Idgie in the popular movie *Fried Green Tomatoes*. She also had a key role in *The Prince of Tides*, and other cinema and made-for-T.V. movies since.)

Julian again gives credit to his own parents: "Like most children," he says, "I'm a mixture of both my mother and my dad, but I am also my independent self, as are my children. What I value most of my mother's is her warm personality, her devotion to family, and her persistence."

Of the many values he absorbed from his father, Julian says, one stands out: "Dad was always telling me, 'Dignity is important. We all have different roles to play, and there's great dignity in every job, whether you're the president or a street-sweeper. The dignity is the same.'"

Today, the first thing a visitor to Julian's law office sees is a framed poster: it's a photograph of a Native American face, with a tribal proverb printed beneath: "To give dignity to a man is above all things."

At times, through the years, Julian's literal and emotional bond with his father has involved some eerie parallels.

Besides sharing the same name and the same birthdate, both men also (a) were "double-promoted" from the sixth to the eighth grade, (b) suffered a broken leg in competitive sports (Julian Sr. in boxing, Julian Jr. in wrestling), and, Julian adds with a chuckle, (c) had childhood crushes on first cousins. Young Julian's involved Libby McPhillips, daughter of his uncle Warren, who also grew up in Cullman in the mid-1950s; the elder Julian's was Rosemary McPhillips, daughter of Julian Sr.'s uncle Manning, who grew up in Mobile during the 1920s and '30s.

Julian was also the third generation of the McPhillips family to participate in the family tradition of stamp collecting; he still has a stamp book on which he inscribed "I received this on my eighth birthday, November 13, 1954." Julian's mom and dad routinely talked about the historical figures, places, and events that were memorialized by the stamps, instilling in him a strong sense of history, culture, and geography at an early age. Julian has tried to pass the tradition and hobby down to his son David.

Another parallel, Julian points out, is that both he and his father see their life's work as a type of ministry—the elder Julian as an ordained Episcopal priest in his second career, the younger Julian in the legal arena.

"PEOPLE SOMETIMES get my father and me confused," Julian says, "and I tell them, 'Dad's the Reverend, I'm the Irreverend.' I say it as a joke, but there's more than a grain of truth to it. Unfortunately, standing up to governors, attorney generals, mayors, a Congressman, and corporations like GE and Westinghouse, sometimes requires a pretty heavy dose of irreverence."

Julian has enjoyed a close relationship with his brother Frank over the years, despite Frank's being seven and a half years his junior. Highlights in their bonding were a summer of 1968 trip for three weeks around Western Europe and a month-long camping journey around the western United States in 1971. The two brothers still enjoy regaling one another with humourous tales of episodes of those travels.

Their misadventures during the summer of 1968 included running in front of the bulls in Pamplona, Spain, having their suitcases stolen in Barcelona, getting separated for hours in a Bastille Day riot in Paris, and quickly leaving a hotel at midnight in Basel, Switzerland. That was some hotel, Julian remembers. The brothers picked it because it was cheap and convenient. However, after they checked in, they noticed a steady stream of men coming and going through the hallways at frequent intervals, and the female residents of the hotel seemed eager to get to know Julian and Frank. When one woman kept knocking on their door at midnight, they decided it was time to check out.

Julian and Frank are next-door neighbors at Lake Martin, where their families are one big extended family on many weekends of the warm weather season. Frank, his wife Louise, and sons Jamie, Alex, and Dixon join with Rachel, Grace, David, Leslie and Julian in a family compound Julian calls "The McP Retreat."

In September-October 1995, the extended McPhillips family faced a crisis when eight-year-old Dixon came down with a rare brain virus. At one critical point, it appeared he might die. "With excellent medical help and awesome prayer support," Julian says, "Dixon eventually rallied from the brink and today is a healthy twelve year old."

Julian's dear sisters are Sandy McPhillips Pitre, four years older, and Betsy McPhillips Williams, three years younger. Sandy, married for thirty-seven years to Charles Pitre and living in New Mexico, has two grown children, son David Pitre, married to Katie, and daughter Lenwood, married to Michael Anthon of St. Louis, and six strapping grandchildren, Zachery, Julia Claire, and Henry Pitre, and Patrick, Dixon, and Andrew Anthon. Betsy, married for years to businessman John Williams, (supplier of family genealogy information) has three beautiful daughters, Eleanor (married to Randy Garver), Ann, and Julia, and a dynamic son, Gordon, according to their proud Uncle Julian.

Julian's brother David, twenty months his junior, suffered from and could not overcome clinical depression. In 1970, at age twenty-one, he attempted suicide with carbon monoxide. He was found unconscious in his parents' garage and revived, though he was severely injured from the attempt. David made a brave and valiant recovery during the next five years, but in May 1976, two and a half months after getting married, he succeeded in a second suicide attempt by carbon monoxide. David left no children. Julian and Leslie remain good friends with his widow, Sue, who married Mike Staff of Birmingham some years later. David's premature death was a deep emotional blow to Julian, but the passage of time, the annual awarding of the David McPhillips scholarships, and the arrival of Julian's son, David, have helped to heal the wound.

On David's first suicide attempt, he was found and saved from death by Irene "Roonie" Landwehr, an Anglo-Indian who served as Julian Sr.'s secretary in Calcutta while he directed the American Peace Corps in India. Roonie followed the senior McPhillipses to America in 1969, lived in their home in Alexandria, Virginia, and stayed in the D.C. area when Eleanor and Julian Sr. returned to Alabama. She is treated like family at reunions and weddings (she was a bridesmaid at Julian and Leslie's 1974 nuptials). Roonie meanwhile began a successful career at the World Bank, married Richard Landwehr, and raised a daughter Rahlina who graduated from Brown.

For years, going back to the '60s, Julian and his siblings encouraged their parents (both born in 1920) to make it to the year 2000 with them. Though infirm, Julian Sr. and Eleanor reached the milestone, celebrating New Year's Eve and Day at Frank's Mountain Brook home with Leslie and Julian Jr., Louise and Frank, and grandchildren Rachel, Grace, David, Jamie, Alex, and Dixon. On January 28, 2000 the family joined Eleanor to celebrate her eightieth birthday. Two weeks later, her Alzheimer's illness had worsened to the point that she was placed at the Fairhaven Nursing Home in Birmingham. Julian Sr. remains only a mile away at St. Martin's in the Pines, an independent living facility, and devotedly visits Eleanor daily. At this writing, the family was planning an eightieth birthday celebration for Julian Sr. in November 2000.

A strong "role model" influence that Julian credits over the years is a close uncle on his mother's side: Dave Dixon of New Orleans, his mother's only sibling. Dixon, often recognized as the "father of the Superdome," was a leader of a group of businessmen who launched the New Orleans Saints football team in 1964. Dixon also co-founded, with Lamar Hunt, the pro tennis circuit in the 1960s. "Uncle Dave" also founded the United States Football League, for which he was rewarded with expansion rights to both the New Orleans and Houston franchises. Dixon sold the Houston rights to attorney Jerry Argovitz in the early 1980s for $6 million, and used the proceeds to open "Dixon and Dixon Art and Antiques" in the French Quarter.

In the years since, Julian says, with the help of Aunt Mary and cousins Frank, Shea, and Stuart, the Dixon enterprise has grown into the Quarter's biggest art and antique business, and the third largest in the U.S.

"My earliest memories of Uncle Dave are of him taking me to games of the New Orleans Pelicans baseball team in the late 1940s and early 1950s," Julian says. He also remembers traveling with Dave to Baton Rouge in 1959 to recruit football star Billy Cannon when Dixon was pushing for the organization of the New Orleans Saints.

"I have no doubt," says Julian, "that much of whatever drive and ideas I have come from my mother's Dixon side, especially the Bocock branch. Uncle Dave, following his mother's instincts, has also been a generous philanthropist over the years, and he's unquestionably been an inspiration to me in that regard."

Uncle Warren McPhillips, the only sibling of Julian Sr., succeeded his older brother as president of King Pharr Canning Company in 1959, when Julian Sr. went to seminary. Uncle Warren chaired his nephew's campaign for attorney general in 1978 and later became one of his law clients after Julian set up in private practice. Aunt Sara Frances, known for her infectious laughter, raised four daughters (Frances, Libby, Mary Morrow, and Emily) and two sons (Warren Jr. and John), before succumbing to Alzheimer's during the 1980s; she died in 1991.

Julian is also proud of his friend and cousin Rosie McPhillips, a Mobile attorney who won the Democratic nomination for probate judge of Mobile County in June 2000. At this writing, she faced a Republican in the November 2000 general election for the open seat.

A whole upstairs wall of Julian's and Leslie's house is composed of a pictorial "family tree" of generations dating back well before the Civil War, and into the mid-1700s. Julian made it a habit to stay in touch with relatives on both sides of his family, even though some of them are far away, like cousin Joe McPhillips III, for years the headmaster of the American School in

Tangiers, Morocco. Second cousin Michael Smith, an attorney-priest in Mississippi, and his attorney-wife, Peggy, are among Julian's favorite cousins on his mother's Dixon side.

"One thing my parents instilled in me very early on," he says, "was the concept of 'extended family,' the fact that all mankind is basically one big extended family anyway. I think a lot about what a different world it would be if we all treated each other that way."

Julian chuckles, however, about the six reasons he's remained faithful to Leslie over twenty-six years of marriage: "First, I love her, and this makes the rest of it easy. Secondly, I take my marriage oath seriously. Third, the Bible says something. Fourth, I've seen too many people come into my law office who got into trouble taking short-cuts. Fifth, Leslie has eyes in the back of her head, and radar. Sixth, I talk in my sleep, and would "spill the beans" if I ever did anything. Summing it all up, a happy marriage is a foundation for so many other good things, including a stable family and stable society. I've been blessed."

Postlude

PeeWee's Case, Circuit Court Criminal Appeal and Aftermath

L ATE MONDAY morning, the Circuit Court jury is officially empaneled in Reginald (PeeWee) Jones's appeal of his Municipal Court conviction for failure to obey a police officer.

Reginald looks across the room at the seated group of twelve in disbelief. "Oh, man. Oh, man," he groans to himself. "This is a jury of my *peers*?"

He has a point. None of the jurors appear to be under thirty-five. There are eleven whites and one black: the latter, a middle-aged professional woman with the stern countenance of a strict school-teacher.

"Oh, man," Reginald groans, one last time. "This ain't good." Sim Pettway lays a consoling hand on Reggie's shoulder, but Sim's mood is glum, too, as is that of the two attorneys – Julian has associated Montgomery lawyer Mickey McDermott on the case, a former Montgomery Police officer who has a wealth of experience with young people in the justice system – at the table on Reginald's side.

The makeup of the jury is not from lack of effort on the part of the defense team. It was a hard-fought morning, with the city's attorneys striking black juror after black juror – including two black law enforcement officers, one a Montgomery County deputy sheriff, the other a state trooper, with the Alabama Department of Public Safety. Julian repeatedly invoked the *Batson* rule, a precedent intended to prevent attorneys on either side from striking jurors based solely on race or ethnic background. The judge repeatedly rejected the *Batson* challenge.

"Your Honor," Julian said in exasperation, at one point, "none of these jurors even live anywhere near the *part of town* where my client lives!"

Now, over lunch at a bustling sandwich shop near the courthouse, Reginald's defenders (the group has just been joined by "Car Wash," the key witness on Reginald's behalf to the events of January 13, 1999) are trying to be upbeat as they methodically go over their options for the afternoon trial. But one question, much larger than all the others, hangs in the air unspoken over the five men: should Reginald take the witness stand in his own defense?

Finally, with the clock ticking toward 1:30 and court scheduled to resume at 2:00, Julian openly broaches what everybody is thinking, for Mickey's and Sim's reaction. "Should we?" he asks, with a neutral expression.

Reggie and Car Wash sit staring into the distance, thinking their own thoughts. But both Sim and Mickey vigorously shake their heads in unison.

"Unh-*unh*," says Sim, shutting his eyes tightly against the possibility.

"They'd kill us," Mickey agrees.

Julian nods, rests his chin in his hand, and stares for several seconds at the same distant point that Car Wash's and Reggie's eyes are fixed on.

The downside to Reggie testifying, as everybody at the table is aware, is that it would open the door for the prosecution to bring in Reggie's whole criminal history (which is by no means negligible, and includes four years in Atmore Prison on a manslaughter conviction) as it relates to his credibility as a witness. If Reggie *doesn't* take the witness stand, the city's attorneys are forbidden by law to even bring the matter up.

Another question concerns the photograph that might be entered into evidence. Sim takes from his briefcase a large mounted color print that was taken by a news photographer at the scene, just minutes after Reginald was run over, and places it on the table.

It's a dramatic image, to say the least. Reggie has not yet been extricated from underneath the truck, and a circle of neighborhood residents watch the rescue efforts with looks of shock and fear frozen on their faces.

There's only one problem. In one corner of the photo, an unidentified police officer wears a vest with the reflective white letters "POLICE" on the front. Though the officer is not Steelman nor DeJohn, Reggie's initial pursuers in the Suburban when it ran him down, the prosecution might pounce on the vest to cast doubt about Reggie's insistence that the officers chasing him wore no identification.

Julian and Mickey both look at the picture, then each other, and shrug. "Yeah, it cuts both ways," Julian says. "Let's just play it by ear." Sim and Mickey nod in agreement.

Julian looks at his watch. "I guess we'd better head on back," he says.

"Okay, ladies and gentlemen," says Judge Tracey McCooey to the jurors as she sits down at the bench. "Looks like we've got everybody back. I hope you enjoyed your lunch. You can have a seat."

The dour black robe looks incongruous on McCooey, a pert, blonde woman in her mid-thirties, whose cheery, outgoing manner reflects the personality of her father, Bill Stewart, Julian's eighth-grade football coach at Sewanee Military Academy in 1959, two years before McCooey was born.

"Before we get started," she says, "I'm going to tell y'all just a little bit about how this case is going to proceed, so you'll know what's going on, here . . ."

She goes pleasantly through the obligatory, routine information about the three different parts of a trial – the attorneys' opening statements, the actual trying of the case with witnesses and exhibits, and the attorneys' closing arguments – and admonishes the jury that what the attorneys themselves say is *not* evidence, and should not be considered when the jurors are deliberating the outcome.

She explains the concept of reasonable doubt, and instructs the jurors to use "plain common sense" in deciding which testimony is credible and which isn't. She asks them not to discuss the case when they take their hourly breaks, but to save it for the jury room.

She tells the jurors (prophetically, as it turns out) that any or all of the attorneys may make objections during the trial, and in doing so, they're "not trying to be obstructionist, or difficult, they're just doing their jobs as officers of the court, and it's my job as the judge to rule on these objections. If I 'sustain' an objection, that means you don't hear the answer to that question. If I 'over-rule' an objection, that means you *do* get to hear the answer. All right?

"And there may also be times," she continues (again, prophetically), "when these lawyers need to confer with me up here, outside of your presence. Again, they're not trying to be sneaky, or to hide anything. They're doing their jobs as officers of the court."

Finally, she tells the jurors, the main thing they need to keep in mind "is the fact that Mr. Jones sits here, before you, presumed to be *innocent*. And he carries with him that presumption of innocence throughout everything we do, until . . . and *only if* . . . the City of Montgomery proves to you his guilt beyond a reasonable doubt."

Judge McCooey looks at the jury and pauses for consensus, which she gets in the form of nods or well-informed smiles from the jurors silently telling her they're ready to proceed. She asks the city's attorneys for their opening statement.

City attorney Paul Burkett rises. "Ladies and gentlemen of the jury," he says, "this case is about a violation of a Montgomery municipal ordinance . . . a municipal ordinance of the City of Montgomery to obey the order of a police officer."

He reads the ordinance to them (Section 2944, to be precise) straight from the Code of Montgomery: "It shall be unlawful for anyone to fail to obey the direction of an order of a member of a police department of the city, of all such members acting in an official capacity in carrying out their duties."

"These were police officers performing their duties," Burkett says. "They were investigating a report they had just received, and because Mr. Jones was wearing clothing similar to the clothes of the supposed subjects the police were looking for, one officer told Mr.

324 THE PEOPLE'S LAWYER

Jones to 'come here,' and another officer said, 'Stop, police!' Mr. Jones didn't stop," Burkett tells the jury, "though the officers were out of their vehicle by then, only about ten feet away. Moreover," he says, "they were outside of their vehicle by that time and he could see they had the word 'Police' on them, and would have had no question as to who they were."

He continues through the same scenario city attorneys did in the Municipal Court trial, including Reggie's "suspicious activity of ducking behind some steps and placing something down," that led to Steelman, DeJohn, and eventually other officers chasing him both on foot and by vehicle.

"Municipal ordinances are enacted for a reason," Burkett begins wrapping up, "and if there's a violation of those ordinances, we need to uphold those ordinances."

Burkett sits down, and the judge recognizes Julian.

After his preliminary remarks, including that he's proud to represent Reggie Jones in this matter, and that both attorney McDermott (a former Montgomery police officer) and Julian himself (a former assistant attorney general) have law enforcement backgrounds, he cuts quickly to the chase:

"You might wonder," Julian says, "why a jury would be impaneled over a case that's 'just' a failure to obey a police officer, as the esteemed prosecution counsel has told you.

"But as you probably know, there's a very important *mother* body of law in this country, and it's called the United States Constitution. Under that Constitution, there's a Fourth Amendment right to be free from an 'unreasonable search and seizure.' And in fact, that's something that really distinguishes our country from many other countries around the world – that important protection that applies to *all* American citizens, regardless of background.

"So, just why *are* we here today? Well, we're here because of an unusual set of facts that will unfold themselves for you. Normally, this kind of case rarely makes it to a jury. What happened on that day back in January of 1999 is that Reggie Jones . . ."

Julian recounts the scenario, of Reggie, Car Wash, and other

CARROLL DALE SHORT

people in the vicinity being startled by an unmarked Suburban van barreling towards them, "and dispersing in all different directions, as people in that vicinity have good reason to, given its history. To protect themselves against drive-by shootings, or who knows what else . . ."

The only officer who testified to giving anything of an order to be violated by Reggie, Julian says, was Steelman: "And he said simply, according to prior testimony, 'Come here.'

"All of you, as citizens of Montgomery, are *not* required by law to do everything a police officer tells you to do. What if he told one of you to drop down and give him ten push-ups, and you didn't do it? Do you think you should be guilty of failure to obey a police officer? And thousands of other such examples come to mind."

In fact, Julian tells the jury, he expects Corporals Steelman and DeJohn to be the two best witnesses the defense has . . . *if* (and he makes this distinction twice, for emphasis) . . . *if* their testimony here today is consistent with what they said previously.

"At a prior proceeding," Julian says, "we asked officer Steelman, 'Y'all actually had him cornered, didn't you?' And Steelman answered, 'Yes, that's correct.' Reggie was standing there with his hands up. And at that point, Raymond DeJohn, who is still in the Suburban van, jumps the curb with it, accelerates, and drives *right into him*." He loudly smacks one fist into the other hand for emphasis. "DeJohn *hits* him, *runs* over him, and *leaves him wounded* under the vehicle while DeJohn jumps out and starts giving him a hard time, using some racial expressions."

The area wasn't searched for drugs or guns, he reminds the jury. And though a lot of other people took off running, none of them were charged with anything. In fact, Julian says, the warrant against Reggie for failure to obey was not even written until *after* he and Reggie appeared on the TV news, at the press conference announcing they were going to file a lawsuit against the city.

"So that's why we're here, ladies and gentlemen," he begins wrapping up. "It's a *shame* we have to be here. But after you consider all the evidence, I respectfully submit and respectfully request that you bring back a 'not guilty' verdict. I thank you for your consideration." He returns to the defense table.

"Thank you, Mr. McPhillips," the judge says. "Mr. Burkett, Ms. Mullins, I'm ready for your first witness.

Burkett calls Corporal Steelman, and while Steelman is taking the stand Burkett offers a certified copy of the Municipal Ordinance 9422 as Court's Exhibit No. 1.

The prosecutor asks Steelman to point out the defendant, Mr. Jones. He does. Then Burkett walks the witness slowly and methodically through the whole arrest scenario from scratch. At one point Julian objects on grounds of hearsay. The judge reminds Steelman to testify only to what he saw and did. "Yes, ma'am," the officer says. At another point Julian objects on grounds of leading the witness. Overruled. Several minutes of dry, detailed testimony pass unquestioned, before Julian objects again to leading. Burkett re-phrases the question. More dry minutes. Julian objects again to leading. The judge sustains.

"That's all for Corporal Steelman at this time," Burkett says.

Burkett sits down, and Julian gets up and begins his cross-examination, pointing out inconsistencies with today's testimony and what Steelman said in an earlier deposition. Today he says he remembers "maybe one other person" in the vicinity of Reggie and Car Wash, but earlier he said "three or four." Today he says he had on his uniform at the time, including a detachable Velcro "Police" vest, but earlier he said he was not in uniform. "You . . . you took that out of context," Steelman says.

Julian reads from the deposition transcript: "Question: 'You didn't have your uniform on that day, did you?' Answer: 'No.'"

"But if you read up there earlier, where I talk about name plates and badges and stuff, that was what you asked."

Julian lets it ride, and moves to other territory. Did the Suburban ever turn on its siren or blue light during the chase? No. Do people in the projects ever run from an unmarked vehicle that approaches them? Possibly. Does Steelman make it a practice of charging everyone who runs from an unmarked vehicle with resisting arrest? No. Steelman didn't personally charge Reggie with anything at all, did he? No.

"Isn't it true, sir, that at one point the officers had Reggie Jones cornered from three sides?"

"No."

"You did not? Just a moment . . .' Julian asks to approach the witness, and shows him his deposition testimony from the previous July, as he reads it aloud. In three consecutive questions, Steelman testified at the time that Reggie was cornered, was finally stopped, and was not running when the Suburban hit him.

"So Reggie had stopped running before he got hit, correct?" Julian asks.

"No," Steelman says. "He was still trying to . . . he tried to dart in front of the truck, and that's when he . . . his hands went up onto the hood."

A few of the jurors have quizzical looks.

"But in a prior proceeding last July," Julian says, "you testified under oath that he ultimately surrendered by putting his hands up into the air."

"Yes. Up in the air, and onto the hood of the car."

"But 'ultimately surrendered' is what you said before."

"You had five questions in there," Steelman says with irritation. "What I'm saying is, he had his hands up in the air and then got them on the hood, and that's when he stopped running."

Julian raises an eyebrow. "I think that's all for right now, your honor."

Burkett does a re-direct, Julian does a re-cross, and no surprising revelations come from either. Some of the jurors begin shifting restlessly, looking at their watches. Burkett does a short re-re-direct, Julian does a short re-re-cross.

The judge thanks the witness, and tells jurors they can take a five-minute break.

When court resumes, the city calls Police Sergeant G. P. Shirley, the officer who reported on the police radio that he'd seen two young men run into the court with a bag of marijuana. He recounts the events leading up to the chase, but says he was too far away from the action to see anything until after it was over.

Next up is Raymond DeJohn. With a fresh haircut, and now the only officer in the courtroom, he looks younger, nervous, and more vulnerable than at Judge Reaves's proceedings back in September, where he sat in the front row of benches with other officers. In contrast to his snappy military movements during the previous trial, this time he takes the stand almost meekly, his eyes slightly downcast.

Attorney Burkett leads him through a fairly long direct, blow-by-blow, of the events of January 11. The jury hears, for the first time, DeJohn's simple explanation of why the accident happened: his brakes failed.

Nothing draws an objection from Julian until DeJohn says, "When I slammed on the brakes, I felt it wasn't stopping at all. It made a spring noise, and I was later told that when anti-lock brakes . . . if you . . ."

"I object to what he was told."

"Just say what *you* said, Officer DeJohn," the judge tells him, "not what someone else . . ."

Burkett leads DeJohn almost microscopically, second by second, through the incident of the brake failure. A couple of jurors begin to stretch their necks stiffly. One older man looks at the ceiling, as though contemplating where else he'd like to be.

Then, suddenly, Burkett's questioning totally changes direction.

"Corporal, at any time *after* this incident, did you find out more about the defendant's motive to run?"

Julian leaps to his feet. "Objection!"

There's a long beat of silence. The proceeding suddenly has the jurors' rapt attention.

"Your honor," Burkett says, "he didn't state any grounds."

"Well," Julian says offendedly, as if the grounds were obvious, "it opens up the door for a lot of hearsay."

"Overruled," says Judge McCooey. "You can answer."

"Okay," DeJohn says. "I later learned by conducting a check of the subject that he had two outstanding . . ."

Julian is up again. "*Objection,* your honor!! I mean, you know . . ."

"I understand," the judge says. Burkett carefully examines his fingernails.

"We *object,* your honor," Julian goes on angrily. "He's clearly trying to prejudice the jury."

"It goes direct to the motive," Burkett interrupts.

Julian doesn't slow down. "He's bringing in something he learned *after* the fact that prejudices this defendant. It's just highly objectionable, your honor. We move to strike it, and we respectfully move for a mistrial."

"We're not doing a mistrial," the judge says calmly. "Mr. Burkett, this is a road we're not going to go down, okay?"

"Yes, your honor," Burkett says, chastened. The rest of DeJohn's direct is an anti-climax, though Burkett does get the officer to say how concerned he was for Reggie's well-being, and how unfortunate it was "that he ran out in front of me like that. I don't want to see anybody get hurt."

It's Julian's turn to cross. He enters Defendant's Exhibit No. 1, the arrest warrant for Reggie as written by DeJohn the day after the incident, and goes over it with the witness, word for word.

"Corporal DeJohn, sir, you've previously testified on the direct that you yourself said, 'Halt! Stop!' a couple of times. Let's take a look at this warrant and affidavit you've written, and which you signed under oath in front of the magistrate on the 12th of January, and see if we can find that fact any place in them, okay?"

Julian reads the affidavit aloud. It's short and to the point, less than a page.

" . . . At this time Corporal Steelman asked the defendant to come here. The defendant took off running and refused to comply with several orders to stop . . ."

DeJohn looks deep in thought.

"You never said once in this thing that *you* gave orders for him to stop or halt, did you?"

"Can I see that paper, sir?"

"Sure." He hands Steelman the affidavit. "So in this," Julian says, gesturing at the piece of paper, "you put it all on Steelman, don't you?"

"Well, when . . . yeah, I . . . what I put in here was that Corporal Steelman asked the defendant to stop," DeJohn says, handing the page back to Julian. "The defendant took off running and refused to comply with several orders to stop. Okay? That was . . . that was me. Corporal Steelman just asked him to come here."

"Right, right. But you don't say in here that *you* told him to stop or halt at any time, do you?"

"Well, when I'm writing that, I'm writing it as in first person. So when I say he refused to stop after several orders, that's coming from me. My orders."

"But the only person to whom you refer in *here* is Corporal Steelman, correct? You don't use the word 'I' at any point."

"No, and again, that . . . can I see that again, please?" Julian hands him the affidavit and he scans it for several seconds.

"No," DeJohn says finally. "I just put that the defendant refused to comply with several orders to stop."

"And that suggests," Julian goes on, "that you're talking about Corporal Steelman, doesn't it?"

"Yes. Corporal Steelman testified to saying 'Come here.'"

"So why didn't Corporal *Steelman* swear out the warrant, since it was *his* order that wasn't complied with?"

"I also gave an order for him to stop."

Julian switches direction. "You never found any drugs on Reggie, did you?"

"No, sir."

"And you never saw that 'suspicious motion' that Steelman talked about, did you?"

"No."

"And you never checked the area where he supposedly dropped something, did you?"

"No, I didn't."

"Did any other officer check that area?"

"Not to my knowledge."

"And you agree that your car, the Suburban, had no identification on it."

"That's correct."

"I notice the black T-shirts that you and Sergeant Shirley have on . . . the word 'Police' is on there, but it's not very big, from a distance, is it?"

"On *this* shirt? Yeah, correct."

"And isn't it true that by the time you actually got to the vicinity of where Reggie was, even before you got out of the car, Reggie was already running?"

"That's not true."

Julian looks confounded. "Not true," he repeats, scratching his chin. "But didn't you get disciplined by the Montgomery Police Department over this whole incident?"

"No, I did not."

"You didn't receive a reprimand?"

"No, I didn't."

Julian opens the depositions again. "Under oath, I asked you earlier, 'Were you disciplined for this?' Answer: 'Yes, sir.' Question: 'Reprimand, warning, suspension?' Answer: 'Yes. I got a letter of reprimand over a traffic accident.'

"Then I asked, 'The one involving Reggie Jones?' And your answer was . . . do you remember your answer?"

"'Yes.'"

"So according to your deposition, under oath, you were reprimanded for the incident involving Reggie Jones, were you not?"

"Under . . . under the circumstances, I thought I received a reprimand, but I was mistaken. I'd never had one before, so I didn't know what the piece of paper was that I received. Honest. I thought it was one, but it wasn't."

Julian reads from the deposition again. "I asked you, 'What was the basis of the reprimand?' Answer: 'I don't remember the exact wording. It was basically because I struck the tree.'"

Julian looks incredulous. "Struck the *tree*?"

"And . . . uh . . ."

"Meaning, the tree you struck *after* you struck *Reggie*."

"Correct."

Julian asks DeJohn if he used profanity on Regie after the accident. No. Did he use the "N" word? No. Did he call him a "n-i-g-g-e-r?" No.

Julian changes course. "Let's see. The accident wouldn't have happened if your brakes had been working correctly, is that what you're saing?"

"No. It would have happened anyway, because the defendant chose to run in front of the vehicle."

"But Reggie was a good *twenty feet* from the vehicle when you first saw him, wasn't he?"

"Negative. I never said that."

Julian opens the deposition again and holds it out for DeJohn to read. "Here at the bottom of Page 62," Julian prompts him. "I asked you, 'At the time you jumped the curb, Reggie Jones wasn't very far from you, was he?' And you answered . . ."

"No."

"Then I said, 'How far?' Answer: 'He was probably . . . before I jumped the curb . . . about twenty yards.'"

DeJohn looks agitated. "You're taking . . . you're taking what I say at one point and another point as two different . . . different things."

"Jumping the curb is sort of an emergency use of that vehicle, isn't it?"

"That's correct."

"And yet you didn't use blue lights or sirens, did you?"

"We're not required to."

"Maybe not, but if you were going to jump a curb to go after somebody in a big project area with a lot of folks around, wouldn't a light and siren have been a good thing?"

"I was, you know, negotiating the vehicle between two parked vehicles. I wasn't directly chasing him. He ran towards me. I was just trying to get to an area where I could assist my partner."

Julian looks befuddled. "You're saying that after you jumped the curb, and he's twenty yards away, *he* runs straight into *your* vehicle?"

"He . . . I didn't . . . the next thing I know, he ran up to the side of my vehicle. That's when, again, I slammed on the brakes and yelled at him to stop, because I was . . . he was too close to the vehicle. I yelled 'Stop,' and that's when he chose to run in front of the vehicle while I was trying to bring it to a stop."

Julian lets this hang in the air for a while. He finishes the cross by going over details of why the warrant wasn't filed the day of the incident. DeJohn says Sergeant Shirley told him to go home and not worry about it until tomorrow.

Burkett asks the judge for "a couple of quick ones" on re-direct.

"You weren't driving real fast when you had to go into that area where the defendant was ultimately apprehended, were you?"

"That's correct."

"How fast were you driving?"

"I . . . never really took note of the exact speed. An accident investigator estimated . . . I think he put five miles an hour."

Eyebrows go up at the defense table, but nothing is said. When Burkett concludes a few minutes later, Julian asks Judge McCooey for "Just a little follow-up." He elicits the fact that, no, DeJohn has not filed warrants on every suspect who ever ran from him.

"Nothing further at this time, your honor," Julian says.

"Mr. Burkett," the judge says, "next witness?"

"That's it, your honor. The city rests."

A couple of the jurors look around concerned, as if they've missed something.

"Ladies and gentlemen," the judge says, "at this time we're going to take a five-minute break. Please don't discuss the case with each other or anybody else. When you come back, we'll be ready for the defense to put on their case."

During the break, Julian asks the judge for a directed verdict of acquittal, and states his reasons in detail. "I hate to sound disrespectful, your honor," he says at one point, "but this is really one of the sloppiest pieces of police work I've ever . . . I mean, an un-marked car, no blue light, no siren? I'm just saying the evidence doesn't rise, and shouldn't rise, to the level required for a convic-tion, and so we ask you to . . ."

"We'll hope the jury agrees with you, for your sake," the judge interrupts. "But I think we've definitely got a jury question. It's up to them. Motion denied.

"Your first witness, Mr. McPhillips?"

"Your honor, we'd like to call Wilbert Brooks."

"Car Wash" has a name! The slender, nondescript black man, wearing slacks and a sports shirt, calmly takes the stand and is sworn in.

Julian talks him through the scenario of January 11, up to the point where Reggie was about to pay Wilbert for washing his car.

"I was ready to get paid from him," Brooks says matter-of-factly, "and then I heard this 'boop, boop' and Reggie took off running."

"A 'boop, boop'?" Julian asks. "What kind of sound is that?"

"It's a loud sound, like something jumping a curb."

"Were there other people around in the project at that time?"

"Maybe ten or fifteen people outside. Standing around."

"And what vehicle did you see come boop-booping over the curb?"

"A black Suburban."

"Was it marked in any way as belonging to the Montgomery police?"

"No."

"Okay. Did anybody take off running besides Reggie Jones?"

"It was a heap of folks took off."

Several jurors are smiling, apparently warming to Car Wash's guileless manner.

"And how many," Julian asks, "would you say were a 'heap of folks?'"

"Ten or fifteen."

"Okay. And did you take off running?"

"No. I hit the ground."

"Why did you hit the ground?"

"I thought it was a drive-by."

"What do you mean?"

"Well, just that in my neighborhood, when you hear a bump that loud, you gotta do one of two things – hit the ground, or run."

"And at that point, did you hear anybody in the vehicle say anything? In that vicinity?"

"No."

"Later on, after Reggie took off running, did you ever see him finally cornered in any place?"

"Yes. I seen him cornered."

"He had stopped?"

"Yeah, he had stopped."

"And what did he do after he stopped?"

Brooks shrugs. "Nothing but get hit by a truck."

Soft laughter in the courtroom.

"So the Suburban jumped the other curb and hit Reggie?"

"Yes."

"Did he run in front of it, like he was trying to get run over or something?"

"No."

"And how far away was Reggie from the vehicle, with his hands up, when it jumped the curb?"

He ponders. "About from . . . from me, to that door right there." The jurors all turn their heads toward the side door, about thirty feet from the witness stand.

"And you observed the Suburban hit him?"

Brooks looks down. "Yeah. And that's something I don't want to see again."

"Did you also see the Suburban hit a tree?"

"It hit Reggie first. Reggie was up under . . . well, the tree was up under Reggie, and the Suburban was on top of Reggie."

"Okay. And the other people you mentioned that were running, do you know where they ran to?"

"No, they just scattered."

"Just scattered," Julian says. "Nothing further, your honor."

Mr. Burkett asks for "just a few" on cross.

"Mr. Brooks," he asks, "Have you ever heard of a drive-by where they shoot through the *front* windshield?"

"No, sir."

"Didn't the *front* of the vehicle approach you?"

"I don't know what approached me. I was duckin'."

Scattered laughter.

"Okay. And how many people did you say were around?"

"It was a bunch of people."

"Okay. And can you name any of the people who were standing around?"

"Not really, no."

"You said 'they' all ran, but you don't know who 'they' were?"

"It was a bunch of people in the neighborhood just standing around."

McPhillips and Burkett spar very briefly on re-direct, re-cross, re-re-direct, and re-re-cross. Jurors are looking at their watches again.

"Your honor," Julian says finally, "at this point the defense rests."

"Ladies and gentlemen," the judge tells the jury, "we're going to be finished here today. If y'all will give me five minutes to talk to these lawyers about a few things, then they'll be ready to give their closing statements and we can get this case wound up. Thank you."

With the jury gone, Julian renews his motion for directed verdict.

"I knew you'd want to," the judge says. "But I'm going to deny it."

Attorneys on both sides wrangle over what the jury's instructions should be. Julian's side feels strongly that the "element of intent" should be mentioned as a requisite for deciding Reggie's guilt on the charge of failing to obey, specifically since there's no evidence that Reggie heard anything the officers said to him before the chase began.

Burkett feels strongly otherwise. "Your honor, if he believes this statute to be unconstitutional the way it's written, that's a different matter entirely."

Julian suggests adding the word "willfully" to the charge of failure to refuse to comply. Burkett is adamant.

"Your honor," Julian says, in a very somber tone, "I respectfully submit that I believe it would be reversible error not to have an element of intent or willfulness, because there are too many examples of where a person could be given an order but not hear it, or have noise, or something like that. And without the *mens rea*, the guilty intent, it just can't be a violation."

The judge reads over Julian's suggested language again, with intense concentration. Finally she says, "I don't mind saying to them that, 'in other words the City of Montgomery has to prove that the defendant heard and understood the directive or order, period."

Burkett points out that hearing and understanding are two different things. This wrangle goes back and forth.

"Heard and understood," the judge repeats to the attorneys.

Julian mulls this. "Yeah. That would certainly imply willfulness or intent."

"I'm not going to say 'willfulness,'" the judge repeats patiently, kneading her brow. "But I mean, there's your intent, right there in that sentence.

"Sure," Julian says.

"Mr. Burkett," the judge asks, "do you have a problem with that?"

Burkett looks pained. "'Heard *or* understood' would be great. I just don't want it to be heard *and* understood."

Julian counters, "I think 'heard and understood' is fine."

The judge looks exasperated. "Well, he can't understand it if he didn't hear it," she says.

Burkett argues, "But he could have *seen* and not heard, so I just . . . I'd just say, 'heard or understood.'

"I see what you're saying," the judge relents.

Julian doesn't budge. "No, your honor. We would insist."

Burkett, McPhillips, and the judge discuss various scenarios involving seeing, hearing, and understanding. The clock is ticking, and the jurors have been out for almost twenty minutes instead of five.

Finally the judge says, "I think it's 'heard and/or understood.' And that's what I'm going to say. I think that covers the intent."

Julian hangs in. "Again, judge, I think it's not clear about the intent unless he both heard *and* understood."

"It's going to be 'and/or,'" the judge says flatly. "It's not going to be 'and.'"

"Then let me," Julian says, "supplement my previous challenge to the statute and say that since the city ordinance that's being used here apparently does not include language for willfulness or intent, that's another ground upon which we seek to have it declared unconstitutional. It's vague, and thereby void, due to its vagueness."

"I'll note that objection," McCooey says, gesturing to the bailiff to bring the jurors back. "Everybody ready?"

Burkett recaps for the jury the testimony from the prosecution's perspective. He concludes by saying, "We think you'll find that the statute that requires people to obey a member of the Montgomery Police Department was, in fact, violated. I'm sure there's a *reason* why it was violated, but we're not here about that reason. We're here because, in a routine investigation, the defendant, Mr. Jones, in fact disobeyed an officer of the Montgomery Police Department. Thank you."

Mickey and Julian split their closing argument, Mickey going first.

"Ladies and gentlemen," he says, positioning himself before the jury box, "here in the cold light of day, in these nice surroundings, we have to paint the picture for you of what that day was like. And what's important for you to remember is that those housing projects are different. They're different because of the fact that the police department *can't . . . control . . .* the crime that occurs there.

"They couldn't control it when I was a police officer years ago, and there's probably going to still be crime in those neighborhoods for many years to come. But that doesn't mean that the people who live in those neighborhoods, or who visit those neighborhoods, are any better or any worse than the rest of us. What we need to remember is that you have to conduct yourself differently when you live there, or when you visit there. When Reggie Jones heard those sounds, when other people heard those sounds, what did they do? They either dropped or they ran. You either protect *yourself* or you take the consequences, because all of the police with all of their resources are not able to stop crime in those neighborhoods.

"Reggie's reaction was perfectly reasonable. Drop, or run. And he ran quite well. All of this other stuff you've heard, about trees and cars, it boils down to one thing: Did Reggie hear? Did he understand that the police were telling him to stop? No. He kept running. Just like everybody else kept running. Everybody else who ran just disappeared.

"All of a sudden he's got police all around him and a car coming at him. He stops. It dawns on him that the police are right behind him. *Before* then, was it reasonable for him to run? Absolutely. Everybody else ran. Was Reggie charged with any other offense? No. Was anybody else charged with anything else? No.

"Was it reasonable for Mr. Jones to have run, under these circumstances? Was it reasonable for Mr. Brooks to drop to the ground, given those sounds and that neighborhood, given an unmarked . . . an *unmarked*, big black car with tinted windows? Absolutely. If Reggie didn't think 'police' at that moment, then he's not guilty of any crime, ladies and gentlemen. Thank you."

Julian goes next, reminding the jury that "burden of proof" in a criminal trial is a much higher standard than in a civil suit. He goes, one by one, over the contradictory statements of Steelman and DeJohn: "'Did you have him cornered?' Answer: 'Yes, that's correct.' 'Do you recall him throwing his hands up like that?' Answer: 'Yes.'

"Mr. McDermott talked to you a bit about the history of the projects. But those people are entitled to the same constitutional rights and freedoms as any other citizen. And if you start chipping away at those freedoms *there*, it'll come home and chip away at all of us some day.

"My point to you is this . . . this is a reasonable doubt case. And compared to some other cases where folks are acquitted, I mean, this is a *trainload* of reasonable doubt. A *trainload* of evidence in this defendant's behalf. And when the rights of one person are diminished, it ultimately affects us all.

"The day this all happened, Reginald Jones was not charged with anything. It was only the *next* day, after they had a chance to consider the consequences of Raymond DeJohn's running over Reginald Jones, that he swore out the warrant.

"Because of all these facts, I respectfully submit . . . I humbly submit . . .our request for an acquittal in this case. I thank you for your kind consideration and attention."

Burkett uses his final few minutes to remind the jury that this case is not about whether or not a municipal ordinance is constitutional, but whether it's obeyed, because think of the alternative, if nobody had to obey an officer of the law.

The judge gives the jury its detailed instructions. Near the end, the contested "and/or" sentence is read with no special inflection.

The jury is charged. It's 5:18 p.m., and beginning to get dark outside.

After the jury leaves, Julian approaches the judge to renew all his previous challenges, including the constitutionality of the statute.

"All right, Mr. McPhillips," McCooey says, "we've got that on the record."

The muffled sounds of noises in the jury room resonate. In eighteen minutes, the jury is back.

"Okay," the judge says. "Has the jury reached a verdict?"

"We have, your honor," the foreperson says.

"Could you give the jury form to Deputy Riggins, please?"

The deputy carries the sheet of paper to the judge.

"Okay," she says. "Is it the verdict of the jury that you find the defendant guilty of failure to obey a police officer?"

"Yes, it is."

"Ladies and gentlemen, at this time you're dismissed. I appreciate your service with me today. Riggins will make sure to walk you out so everybody gets to their car safely. Thank you again, and have a nice evening."

JUDGE MCCOOEY sentenced Reggie to the $200 fine originally issued in Municipal Court.

In a *Montgomery Advertiser* article on March 1, 2000, Julian was quoted as saying, "The ruling, however, will not affect the civil suit filed by Jones last year against the City of Montgomery and police officer Raymond DeJohn."

As is often the case with civil suits, attorneys began settlement discussions as the May 1 trial date approached. On April 25, a Stipulation for Dismissal in Reggie's civil case was filed in Montgomery County Circuit Court, and a story in The Advertiser reported that the case was settled.

Julian, when contacted for comment about the outcome of the case, said that the terms of the agreement limited him to saying, "No comment. Nothing less, nothing more."

"Cases like this one are tough," Julian says now, looking back. "That's why we're virtually the only firm in town who takes on police brutality. But somebody has to.

"Basically, Reggie took off running. Whether that action was smart or dumb by white or black middle-class standards, the fact was that Reggie had been roughed up by the police just a few weeks earlier. He's also small in stature, and he didn't want another beating from anybody – be it hoodlum or policeman.

"But running away doesn't give a policeman license to run over you with his Suburban, especially when Reggie had stopped, with his hands in the air.'

Julian calls the initial "failure to obey an officer" case a "tempest in a teapot," a jockeying for legal position by the city. "Frankly, it was helpful to us," he says, "in getting our client to temper his expectations.

The jury was a typical one for Montgomery, Julian says: eleven whites, from middle-aged to elderly, and from middle class to upper class. The one black juror, a female, was from the same socio-economic background.

"There were no young, black males, especially none from the projects," Julian says. "And there aren't likely to be, any time soon. The system calls for a jury of your peers. But that's dreaming.

"Given the circumstances, Reggie's satisfied. And having a happy client makes me a happy lawyer."

*When this book went to press in 2000, REGGIE JONES was sharing a home with his girlfriend, their one-year-old daughter, and Reggie's disabled mother. He was pursuing a GED at Trenholm State University while awaiting a ruling on his application for Social Security disability benefits. The family attends Weeping Willow Baptist Church, and Reggie was hoping that his life "will take an upward turn."

28

Closing Arguments

ONE OF the problems of writing a biography of a contemporary figure is finding a stopping point. This was especially true in Julian's case, for the lawsuits keep coming, and his political, community, and religious involvements don't slow up. This book covered a lot of miles, and it introduced a number of interesting people. As it went to press in 2000, I wrote some short summaries updating what was then happening to some of the people and situations that had been mentioned. Now, in 2005, when a revised edition of the book was prepared, some of those updates became asterisked notes at the ends of the preceding chapters.

But the first five years of the twenty-first century, as Julian points in out his "Preface to the Revised Edition" on page 9, have been momentous ones in the McPhillips household and law firm. Many of the ongoing developments were too extensive to be covered by brief notes, so in the new Part V that follows, we go straight to the source, as it were. Julian himself has written the updated material in this new section. This may be an unorthodox treatment for a book that started out as a creative nonfiction biography, but then no one has ever accused Julian of being orthodox.

In closing, then, and in his own words, the following new chapters bring the latest in the colorful life and times of Julian L. McPhillips, Jr., people's lawyer.

V.

The Next Five Years

By Julian L. McPhillips, Jr.

29

My Parents

EVERYTHING I HAVE DONE in life seems to have been influenced by, to one degree or another, my parents. In 2000, when the first edition of this book was written, both were still physically present in my life, although my mother, Eleanor, had advancing Alzheimer's disease and was in a residential nursing care facility near her home in Birmingham. My father, Julian Sr., visited her every day. Now, five years later, both are gone, though I still vividly feel their presence.

Dad's Big Move

In late November 2000, shortly after Dad's eightieth birthday, I received some woeful news. Long troubled by back pain, Dad announced he was having back surgery. It would be on January 30, 2001. The doctor, a member of Dad's church, would give him three new discs in the lower part of his back. I immediately had this awful sensation, as in a prophetic insight, that this invasive surgery would kill Dad. I told him so, but Dad ignored my concerns.

My premonition was so strong that I urgently tried to talk Dad out of it. I gave him written material about prolotherapy, which had worked so well for my own back problems in 1999. (This treatment, involving dextrose 50 percent injections in the muscle tissue near the discs, strengthens the surrounding tendons and ligaments, allowing the discs to heal naturally.) I paid Dr. Teresa Allen of Montgomery, who had successfully treated me, to visit Mom and Dad at their Birmingham home of St. Martin's in the Pines. Teresa did visit them to explain the benefits of prolotherapy for Dad and chelation therapy (artery-cleansing) for Mom's Alzheimer's. But to no avail.

Despite a Christmas-week trip to New Orleans and Gulf Shores, I kept trying to persuade Dad not to have the surgery. He would not listen. The complications I feared most were cardiac, respiratory, or staph infection. Two of my senior friends, Dr. Grover Murchison at seventy-five, and fellow church member George Hipp at eighty, had died in recent years of staph infections. One need not be a great prophet to know how precarious surgery at age eighty is for anyone. But Dad would not listen.

I tried praying with Dad about his surgery in January 2001, but the strangest thing happened. It was like my words were paralyzed. I couldn't pray. At least I could not pray with Dad at that moment, although I tried. This had never happened to me before. I tried to convince Dad not to have the surgery, even though I knew he was in great pain. I had experienced such great results only two years earlier with my bulging discs pain and sciatica, by using prolotherapy, a wonderful alternative to surgery.

Dad diluted my concerns by telling me he would only have the surgery if both his regular doctor and his heart doctor said it was okay. (I thought to myself at the time that surely those doctors wouldn't agree.) Dad's surgeon was to be Mark Hadley, star of the UAB (University of Alabama at Birmingham) faculty, and a member of St. Luke's Episcopal Church, where Dad had been senior priest associate.

From afar, I was praying double time. Finally, I succumbed. Dad lulled me into a false sense of security. Minor surgery, he said. No big deal. Don't worry. It momentarily occurred to me that maybe Dad knew something I didn't. Momentarily occurred.

In mid-January, Dad called us, his children and grandchildren, together. He divided up most of his material possessions, parceling them out in order of a draw. Ten days before surgery, Dad also completed a sequel to the four-volume autobiography he and Mom had written over the previous twenty-five years. About the same time, Dad sent me a wonderful two-page letter, chock full of excellent advice about the Senate campaign. Dad was proud of my running, and spurred me on. He made no bones about it. He was a great encourager.

Indeed, I must share the encouraging words of his letter to me, written by hand on Saturday, January 11, 2001:

> In order to be successful in your campaign, you will have to come across and be perceived as *not a politician* but as a leader pushing for "Justice" in the American sense and in the Christian sense, and *Justice for All* citizens—*white*

and black! And your *conviction* and courage must be based on your *faith*—not *politics.*

If you are only perceived as a trial lawyer and a "*civil rights*" lawyer you will not succeed. You must be a *new breed*—a new generation—*a faith-based leader* for a new America.

Alabama doesn't have that now.

Alabama deserves better.

You can provide this—where Sessions by his record has *failed.*

Dad

(emphasis in Dad's original)

Tears still come to my eyes when I look at this letter, as I occasionally do. The letter, with a picture of Dad, is framed and hanging on my inner office wall.

In hindsight, it is easy to see how these preparations, and Dad's words in the few days following surgery, revealed that Dad himself must have believed I was right. My father was a man of great faith. For him, earthly death, at least subconsciously, might have seemed the better outcome of the surgery. How else can one explain that when Dad woke up on January 30, 2001, on the hospital bed, following surgery, he told my sister Sandy that he was "surprised" to be alive. How else to explain that Dad told my wife Leslie in Birmingham, several days later, that he didn't expect to survive the surgery? Dad must have believed I was telling him the truth, but wanted to have the operation anyway.

No, the surgery was not suicidal. Dad would have been happy to survive the surgery, with a pain-free back and continued life. However, in hindsight, it appears that Dad saw going to Heaven an even better outcome of the surgery.

I had planned to be with Dad at the surgery. An important business trip to St. Louis sprung up at the last moment. But sister Sandy was there. My brother Frank was also nearby. Dad urged me to go on to St. Louis and stop back by Birmingham afterwards. Upon returning to Montgomery late that Tuesday evening, January 30, Sandy told me the surgery was a success. Dad was resting comfortably.

Not so, however, was my son David, then ten years old! David was experiencing a mysterious pain. Appendicitis and other normal ailments had been ruled out. The pain worsened. Upon my return from St. Louis, Leslie insisted that I spend the night with David at Baptist hospital in Montgomery, relieving her. I was only too happy to do so with my only son. Besides Dad was resting comfortably.

It had been my plan to get up to Birmingham to visit with Dad the immediate weekend following surgery. Unfortunately, I caught something at David's hospital. That Saturday, as I planned to drive up to Birmingham, I was feeling awful. The next day, Sunday, was the worst I had felt in many a moon, with a bad flu. I certainly didn't want to expose Dad to this. Thus, I didn't make it up to Birmingham that weekend, as intended.

The next day, Monday, campaign consultant Ben Eley flew in from Miami. He was being paid big bucks by my campaign to help raise money. Unfortunately, the routine depended upon my being present to make the phone calls. Ben couldn't do it without me. So my revised plan was to work hard that week, and see Dad in Birmingham the next weekend.

Dad and I spoke several times during the ten-day period following his surgery. Each time I told Dad how delighted I was to have been proven wrong in my fears about his surgery.

The last time I talked to Dad was Wednesday night, February 7. The last words we spoke to each other were, "I love you." How fortuitous. I was always comfortable with the expression and used it freely. Dad was "old school," more reserved than me. Surprisingly for a minister, he did not use that expression easily. Yet those were Dad's last words to me. I still cry inside, when I think about it. We were so close.

The next night, just hours before his fatal stroke, Dad called to talk to me. Unfortunately, David's fourth-grade St. James School teacher telephoned just before, at the unusually late hour of 10:00. Unintentionally, she blocked Dad's call. Dad left a message, but we didn't discover his words until the next morning. By that time, he had suffered his stroke, in the early morning hours of Friday, February 9, 2001.

For me that Friday morning started off like any other until I received a call from my brother Frank. He informed me that Dad had been discovered unconscious in his apartment at St. Martin's in the Pines in Birmingham. Dad was taken by ambulance to the UAB Hospital, where he was being examined and treated. I jumped into my car and rushed up to Birmingham, hoping and praying to God that Dad would be okay.

Upon arriving, it was soon clear that Dad's stroke was massive. I knew instinctively it was the result of surgery. In the aftermath, a blood clot formed, broke loose and traveled up the brain stem to the cerebellum, we were informed at UAB. The clot blocked the flow of blood to a key part of the brain, causing the stroke.

Oh, how painful, how painful, how very, very painful it was to be proven right! My foreboding had been correct, just delayed in happening. One doesn't have to be much of a prophet to foresee adverse possibilities when one's own father, at eighty, is having surgery to give him three new discs. At eighty? New discs?

But at what price? His life? What a price! Oh, how I had tried to persuade him not to have the surgery.

To say I was shocked, devastated, overwhelmed, and knocked from my foundation, would be an understatement. I had always enjoyed an extraordinarily close tie with my father. We had the same name, Julian Lenwood McPhillips. His father, my grandfather, also had the same first name, but a different middle name. We three Julians were a close threesome. At thirty-two years of age in 1978, I was at my grandfather's side in Mobile when he died. Grandfather Julian and father Julian both helped me campaign for state attorney general that year. On the back cover of *The People's Lawyer* is a great 1977 picture of the three of us standing together.

The many uncanny similarities Dad and I shared [see Chapter 27] cemented our bond. Yet, I am certain Dad loved my two brothers and two sisters equally as much as he loved me. He loved each of the five of us greatly.

Dad was my foundation, my alter ego, my older half. All that was crumbling. I was scrambling as hard as I could in the next two days, to keep it from happening. It was Saturday, February 10, 2001, just twenty-four hours after the stroke, and we had a grim prognosis from his surgeon, Dr. Hadley, leaving us with the terrible question of whether to remove Dad from the life-support system. I strongly fought against it. Amidst many tears, I finally convinced the doctors and my siblings to wait another twenty-four hours.

And yet, by Sunday, February 11, 2001, the prognosis was the same, meaning that Dad was not likely to survive. If he did survive, he would be in a vegetative state, we were told. I was so overwhelmed and devastated. A family member tried to console me with a compliment: "Oh, Jutsy, you're such a fighter, and you believe in the healing ministry."

Yes, I am a fighter, and yes, I do believe in the healing ministry. I make no apologies about either. I have seen great miracles of healing. I also know that when God calls you home, He calls you to the greatest, biggest healing of all.

Bishop Bill Stough led a wonderfully inspirational service, full of tearful hymns and spiritual songs, in Dad's hospital room. Most of the immediate family of children and grandchildren were present. We were knocking on the doors of Heaven. When we finished, the plugs were pulled. Five minutes later, Dad was pronounced dead. This was on Sunday, February 11, 2001.

As a faithful Christian, I was doing my best to rejoice for Dad. He had graduated. He was seeing grand and glorious things, getting his reward. In my book, Dad was a modern day saint. But, I was devastated—coping, struggling, grieving. Not ready! Surprisingly unprepared for this sudden turn in events. In a brave new world. At the very mature age of fifty-four, I was like a baby. I felt a little guilty, feeling this way, because I knew how many others had lost their fathers at much younger ages. And think of the people who never had fathers! Or never knew them!

Given my own strong feeling about how unnecessary and how totally avoidable Dad's death was, I found it tough to stick around Birmingham, and talk things out with my siblings. That apparently is the traditional way to deal with grief. I was afraid that in my own tortured grief I would say something inconsiderate or inappropriate to one or more of my siblings about the circumstances of Dad's death. So I took off the next morning for Montgomery and then headed south. Together with my loyal law clerk and friend, Sim Pettway, we drove down to Mobile, Dad's hometown. We then drove on to New Orleans, where Dad had met Mom. I was crying much of the way, hurting deeply inside. At a loss for words, a flood of emotion surged through me.

Two days after Dad's death, I attended a book-signing reception for *The People's Lawyer* at a downtown New Orleans hotel, which was hosting a national conference of the Association of Trial Lawyers of America. While in New Orleans, I spoke with my old friend James H. Cohen, who operates a coin and curio shop on Royal Street. I shared with him what had just happened to Dad. Mr. Cohen was sympathetic. He said he had just lost his own father the previous week and he knew how I felt. I said, Mr. Cohen, how old are you? He answered, "Seventy-five." I said, "How old was your father?" "Ninety-seven," he replied. I responded to Mr. Cohen, "Yes, I guess you do know how I feel." But deep inside, I knew that, without the surgery, Dad might have lived as long as the older Mr. Cohen.

I knew in my gut that Dad could easily have lived into his nineties. I felt robbed of those additional years. I was especially disturbed not to be able to say my good-byes to him. I was further disturbed that I hadn't spent more time with Dad during the last week of his life, and during the last years of his life. How messed up I felt. How much empathy I gained for others who suffer similar losses.

From an unselfish perspective, I have gradually learned to "let Dad go."

Nonetheless, I frequently share with others, and often think myself, about what Dad said in 1959 when I asked him why he was leaving the prosperous family business, King Pharr Canning Company in Cullman, to go to seminary for three years in Sewanee, Tennessee. I pointed out the obvious, that Dad wouldn't be making any money during that time, and with five children, and my sister Sandy, the oldest, a year shy of college, it would be an enormous financial sacrifice.

Dad's answer, which has rung in my consciousness ever since, was that *"I have decided to bet my life on the fact that everything Jesus Christ said about Himself in the Gospels is true, and at the end of my life if I discover that maybe everything was not true, I am still convinced that I'd lead a far better life believing and acting as if everything were true."*

Dad called this the "leap of faith," and his statement has enormously influenced my own faith walk and spiritual journey in life, for the better.

The Dad who encouraged me to play sports, to love learning, to cherish family, and to adore the Lord was called home. Too early for me, but maybe on time for him. I cheer him regularly, wonder about him often, and pray for him and Mom twice a day. I still want to honor them both any way I can.

Mom's More Extended Departure

While Dad's death was sudden and without warning, my dear Mom's departure was just the opposite. Bless her heart, she fought Alzheimer's as long, and as hard, and as bravely, as she could.

If God had presented a catalog and asked me to order a type of mother, I couldn't have chosen one better than He sent me. She came from great people: the Sandersons and Bococks on her mother's side were pioneer educators, and the Dixons and Pooles on her father's side were hard-working, conscientious people. Both Mom's parents were brilliant, and the acorn didn't fall far from the tree when their only daughter, Eleanor Dixon, graduated dean's list from Tulane in 1941.

Mom met Dad in 1939 at Tulane. They were married in November 1941, just before Pearl Harbor. After serving four years as an officer in the U.S. Navy, Dad took Mom with him from New Orleans up to a sleepy north Alabama town, Cullman. There I first peeked out at the world in 1946 [see chapter 2].

I remember Mom as the beautiful young woman that she was. When she was twenty-nine, she carried on about turning the old age of thirty. Her sparkling personality, her enthusiasm, her use of the expletive "plague take it" when she wasn't happy, well, all that nurtured her children well.

Mom read to us early, pointing out words and meanings. She regaled us with colorful Bible stories shared around the rocking chair. She led her little brood in singing songs like "Oh, Suzanna" and "She'll Be Comin' Round the Mountain." This was in the late 1940s and early 1950s.

Mom got us off to school, to camps, and to life in general with gusto. She modeled what a mother and a wife should be. I fight back tears, as I write these words.

And what a good writer Mom was. Dad would describe things in a more business-like way. Mom used her pen as a paint brush, evoking images and emotions with colorful, poignant words. My brother Frank and I have inherited her writing style.

Mom was the major inspiration and the primary craftsman of her and Dad's four-volume unpublished joint autobiography, *The Drummer's Beat: Our Life and Times*. She and Dad co-authored it from 1975 to 1995. It is a fascinating account of the ups and downs of their lives, mostly experienced together.

Mom gave me the backbone to endure and eventually to flourish through five tough years at Sewanee Military Academy, from 1959–64. She kept me on track at Princeton, and at my emotional low point in 1966 when my second broken leg in ten weeks threatened my identity as an athlete, Mom prophetically declared, "This may turn out to be a lucky break."

Indeed, it was, because it kept me out of the Vietnam War we all abhorred. My daughters Rachel and Grace and son David cherish the photograph of Mom, about 1970, on her knees in Lafayette Park, across from the White House in Washington, D.C. She is looking up at a law enforcement officer, and apparently lecturing him about how bad the war was. She and Dad, both members of Clergy and Laymen Concerned About Vietnam, were briefly arrested and detained. They were the daring participants of a prayer vigil. The charges were later dropped.

Mom and Dad, at that moment, modeled for all their children that we must sometimes be sacrificial, when issues of grave moral concern are involved.

Mom's support of Dad's career was legendary. She shaped and corrected his sermons. He practiced them in advance on her, before preaching to the congregation. She was constructively critical. The final product was the work of them both.

Mom had her own separate ministries, from teaching youngsters struggling academically in Cullman in the 1950s, to her work with Mother Teresa in the late 1960s in Calcutta, India. I frequently point out to clients in my law firm hallway the wonderful picture of Mom with Mother Teresa, caring for a little baby. Mom countenanced an angelic spirit in describing this "poorest of the poor" ministry to various church groups in 1970s–80s.

The most difficult blow life dealt Mom was the tragedy of her third child, my brother David. Growing up, he was just as sharp, normal, and balanced as the other four of us. But an unsuccessful suicide attempt, via carbon monoxide in 1970, maimed David. His final suicide attempt succeeded on Mother's Day weekend in 1976. It crushed Mom and Dad. If Mom didn't have a nervous breakdown in the months following, she was so close that no one could tell the difference.

But she survived. Mom was, in my opinion, one of life's greatest survivors and modeled that role for her other children, including me. Despite her heartaches, Mom was steadfastly an encourager, first to Dad, then to her children, finally to others.

Mom's Alzheimer's began about 1993, in her seventy-third year. She lived on with the disease for ten more years. It was sad to see this beautiful, brilliant person deteriorate as she did. With her graciousness and charm, Eleanor Dixon McPhillips covered it up as best as she could for the balance of the 1990s.

Mom celebrated the New Millennium with us at my brother Frank's home on January 1, 2000. The picture on page B-16 of this book shows her in a distant stare. Mom just wasn't all there.

Mom turned eighty on January 28, 2000. Within two weeks, she suffered another mini-stroke, complicating her Alzheimer's. Dad was in tears when he acknowledged that he couldn't properly take care of her anymore. We helped Dad move her to Fairhaven Nursing Home, just a mile down the road from the St. Martin's in the Pines, the residential facility where Dad remained.

Although Leslie, the kids, and I saw Mom frequently, and although I called Dad more often than ever, I didn't realize at the time how depressed Dad had become. He was beginning to snap out of it by late 2000. On his eightieth birthday on November 13, 2000, we had a grand celebration. Except for Mother, down the road at the nursing home.

When Dad died in February 2001, my brother Frank and sister Betsy were delegated the duty of breaking the news to her. They tried to sugarcoat it. Frank said to Mom: "Good news, Dad's gone home to Heaven." Mom's reply was. "What's so good about that? What happened?" Clearly she understood, but with her greatly diminished mental capacity, Mom couldn't properly process Dad's death. Which was a blessing.

As the months of 2001 passed after Dad's death, the amazing thing is that, as disabled as Mom was, she still managed to inspire and uplift me and her other children. She was such a source of strength for us all. She would immediately "light up" when we came to see her. That, in turn, captivated, and energized me as well. Frail though Mom was, she always reignited the "little boy" inside me.

She was always there when I needed her. Despite a busy campaign for the U.S. Senate, combined with a never-ending law practice from my Montgomery base, I still managed to see Mom once a week in Birmingham until December 1, 2002, the day she died.

All legal and political endeavors came to a screeching halt in late November and early December 2002. That was when Mom finally went home to be with the Lord. I was in the clouds emotionally. Appropriately, on Thanksgiving Day, November 29, 2002, Rachel, Grace, and I had visited Mom at Fairhaven in Birmingham. This was Mom's last day of consciousness. Leslie and David were back in Montgomery, attending to her Burton family reunion.

I'll never forget that day. Mom, with her hand, playfully batted a balloon tied to the side of her bed. I cried most of the time. Tears of sadness, tears of joy. At least I had time to tell Mother my good-bye. I told her how much I loved her, how grateful I was, and how she would be soon rejoining Dad and my brother David .

Mom's memorial service, the same as with Dad's, was a glimpse of heaven. To this day, I still pray for Mom and Dad, twice a day. I am still warmed and strengthened every day by their memory.

Both were absolutely as good, and as decent, and as loving, and as helpful, and as inspirational, as any parents could ever be. They gave us an awesome heritage.

30

The Senate Campaign

M Y SON DAVID asked me on Sunday, February 11, 2001, just after Dad died, while we were packing to go home, "What are you going to do, Dad?" I replied, "What do you mean, David?" He responded, "I mean about the campaign, Dad." I answered back, "What do you think I should do, David? I'm really not sure." David's quick reply was, "I think you should continue, Dad, because your father would have wanted you to."

That statement from David spoke an instant truth to me that kept me in the campaign. It was like Dad was speaking through David, or the Holy Spirit speaking through David. My campaign was still at such a beginning stage, a year and a half before the election. We could easily have discontinued, before really starting. Few, if any, would remember long-term that I had even considered the race.

My giving the eulogy at Dad's memorial service was therapeutic. This I did jointly with my brother Frank, on Friday, February 17, 2001, at St. Luke's Episcopal Church in Mountain Brook. Frank spoke appropriate, sensitive words that greatly honored Dad. The Reverend Doug Carpenter gave a touching sermon in a church packed with a long procession of vested clergy (Dad had served as rector at St. Luke's from 1964-66 and was a senior priest there again in the 1990s). This emotional experience would repeat itself twenty-one months later at Mom's memorial service, when Bishop Stough gave the sermon, and I gave the eulogy. Both times, I walked down the aisle at St. Luke's, together with my siblings and family. It was like walking on clouds. It was as if we first saw Dad, and then Mom, off to Heaven. It was just like that. It felt like that.

The one good thing coming out of this was that now I could do much more than sympathize with the others who have lost their parents. I could "empa-

357

thize." I had now walked in the moccasins of so many others who grieve over the loss of their parents. This has helped me in my law practice. It has made my heart more tender.

But, oh what a struggle the next few months of 2001 were. How I made fundraising calls, how I practiced law, how I did anything, I don't know. Sim Pettway has heard me tell him this several times, but I want to say it again, for all the world to hear. I couldn't have made those calls, couldn't have maintained my sanity, if Sim Pettway, Jr., my fundraising assistant, campaign manager, and law clerk, hadn't been there to cheer me on with humorous comments. Sim knew my Dad. Sim once drove Dad from Mobile to Montgomery, had a good visit with him, and knew what an awesome father Dad was.

Sim placed the calls to fundraising prospects. We developed a system that made it less painful, or more fun. God bless Sim for keeping me a little more light-hearted, helping to ease the grief.

And God bless my office manager-paralegal-secretary-campaign treasurer Amy Strickland for stepping up and helping out in so many ways. She also wears about five other hats of responsibility. Amy is no-nonsense and a bulwark of strength, despite health concerns of her own.

And God bless my law partners, Kenneth Shinbaum, Mary Goldthwaite, William Gill, Aaron Luck, Karen Rodgers, Jim Bodin, and Joe Guillot for helping carry the load of the firm's practice during the campaign, and during the extended grief following my father's death. They were all invaluable as both lawyers and friends. They all made it to Dad's and Mom's memorial services in Birmingham. They are all people of great integrity as well as skill.

All these law partners, and Amy, Sim, Kaylon Jenkins and the three wonderful Pucketts (Carroll, Betty, and Paul), I simply can't say enough good about them. They were with me at the beginning of 2001, when the campaign began. They were still with me three years later, when 2004 arrived. Except for William, who moved from a partnership to an "of counsel" relationship in mid-2004, all are still with me today. And William is working closely with us on certain big cases.

Carroll Puckett, bless his heart, started working with me in 1978 as a client. By 1979, he was helping me find real estate investments. By 1981, he had become my paralegal. To this day, at age seventy-one, he is still with us, together with his wife Betty and son, Paul.

How I got through the next six to nine months, leading up to September 11, how we continued both the campaign and the law practice, only God knows. But great credit goes first to an awesome God for his wondrous miracle of healing. Foremost among others deserving credit was my devoted wife Leslie and three wonderful children, Rachel, Grace, and David. I thank them enormously.

Leslie is clearly my better half. Level-headed, practical, patient, a great mother, a partner in our Christian faith, and still beautiful at fifty-seven, I have been extraordinarily blessed by her. Thank you, Lord!

Surprising to some, Leslie actually encouraged me to make the U.S. Senate race both in 1998 and 2002. It wasn's that she wanted to be a senator's wife, or go to Washington. It's just that she believed that deep down, this was something I had always wanted to do. Her motivation was simply loyalty to me, to the highest degree.

Also, undergirding the foundation of my campaign, continually inspiring me and helping me endure the losses of Dad and Mom was my dear friend, the Rev. John Alford. The indefatigable pastor of Mt. Gilliard Baptist Church for thirty years and still the president of the Montgomery chapter of the Southern Christian Leadership Conference (SCLC), John frequently traveled with me to campaign stops. His official title was "clergy coordinator" but unofficially he did so much more.

And guess who Rev. Alford brought into leadership roles in my campaign? None other than Martin Luther King III, the Rev. Dr. Fred Shuttlesworth (hero of the Birmingham Civil Rights Movement), and the Rev. Dr. Andrew Young (Jimmy Carter's United Nations ambassador). John also introduced me to both State Senator Sundra Escott of Birmingham and former State Senator Charles Steele of Tuscaloosa. Each was enormously helpful in the campaign, and both are the closest of friends today. Steele is now the National SCLC president. John also introduced me to Rev. T. L. Lewis and many other ministers, leaders, and luminaries from the "black church" statewide. Indeed, the black church became a foundation of my campaign.

If there were a most valuable player award, then surely John Alford would have to be the winner. He also ministered and pastored to me, and counseled me, not just politically but spiritually, throughout the campaign. At one low point in September 2001 that I'll never forget, I went out to John's house in west Montgomery seeking advice. The words of wisdom he gave me were from Proverbs 3:5-6, which says: "Trust in the Lord with all your heart and lean not on your own understanding. In all your ways acknowledge Him, and He will direct your paths." This verse, one of my favorites, has become a frequent source of inspiration.

John is now the executive director of our family foundation, The Rev. Julian and Eleanor McPhillips International Center for Racial and Religious Reconciliation (also called the McPhillips International Reconciliation Center, or MIRC). Founded in 2003, it has a special outreach to Africa, because that is where "the poorest of the poor" are now located, to use a Mother Teresa phrase.

John Alford was also the conduit for the several major cases coming to the law firm. In turn, I have represented John, the SCLC, and others at his request, frequently on a pro bono basis. Together with Charles Steele, John and I fought on the front lines against police brutality and other injustices perpetrated against a diversity of citizens.

WHY WAS I RUNNING for the U.S. Senate in the first place? I had thought long and hard and prayed about this over the years. My interest in public service originated at Princeton and Columbia through my contact with stimulating national and international issues. J.F.K.'s "Ask not what this country can do for you, but what you can do for this country" speech fed a desire to serve in national government. The motivation grew with travels to Europe and the Middle East, en route to India, where my family lived in the late 1960s, and with additional international travel over the years.

Mom and Dad encouraged my public service leanings. My own faith walk as a Christian kindled a desire to practice the "Sermon on the Mount" ideal in the public arena.

My law practice succeeded beyond expectations, both financially and in terms of professional satisfaction. Accordingly, I concluded that it was "time to give back," to America, to Alabama, and to people who were hurting. My own money expended was more than an investment. Coming from contingency fees representing ordinary people wronged by powerful interests, I considered the funds equivalent to a "public trust." I knew the total financial sacrifice would be more than out-of-pocket campaign costs. The campaign also interfered with family time. An occupational hazard I anticipated. And, as expected, the firm's revenues nose-dived in 2001 and 2002, due to my immersion in the campaign.

Further, raising money requires a "true grit" that is difficult to summon up, unless one is truly inspired. Fortunately, I was that inspired.

Another downside of politics is the jealousies and rivalries it spawns. Armchair cynics skeptically attack a political candidate's motives, or dismiss them as pure ego. Just look at Clinton and Bush. I was no exception. There is an old saying in politics, however, that "if you can't take the heat, get out of the kitchen." Teddy Roosevelt said it similarly in his famous quote about those who get into the arena and get bruised, versus those who do not.

At all levels of consciousness, I felt called by God to get into the arena. Many may not understand this. Nonetheless, I felt called to step up and go to bat for the less powerful in society, the "least of these my brethren." That included Alabamians out of work, people with no health insurance, folks hurt by crumbling public education resources, and the elderly and infirm plagued by inadequate Medicare or Social Security. Namely, "people hurting."

Yes, "the least of these" also included, in my humble opinion, "unborn children" whose mothers didn't want them. This view caused me to be attacked not only by liberal Democrats and rival interests, but more painfully by certain people close to me for years. Towards that end, I consider Matthew 5, 11-12, and take solace in it.

IN OCTOBER 2000, upon the strong recommendation of my campaign manager Sim Pettway, I settled on Doc Sweitzer of Philadelphia as my campaign strategist and media guru for my 2002 U.S. Senate campaign. Upon Sweitzer's recommendation, I chose Ben Eley of Miami to be my fundraiser. Both Sweitzer and Eley brought impressive credentials to the table. Sweitzer touted himself as "outside the box," sublimely suggesting that other national media strategists were "cookie cutters." These terms were relatively new to me at the time, and seemed impressive, as did Sweitzer's national won-lost record, the highest of national Democratic media firms.

With Ben Eley's professional help, in mid-January 2001, after releasing a public statement about my U.S. Senate campaign committee in Washington, D.C., I kicked off my fundraising efforts. The announcement was intended to "jump start" the all-important financial part of the campaign. Instead, Phil Rawls's Associated Press article emphasized my pro-life legal work, upsetting my media guru, Doc Sweitzer. Phil, as was his prerogative, ignored my news release statements about reforming health insurance (the central plank of my platform), promoting economic development, and improving education. Sweitzer was livid. He said, "You need to define yourself, but don't let them define you." Of course, I intended to be what I was, namely, pro-life, but not quite so loudly so, at least not until the general election.

The national economy was already on a downward spiral in the summer of 2001 when the earthshaking 9/11 terrorism attacks occurred. Even before that disastrous milestone, prospective contributors were complaining about how much their stock portfolios had shrunk in 2001. Of course, the complaints intensified after September 11, 2001.

My law partner Jim Bodin and I had installed a good jury on September 10, 2001, defending a criminal case in Opelika, Alabama. We were into our second day of trial on that fateful Tuesday. That morning, while driving east on I-85 to court, I received a call from Leslie. She told us about the first plane. We hoped it was an accident. By the time we arrived in Opelika, the second plane had hit. The court nonetheless started us on the second day of trial. During the next hour, however, Judge Jacob Walker kept receiving messages delivered to him at the bench. At the first break, he declared a mistrial, due solely to the national emergency, saying some jurors might have family or friends who were affected. Jim and I hustled back to Montgomery. I soon gathered all of the firm employees and campaign workers in the "Oak Room" on the first floor.

We all joined hands in prayer, fighting back tears, as increasingly agonizing details came in on the doleful tube. No one could believe it. It seemed unreal, or rather surreal. But we knew it was happening, undeniably.

For me, the aftermath of 9/11 was a "multi-whammy," to coin a phrase. That is, I had a multi-level reaction. Like everyone else, I was deeply concerned about our nation's security and was upset about the enormous loss of life and suffering of victims and their families. Yet the attacks emboldened my sense of purpose and validated my decision to run for the U.S. Senate. I was doing my part.

On a more personal level, Leslie and I lost a dear friend on the hundredth floor of the first World Trade Center tower. Charlie McCrann, a Princeton classmate, had invited Leslie to the party where she and I met on March 30, 1973. Charlie's roommate at his eastside Manhattan apartment, Bob Wise, was a fellow associate lawyer with me at Davis, Polk, and Wardwell, a Wall Street law firm. Bob had invited me to the same party.

After Leslie and I met, as they say, the rest is history. At least until September 11, 2001, when Charlie perished in a moment. Mercifully, he probably never knew what hit him. His office was very close to where the plane struck. In November 2001, I traveled to New York to express my sympathies to Charlie's widow and children at their Soho flat in lower Manhattan. Upon entering their apartment, I was touched by the "glazed-over" look on their faces. It was like they had cried so hard, they couldn't cry anymore.

Fundraising for the U.S. Senate Campaign was extremely difficult the several months following September 11. The nation's business slowed down. Our law practice was no exception. Actually, performing the firm's legal work was healthy for me. However, many prospective campaign donors saw their net worth nosedive after 9/11. They were frightened, and their pockets tightened. They were understandably hesitant about discretionary giving. I couldn't blame them. My own net worth also plunged.

Throughout the campaign, especially after David's sickness in early 2001, I prioritized my time with my only son. He is very dear to me. I drove David to school every morning, and we had special time every night before bed. We read things together. We prayed together. We played together. If I was on the road late coming home, we prayed over the telephone. We had this "special deal" when one of us was feeling ill, to effectively pray for the other's healing. This often produced great results. We reserved one school night each week as a "Big Night." We usually went bowling or played pool. I left political banquets early to fulfill this commitment. It was more than an obligation. It met my own deep emotional need, especially after losing my father. It seemed to benefit David as well.

One time I asked David what his best moment in life was. He quickly replied, "It was seeing your tears when I gave you that trophy." David was referring to the three-foot-high trophy, with wrestlers on top, he gave me on Father's Day Weekend early in the campaign. It stated:

Julian L. McPhillips
Best Father
EVER
Love, David
June 17, 2001

David bought it at a yard sale, had the top corrected, and a plaque inscribed. It is resting on a cabinet in my law office. I look at it often.

The twin pressures of campaign and law firm, amidst the usual demands of family, church and community, kept me spinning. It made the Christmas break of 2001 especially welcome. We flew as a family to Bermuda on December 26, returning January 2, 2002. What an awesome time together we had, refreshingly good for the soul and heart, and nourishing of family bonds.

Returning, the six-month countdown to election day accelerated our pace. Other full-time campaign workers, besides Sim and John Alford, were press secretary Hunter Ford, scheduler Lisa Warren, and field coordinator Robert Smith. During the last two months, new energy and insight arrived with the Rev. Jim Webb, an African Methodist Episcopal (AME) minister. He became campaign director, while Sim remained campaign manager. We tried to start every campaign day at the office with prayer. It helped to keep us stable, focused, and motivated. We needed that, because our campaign, like all political campaigns, had its tensions and rivalries.

The campaign wasn't all serious. Comic relief has its place and may be necessary to keep a candidate's sanity intact. When Leslie traveled with me, a campaign line that always got the audience to laugh in response was my saying that "we have one child born in the '70s, one in the '80s, and one in the '90s." After the chuckling died down, I added that "if you ask me about this decade, I'll hem, and I'll haw, and tell you it ain't over yet . . . " Leslie always loudly interjected, "Oh, yes, it is." Her response always left everyone laughing.

Our campaign made its efforts among the traditional Democratic labor organizations. I related well to most labor leaders. My background as an assistant attorney general under Bill Baxley helped. However, Susan Parker and her husband Paul had prior relationships consolidating their support with most labor groups. Pete Wethington helped me keep central Alabama.

This proved especially problematic when campaign worker Hunter Ford took "McPhillips for U.S. Senate" t-shirts up to a labor rally in North Alabama. The shirts were ordered by Robert Smith of my campaign, and I had not yet examined them. Although there was a label on the shirt stating "Assembled in the U.S.", another label said "Made in Honduras." At the rally Hunter covered for me, pro-Parker labor people seized upon the t-shirt, and criticized us for it. The Parkers' campaign organization sent out letters and videos to labor groups all over Alabama, hitting me about the t-shirts not being made in the U.S. Such is the game of politics—as former U.S. House Speaker Rep. Tip O'Neill famously said, "It ain't beanbag."

Helping us build the fort as major volunteer leaders in Mobile were Ed Kahalley, Sr., my cousin Rosie McPhillips, and the Revs. J. J. Phillips and Howard Johnson. A father-son team of John Knight Sr. and Jr. energized my Cullman base. Chris Mosley, Chris Cummings, Mark Reynolds, and Rev. T. L. Lewis kept Birmingham popping, while former State Senator Doug Ghee provided a steady hand in Anniston. Dear SCLC friend and State Senator Charles Steele, though busy with his own reelection campaign, used his leadership team to help me in Tuscaloosa and the Black Belt. Spiver Gordon and Bobby Singleton also provided valuable help in the Black Belt.

The Rhea law firm and NewSouth leader Robert Avery were my leaders in Gadsden, and the Rev. James Smith, Jr. led our efforts in Dothan and the Wiregrass. Stuart DuBose and his family were enormously helpful in Clark, Monroe, and Washington counties, as was Barbara Turner in Monroe.

Two first cousins in Huntsville and Decatur, Rex and Garland Cheatham, provided great leadership in north Alabama, and Rex, an Alabama Education Association (AEA) Uniserv director and former client, helped me in education circles. Providing awesome leadership in the black communities of Madison and Morgan counties was William Smothers, the publisher of *Speaking Out News*.

Meanwhile, Cubie Rae Gilmer and Janet May of Montgomery and Pete Wethington and Tom Edwards of Wetumpka galvanized my Greater Montgomery base and the central Alabama area. Tom also helped with trial lawyers and Pete worked local labor leaders. Many others made substantial contributions throughout Alabama, including especially State Senator Sundra Escott, the Rev. Abraham Woods, and Gwen Webb in Birmingham, and Robert Smith in Mobile, and Jimmy McCurdy in Montgomery and statewide.

Ron and Loraine Williams of Tuskegee deserve the prize for covering the most territory for me statewide. During the last months of the campaign they traveled by car to every county of Alabama, passing out campaign literature and putting up signs. Ron, former mayor of Tuskegee, contributed substantially to the large margin of victory in Macon County.

Yet we had spots and places where we had no great organizational help. We had to rely on advertising. Probably most helpful in obtaining votes in central Alabama were my years of recognition and work as an attorney.

I recall that before the campaign started, back in November 2000, my media man Doc Sweitzer, Sim Pettway, and I visited with Democratic powerbroker Paul Hubbert of AEA. Present also was AEA pollster-guru Gerald Johnson, a retired Auburn University professor. AEA has long prided itself on the professionalism and accuracy of its polling operations. The signals given us at that time were that my candidacy was welcome, and that AEA would be relatively neutral in the race between Susan Parker and me.

Perhaps out of over-optimism or naivete, I misread AEA's intentions. As the campaign worn on, it became increasingly clear that AEA was doing everything it could to help State Auditor Susan Parker. I also underestimated the value of her husband Paul Parker's help. His sixteen years in the Alabama House of Representatives, doing the bidding of AEA and organized labor, gave both Parkers many IOUs from those two camps. And Paul Hubbert's punch is legendary.

Susan had also been very visible as a statewide elected official. She was also smart. She had appointed key Democrats and minority leaders to vacant Board of Registrar seats around Alabama. She was expecting, and received, a "quid pro quo" (the old "you scratch my back, and I scratch yours"). Susan knew where her bread was buttered. This part was legitimate politics.

Susan used her office well for campaign work, devoting most of her waking hours to making telephone calls, visiting people, and raising money. I give both Parkers credit for working night and day, non-stop. Neither had children or daytime jobs to slow them down. They had few distractions. This turned out to be a big advantage, I realize in hindsight.

It soon became apparent that my competitors in this race were not just incumbent Republican U.S. Senator Jeff Sessions and Democratic primary candidate Susan Parker. I had been hearing rumors and rumblings of it, but then U.S. Attorney Doug Jones of Birmingham announced that he, too, was running for U.S. Senate. He made his announcement immediately after successfully prosecuting the second of the three church bombers (Bill Baxley convicted the first in 1977). A third Democratic candidate, and a strong one at that, Jones was awash in much favorable publicity, including a full-page picture and story in *Newsweek* magazine.

Thus, many Birmingham trial lawyers, who should have been a natural base of support for me, got conflicted out by Doug's candidacy. Many had practiced law closely with Doug and the massive publicity gave Doug a strong base of support in Birmingham, and elsewhere in Alabama. Through his law firm, which represented many labor unions, Doug also had a strong base of labor support.

Meanwhile, much of the Birmingham civil rights leadership, led by Rev. Abraham Woods, raised serious questions about Doug's agreement with a defense lawyer to shelve the third case, or put it on hold. The reason given publicly was that the bomber, Bobby Frank Cherry, was incompetent to stand trial.

Doug Jones's flippant statement that "two out of three ain't bad" played poorly with Rev. Woods, Rev. Lewis, and many other Birmingham "civil righters" in the black community. Many of them came to me for help. I agreed to file, and did file, a motion on behalf of ex-Jefferson County Commissioner Chris McNair, father of one of the four girls killed. I also filed a motion on behalf of the Birmingham chapter of the Southern Christian Leadership Conference. We challenged the Court's decision to allow the third case to be put on hold. Eventually, after a month of legal maneuvering and street support by Rev. Woods and company, we got the case back on track. Rev. Woods and his friends gave me great credit, which helped me politically, but hurt Doug Jones.

Nonetheless, Doug stayed in the race for eight to nine months as a third "major" candidate. In doing so, until he realized that he had no chance to win, he drained away valuable momentum and financial support from me. In the end, Rev. T. L. "Tommy" Lewis called it right when he said that I had muscled Doug out of the Birmingham civil rights community's support and out of the race. Doug had no chance of winning and knew it, which is why he withdrew, but he obviously resented me for it.

Notwithstanding his late withdrawal, Doug caused me much damage, competitively criticizing me to potential supporters. It trickled back to me that Doug was telling these people that I had no chance of beating Sessions because I had stood up too strongly against police brutality in Alabama.

Thus, Jones's withdrawal didn't lend itself to his supporters running in our direction. Some did; some went to Parker, but most, having wasted their money on Jones, were not ready to sign up with anyone else. At least not until after the Democratic primary produced a winner, they said.

The "black base" of my campaign was strong from the beginning. This was more than strategy. It was who I was most comfortable with. Throughout my law practice, I have represented many minorities in difficult situations, and many rallied to help me in my campaign. I had also represented many women in breaking glass ceilings or other gender-based legal cases. Some women voters stayed with me, but many, especially white Democratic women, went to Susan Parker, solely due to her gender.

Susan astutely encouraged this, making her gender the largest asset of her candidacy. At rallies or banquets we jointly attended, she was always touting her gender, not only for making her more electable. It also made her better qualified on issues related to families and children, she said. It was difficult to respond to this. I tried to be gracious.

Much of the leadership of my campaign was black, including former Alabama Democratic Conference field coordinator Robert Smith, campaign manager Sim Pettway, and such Alabama civil rights leaders as Rev. John Alford, Rev. T. L. Lewis, Sen. Charles Steele, former Tuskegee Mayor Ron Williams, and Rev. Jim Webb. They believed my civil rights record was so strong that singular endorsements from the leading black political organizations would surely be mine. That is, that the Alabama Democratic Conference and Alabama New South Coalition could not deny me their support.

An early boost of momentum came in September 2001, after 9/11, when Birmingham civil rights legend Dr. Fred Shuttlesworth publicly endorsed me in front of the Birmingham Civil Rights Museum. A number of other clergy, black and white, attended the announcement. The friendship between Rev. Shuttlesworth and me grew during the campaign and continues strongly to this day. My dear friend, the legendary J. L. Chestnut, Jr., senior partner of New South leader Hank Sanders, issued an enthusiastic endorsement of me at a Selma banquet early in the campaign, adding to the "Big Mo."

On the other hand, foreshadowing future difficulties with New South Coalition President Sanders was the discipline Sanders imposed upon Janet May, a long-time friend and supporter of my campaign. In her capacity as a public relations professional, Janet organized a McPhillips campaign reception in early 2002 at the Kellogg Center in Tuskegee. At that time, Janet was also president of Montgomery's New South chapter.

Citing the reception and other reasons, Sanders decided that Janet had engaged in "unauthorized activity," and removed her as Montgomery chapter president. In an exchange of letters, Sanders reassured me that this was "nothing against me." Nonetheless, Janet was livid, and shortly thereafter transferred to the rival ADC organization headed by Joe Reed. That proved beneficial to her, when Reed returned the favor in the 2003 municipal elections, helping her win election as Montgomery's second-ever black female city council member. I think Janet would make a great future mayor of Montgomery.

We took nothing for granted in the campaigns. April of 2002 brought us to the first large black political convention, the Alabama New South Coalition meeting in Birmingham. A good 80 to 90 percent of New South's county leaders were poised to vote for us, we were informed. At the screening committee meetings, approximately ninety percent of those present expressed their support for me, according to former Tuskegee Mayor Ron Williams, present at the meeting. Unfortunately, New South chairman and State Senator Sanders came in just before the committee was to vote to endorse me. He instead recommended a joint endorsement, or "co-endorsement."

New South had reasons to be indebted to Susan, for appointing voting registrar members in certain counties, Sanders said. New South had reasons to prefer me, because of my strong civil rights record, Sanders added. This way, they avoided a problem for themselves, by endorsing us both, he concluded. Suddenly, the "fix was on." My many enthusiastic supporters endeavored to retain the sole endorsement for me, despite Sanders's recommendation. Unfortunately, the committee's vote to override Sanders's recommendation lost 15-17.

Our team worked hard to change the endorsement on the full floor. Unfortunately, Sanders had instructed the chair of the plenary session to ignore my New South supporters. They knew my leaders were attempting to override the screening committee's co-endorsement. Ignore them, they did. My leaders were denied the right to even speak out on my behalf, or to persuade the entire body otherwise. What a democracy! My supporters' waving arms went unrecognized.

I remembered the big reception in 1986 that I gave for Hank Sanders in my Montgomery home, when he first ran for the State Senate. I remembered how in 1990 I strongly supported Sanders with a large contribution for his U.S. Congressional race. Earl Hilliard won the race, but I thought Sanders would remember my support. I had supported Hank's New South organization strongly as well as other causes of his over the years. I thought Hank would remember. If he did, he sure didn't show it, when I called on him for help in 2002. Often, his brush-off response was "Oh, quit trying to impress me."

To say I was disappointed by the "co-endorsement" would be a vast understatement. In all fairness, based on my strong civil rights record, versus Susan's non-existent record, the singular endorsement should have been ours. Also, since I was more conservative than Susan on faith and family issues, I was more electable. The black leaders knew, or should have known, that I was more electable and could take the fight much better to Sessions, whom they really wanted to beat.

Not surprisingly, New South's action had a domino effect, unraveling a solid string of singular endorsements that should have been ours. A few weeks later, the Alabama Democratic Conference met in Montgomery. It issued a co-endorsement as well. Susan Parker was spotted crying. Apparently, given her strong AEA ties, and given the close connection between ADC and AEA, Susan naively believed the ADC's sole endorsement was hers. I guess we were both a little naive.

Thus the two largest political black groups in the state, once thought solidly behind me, were effectively "neutralized" by these co-endorsements. Susan and I were the two main candidates in the race. Co-endorsements were the same as no endorsement. With both our names on thousands of ballots distributed, we canceled each other out.

The large majority of New South county leaders were still enthusiastically with me. Aided by years of building a reputation in the black community, I still expected the lion's share of the black vote. However, had the sole endorsements remained firm, we would have had 10-15 percent more, avoiding a run-off. Moreover, a first-round win would have been a strong springboard into the general election.

We were also working the white Democratic vote in various and sundry ways. We organized as many counties as we could, but we were also counting on our T.V. advertising for reaching a broad array of voters.

Also boosting the campaign at this later stage (spring of 2002) were timely endorsements from Martin Luther King III, and the Rev. Dr. Andrew Young. Dr. Young came to Montgomery and, at a reception in my home, lent his national prestige with a very complimentary endorsement. Martin King joined Dr. Shuttlesworth, my daughter Grace, and me for a whistlestop tour of the Black Belt late in the campaign. The tour began in Tuscaloosa, with Sen. Charles Steele joining in, and continued on with stops in Greensboro, Demopolis, Uniontown, Selma, and Mobile.

In a subsequent front-page story just before the election, the Tuscaloosa News "accidentally" placed my name under the photograph of black candidate Wayne Sowell, and placed Sowell's name under my photograph. Only Susan Parker was correctly identified. Sen. Steele felt that this was no mistake, that it was meant to hurt me. The error was corrected in the interior pages of a subsequent edition of the Tuscaloosa News, but the confusion was clearly not helpful to my candidacy in that part of the state. Shortly thereafter, the News endorsed Susan Parker.

We had a strong challenge plan against Sessions. But we never got to use it. The best laid plans of mice and men often go astray.

There was another, supposedly "non-serious," candidate, namely Wayne Sowell. A black male, he also qualified for the Democratic primary. All my black supporters put him down as the "perennial candidate." They told me not to concern myself with Sowell. He would be only a 1 or 2 percent vote-getter, they added. Originally a fourth candidate, he became a distant third after Jones dropped out of the race.

The two large black political groups in Birmingham were the Jefferson County Citizens' Coalition and the Jefferson County Progressive Democrats. We received the unanimous endorsement of the Citizens Coalition, otherwise known as "Arrington's group" (because four-time Birmingham mayor Richard Arrington organized and developed it). My Birmingham coordinator, Chris

Mosley, a Coalition leader, did his work exceptionally well. I supplemented his work with telephone calls to key leaders.

The support of the Progressive Democrats was supposedly even more solid, based on reliable "commitments." As the Progressive Democrats' endorsement meeting approached, my other Birmingham coordinator, Chris Cummings, told me "Julian, you have nothing to worry about. You got it locked solid."

I recall, however, that a few weeks *before* the Progressive Democrats' endorsement of May 2002, a top leader of their organization, an attorney in Birmingham, called me. He inquired about how much I could "donate" to get out the vote. "My fair share," I answered, thinking that was a good answer. In hindsight, it was a bad answer. A more solid figure would have been better. But how much? We were not unlimited financially. I didn't realize until later how much this endorsement was "for sale."

After Susan Parker shocked us with the Progressive Democrats' endorsement, we were informed that Paul Hubbert and AEA had swept in at the last moment, infusing the Progressive Democrats with a large sum of "get out the vote" money. We heard that it was a ton of money—one person told us it was in the neighborhood of half a million. The only reciprocal consideration was that the Progressive Democrats support Hubbert's and AEA's statewide list of endorsed candidates, we also heard. That included Susan Parker for U.S. Senate.

Thus, a split of the two large black political groups developed in Birmingham. Rather than winning Jefferson County by 2 to 1, as originally expected, we ended up in a photo finish tie of 26,884 to 26,627. This development, more than anything else, cost me a win without a run-off in the Democratic primary.

Another problem was that Sen. Hank Sanders of Selma, president of the New South Coalition, wanted me to give $10,000 to the cost of putting out their worthless co-endorsement ballot. When I challenged him about why I should pay anything to promote the election prospects of my opponent, Sanders became very defensive. Through intermediaries, Sanders made it clear that if I didn't pay the money, I might be stripped of my co-endorsement. "That stinks! Is that legal?" our campaign workers exclaimed.

But Sen. Charles Steele, a great friend and supporter, said, "Hey, that's politics." A compromise was reached in the first primary with a payment of $7,000. In the runoff, however, I was told that I better come up with $10,000 or suffer the consequences. When I didn't come up with it quickly enough in the run-off, although I was getting ready to pay it, the New South leaders followed through on their threat and gave the endorsement to Susan only. I was livid, but already on a slippery, downhill slope. I almost went public with my criticism about the unethical nature of all this but I knew the futility of doing so. I realized some would have dismissed my comments as "sour grapes."

By contrast, the Alabama Democratic Conference (ADC) and Joe Reed, to their credit, did not try to extract money from me for their co-endorsement. Nor did the ADC attempt to remove the co-endorsement in the run-off.

As we went into the final two weeks of the campaign leading up to Tuesday, June 2, it was a horse race. We had energetic get-out-the-vote efforts in Montgomery, Mobile, Cullman, and Birmingham, and strategic efforts in the black neighborhoods of Huntsville, Gadsden, Selma, Anniston, the Wiregrass, and the Black Belt, but unfortunately in few other places. We had a statewide telephone campaign to identified black voters to play the recorded endorsements of Martin Luther King III and Fred Shuttlesworth.

Even knowing that we had "organized labor" and "organized education" (AEA) against us in the primary, we still believed we could win without a run-off. One of our big strengths seemed to be good T.V. advertising. We were getting much positive feedback and our polling showed that our percentage of the vote was rising rapidly in the final weeks of the campaign.

Doc Sweitzer put together a set of eight television ads. The only ad that was "out of the box" was one that had my daughter Grace saying the blessing at the family table before dinner. That ad had a sensationally positive response in the black community. Everywhere I went black voters were exclaiming about how much they liked it. Moderate to conservative whites reacted similarly, but unfortunately most of them were voting in the Republican primary and their support was thus lost to me.

The reaction of liberal whites to Grace's blessing ad was mixed. Of those who knew me but might otherwise have questioned the ad, there was less of a problem. They knew the real me, and the good intent of the ad, and voted for me. But among some liberal whites, especially those who didn't know me, there was some adverse reaction. Even though the blessing was generic and didn't mention Jesus, some thought we were too "out front" in our Christian faith. After the campaign was over, my brother Frank echoed this view. Others thought one should only pray in the privacy of one's closet. Some editorialists, skeptics at heart, took condescending swipes. My daughter Grace, bless her heart, wrote a letter to the editor, defending the ad, making the point that I hadn't made her say the blessing for political reasons, as an earlier letter to the editor had charged.

Wiser heads in the Democratic party complimented the ad. Indeed, Lucy Baxley, campaigning for election as lieutenant governor, said at an August, 2002 Montgomery County Democratic Executive Committee meeting that "Julian's blessing ad is the best thing that's happened to the Democratic party in some time." She added that "we need more like this." In agreement was Democratic secretary of state candidate Nancy Worley, who initially told me what Lucy said. Lucy subsequently confirmed the accuracy of that quote.

On the whole, I believe the famous Grace blessing ad was much more positive than negative. The same ad helped elect Democrat Mark Pryor as new U.S. Senator in Arkansas in 2002. At least the ad was memorable and surely caused a public reaction, one way or the other. One reaction, especially among young men, was "Oh, what beautiful daughters you have." Of course, I was most pleased to hear that.

The Abortion Issue

Another major factor at work during the primary campaign was my position on the abortion issue. Ironically, it would have helped me in the general election, but it proved troublesome in the primary.

From the beginning of the campaign, this was a delicate subject. Everyone knew I was unapologetically pro-life. My son David had been saved from an abortion at the last moment, despite the fact that his biological parents were a young married couple. Like so many other Americans, they didn't realize what was at stake. Fortunately, I persuaded them that adoption was a better alternative.

Unfortunately, 40 percent of the millions of abortions that occur in America annually take place among married couples for reasons of convenience. This travesty is a national tragedy, in my opinion.

If David's story was the extent of my involvement in the pro-life fight, I might not have been so vulnerable to the pro-choice attack which developed from the political left.

The position I tried to articulate was that, yes, I am pro-life, but my objective is to raise the public consciousness to a level where more and more people would "choose life."

There is great life inside the womb at two months. Every organ and limb are in place, and only need to grow more. There is a strong heart beat, and a brain wave so strong that, if the unborn child were an adult, the law could not allow removal from life support. All this I stated, when questioned at debates, to show why I took the position I did. My position wasn't just religious; it was scientific.

Of course, my famous case representing an unborn child, a case to which I was appointed by a Montgomery County Circuit judge, had made me something of a hero to the pro-life community, nationally and locally. But it also made me a danger to the pro-abortion crowd [see chapter 26], especially people like Southern Poverty Law Center founder Morris Dees, who had used the Center's unlimited resources to file suits against the pro-life community in Florida and elsewhere.

Not surprisingly, Susan Parker and her husband made my abortion view the primary focal point of their attacks on me. We heard it everywhere. It was not generally in the press during the primary's first round. It was a "tongue-wagging" effort. "Oh, he's really a Republican," was how it came back to us. Paul and Susan Parker were saying that about me to Democrats everywhere.

Just as Susan made her gender one of her two main biographical strengths (the other was that she "picked cotton" until she was sixteen), the Parkers stepped up their attack on my abortion position as the June 2 primary date drew near.

On May 7, 2002, Susan sent a letter to what must have been every women's group in Alabama. My wife Leslie was on one such list, and she received a letter in which Susan stated:

> . . . I am also concerned with the rights of women's reproductive care. Simply put, I support a woman's right to choose.
>
> My major opponent in the Democratic primary for the United States Senator, Julian McPhillips, voices his beliefs loudly in his book, *The People's Lawyer: The Life and Times of Julian L. McPhillips*. Take a look at the following excerpts.

"What really galls me is the cruel irony that there are people out there who are trying to save whales and save the field mice but who are not in favor of saving children. And this is what we have here- a real, live human life, if you have a conflict between a woman's right to privacy and the right of a person to live... if there's the constitutional rights to life and privacy, I say the right to life should be greater." (Page 320)

"I think it is known that I have a heart for unborn children, and I'm proud of that." (Page 320)

"I say there is no greater underdog, or victim, in life . . . and I emphasize the words 'in life' . . . than a baby who's about to be killed in his or her mother's own womb. It's just consistent with my overall philosophy and clientele. I'm just proud to be able to do what I can." (Page 320-21).

As you can see, we have a potential problem on our hands. We must do everything possible to protect our right to choose. *As your next United States Senator, I will certainly do just that.*

With these inflammatory words, Susan made a strong pitch for financial and other support.

I had significant disagreements within my own extended family about this issue. I try to respect different views but my conscience wouldn't allow me to compromise my belief that there is great life inside the womb, even at two months, when most abortions take place.

There were significant numbers of other liberals out there who greatly appreciated my civil rights record but raised their eyebrows about my pro-life views. How dare I not be a liberal doctrinaire? How dare I not fit into their box?

As the last six weeks of the primary ensued, we noticed an increasing number of letters attacking us from Susan Parker supporters. Fictitious names were often used. Some attacked "the fancy schools" my children and I had attended. This was an obvious effort to attract the public school vote and play the "class card" against me. That is, I was "too privileged" to be a Democrat, the Parkers were saying, with the message coming from their friends writing letters to editors.

Some letters attacked Grace's blessing ad. One letter completely misrepresented the source of my fundraising, saying that two-thirds of my money raised came from out-of-state. The truth was that only one-third came from outside of Alabama. The other two-thirds came from Alabamians.

We also heard that the Parkers were playing the "race card" against me, saying in largely white union halls that, "Oh, you don't want him. He's that civil rights attorney."

As they say, all's fair in love, war, and politics. But I had gone out of my way, everywhere I went, to say nice things about Susan Parker, Obviously this was not being reciprocated. The irony is that I truly was much nicer to her than vice-versa. Yet in the run-off election, I was the one wrongfully portrayed as unfairly attacking her. It was a downer.

Class card. Race card. Gender card. Maybe Susan just played her political cards better than I did.

Election Night

Election night was surprising. As vote totals mounted on T.V., Susan Parker maintained a small lead, but I was "in the forties," percentile-wise. The final vote was 48 percent for Susan, and 43 percent for me. Amazingly, there was a 9 percent tally for the supposed "non-entity," the perennial candidate Wayne Sowell whom my black leadership had told me to disregard. Yet given the black base of my support, Sowell, as the only black candidate, ate into my vote much more than into Susan's.

Although Sowell had little advertising, he enjoyed some underground support from voters who agreed with his "legalization of marijuana" position. How else can one explain the 884 votes he got in almost all-white Cullman County? Such a stance, if widely known, would have caused a backlash in conservative Alabama. Sowell had zero chance of ever winning. Unfortunately, Sowell's quiet pro-marijuana stance, his presence as the only black candidate in the race, and his hobbyist candidacy in every election since the mid-1980s gave him enough voters to be a spoiler. Spoil us he did, putting Susan and me into a run-off.

When the votes were counted on election night, June 4, 2002, I won most of south Alabama, including my home county of Montgomery by 3 to 1. This was gratifying, as these voters knew me best. We also won my "ancestral roots" county of Mobile by 2 to 1. This, too, was gratifying. I know my grandfather and father would have been proud. We won 78 percent of the vote in Macon County, one of the counties in the state with the highest percentage of black voters. We won the counties around Montgomery by large margins, and the counties around Mobile by smaller margins.

Unfortunately, the "tie vote" in populous Jefferson County killed us. Further, I was clobbered in white north Alabama except in Cullman County, where I grew up as a child (1946–59). It was sweet to win Cullman by exactly 1,000 votes over Susan Parker. Her hometown of Eva, virtually on the Cullman-Morgan line, gave Susan a strong Cullman County base, further developed during her four years as a statewide elected official.

I was disappointed that my "out-of-the-box" media man, Doc Sweitzer, did not speak to me until six days after the first primary election date, or not until Monday, June 10, 2002. As it turned out, I could have used some helpful guidance in advance on how to respond to the press in the next several weeks.

The Run-Off

So we ended up in a run-off, for which I was unprepared. I had expected either Susan or me to win outright as we were supposed to be the only two real candidates. Sowell was not supposed to be a factor.

I got little sleep on election night and the next day. We began the anti-climatic task of organizing a run-off campaign. Although Wayne Sowell messed us up, greater shenanigans, of a nature I had never before experienced, were just around the corner. And the perpetrator was one I would never have expected.

The *Birmingham News*'s Sabotage

The *Birmingham News* assigned a young white reporter, Katherine Bouma, to do a story on the U.S. Senate race. Bouma's personal demographics were identical to Susan's, namely female, younger, white, and childless. Little did I realize that she was allied with forces wanting to "do me in." It was a sabotage job, pure and simple. The newspaper's motivation came from variety of sources. It included editors favorable to Susan Parker, and other powers-that-be in the *News* connected philosophically if not personally to Jeff Sessions. The primary negative influence, we believe, was former *News* Publisher Clarence Hanson, father of young Victor Hanson, the current publisher. The younger

Hanson had taken over his father's position, a family sinecure, not too many years earlier.

Victor was publisher at the time we initially received the *Birmingham News'* endorsement for the first-round primary. Young Victor, a close friend of my brother Frank and a decent fellow who apparently agreed with me on the abortion issue, initially favored me himself. I'm sure Frank helped. I believe senior editor Tom Scaritt also initially favored me, for personal reasons. There may have been a few others. They helped me get the *News* endorsement for the first primary, which would make some wonder why the *News* had a motive to sabotage me later.

Frankly, I don't think Victor Hanson or Tom Scaritt were a part of the original sabotage scheme, but they got swept up into it, without realizing what was going on. Later on, they were forced to defend the *News* and are likely still in denial about what happened.

Unfortunately, the initial endorsement created a backlash among friends of Clarence Hanson, I was later informed. Although no longer publisher himself, Clarence Hanson was well connected to the Birmingham business community, a segment of which truly feared me. Some in that group wanted to stop me at all costs. They correctly considered me a much stronger threat to Jeff Sessions and his Big Business string-pullers than Susan Parker ever would be. The senior Hanson still had his influence within the newspaper.

I was floored when I received a call Thursday morning, June 6, two days after the election, from a close personal friend who asked if I had seen the article in the *Birmingham News* that morning. He said the article was the "final nail in my coffin," and added that he could no longer support me in the campaign. Coming from someone so close, it took the wind out of my sails, and left me staggering.

How this nefarious episode developed needs to be told. It started with the young Bouma, the day after the first-round election, baiting me with a question about Susan Parker's advantage on children's and family issues. It was about the seventeenth out of twenty subjects I talked to Bouma about. I was unaware of the trap being laid. Bouma said that Susan claimed to be better on these issues, due to her gender. I said, "Yes, I know. I had been hearing that throughout the campaign." But I responded, "How can that be? I'm the only one who's ever raised children. I don't think she has ever raised a single child.

I know as much, if not more, than she does about these issues."

I was simply defending myself from Susan's implied criticism of me as a male.

The article Bouma wrote, surely tweaked masterfully by editors, was a Machiavellian effort designed to discredit my candidacy. It succeeded beyond their greatest expectations.

The Thursday, June 4, 2002, *Birmingham News* had an innocent enough headline, *"McPhillips Makes Family an Issue."* The subtitle ominously read *"Says Childless Parker Can't Understand."*

The newspaper's cleverly written first sentence said: *"Democratic Senate Candidate Julian McPhillips said on the first day of his runoff race that he understands children's issues better than opponent Susan Parker, because he had three children, and she has none."*

The tricky next sentence began with the words, *"He also attacked her,"* suggesting that the first sentence was an initial attack upon Parker because she was childless. Of course, I had not attacked her, and neither said nor meant anything of the sort. The *Birmingham News* knew that. Otherwise, it would be like me attacking anyone, and everyone, who had never had children.

As the old saying goes, "I may be dumb, but I ain't stupid." Certainly not that stupid.

The article next quoted me as saying Susan Parker was *"leading primarily because her husband was a water boy for the Alabama Education Association."* This quote was largely out of context, although technically correct.

The next sentence of the article quoted me as saying: *"I am a family person and she's not had any children. She's never ever had any children. I have three. I can understand the concerns of children both born and unborn."*

This quote subtly but grossly twisted out of context what I actually said, suggesting that Susan was *not* a "family person," something I never said. This sentence drove a verbal knife deeper, creating enormous damage to my candidacy.

The next part of the story sympathetically quoted Susan Parker as saying, *"I lost a child and was told by doctors that I shouldn't try to have children again. It wasn't that I didn't want to have children. That's very hurtful."*

Oh, what a villain this cleverly nuanced response made me look like. Yet, none of my comments were ever directed at Susan Parker herself. My words were only in response to reporter Bouma's questions. Ms. Bouma, in turn, spoke with co-reporter Anna Velasco, who then spoke with Susan Parker. By the time my original words got back to Susan, they were "triple hearsay," and Susan's words back to me were triple hearsay. Any judge will tell you that hearsay is unreliable, and will not be allowed into evidence. This is all the more true for double or triple hearsay. I was not talking directly to Susan.

Accuracy of quotes was of no concern to the *Birmingham News* nor was the reliability of its facts. Influencing the outcome of the election was the *Birmingham News'* desire. It was great sport to them. The Birmingham paper was not reporting the news; it was making the news, and that is not good journalistic ethics.

Susan Parker's statement that my words were "very hurtful" portrayed me as a big bully. Here I was, an older man beating up on a younger woman, or so the *Birmingham News* painted me. Voters immediately flocked her way.

Unfortunately, the *Birmingham News* never disclosed that I did not speak directly to Susan. I spoke only to Ms. Bouma, who then spoke to Ms. Velasco, who then spoke to Susan. With the reporters' slanted reconstruction of my words, if Susan experienced any hurt, it was due to the reporter's words, not mine. Some political observers doubted that Susan was "hurt" at all. They believed she was capitalizing for political gain.

Cleverly, this masterful piece of "so-called journalism" continued by saying: *"Parker, now state auditor, said she admired McPhillips for his adoption of his third child."*

Here the trickery was thick. That sentence made Susan look gracious and forgiving, while portraying me as an insensitive oaf. It was a purposeful twisting, an artful slant, with a deadly accurate aim.

The hatchet job still wasn't over. The next part of the article, continuing to build sympathy for the Parkers, stated: *"She said she and her husband considered adoption, but did not know if their income would be sufficient to get through the adoption process."*

What a ploy! Here the *News* was bolstering Susan's own projected image as "the poor country girl made good."

The *Birmingham News* then outrageously misquoted me as saying: *"Parker could have adopted a child with the $75,000 she recently donated to her campaign."*

My correct statement, in response to the reporter's question was: *"It doesn't sound like someone who couldn't afford to adopt, since she gave $75,000 to her own campaign."* A huge difference!

There is a big distinction between saying a person could afford to adopt, and implying that one should have done so, which is a highly personal decision and none of my business. Oh, how the nuances can spin things in a different direction, and make the intended target look villainous.

The *Birmingham News* still wasn't finished. Next, the hatchet job incorrectly said I loaned $1.3 million to my campaign. Although the true amount was $300,000 less, the worst part was the deliberate *News* omission of my raising about $450,000 from approximately one thousand contributors. The *News* article also failed to point out that Susan Parker's campaign had benefitted from a huge amount of unreported AEA money used to help secure key endorsements and other campaign assistance. Some knowledgeable insiders speculated that this assistance was easily worth $1 million.

The final "nail in my coffin," to use my friend's words, came when the *News* printed: *"McPhillips, 55, said he . . . would vote for laws to repeal abortion rights."*

Although I had been unapologetically pro-life throughout the campaign, I had *never, ever,* used the word *"repeal."* This confirmed how fabricated the whole story was. What I said to Ms. Bouma, in response to her question, was precisely that I "favored legislation supportive of mother and child." Throughout the campaign, I consistently stated that I recognized and respected the U.S. Supreme Court's decision upholding choice. I added that my goal, as I described above, was to elevate public consciousness so more people would choose life.

After this initial article, the attack against me from editors and reporters was relentless and mean-spirited. The two most vicious "attack dog" columns came from Elaine Witt of the *Birmingham Post-Herald.* Another liberal white female journalist, without children, she obviously took great personal offense at my alleged comments, and hammered me unmercifully.

The "letters to the editor" which *News* editors "chose" to publish were also ugly. They reduced my oldest daughter Rachel to tears. It was not until sweet Rachel's own letter defending me was published nine days later that the editors finally stopped that form of attack. But the damage was done, and it was too late to undo it, with so little time left in the run-off.

My precious older daughter Rachel wrote, as part of her five-paragraph letter:

> My father is the greatest man I know. He has always stood up for people regardless of their gender or race. There is no one who cares more for powerless people than my father. He has raised my sister, brother and me to reach out to hurting people. My father has a very big heart. That is why the attack on my father hurts so much. Numerous times, his opponent has stressed the importance of her being a woman. She has cited research about the typical records of women to put herself out as the better candidate.

No doubt I was remiss for ever mentioning that Susan Parker had no children, even if I was trying at the time to make the equalitarian point that men as well as women have stakes in and can have expertise in family matters. I have been a devoted father and still believe that, having raised three children, I know as much about childrearing as do most women and, logically, more than women who have not raised children. But I admit my fault in the way the comment came out. I was tired the morning after the election, was caught off guard, and should have been more careful.

I immediately apologized to Susan. However, I certainly was not trying to criticize Susan or any woman for her having children or not having children. Instead, the embellishment, the cleverly crafted article, which made me look like I was attacking Susan for her not having children, was a vicious and deliberate sabotage attack on me. Adding to the pain, the *Birmingham News* switched its endorsement to Susan for the run-off.

The repercussions throughout the Democratic party were immediate, very negative, and irreversible at that late date. At a state capitol introduction of the run-off candidates, Alabama Democratic Party chairman Redding Pitt heaped praise on Susan Parker. He looked at me with a cold stare, and said, "The other candidate is Julian McPhillips."

At that rally, I walked over to Steven Black, a run-off candidate for state treasurer. Steven looked like he was embarrassed to be seen talking with me, and said, "Did you really say Susan Parker should adopt with $75,000 of her own money?" I groaned and said no, I didn't say that.

Others, from Democratic secretary of state candidate Chris Pitts to state attorney general Bill Pryor, were also quoted publicly as saying ugly things about me.

The worst attack, kicking me while I was down, came from former U.S. Senate candidate Doug Jones. Doug called a press conference and said my comments about Susan were outrageous. He didn't stop there, however. He attacked me for misrepresenting my role in the Bobby Frank Cherry case.

My law partner Kenneth Shinbaum quickly responded publicly, defending me, and demonstrating correctly how my motion on behalf of Chris McNair and the SCLC got the Cherry case back on track. Moreover, it was actually the Revs. Fred Shuttlesworth, Abraham Woods, and T. L. Lewis, not me, who commented publicly about how helpful I was in the Cherry case. But Jones was not concerned with accuracy and had a sympathetic audience with the *Birmingham News* editors, who gave his attack a substantial play, and my response much less coverage.

Amazingly, however, many Republicans were speaking well of me for what they perceived as a truth, that yes, a man can be just as good as a woman on family and children issues, especially where the man has raised three children and the woman none. These Republicans said I was a victim of the political correctness doctrine. Maybe I was, although I know it was my own fault for not being more careful.

On the other hand, Democratic state senators Charles Steele and Sundra Escott could not have been more helpful. They have each been through clever newspaper sabotage attacks themselves. They knew the *Birmingham News* article on me was a "set-up" and a distortion. Sundra, bless her heart, even had my name placed on ballots her campaign printed up and distributed in her electoral district during the run-off campaign in Birmingham, Alabama.

Although I strongly believe the New South Coalition removed my co-endorsement in the run-off for not paying an additional $10,000 fast enough, some of its leaders pointed out another rationale, the so-called "gender insensitive" comments attributed to me by the Birmingham News. After all, Hank Sanders's top echelon of assistant leaders was overwhelmingly female, which helped cause the co-endorsement in the first place.

Despite attempts by some black female leaders in Birmingham to help me repair the damage, it was too late. I still won Montgomery and Mobile, but lost

Birmingham by a large margin in the run-off. Statewide, Susan won by a significant margin.

I will always remember, and be comforted by the fact, that my cousin Frank Dixon of New Orleans showed up on the last two days of the run-off and campaigned hard for me in some of Birmingham's black precincts. We had too much to overcome at that late date, however.

As the campaign ended, all I did to recover was take one long weekend at Lake Martin. I was battered and bruised, more emotionally than physically, but grateful to be alive. I was still blessed in many other ways.

I wrote Victor Hanson on July 1, 2002, told him the *Birmingham News* had "grievously wronged" me and asked for an apology. All I received was a brief reply wishing me the best of luck, as I returned to the practice of law.

The first two weeks of July 2002 were the most productive two weeks of my law practice in quite a while. It was good to be back in the saddle, even though I was in need of more rest. I knew that later in July we'd be attending one of Mahesh and Bonnie Chavda's healing conferences in Charlotte, North Carolina. I knew that would be spiritually refreshing. I also knew that a week up in New Hampshire, visiting our actress daughter Grace at a summerstock theater, would also relax us, and it did.

While the law practice was zipping along in the late summer of 2002, I continued to feel wronged by the *Birmingham News*. I therefore sent Victor Hanson a second letter, on September 5, 2002, this time asking for a retraction and public apology. Not surprisingly, the young publisher gave none. Although I briefly considered suing the *News*, after giving it prayerful consideration, I decided not to do so, and turned it over to God.

Nonetheless, two late-summer letters to the editors of the *Birmingham News*, summed up well what happened. On August 8, 2002, Elinor Staff of Mountain Brook wrote:

> After seeing your ugly, unflattering cartoon of Susan Parker in The Birmingham News on July 19, it now appears that your paper's attack against U.S. Senate candidate Julian McPhillips in the runoff election was calculated to help secure Parker's victory because she would be a weaker candidate against U.S. Senator Jeff Sessions. I also find it interesting that you hammered McPhillips so unmercifully for alleged insensitivity over Parker's childlessness

yet, hypocritically, you draw a picture of Parker as a big, muscular, overweight man in a woman's clothing. Is that not much more crass and insensitive than anything attributed to McPhillips? Otherwise, why would you attack both candidates that you also endorsed, except for the planned purpose of helping Sessions?

On September 9, 2002, Republican state representative Dick Brewbaker of Montgomery wrote:

> I am a Republican. I am voting for U.S. Sen. Jeff Sessions. Even so, I watched with regret the hatchet job The Birmingham News chose to do on Julian McPhillips. Apparently, the guardians of political correctness at The News were horrified that McPhillips would dare suggest that a man who has actually raised children has at least as much understanding of children's issues as a woman who has not. McPhillips' unapologetic pro-life stance and his claim that religious values have relevance even in politics must have been so offensive to the political editors at The News that they decided to do everything in their power to damage his candidacy. Perhaps they were right to do so. If McPhillips had been allowed to go on, he might have started suggesting that character is more important than political correctness. We certainly can't have that.

I was grateful for both letters. They accurately told the story. My campaign leaders from Rev. John Alford in Montgomery to Rev. T. L. Lewis in Birmingham to Rex Cheatham in Huntsville all stated that the *Birmingham News* hatchet job cost me the run-off. As much as I didn't want to admit it at the time, I have come to realize they were correct.

While proving the conspiratorial involvement of everyone to a certainty would be difficult, I nonetheless believe, based on the overwhelming circumstantial evidence, that I was targeted by the *Birmingham News*. Perhaps the *News* believes that "all is fair in love, war, and politics" was its justification, or license, to influence the outcome of my run-off contest. Whatever its rationale, the *News's* sabotage story had a devastating impact on my candidacy.

Although I was burned by the *Birmingham News* and have had other friends treated similarly by it, including Don Siegelman, Sundra Escott, and

Richard Scrushy, I'm well aware of the newspaper's long history and redeeming journalistic accomplishments. I've been reading the paper myself since I was six, when my father taught me to follow my athletic heroes in the *News'* sports pages in the early 1950s. Once I became a sports reader, I moved on to other articles. I remember when I was only nine reading the *News'* fascinating accounts of the Montgomery Bus Boycott. I concede that even today the *News* has the broadest overall coverage of any newspaper in the state, with many fine journalists and editors.

Like many news organizations, however, they like sensationalism and this can lead to negative "feeding frenzies." And the *Birmingham News*, like most human institutions, can also be hypocritical. When the Birmingham News Company, the publisher of the *News,* was hit by a $20 million fraud judgment in 2003, there was a small article about the case in the business section. Had the case been about anyone else, it would have been a front-page headline. The company appealed the award to the Alabama Supreme Court, but it was upheld. Naturally, there was no article in the *News* about that decision.

Aftermath of the Campaign

To avoid becoming a Biblical pillar of salt, one should not look back too much. Nonetheless, a little constructive self-criticism can be good for the soul. What could I have done different, or better?

First, I spent too much time raising money. I could have easily made three times the $450,000 I raised if I'd spent the same amount of hours practicing law. Better still, if I had used equal time meeting politically savvy people in the neighborhoods of Alabama, maybe it would have translated into more votes. After all, I still had plenty to spend on advertising from the million dollars of my own money set aside for that purpose.

A year before the election, former state senator Doug Ghee advised me that to win I would need to take off fulltime from the law practice the next year to campaign. I simply wasn't able to do so, as the head of a firm of eight lawyers and more than twenty employees. There were times, especially after September 11, when my presence at the law practice was badly needed. Indeed, law partners Mary Goldthwaite and Karen Rodgers were both giving birth about the time of the June 2002 primary election.

Besides, I rationalized, I'd be off full-time between getting the nomination on June 4 and the November general election, and a year and a half was perhaps an unnecessary amount of time away from the practice.

Also, I should have had more full-time white leadership in my campaign. I heard that advice from the black leadership of my campaign.

However, we had unprecedented strong support from local, state, and national civil rights leaders. As it turned out, that didn't guarantee me the endorsements of all the black political organizations in Alabama.

It would have been helpful to have brought in a full time "pro," even from outside of Alabama, who had run a U.S. Senate campaign. We had the money to pay one. But we never found him or her. We should have tried harder.

We did a lot of things right in our message, in our organization, and in our enthusiasm. The overwhelming majority of past presidents of the Alabama Trial Lawyers supported me, each making the maximum $1,000 contribution to my campaign.

But we had stronger primary opposition than anticipated, not just from Susan Parker but also from Doug Jones and Wayne Sowell. We had to spend too much of our time and resources fighting for the nomination, and were not able to focus enough on Jeff Sessions.

Obviously, I needed better advice and coaching on how to handle the gender issue. I received little or none from my strategist Doc Sweitzer up in Pennsylvania. As it turned out, this was very tricky and ended up hurting me greatly, especially in a Democratic primary whose turnout was 60 percent female.

In hindsight, I believe we should have spent less money on media, and more on get-out-the-vote (GOTV). Wherever we devoted resources to GOTV, it paid royal dividends.

We learned a lot, but it took enormous energy and enormous resources.

It wasn't just *the Birmingham News* sabotage job that killed me. I lost the nomination when the New South Coalition co-endorsed Susan Parker and me and set the dominos in motion.

For the record, Susan lost the general election to incumbent Jeff Sessions by almost 20 percent of the vote, or 253,668 votes. Many politically savvy Alabamians said I would have made the race much closer, and might have beaten Jeff. Susan, on the other hand, spent all she had raised in the primary, appeared worn out heading into the general election campaign, never attacked

Sessions, and virtually conceded months before the November election.

Despite the tribulations and sacrifices, the U.S. Senate campaign was exhilarating for me in many ways. Addressing national issues was thrilling. Meeting new people and organizing all over Alabama was exciting. The three debates Susan and I had in Birmingham, Tuscaloosa, and Montgomery were fun. There were ups and downs almost every day. But it was exciting. And faith-building.

I forgive those who wronged me in the campaign. Unforgiveness, after all, generally hurts more the one who holds such feeling in his heart than it does those who are the object of such unforgiveness.

Despite what happened with Hank Sanders, I commend him and his energetic wife Rose for supporting many good things in their professional careers, especially advocating the causes of poor folks and minorities. I wish them well. Ultimately, we are allies in wanting to make Alabama a better place for all its people. Similarly, Doug Jones is an exceptionally capable attorney, and I hope he does very well in defending my old friend and former client, Chris McNair, recently indicted in Birmingham on seemingly preposterous charges of bribery. Susan Parker and her husband Paul are good people. I hope they have many happy years together in the future. As for the Birmingham News, I read it daily, and long ago wrote Victor Hanson that I forgave his newspaper. That doesn't mean I can't take them on in a case or two for other clients.

As my good friend Joe Turnham, twice-defeated but undaunted candidate for U.S. Congress, has said: "One can be legitimately called by God to run for office. That does not mean one is called to win the election." I take solace from that statement and believe that I won in many other ways. Among other blessings, the Lord used the results to humble me, and that is a good thing.

In the end, the campaign reminded me how much more important my relationships with God and with my family were than winning any political office, or accomplishing any professional goal.

31

Back Into Law Practice

A S THE CAMPAIGN ENDED, it was good to get back into the full-time practice of law. Our firm is like a family. All my law partners are good people, and they are smart lawyers. Most, if not all, share my view that law practice is not just a business, not just a profession, but a ministry as well. All have been active in their church or synagogue. My long-time partner Kenneth Shinbaum is a past president of Agudath Israel Synagogue.

Speaking of Kenneth, what a wonderful example of assistance he has been to our lawyers and personnel! Although he has more than one hundred cases on his own docket, he goes around the firm helping other lawyers, or they come to him. Ken answers their questions and provides insight and strategy. Unselfish, honest, and loyal to the highest degree, Kenneth has been a wonderful complement, in personality and skills, to me.

Of course, the firm's lawyers all have different personalities. Like pieces of a puzzle, we fit together. My former "name" law partner William Gill decided a year ago to peel away from the partnership. Although now at a different location, he remains "of counsel" to us and is so listed on the firm letterhead. He still works with us on a few big cases. William's rationale in stepping away from the partnership was to free himself to devote at least half of his time to missionary work, and eventually all of his time. Such a laudatory motive is understood and applauded by all.

Mary Goldthwaite is the next partner in the pecking order. What a blessing she has been since she joined us in 1992. We offered to add her name to the firm name upon William's departure. Mary, always modest, declined. After discussion with the other partners, the firm's name was amended in April 2004 to the shorter "McPhillips Shinbaum, L.L.P." Mary works more hours than anyone. Her diligence has paid off handsomely in major cases, especially where she represented four young female students sexually abused by a Selma school teacher. In May 2005, she obtained a $1 million judgment from the federal court in Mobile. In late 2004, she had settled claims against the other defendants for $600,000, most of which was paid for by insurance.

The four junior partners—Karen Sampson Rodgers, Aaron Luck, Jim Bodin, and Joe Guillot—have all emerged as first-rate lawyers. The last three went to Jones School of Law. When I mentioned to Jones law professor Shirley Howell that we had "three of Jones Law's best" in Aaron, Jim, and Joe, the professor quickly said, "No, you have the three best."

Aaron, an ex-Marine, and Jim, a former history professor, are in their mid-thirties. Both are bright, unpretentious, reliable, and faithful to God and their families. They are loyal to the law firm family. Both get things done quickly. Each has been a great blessing, specializing in personal injury, keeping the firm's cash register ringing, and earning well-deserved bonuses.

Joe Guillot, a retired Air Force lieutenant colonel, has been a triple blessing. He's not only a fine lawyer, with a wide array of legal skills, but has become especially astute in employment law and criminal defense. With his accounting skills he checks our firm's books monthly, to reconcile accounts. Thirdly, at Christ the Redeemer Episcopal Church, Joe is our church's treasurer, past senior warden, and solid lay leader.

Karen Sampson Rodgers is a dear, well-rounded attorney. She has developed into a fierce advocate in the nine years since she joined the firm in 1996. Karen is especially adept at employment law and is improving her knowledge in personal injury and criminal defense. Karen is also a licensed, ordained co-minister, along with her husband Thomas, at a local church. Karen is a "sister-in-the Lord" with me, sometimes helping me pray for (and with) firm clients or firm employees.

Joe Marston, a retired assistant attorney general after thirty-three years of specializing in criminal appellate work, and a friend from my own days in that office, came on board as a staff attorney with our office in November, 2004. He was very helpful to us as a "senior statesmen" of the law. In April 2005, he converted to an "of counsel" status and assists us on several cases, working out of his Prattville home.

Elizabeth Bern Spear, who took the bar exam in July 2005, is our newest "attorney-to-be." An outstanding student at both Jones Law School and Auburn University, and a friend of my daughter Grace from St. James School,

Elizabeth is scheduled to start working for our firm in mid-August 2005. She will join long-time law clerk Sim Pettway Jr., who also took the bar exam in July, as new lawyers in the firm.

Amy Strickland, office manager, bookkeeper, computer guru, advertising manager, paralegal, and secretary is my right arm. We sometimes call her "Superwoman" or "Wonder Woman." When she is out for health or personal reasons, we feel the pinch.

Finally, I'd be remiss to not mention such stalwart firm employees as the legal assistant Puckett family team of Carroll, Betty and Paul. Paul also backs Amy up in bookkeeping. Likewise, secretary-paralegals Page McKee, Suzanne Clemens, Patricia Williams, Carol Thomas, Jennifer Lee, and Sharon Duke are valuable support staff. Chelsi Hudson keeps our telephones answered properly, while Kaylon Jenkins is in his eighth year as a runner, efficiently serving subpoenas, and making bank, courthouse, and other deliveries.

Young Andy Akin has brought new energy to this firm as a joyful and competent law clerk. Finally, Donna Puckett, daughter-in-law of Carroll and Betty, joined us in June 2005, working directly for me as a secretary-paralegal. She has been a big help, keeping me straight and relieving Amy, enabling her to concentrate on office management, bookkeeping, and fixing computers.

Because our law firm is like a family, as with any family sometimes there are are joyful moments to be celebrated and sometimes painful episodes to be endured. One such episode for me involved Jim Webb, a firm employee from the fall of 2002 until he resigned in August 2004. The week of my daughter Grace's wedding we discovered, and Jim admitted, that he had been embezzling advertising funds at our firm for months. Jim did some excellent work for the firm as an investigator. And getting us into television advertising, which has helped the firm, was Jim's idea. He created several of our better ads. His infectious laughter and keen insight frequently lifted my spirits. He was a dear friend.

However, stealing from the firm can't be sugarcoated. Jim first agreed to pay the money back in monthly installments, but he made no payments, offered no explanation, and then took off to Africa. His behavior left us with no alternative. The final tally of $23,000 was mostly covered by insurance, but as a condition to receiving insurance proceeds, office manager Amy Strickland signed a warrant against Jim for "Theft of Property I" in late September 2004.

Ten months later Jim remained a fugitive from justice.

BY THE END OF THE SUMMER OF 2002, I was back in full throttle as "The People's Lawyer," handling a variety of cases. Some were more newsworthy, some less so. Among the more significant cases are the following:

Hostile Work Environment at Selma Plant

After the campaign ended in late June 2002, I started receiving numerous complaints from African-American employees in Selma that Globe Metallurgical Plant was subjecting them to a hostile racial work environment. Representing forty-eight plaintiffs whose work experience ranged from ten to thirty-eight years, my clients claimed that Globe had consistently refused to promote them to supervisory, management, or foreman positions, while hiring and promoting less qualified white employees.

Mayor James Perkins, the excellent, conscientious new mayor of Selma—the city's first African American mayor—called me in late 2002, and urged me to help resolve the case. Apparently, it was affecting efforts to attract new industry to Selma.

After battling it out for several months, we settled the case for a significant, confidential amount for each employee, with express provisions concerning promotions, and a good attorney's fee. Law partners Joe Guillot and Karen Rodgers helped bake this pie, and firm investigator Jim Webb was a big help. When my clients are happy, and these clients were delighted, then I am happy.

On my office wall hangs the photograph of an American Indian with the motto beneath, "To give dignity to a person is above all things." The inspiration for this came from my father telling me in the early 1950s something very important. He said, "There is just as much worth, dignity and value in a street sweeper's job, in God's eyes, as there is in my job." At the time Dad was president of King Pharr Canning Company, headquartered in Cullman, with plants also in Selma and Uniontown, Alabama, and one in Georgia and one in Louisiana. At its peak King Pharr employed a thousand workers. Somehow these words, I believe, influenced me in this case with Globe Metallurgical and numerous other cases I have handled.

Food Stamps and Fired Deputies

During October, 2002, we also filed suit against the U.S. Department of Agriculture for denying Fannin Grocery in Shorter the right to accept food stamps. That case is still pending. The same month, we took on Bullock County Sheriff Charles Hudson for wrongfully terminating a deputy. The case was later settled.

Samimah Aziz vs. Ford and Firestone

The U.S. Senate campaign cost me dearly, both in out-of-pocket expenses and in reduced law firm financial returns. Yet one case came in from the campaign, through campaign coordinator Rev. John Alford, which helped reimburse all my own money spent in the campaign.

How it began is that in June 2000, during the early stages of my pre-campaign organization, a caravan of nine cars, with a state trooper escort, made its way from the Atlanta airport to Montgomery. The First Lady of Liberia, Mrs. Charles Taylor, was in one car. In another car was Earl Shinhoster, executive director of the NAACP, and Ms. Samimah Aziz, daughter of Akbar Mohammed, a high official in the Nation of Islam.

Unfortunately, the Shinhoster-Aziz car, a Ford sport utility vehicle, blew a Firestone tire, and slammed into a tree, killing Shinhoster and gravely wounding Aziz. Since it happened in the Macon County portion of I-85, we had an excellent venue, given that Macon County is about 90 percent black, as are its juries, which are sympathetic to plaintiffs. Through John Alford's friendship with Mr. Mohammed, the case of Ms. Aziz came to our law firm.

I assigned my younger law partner, William Gill, to take the lead. He did a wonderful job on the case from the summer of 2000 until January 2003, when the case finally settled. Unfortunately, we had to fight off attempts along the way by unethical Texas lawyers to steal the case away from us.

Long story short, following protracted depositions and pre-trial discovery, and just after the jury was struck, both the Shinhoster and Aziz cases settled for record amounts. Coming just after an expensive campaign, it was a vindication of sorts, a sign from God that He was restoring my warehouse after a sacrificial campaign. My discernment was that God had strongly encouraged me in the campaign in the first place, and appreciated my efforts.

Saving Schools

In February 2003, I intervened on behalf of a group of parents to stop the Montgomery County Board of Education from closing South Montgomery County High School. While not ultimately successful in saving the school, our efforts bore fruit for the parents in other ways. We stopped long bus rides to alternative schools, with a compromise solution allowing students to attend schools closer to home.

Representing Prattville and Phenix City Firemen

Unfortunately, the lives of fireman often involve more than putting out fires. Hence, I found myself taking the lead in representing former Prattville fireman Corey Houston against the Prattville Fire Department. I also assisted my law partner Kenneth Shinbaum in representing former Phenix City firemen Dennis Duty and Randy Doster.

The case against Prattville ended quite successfully for Houston in a settlement. Unfortunately, the cases of Duty and Doster, after more than two years of preparation and a week-long trial, ended in a defense verdict in May 2005.

The Coaches Cole and Alabama State University

When Donald Watkins was on the Board of Trustees of Alabama State University, he dreamed of building up his alma mater into a Division 1-A football team. His first step was to recruit a pair of brothers, L. C. Cole and J. C. Cole, away from Tennessee State University. At that school, the brothers had dominated their league with a pair of conference championships. It was a coup to get such great coaching talent to come to ASU.

The Cole brothers immediately turned football around at ASU, leaping from the bottom to the top of the Southwestern Athletic Conference (SWAC). Their only problem was that ASU power (some call him "tyrant") Joe Reed had not blessed the Coles' coming. In fact he had opposed them. Reed's initial opposition was not a problem since it came during a brief time of Reed's exile from the ASU Board. Reed couldn't stop them then. It became abundantly clear, however, that the primary basis for Reed's opposition to the Coles, upon his return, was simply that Donald Watkins, Reed's arch-rival, was the Coles' chief sponsor. By this time, Joe Reed had developed a hatred for Donald Watkins, and vice-versa.

A conspiracy developed on the ASU campus to get rid of the Coles, and Joe Reed was behind it. As finance chairman of the ASU Board, Reed had virtually unlimited resources to fight the coaches, and ended up spending nearly $1 million of ASU's money in attorney fees to oust the Coles.

It started with bogus, anonymous charges against the Coles, attributed to a disgruntled assistant football coach fired by the Coles. Some charges were fabricated completely, other were grossly exaggerated or blown up way out of proportion to the facts.

My law partner Kenneth Shinbaum and I, paid very modestly but with the expectation of more to come (that never came), fought these trumped-up charges long and hard. In the process, we fought three law firms at one time, one from Mobile, one from Birmingham, and a third from Montgomery-Tuskegee, namely Fred Gray's law firm.

The biggest opposition came from a fourth source, namely New Orleans attorney, Robert Clayton, a so-called expert on NCAA football investigations. He was also the greatest money drain, as he testified at a hearing that he was paid $250 per hour by ASU for his work. Clayton milked this cow for every ounce that it was worth, working several months non-stop, building a huge file against the Coles, most of it exaggerated. Clayton's bill was probably closer to three quarters of a million dollars, and the fees of the other attorneys brought the total up to near a million.

When it first started, Kenneth and I naively hoped we could head this off and save the coaches' jobs. A rule one must forever relearn is to never underestimate Joe Reed and his sheer will power, aided by unlimited financial resources, since he controls the ASU pursestrings. The Coaches Cole were treated miserably and undeservedly by ASU. The Coles had been ultra-careful to follow all NCAA rules. It went unappreciated by ASU's two Joes, namely Reed and President Joe Lee. If there was any violation during the Coles' tenure, it was in the school's compliance officer's paperwork. But it was a "tale of two Joes," to the detriment of the two Coles.

We had to get creative. At one point, so many football players came to us, wanting to help the Coles, that we prepared and filed a lawsuit on their behalf. The story about it and a picture of Coach L. C. Cole and me appeared in *USA*

Today and the *Montgomery Advertiser*. My famous sports relative, Uncle Dave Dixon of New Orleans, called to tell me he had seen it.

We also filed a second suit in Montgomery County Circuit Court for defamation against a fired former assistant coach, ASU athletic director Richard Cosby, ASU President Joe Lee, and unnamed conspirators. We hinted loudly that Joe Reed might be added.

Meanwhile, a hearing was finally scheduled at ASU. It lasted about two weeks. Kenneth Shinbaum took the lead, assisted by Donald Jackson, a black Montgomery attorney experienced in sports law, and by me. The final ruling from the ASU hearing officer, a faculty member, was most encouraging. He could not find where the Coles had violated any NCAA or school rules.

The hearing officer's recommendations had to go to the full ASU Board of Trustees for review. That is where Joe Reed's crowd held the trump cards, even to the point of keeping off the Board a duly elected member favorable to the Coles. The Board rubber-stamped the ASU president's proposed termination, notwithstanding the lack of evidence. It was bush-league justice.

At one point the Coles' pending law suit against ASU had become such a "hot potato" that every Montgomery County circuit judge had recused himself or herself until the final judge, Chief Judge Charles Price, said he was ready to hear the case.

Just as we were about to reactivate the lawsuit, L. C. Cole advised us that he could not afford to fight the firing any longer. Instead, he accepted a coaching job in Minnesota. Earlier, his younger brother J. C. had done the same in Texas.

A grave injustice was inflicted upon not only the Coles but the entire ASU football family. Easily ninety-five percent of ASU's alumni, students and faculty were with us. It has always been difficult to understand how one man can so thoroughly and wrongfully dominate one major university. With no check on how Joe Reed uses ASU's money, he wears people down.

Taking on the Chicago Cubs and Major League Baseball

In April 2003, former governor Don Siegelman called me, stating that he had a potential case he wanted me to consider. I drove over to Don's office and was introduced to Ms. J. D. Patton, a ten-year assistant scout of the Chicago Cubs, until she was non-renewed in December, 2002.

Ms. Patton's non-renewal as a part-time scout was directly related to her seeking the full-time amateur scouting position being vacated by her immediate boss, Jim Crawford. Ms. Patton had extensive scouting experience in Alabama, Tennessee, and Florida, and Mr. Crawford had spoken well of her abilities, as had many others.

The only problem was that J. D. Patton was a female, and the macho management of the Cubs and their parent Tribune Company wanted a male. I helped Ms. Patton amend her EEOC charge, and we were off to the races.

The Cubs hired one of Chicago's top law firms to fight us, and we slugged it out. Their legal counsel was as condescending and arrogant as the management. The defense tried to whip us around in the discovery process, but U.S. Magistrate Judge Vanzetta McPherson ruled in our favor.

Depositions once scheduled for Chicago during mid-January zero weather were rescheduled for the Spring training camp in Phoenix, Arizona. Client J. D. and I flew out to this desert oasis and took in a Cubs-Giants spring training game, and the local scenery. The only problem was that the Sammy Sosa-Barry Bonds slugfest we excitedly anticipated did not materialize. Neither played that day.

The case rocked and rolled along for a year and a half. Judge Harold Albritton ruled in our favor, denying a summary judgment the Cubs' attorney believed was theirs. However, some of our key claims were "gutted," to use a lawyer's jargon. By late November 2003, we reached a confidential settlement that pleased client J. D. Patton. Referring attorney Don Siegelman was happy, and so was I.

Defending Birmingham Municipal Court Judge David Barnes

Spurred by the *Birmingham News*, an anonymous complaint was filed in 2003 against the Birmingham Municipal Court Judge David Barnes for failure to recuse himself in an animal cruelty case involving City Councilman Lee Loder. The complaint was that Barnes had a conflict of interest. The ulterior motive appeared more to hurt mayoral candidate Loder's election prospects.

David Barnes hired me to represent himself, and I took the leadership at the Judicial Inquiry Commission hearing in Orange Beach, Alabama, that September 2003. Meanwhile, another Birmingham attorney, Charlie Waldrop, volunteered his services to help Judge Barnes. At Orange Beach, Waldrop advised Judge Barnes to plead guilty and take a thirty-day suspension. I advised him to fight.

Judge Barnes, in tears, told me that he felt any suspension would be a grave injustice. Therefore, we prepared to fight the charges. At the last moment, the Commission backed down. We worked out a deal that allowed Barnes to take a slap-on-the-wrist "reprimand," but no suspension. To my surprise, in a later front-page story in the *Birmingham Post-Herald*, attorney Waldrop claimed credit for the outcome and conveniently forgot to mention me. I was miffed, but chalked that up to experience. My client was happy. He knows which lawyer helped him achieve his successful outcome.

The People's Baptist Church Against ASU and Joe Reed

Overlapping my representation of the Coaches Cole was another case taking on both Alabama State University and Joe Reed. This time, my client was the People's Baptist Church. Situated on the major part of a city block across Hall Street from ASU, the church's property had long been coveted by the University for expansion. Indeed, ASU had already bought up most of the residential lots in the multi-block area surrounding the church.

Thus, the neighborhood had become something of a "no-man's land." The church was in a "damned if they did sell, and damned if they didn't sell" situation. If the church were sold, market pressures, including the fact that no one wanted property ASU could so easily condemn, meant that ASU was the only interested buyer. The church was in a "take it or leave it" position. At its present location, the church was losing members and couldn't afford to move unless it sold its property.

Due to its ability to condemn the property via eminent domain, ASU (or rather Joe Reed) thought ASU could get the property for peanuts, or for something like $125,000. The property was really worth much more, and the church needed a fair price to continue functioning at a new location.

In September 2003, we filed lawsuit against ASU. But getting the case on the legal track was not easy. There were all kinds of mountains, moguls, and potholes to get around.

Legal motions, counter-motions, and briefs brought the case to a logjam in front of Judge William Shashy. By early 2004, Shashy referred the case for mediation to renowned former circuit judge Randall Thomas.

This was a mediation that perhaps only Judge Thomas could successfully perform, and one he had to pull out of the hat. Randy is very spiritual, and always turns mediation sessions into opportunities to share his faith. That is fine with me. Long story short, Judge Thomas, using spiritual arguments, finally persuaded Joe Reed to do the right thing. Notwithstanding that money was very tight at ASU, we structured a deal that, over a period of several years, would make the total settlement worth close to $500,000. The People's Baptist Church has since been organizing to move to a better location.

Brandi Timmons Dies in Medical Malpractice

One of the most heart-breaking cases I have ever worked on began in late 1998 and continues to this date. It involves Brandi Timmons, who in 1998 was a seventeen-year-old senior at the Loveless Academic Magnet Program (LAMP) school in Montgomery. A talented student citizen, Brandi was selected for the Alabama Junior Miss program that year, as was my daughter Grace who remembers Brandi's unselfishness during the pageant competition.

Brandi was the only child of Ms. Johnnie Timmons, a saintly lady given the heroic way she has handled this enormous loss.

Unfortunately, Brandi had an overbite and occlusion problem with her teeth that needed surgery to fix her jaw. It should have been routine, and the dentist, Dr. Bradford, performed his surgery well. Unfortunately, Brandi received too much anesthesia, and Anesthesiology and Pain Management of Montgomery, P.C., failed to monitor her condition after her breathing tube was removed. This caused her to suffocate for about ten minutes.

Thereafter, Brandi fell into a coma, with serious brain damage. She would have been in a permanent vegetive state, had she survived. Perhaps mercifully, Brandi lapsed from the coma into death in late December 1998, just before the New Year.

Her family was heartbroken, and first Brandi's uncle, Albert Hardy, then Ms. Timmons, came to see me about it. Although I do not specialize in medical malpractice cases, I work in an associated capacity with firms that do. I therefore associated Cunningham Bounds Yance Crowder & Brown of Mobile, arguably the best medical malpractice firm in Alabama. They only take one out of every twenty-five potential cases. (The Birmingham firms of Hare Wynn; Pittman Hooks; and Ralph Bohannan are also excellent.) When I spoke with Cunningham partner John Crowder, he was excited about this case's potential. His firm went to work immediately. Long story short, after a "battle of experts" and discovery costs exceeding $250,000, the case was finally tried in Montgomery County Circuit Court over three weeks in June 2003, before Judge Charles Price.

Cunningham lawyers Buddy Brown, Greg Breedlove, and David Wirtes did a superb job. The jury returned a record verdict of $14.5 million. The Cunningham firm deserves all the credit, but our firm did assist in minor ways, and contributed to the equation leading to the result.

Regrettably, the battle was not over in June 2003. Post-judgment motions and appellant briefs have continued for more than two years.

In April 2005, Buddy Brown of Mobile gave one of the most outstanding appellate arguments I have ever heard before the Alabama Supreme Court, sitting in special session at the Cumberland Law School in Birmingham. As of July 2005, we are awaiting a ruling from the higher court.

We settled with Baptist Hospital for $800,000 in 2003 and the anesthesia firm is entitled to a credit for that amount against the judgment. We hope the Supreme Court will uphold the verdict, or at least not reduce it too much. Civil justice is needed for a precious life cut too short, so unnecessarily.

Every year, at the David Dixon McPhillips Scholarship Award presentation at LAMP in Montgomery, I give an update on Brandi Timmons's case. I have also presented the Timmons scholarship several times.

Defending Auburn Professor David Laband

Professor David Laband had the insight and courage to challenge the Auburn University Board of Trustees when it eliminated the PhD program in economics in 1999. This may have been one reason the Southern Association of Colleges and Schools put Auburn on probation, or allowed it to remain on such a suspect status. The Auburn administration was not thrilled with Laband's audacity, and retaliated against him by denying him summer teaching opportunities, Laband charged.

I sent a letter that fall to all members of Auburn's Board of Trustees about the wrongful retaliation again Professor Laband. Naturally, the Auburn administration was not pleased with this, either. Professor Laband also intervened in an ongoing SACS lawsuit before the Georgia courts.

Eventually Auburn got off probation, and it appears the Auburn administration is messing no more with David Laband. Our efforts played a part in the outcome. Poetic justice, no doubt.

Abuse of Rev. Leon Henderson by Montgomery Police

On February 4, 2004, Rev. Leon Henderson was in the privacy of his own home when the Montgomery police, without a warrant, barged in. Actually, it was far worse than that, and there is no delicate way to put it: When the police accosted him, Rev. Henderson was in his bathroom, sitting on the toilet. Not allowed to clean himself or to put on his pajama pants, Henderson was handcuffed and exposed in front of his twenty-year-old granddaughter. Unbelievably, the City of Montgomery later had to admit that Henderson had done nothing wrong. He was not arrested or charged with any crime. Nor was his granddaughter handcuffed or secured. The police officers who frightened and embarrassed and roughed Rev. Henderson up had come into his home looking for his step-grandson, *whom they had already apprehended before they came back to Henderson's bathroom!*

Henderson seeks compensation because he was humiliated and his back and wrists were injured by the unnecessary roughness of the police, invading his privacy. Henderson considers himself a victim of racial profiling, believing the MPD would not have treated a middle class white man similarly. A group of black ministers supported Rev. Henderson at a news conference.

Stated Rev. Henderson, as he filed suit a day after the incident, "It's time these gestapo and illegal tactics stop." Depositions have been taken, other discovery is progressing, and this case remains pending before Montgomery Circuit Court Judge Eugene Reese.

Staying Active Before Alabama Securities Commission

From 1975–1976, I served as counsel to Alabama Securities Commission Director Tommy Krebs. We pursued a number of big cases together. Before that, from 1971–1975, I had done securities litigation work on Wall Street, a background which has been helpful.

In the last two years, 2004–2005, I found myself actively representing before the Alabama Securities Commission several alleged violators of securities laws. My prior experience and reputation have been helpful to these clients.

The first was Terry Harris and his business, Wealth Builders International. Mr. Harris had about five attorneys before me, and two or three after me. Nonetheless, our legal work laid the foundation for a better outcome later.

The second was Nick Autry and his firm, First National Online Processors, a cash machine, or ATM (automatic transfer machine) business. I'm still representing Mr. Autry before the Alabama Securities Commission, which appears to have backed off. I also have a civil lawsuit ongoing against some competitive business entities. Mr. Autry alleges that these competitors tortiously interfered with his business and wrongfully confiscated some of his ATMs.

As recently as May 2005, I was retained by Aruban-American Ivan Shew-a-Tjon and his firm of Caruba International to defend them against alleged securities law violations. An informal meeting with my friend Joe Borg, current director of the Securities Commission, and his staff is moving this case in the right direction for my client.

Representing Heather Scarlett in Police Abuse Case

I have always vigorously opposed police brutality. Usually my clients have been black citizens who were maltreated by white officers. But police brutality has to be challenged, no matter what the race of the involved persons.

On March 19, 2004, a petite, attractive young white professional, Heather Scarlett, was pulled over by a black Prattville policeman, Dexter Emmanuel. When she questioned Emmanuel as to why she had been stopped, Emmanuel roughly threw her against her vehicle, bruising her and causing back and rib pain and severe headaches.

Although Scarlett was not charged with anything related to being stopped in the first place, she was charged with the misdemeanor crimes of resisting arrest and failure to obey a police officer.

The City of Prattville offered to dismiss all charges if Scarlett would give the City and Emmanuel a release of all claims. However, Scarlett felt so strongly about her mistreatment that she refused. She said it was the worst thing that had ever happened to her, next to her father's death. Convicted in a kangarooish Municipal Court, Heather appealed her conviction to the Autauga County Circuit Court, and simultaneously filed suit against Prattville and Emmanuel for damages.

A motion to suppress evidence was denied in June 2005. The trial is coming up in September 2005.

Naturally, Emmanuel and Prattville deny any wrongdoing. Both the criminal and civil cases remain pending, as of July 2005.

Auto Accidents Keep Our Firm Busy

In April 2003, we started advertising on T.V. for the first time. We've always handled many auto accidents and other personal injury cases. However, this new advertising pushed us up to a much higher lever. It definitely increased our share of the market.

My young partners Aaron Luck and Jim Bodin especially enjoy handling this kind of case, and they do it well. My senior partners Kenneth Shinbaum and Mary Goldthwaite are also exceedingly competent in representing injured plaintiffs in personal injury cases. Junior partners Joe Guillot and Karen Rodgers are fast developing their skills in this area also.

I, too, am in the middle of several big auto accident cases, including one with Brenda Kitchens, brain-injured in a disputed-liability auto accident. Another is the wrongful death case of pedestrian Demetrius Hollinquest, run over on Highway 231 near Todd Road by an older woman, who admitted that she was going 60-75 miles per hour in a 45-mph zone. The insurance company had been stonewalling, claiming Mr. Hollinquest jumped out in front of the lady's car at the last moment. However, in late June 2005, via mediation, we settled the case for a satisfactory but confidential amount.

I'm also representing a Mobile attorney, Vivian Beckerle, injured (while she was a student walking on the Jones Law campus) by an older male driver. Naturally, liability is disputed.

Certainly clear liability cases are very productive in terms of compensation versus time spent. However, if anyone thinks all auto accident cases are "easy pickings," they do not know the realities. These are always many issues and details dealing with liability and damages, the key components of any such case.

Mediation is being successfully used in more and more cases. Mediation is good for plaintiffs because either side is free to disagree or agree. Alternatively, arbitration is bad for the average person because it is binding and often unfair, tilted in favor of the more powerful party.

Mohammed Araiinejad vs. O'Charley's, Inc.

The principle of why mediation is desirable, and arbitration is not, is well illustrated in this case now pending in federal court.

Mo Araiinejad of Iranian descent, moved to America in the 1970's. Despite his accent, Mo moved quickly up the managerial chain at O'Charley's, starting in 1992, before becoming an area supervisor in 2000 over several north Alabama restaurants.

Mo did well at O'Charley's until September 11, 2001, or its aftermath, when he started experiencing anti-ethnic comments and slurs from higher O'Charley's management. This harassment increased in frequency and culminated in April, 2002, when Mo was wrongfully accused of several shortcomings. In December, 2002, Mo refused a demotion and was terminated.

That is only half the story. After filing a charge of "national origin" discrimination against O'Charley's with the EEOC in Birmingham, I received the standard "right to sue letter." At that point, however, O'Charley's attorneys advised us that Mr. Araiinejad had signed a binding arbitration agreement.

We filed suit in federal court in February, 2004. Mr. Araiinejad says he was forced to sign the agreement after years of working with O'Charley's, subject to the threat of being fired if he didn't sign it. We claimed "fraud in the inducement" of the agreement, because "it was explained to me that mediation would be allowed first because arbitration was required," said Mr. Araiinejad.

In this case, O'Charley's denied Mr. Araiinejad the right of mediation, and sought a court order compelling arbitration with the American Arbitration Association (AAA). Evidence of O'Charley's long and cozy relationship with the AAA was no secret. Hence, Araiinejad and I filed an "opposition response," stating under oath, "If O'Charley's had explained to me before I signed the arbitration agreement that the mediation provision would not be used or allowed, I may very well have elected not to sign the arbitration agreement, even though it may have cost me the job."

The case was assigned to U.S. District Judge Myron Thompson. The issue of whether to arbitrate was submitted in July 2004. A year later, in July 2005, we are still awaiting a ruling. Judge Thompson is known for being meticulous, and writing landmark opinions.

Given the length of time, and given Judge Thompson's judicial philoso-phy, we are hopeful of receiving a favorable ruling from the federal court. That could be helpful precedent in future cases. All we want is "an even playing field."

Unfortunately arbitration, especially through the AAA, does not afford that, in my opinion.

Nepotism Case Against Two State Departments

In this case, the evidence of nepotism would knock you off your feet. Young Brent Langley, whose father Robert Langley was second-in-command at the Alabama Industrial Relations, was allowed to catapult over my client, Debbie Carter Richbourg, and land a supervisor's job which should have gone to Richbourg. In the process, DIR and the State Personnel Department ignored their own rules and regulations.

I filed two complaints with the State Personnel Department, but adminis-trative law judge Julia Weller ignored the complaints for several months. A justifiable request for recusal was made to that judge, a paid employee of the Personnel Department, since her own boss, Tommy Flowers, was a defendant. However, in late April 2005, Judge Weller denied the request and issued a ruling that no nepotism existed, and that state personnel rules didn't prohibit it anyway. Written exceptions to Judge Weller's ruling were filed on a petition for judicial review with the State Personnel Board, but were denied in late May 2005. The case is currently on appeal to the Circuit Court of Montgomery County.

Representing Embattled CEO in Defamation Case

In 1979, Richard Scrushy, then only twenty-six years old, drove his parents to my law office in connection with an estate dispute involving his parents and aunts and uncles following the deaths of his grandparents.

In 1984, Richard Scrushy had the inspired idea of developing hospital rehab work into an empire named HealthSouth. This meteoric business success at its peak owned hospitals in every state and many foreign countries, and employed fifty thousand.

Coming from a modest background out of Selma, Scrushy is a Horatio Alger story if ever there was one. But such phenomenal success spawned its share of jealous detractors. Richard Scrushy also employed high-level accounting experts as HealthSouth officers under him. Some of these saw a way to enrich themselves with great bonuses and stock option earnings by "playing with the books."

That a fraud occurred involving millions of dollars in wrongful accounting was later mutually agreed upon. Who did it was the question. The feds blew a whistle on it in March 2003, causing HealthSouth stock to plummet from $4 per share to 12 cents a share (the stock has since returned to over $6 per share).

When fifteen former CFOs or other high-level accountant types at HealthSouth pleaded guilty, everyone assumed Scrushy was guilty, too. That is, almost everyone.

Scrushy himself said, "Whoa, wait a minute. Not so fast. I didn't know this stuff was going on. I'm not guilty." He assembled a good defense team of attorneys and accountants and fought the government's charges long and hard.

Unfortunately, certain media outlets, especially the *Birmingham News* treated Scrushy like a pariah, a liar, and a scoundrel in every article printed about him from the initial federal charges in March 2003 on up until early December 2004. On that date, I put a letter requesting retraction upon the *Birmingham News'* publisher and the paper's owner, Newhouse Publications.

When nothing was retracted, I followed up with a lawsuit against the *Birmingham News*, a few days before Christmas 2004. I pointed out thirteen major areas of defamation, when things both untrue and mean-spirited were printed in the *News* about Scrushy. Not surprisingly, the *News*, in its typically haughty way, has failed to retract anything. That case is still pending in the Circuit Court of Jefferson County.

Expressing profound gratitude to me, Scrushy said one of the best things he ever did in his defense was suing the *Birmingham News*. Why? Because the *News'* coverage changed drastically for the better once it was sued. With the jury unsequestered, this was a positive development for Scrushy. Of course, Scrushy sued because he was defamed and damaged.

The *New York Times* also defamed Scrushy badly, quoting selective sources, all of whom had negative, cynical quotes about Scrushy, while ignoring numerous people with things positive to say. The only difference is the *New York Times* is not nearly so widely read in Birmingham, where the jurors were unsequestered for four months of trial and four weeks of deliberations. I have now put three demands for retraction upon the *Times*, but not surprisingly, the *Times* too has failed to issue a single one. We are analyzing and reserving, our options against the *Times*.

Not to be outdone, Scrushy's one-time friend Paul Finebaum, a consummate motor-mouth with a barbed-wire tongue, betrayed Scrushy. Why? Because his listeners liked it. Finebaum has obviously gotten a better audience reaction by dog-cussing Scrushy. After I put a demand letter for a retraction upon Finebaum and his boss, Clear Channel Communications, Finebaum, ever the arrogant know-it-all, started spewing ugly words about me as well, calling me an ambulance-chaser. It doesn't matter that, in thirty-four years of practicing law, I have never done so.

Oh well, that is an occupational hazard one endures as a trial lawyer representing controversial clients. You get called names.

My own research has led me to believe strongly that Richard Scrushy is not only innocent, but that he has been wrongfully vilified by media sources. Richard and his supporters have been a "tower of faith," covering the entire defense for months with prayers.

Scrushy, like everyone else, has his faults. I have mine. We are all human. Yet, even though his great wealth sets him apart from my average clients, the consistent thread is that Scrushy has been bullied and victimized by more powerful entities, namely the U.S. government and the *Birmingham News*, often working together.

It has been my great honor, and one of my foremost professional challenges, to represent Richard Scrushy at a time when his ox is in the ditch. I was overjoyed when Scrushy was acquitted by a federal jury on all thirty-six criminal counts on June 28, 2005. The original indictment had eighty-five counts. Now there are zero.

Scrushy had his own "dream team" of attorneys in court. Managed by the agile and creative Donald Watkins, the lead attorneys were Jim Parkman, with a country charm that appealed to the jury, and the impeccable Art Leach, a former assistant U.S. Attorney from Georgia who once prosecuted white-collar crime. Rounding off the first team was Lewis Gillis, an artful barrister from Montgomery.

Together, these two white and two black attorneys put on a "full court press" of a defense. The jury, equally balanced racially, endured a tough trial.

I was in court for only five days, but observed a spirit, tenacity, and organization by this legal team, and a moral strength among the supporters, which far surpassed the prosecution's efforts and support.

Besides our defamation suit against the *Birmingham News*, and discovery suit versus Paul Finebaum, Scrushy has a number of stockholder suits and an SEC civil action to defend.

Defending Former Montgomery Police Officer

Back in September 2004, it became public news that my client, former Montgomery police officer, George David Salum, was the target of an investigation involving the release of a photograph of another former police officer, Raymond David DeJohn.

It all seemed like making a mountain of a mole hill, because DeJohn's picture was readily obtainable from other internal sources. The infamous DeJohn [see index] was a defendant in my 1999 suit against the City of Montgomery, filed on behalf of client Reggie Jones. In recent years, DeJohn had become an undercover police office for the City of Prattville, his latest job.

In September 2004, my new client, Salum, already in the midst of leaving the MPD after twenty plus years for health reasons, accelerated his withdrawal after catching flak about the picture's release. For a combination of health and legal reasons, and upon my advice, Salum refused to participate in any internal investigation by the MPD in this matter.

In February 2005, I was contacted by an assistant U.S. attorney from the panhandle of Florida, Dixie Morrow, specially appointed to prosecute the matter. She wanted to talk with Salum, but confirmed he was the target of an investigation, and would not be granted immunity. Under such circumstances, I would not allow Salum to talk openly with the prosecutor.

On May 27, 2005, it was announced publicly that Salum had been indicted for obstruction of justice. I met with him and his very helpful wife, Sonya, later that day, to prepare his defense.

On July 26, 2005, I argued before U.S. Magistrate Delores Boyd that the indictment should be dismissed for failure to state a violation of federal law. The trial is set for November 7, 2005, before U.S. District Judge Mark Fuller.

Hurricane Ivan Blew in More Cases

As much as I regretted the damage of Hurricane Ivan, it brought in many cases to our law firm. Either insurance companies were not paying an adequate amount in damages, or they were disputing liability altogether. All of our lawyers, including me, have handled these cases and gotten good results.

Indian Immigrant Mike Patel Needed Our Help

Mike Patel, of East Indian ethnic origin, and of Chicago, spends part of his time in Montgomery. As is well-known, many of the smaller motels nationwide have been owned by East Indians for years. I am informed that the name "Patel" is the Hindu word for "innkeeper."

Mr. Patel called me for legal help when his Day's Inn motel burned down. I assigned my law partner William Gill to take the lead, just before William left our central office. William, now in an "of counsel" capacity, has teamed up with my law partner Jim Bodin to build up a million-dollar claim.

Meanwhile, one of Mr. Patel's former female employees filed a claim against his business for failing to protect her from racial harassment by another white male employee, an independent contractor. Usually I represent the plaintiff in race discrimination cases. This time I found myself representing the management side, in defending Mr. Patel.

Judge Albritton granted summary judgment on two of the three plaintiff claims, but on one of the remaining counts, a two-day trial ensued. The jury was out about twenty minutes before it came back with a verdict in our favor. Whether it is representing a plaintiff or a defendant, it always feels good to get a jury verdict. It felt good to vindicate Mr. Patel.

Defending Auburn Ag Dean Mike Weiss

When Auburn University recruited its new Agriculture College dean out of Idaho, Auburn landed someone who looked like a Paul Bunyan-style lumberjack or a former professional football player. At 6' 5" and three hundred pounds, Dr. Weiss looked less like an academic than an outdoorsman. Although his vita of professional publications and accomplishments was most impressive, the problem he encountered was that he not only looked like a lumberjack, but sounded like one. He was known to use colorful language.

A very decent man, happily married for many years to his best friend Cindy, Dr. Weiss's language supposedly offended certain prim and proper people, including Auburn's president, Dr. Ed Richardson.

What did Dr. Weiss say or do that was so bad? For beginners, he was a little too touchy-feely for some people's taste. He freely gave hugs, and even planted a kiss on the cheek of an employee at a dinner party at the Weisses' home.

Further, Dr. Weiss, at a golf game, in front of polite society, referred to the "knockers" of a well-endowed woman who was some distance away out of earshot but evidently not out of eyesight. There were other trivial transgressions, none relating to Dr. Weiss's academic work, but causing eyebrows to be raised.

The true motivation behind this may well turn out to be a disappointed interim dean who served before Dr. Weiss but who was ineligible to be considered for the permanent dean's post. Instead, he was pushing for a restructuring of the College of Agriculture, and wanted to see himself selected as vice-president of Agriculture for Auburn University. Dr. Weiss wasn't thrilled with this proposal when the predecessor dean presented it to him.

Dr. Richardson sent Dr. Weiss a list of complaints and temporarily suspended him, placing him on paid administrative leave, pending a hearing with the Faculty Investigative Committee.

We quickly gave our responses to the Faculty Investigative Committee, which ruled in Dr. Weiss' favor. Unfortunately, pursuing University process, President Richardson had the right to push it further, insisting on terminating Dr. Weiss, both from his deanship and his tenured faculty status. While Dr. Weiss has been willing to concede the deanship, we are fighting tooth and nail to retain his tenured faculty job.

Just after a hearing began on July 21, 2005 before the Auburn University Faculty Tenure Committee, a settlement was worked out. Dr. Weiss resigned as dean but managed to retain his tenure as a faculty member. Dr. Weiss and his dear wife Cindy were happy.

Isaiah and Johnnie Sankey

I'd be remiss not to mention Isaiah Sankey and his devoted wife, Johnnie. Some folks come to us on a wide range of legal problems. The Sankeys fall into that category.

With the help of a construction company, architect, and sprinkler company, the Sankeys in November 2003 completed an independent living facility (now called The Butterfly Inn), together with an adjacent restaurant, called Isaiah's. The complex is located at the corner of Mildred and Holcombe streets, a block west of the 1870s Sayre Street School, and a block east of where Zelda Sayre Fitzgerald grew up on Pleasant Avenue. Internationally known folk artist Mose T's home is but a stone's throw away. This is "Very Old Montgomery." The Sankeys' business is helping to revitalize this rundown neighborhood, and I am happy to help them.

We helped Isaiah and Johnnie successfully resolve disputes with their architect, and then with the sprinkler system company. We're headed to trial before Judge Eugene Reese in September 2005 with Marshall Construction Company.

We're also representing Isaiah, his son, and nephew against the Montgomery police, who roughed them up one evening, in a mistaken identity case. Our firm has also successfully defended the Sankeys in a subcontractor's suit, and helped them with several other legal matters.

Isaiah and Johnnie are gracious, Spirit-filled people. Independent and hardworking, they add much to the social fabric of Montgomery. I've enjoyed delicious "soul food" lunches at their restaurant, just three blocks away from this firm. I recommend it to everyone.

Judith Ann Neeley

Back in September 1982, I remember reading about how Judith Ann Neeley, then in her teens, brainwashed, and under the influence of an oppressive husband, helped kidnap and kill someone in northeast Alabama. It was a horrible crime. She was convicted of capital murder in DeKalb County. Her husband received a "life with parole" sentence on another murder in Georgia and was not tried in Alabama. In Judith's case, a jury voted ten to two for her punishment to be "life without parole." However, Judge Randall Cole overruled the jury's recommendation, and ordered her put to death.

For the next sixteen years, Neeley's case bounced up and down the appellate chain. Despite her oft-expressed desire to abandon appeals and be executed, young Judith had a support group regularly visiting her at Julia Tutwiler Prison in Wetumpka. She became a grandmother by her late thirties.

She was encouraged to hang in there, and she experienced a genuine Christian conversion, completely changing her character.

Fast forward to 1993. I'm sitting in the Alabama Supreme Court, waiting to give my argument for a taxpayer against Governor Hunt's flying in state aircraft around the South, making money for himself in preaching engagements. I notice another exciting case immediately ahead of me. I hear attorney Barry Ragsdale of Birmingham persuasively arguing about all the due process Judith Ann Neeley was denied at the trial court level. The Supreme Court denied Neeley's appeal, but I was touched.

Fast forward again to late 1998. Judith's appeals have run out. Her execution date is fast approaching in early 1999. At about that time, Governor George Bush of Texas is making headlines denying the clemency appeal of Carla Faye Tucker, despite personal requests from Pope John Paul, Pat Robertson, and Jerry Falwell. These religious leaders were convinced Tucker had experienced a sincere Christian redemption, and deserved a second chance to live. She didn't get it. Bush was running for president, and didn't want to hurt his election prospects.

I teamed up with Sister Helen Prejean of *Dead Man Walking* movie fame to help Judith Ann Neeley not suffer Tucker's fate. With my legal brief in tow, Sister Prejean and I personally visited Governor Fob James at the State Capitol. Fob is compassionate, and he proved it.

After several weeks of lobbying and pro-bono lawyering, I learned that Governor James granted our petition in January 1999, during the last two days of his administration. He commuted Neeley to a life sentence absent any "without parole" restriction. For Governor James, it was a fine moment. We thanked our Governor, and we thanked our God.

My good friend Don Siegelman entered the governor's office the next week. Discovering what had happened, he blasted Governor James. Siegelman made it clear he wouldn't have granted clemency.

The above story almost appeared in the first edition of this book. However, at the last moment, a close friend convinced me to edit it out, saying it would hurt me in the U.S. Senate race. Now that I'm not running for anything, I say "let the truth be known" in this second edition.

Sister Helen Prejean and I began a strong friendship. When Sister returned to Montgomery in early 2004, to rally anti-death penalty forces, she was on my firm's "Law Talk" radio show. We had a lively exchange.

Fast forward a third time to 2005. This story is not yet over. On May 12, 2005, I received a letter from Neeley, now stationed at a female prison in Basile, Louisiana, due to Alabama's overcrowded conditions. She'd been meaning to write me for years, but hadn't. She only recently discovered my role in her 1999 clemency. She humbly wrote, "How does one thank someone for helping to save a life? I do not know why you did it, but I am so very grateful. Thank you so much."

Neeley then revealed how the Alabama legislature, after her commutation, passed a law that anyone coming off death row would not be eligible for parole. The law was made specifically retroactive to apply to Neeley.

Some people call this an *ex post facto* law. If it is, then it is unlawful under the United States Constitution. Since Governor James's commutation sentence was not "life without parole," Neeley would be eligible for parole in 2014. However, with the legislative version intact, Neeley will never be eligible for parole.

Judith asked me if I knew an attorney willing to take her case on a pro-bono basis. She didn't ask me to do it, but wrote, "I need help. My attorney quit a year after I came off death row. I have no help, and no idea how to do it on my own." I plan to help her and have begun legal research. It may be politically unwise, but so what.

I understand the deep anguish of the victim's family. Even if Neeley were to become eligible for parole in 2012 (after thirty years in prison) it doesn't mean she will get it. But Judith is a one hundred percent different person today from the one who committed the crimes. Further, *ex post facto* laws are wrong in our democratic system of government.

Miscellaneous

A. Bobby Segall

In this book's first edition, Bobby Segall's name appears on thirteen pages. (His picture also appears on B-3). As my own attorney, Bobby helped me stay out of trouble in the 1980s and 1990s. We have teamed up on several important cases over the years, with good results.

I first met Bobby in February 1975, just after I took the Alabama bar exam and while Truman Hobbs, Sr., was offering me a job at Hobbs, Copeland, Franco & Screws, where Bobby worked. Although in April 1975 I became an Alabama assistant attorney general, Bobby and I developed a close friendship that remains to this day. In my opinion, there is no finer attorney in Alabama, and no finer person, than Bobby Segall. He also has a sense of humor that will crack you up.

Accordingly, Leslie and I were delighted to be at the Grand Hotel in Point Clear, Alabama, in July 2005 to witness Bobby's elevation as president of the Alabama Bar Association. I kidded Bobby about his "coronation." Bobby has an insightful intellect and even resembles Albert Einstein, but is still generous and humble. He probably handles more cases, and works more hours, than any attorney I know. Notwithstanding, Bobby should be one of the best presidents the Alabama Bar has ever had.

B. Susan Price and Terri Sewell Return to Alabama in 2004

Two of the most outstanding students I ever recruited to Princeton were Susan Price and Terri Sewell. Susan graduated in 1984 and Terri in 1987 from Ole Nassau. Both attended top law schools, Susan at the University of Virginia and Terri at Harvard. Each developed professionally outside of Alabama, Terri in New York City, and Susan in Seattle, Washington. Both have distinguished parents who are friends of mine, namely Coach Andrew Sewell of Selma and wife Nancy, a former Selma city councilwoman, and presiding Montgomery County Circuit Judge Charles Price and his ASU professor-wife, Bernice.

2004 was a great year for talent returning to Alabama, as both young ladies came home. Susan landed the highly responsible position of Alabama vice-chancellor of Post-Secondary Education. Terri became a law partner of my brother Frank at Maynard, Cooper & Gale in Birmingham. I rejoice, and know that Alabama is better off to have them home. They join David Sawyer '87, Shannon Holliday '89, and Rick McBride '93, as other excellent young Alabamians I recruited to Princeton, who later came home to practice law.

C. Jere Beasley and His Law Firm

When you practice plaintiff's law as I do, in Alabama, you can't help being aware of Jere Beasley. The two-time former lieutenant governor of Alabama is the tallest tree in the forest. He's won more million-dollar verdicts than any lawyer I know. I greatly respect Jere's intellect, his organizational skills, his morality, and his leadership in standing up for injured parties and working people.

I'll hand this to Jere. He definitely sets a high standard for the rest of us on the plaintiff's side of the bar. His firm does outstanding work. Secondly, Jere has provided enormous leadership in fighting against arbitration and other roadblocks to civil justice that the business community dreams up. Jere gets criticized by jealous individuals and rival interests, as do I. However, Jere's irrepressible "force of nature" energy has helped level the playing field for injured parties. He is a friend of the little guy. Philosophically and profession-ally our interests are close.

You can appreciate, then, the depth of my disappointment when Jere did not support me in the U.S. Senate race. I had sought his political backing early and carefully, and given our parallel professional philosophies and my better electibility chances against Sessions, I believed then and still do that Jere had good reason to support me. It could have been enormously helpful if he had. At least, Jere let his younger partners make up their own minds, which I appreciate. I'll always be grateful that such leading Beasley partners as Greg Allen, Mike Crow, Tom Methvin, Dee Miles, Graham Esdale, Labarron Boone, Gibson Vance, Lance Gould, and Mark Englehart all supported my candidacy financially and in other ways.

D. Tommy Gallion

The famous "Gallioni," as I like to call him, is truly a colorful character. He is also an extremely capable lawyer, especially in the courtroom, where his flamboyant style is one of the reasons you want him on your side rather than against you. He and I practiced law very closely from 1978-82 (see Chapter 15). We were like "de facto" partners.

I've kept up with Tommy in the twenty-three years since he left our Perry High office building. We always enjoy good laughs together.

Like myself, Tommy can be a bit of a crusader and sometimes tilts at windmills. For the past two years he pursued a case against the National Collegiate Athletic Association (NCAA) and its confidential witness Tom Culpepper for gravely wronging former University of Alabama football coach Ronnie Cottrell, ruining his career. Tommy's colorful press conferences, in deep baritone phrases, have endeared him to the sports media. Amazingly, both Alabama and Auburn fans cheered Tommy on in this case.

As the July 2005 trial date in Tuscaloosa rapidly approached, Tuscaloosa Circuit Judge Thomas Wilson, "gutted" Cottrell's and Gallion's case, dismissing the NCAA, but retaining Culpepper as a defendant on a limited "defamation" count. The jury was not dissuaded, and returned a verdict of $30 million against Culpepper on July 22, 2005. This sent an enormous message to the NCAA. Apparently, that sullied body will no longer be using confidential witnesses.

Three cheers for Gallioni and his co-counsel Delaine Mountain of Tuscaloosa!

HAVING PRACTICED LAW in Montgomery County for more than thirty years, I've developed a yardstick for appreciating, or not appreciating, when a judge is fair, polite, and competent. I've practiced in courts all over Alabama, and I know when I've been hit by "home cooking" and when I've been treated fairly and squarely.

I would be remiss not to acknowledge that we have a most distinguished, bright, and level-headed set of circuit judges in Montgomery County in Presiding Judge Charles Price and Circuit Judges Eugene Reese, Truman Hobbs, Jr., Tracey McCooey, William Shashy, and Johnny Hardwick. All are fair, courteous, and considerate, in my opinion. I no longer practice in domestic relations court, but when I did I was always treated well by Judge John Capell, and I hear good things about Judges Anita Kelly and Pat Warner, both elected in 2004.

Likewise, we have a wonderful set of district court judges in Lynn Clardy Bright, Peggy Givhan, and Lucy McLemore. I have always been treated with great respect by these judges.

In the federal court, where lifetime appointments exist, we have a very professional set of judges in Myron Thompson, Harold Albritton, Truman Hobbs, Sr., Ira DeMent, and Mark Fuller. The same is true for U.S. Magistrate Judges Vanzetta McPherson, Charles Coody, Delores Boyd, and Susan Russ Walker.

All any lawyer should want is an even playing field. We are fortunate to have that at all levels in Montgomery County.

32

Challenges and Opportunities

WHILE MY LAW practice and family obligations consume the largest part of my time, there are other extra-curricular activities that challenge me, and afford great opportunity for mission and ministry. Some of the more organized efforts are as follows:

The McPhillips International Reconciliation Center

While the Rev. Jim Webb was working as an employee of McPhillips Shinbaum, L.L.P., he discussed with me the possibility of creating an international center for racial and religious reconciliation. We agreed that it was a good idea, and I decided to do this in my parents' names. My parents were early activists in the Civil Rights Movement when it was dangerous and courageous to be involved. That was in Montgomery from 1962–64 and Birmingham from 1964–66. One of his sermons from that period is framed and hung in an honored place at the Rosa Parks Museum in Montgomery.

In addition, Dad especially helped achieve reconciliation as an interim rector in troubled Episcopal parishes throughout Alabama.

I've always wanted to honor both parents, so after their deaths I authorized Rev. Webb to prepare the necessary paperwork, and in due time The Rev. Julian and Eleanor McPhillips International Center for Racial and Religious Reconciliation was founded. The short name is "McPhillips International Reconciliation Center." The acronym is "MIRC."

The center was incorporated August 3, 2003, in the Probate Court of Montgomery County, Alabama. The original three incorporators were Rev. Webb, my wife Leslie, and me. The IRS gave MIRC tax-exempt status by a letter dated March 10, 2004.

The first project of MIRC was the donation of $25,000 to Bethany Orphanage in Kafue, Zambia, to build a schoolhouse for aids orphans. This was done in increments in the spring and summer of 2004. It's amazing how much further money goes in Zambia (about ten times more than in the USA). Later, in February 2005, MIRC gave the orphanage an additional $3,500 to complete the roof on the schoolhouse.

This coming February 2006, Leslie and I are planning to visit the new school and Bethany orphanage in Kafue. Our son David will be going with us. While there, we will visit my third cousin, Dr. Elizabeth Stringer (daughter of Dr. Frank and Stella McPhillips) and her husband Dr. Jeff Stringer. The Stringers run an AIDS clinic in Lusaka that employs four hundred Zambians and is on the cutting edge of medical cures for this awful disease.

Rev. Webb departed employment with our law firm in August 2004, and MIRC remained dormant for the better part of the next year. I was approached in early 2005 by the Rev. John Alford, about reactivating the Center. John was knowledgeable about MIRC and its creation. He was on the Center's first board of directors.

After prayerful consideration, I decided to gear up the Center for participation in another project in Benin, a country on the coast and interior of central west Africa. Known until 1970 as the French colony of Dahomey, Benin has grown in international awareness. On February 28, 2005, Leslie and I hosted a reception for a delegation from Benin. Eloquent in his remarks about the "reconciliation renaissance" in Benin was Pastor Romain Zannou, called by some "the spiritual leader of Benin," because he helped guide its president, Mathieu Kerekou, from a Marxist philosophy to a committed Christian faith.

A major conference is set for early August 2005 to promote reconciliation and trade between Benin and Alabama. Leslie and I are planning on being present, along with numerous other Alabamians, predominantly African Americans. There we will meet President Kerekou and will consult with Zannou and other Beninese leaders.

Why Benin? Partly because it was the homeland of the last slaves brought to Alabama from Africa in the late 1840s. (They settled in Africatown, near Mobile.)

After further discernment, I decided, as president of MIRC, to hire Rev. Alford as a part-time executive director of MIRC. His responsibilities and duties, and MIRC's obligations in return, are set forth in an independent contractor agreement.

Rev. Alford and John Smith, former mayor of Pritchard, Alabama, and now head of the Alabama-Benin Project, used our Lake Martin cottage for two weeks in April 2005 to host leaders from Benin while planning the upcoming conference in Africa.

I hope that MIRC will emerge as a useful tool in the growing international reconciliation movement.

Christ the Redeemer Episcopal Church

When Dale Short was updating the newest developments for the "Closing Arguments" chapter of the first edition of this book five years ago, he wrote that "Leslie McPhillips had spent a good part of the past fifteen months handling, in her role as senior warden, the administrative functions of Christ the Redeemer Episcopal Church. In August 2000, Leslie was looking forward to 'turning the reins over' to a new priest, the Rev. Doug McCurry, who was arriving in August 2000 with his wife Cathy Sue and their four young sons."

Well, five years later, Leslie is still working hard on church matters, but the "reins" she turned over to Rev. McCurry remained with him for only four and a half years.

We experienced an unfortunate split at our beloved Christ the Redeemer Episcopal Church on January 23, 2005, when Rev. McCurry announced that he was not only leaving the church that hired and paid him, and to which he owed a great fiduciary loyalty, but he was in fact leaving the entire Episcopal Church in the USA (ECUSA). Unfortunately, McCurry lobbied church members before he left and took about 75 percent of them with him.

I have no loyalty to ECUSA, and I share Rev. McCurry's dismay over ECUSA's consecration of Bishop Gene Robinson of New Hampshire. We also strongly oppose the blessing of same-sex unions. Ironically, Alabama Bishop Henry Parsley voted correctly on this issue, that is, orthodox opposition votes, but he was unable to satisfy conservative demands for a stronger stand. Contrary to the majority, I had no desire to leave Christ the Redeemer. I consider it "holy ground." My children have been baptized, confirmed, and married there. We have seen amazing miracles of healing and redemption there. Our spiritual batteries have been recharged there. We have frequently been very inspired there (see Chapter 24). I know that I have done better professionally because of Christ the Redeemer's spiritual influence.

At the same time, we are opposed to gay-bashing, and believe all people should be treated with dignity and respect, regardless of sexual orientation. Many of us believe that one's sexuality is not an immutable characteristic. That is, unlike race or sex, it is something that can swing from heterosexual to homosexual, or vice-versa, depending on environmental, psychological or spiritual factors in one's background.

I'll never forget a member of Christ the Redeemer ten years ago telling Bishop Miller about his struggle to avoid homosexuality, in connection with drug usage. He said that if the Episcopal Church have been more forthright and clear that homosexuality was wrong, he could have avoided the "gay lifestyle," which had caused him great pain and depression, bringing him to the brink of suicide.

The Episcopal Church of the USA (ECUSA) is losing members in many places, as numerous unhappy conservatives are transferring to various Anglican or other denominations.

I'm very concerned about this issue. While I sympathize more with conservatives, I can understand the concerns of the other side. However, each diocese has a great deal of autonomy within the "national church", and each individual church has much autonomy within the Diocese of Alabama. Further, "if you jump ship, you can't help fix it." Thus, many of us who stayed at Christ the Redeemer hope to see the ship of the Episcopal Church repaired. We can only help accomplish that goal by remaining where we are.

My wife also wanted to stay at the Church, as did Joe and Maria Guillot, John and Carol Murray, Pam Long, Jim McEwen, Jr., and his wife Melissa, Rush Wickes, Eugenia Archer, Libby and Andrew Conner, Elizabeth Murray, and Sandy and Michael Kerr. Others who stayed with us were Rev. Vernon and Lillian Jones, Fiona MacLeod, Janice Morris, Delia Cerpa, and several Hispanics. We also kept some young people, including fourteen-year-olds David McPhillips and Wesley Long, eight-year-old Madison McEwen, and two-and-a-half-year-old Laney Conner, my "adopted grandchild." Several new children have joined us in recent months. So have several adults, including clients Shannon Bedsole Boyd, Betty Benjamen, and Sonya and David Salum.

Although I was already on the vestry, Bishop Parsley appointed me as senior warden, a position I held twice in the 1980s. The previous senior warden, Doug Cairns, left when the congregation split.

Those of us who stayed consider ourselves the "faithful remnant." We're excited about rebuilding the congregation. We have a dynamic new Hispanic ministry, lead by Pam Long, an Auburn University at Montgomery Spanish professor. We're also supporting a Montessori School, which is using our classroom facilities, and allowing a Korean Methodist Church to use our facilities on Sunday afternoons.

For three months, the Diocese of Alabama supplied us with Rev. Rob Morpeth for Sunday services. He preached excellent sermons and helped keep us together. Rev. Bill King of the Diocesan office was a great encourager.

Recently, we brought seventy-nine-year-old Rev. Mark Waldo out of retirement as our interim rector. He is doing a good job. I've known him and his dear wife Ann for forty-three years (Mark recruited my father out of seminary in 1962 to come to Montgomery). We've just found a permanent rector, the Rev. John Paul Thompson. We still love Spirit-filled, dynamic worship. We uphold Jesus as Lord of our lives. We're coming back.

The Healing Ministry

The healing ministry continues to be a big part of our church. In April 2003, before the split, we had Mahesh and Bonnie Chavda back for their fourth "Healing the Nations" conference. I chaired the conference again. Once again, with Christ the Redeemer packed, many were healed, touched, and revived, spiritually and physically.

In the aftermath, my dear friends the Rev. George and Sharon Bretherick talked me into becoming a part of their "Healing Streams—Healing Rooms" ministry, based at the old St. James School campus. From April 2003 to December 2004, I served as Chairman of the Board of this healing ministry.

The Bretherick's enthusiastically pursued this ministry and saw a number of people experience great healings. Unfortunately, they ran into resistance from others, primarily (a) organized religious leaders who had not seen or experienced sudden and dramatic healings and thus considered them "suspect", and (b) rival church healing ministries, who considered Healing Rooms as competition. Personality conflicts also played a role in the Brethericks' decision, by late 2004, to put their ministry on hold and take an "extended sabbatical."

I continue to cherish the healing ministry, generically speaking. I do it on a low-key basis, and don't advertise it. (See also Chapter 25). During Holy

Communion at Christ the Redeemer each Sunday morning, we have a prayer rail in the back where a "prayer team" prays for healings and for other member needs. Leslie and I often do this together. We continue to see wonderful results, but to the Lord be all credit and honor.

Everyone should recognize that God, and God alone, is the Healer. He uses his Son Jesus, alive today in Spiritual form, as the Great Physician. The third person of the Trinity, the Holy Spirit, is always powerfully involved in healings. This is not a "manipulation of God", as some skeptics criticize. Instead, it is taking Jesus seriously, at his Word in the Gospels, about how to pray.

Leslie and I highly value the medical profession. We believe it should be used to its maximum and should be available to all who need it. This was a point I stressed in my U.S. Senate campaign. After all, medicine is God's "gift of wisdom" to us.

Unfortunately, some very wise people in the secular world limit God to what their reason, intellect, and five senses can comprehend. The "realm of the spirit," is something that must be understood by a "sixth sense," deep in one's own spirit. There are big barriers to the flow of God's Holy Spirit. The largest is doubt or unbelief. The next is unforgiveness. There are others.

I have found it helpful, in praying with people, to suggest to the one seeking healing that if he or she has anyone to forgive, including one's own self, then pray that the Holy Spirit will enable him or her to do so. A repentance to God of one's own sins is also helpful. These are foundational spiritual exercises opening up the floodgates from heaven, administering God's healing touch.

I cherish the many opportunities for practicing the healing ministry, which I consider central to our Christian faith. There are many times at church, at work, and at play, to pray for people with physical, mental, or spiritual needs. One can see great results, if one does so with faith.

I cherish the relationship I have developed with Brad and Venita Christian, and the four generations of their family who look out for one another in one household. Brad is in the twelfth year of his Lou Gehrig's disease. He can't move a single muscle except his eyelid, but he is mentally alert, and spiritually vibrant. He communicates with Venita by the number of blinks of his eye.

For two years I visited Brad at his home once a week, to lay hands on, and to pray for him. Now it is once every two weeks. I am inspired by the awesome faithfulness to God and to her husband of his devoted wife, Venita. She is a modern-day saint, in my book, and a one-woman tornado of support for her husband. Venita assures me that my praying regularly with them has greatly blessed Brad and her. I know for certain that it has blessed me—in ways hard to describe.

My mother's six-inch wooden crucifix (Christ on cross) hangs permanently in Brad's room. The Christians' seventeen-year-old daughter Kelli Maria worked in my law office the summer of 2005. She and her fourteen-year-old brother Chase are both star athletes and good students at St. James School. Also at the home are Venita's parents, Vera and Coach Webster, who anchor the household, along with the ninety-one-year-old great-grandmother of the kids. The Christian-Webster family is "like family" to me. They are also an inspiration to many Montgomerians.

I also had one client, Mary Caldwell, whom I prayed for a year ago, who had had blood cancer for years. Immediately after we prayed together, the cancer went away. It has not come back. Ditto for the mother of former employee Echol Nix, Jr., Annie Mae Nix, who has been in remission for ten years. She said this happened shortly after we prayed together at my office. Likewise for my former bookkeeper, Pat Hornberger, whose cancer in her remaining lung disappeared after we prayed together several years ago. As of July 2005, she was still going strong. My father frequently had this experience with cancer patients also. I like to think some measure of his anointing has been passed down to me.

I get criticized occasionally for being too "out-front" in my Christian faith, or too evangelical or charismatic, in the spiritual sense of that word. When that happens, I smile and take solace in Matthew 5:11-12. I also take great comfort in John 8:12 and 8:36.

The Scott and Zelda Fitzgerald Museum Association

Very different from most of my other extra-curricular involvements is the Scott and Zelda Fitzgerald Museum. It is a joy to be a part of.

The Museum is named for both Scott and Zelda and promotes both. It is located within the house, in Montgomery's Old Cloverdale neighborhood, where Scott and Zelda lived briefly in the 1930s, their only Montgomery residence as husband and wife (see Chapter 19). A historic marker erected in

1987 in front of the house contains romantic quotes, from F. Scott on one side and from Zelda on the other.

Art Douglas, Jr., of Los Angeles, son of board member Art Douglas, Sr., and wife Cindy, recently put together a dynamic new video about both Fitzgeralds, complementing the 1988 documentary by WSFA's Bob Howell.

In late June 2004, Leslie and I represented the Fitzgerald Museum at the International Fitzgerald Society Conference in Vevey, Switzerland. We did so at our own expense and also paid the way for Elena and Andy Aleinikov to join us there. Inasmuch as Elena died from cancer six months later, we're especially happy we had the chance to make this trip available for our Russian immigrant friends. Elena nobly served the Fitzgerald Museum as executive director for about eight years. A memorial plaque for her was installed in the Fitzgerald Museum at our last gala in January 2005.

Leslie and I really enjoy the camaraderie with the fifteen other Fitzgerald board members, together with the shared sense of purpose in maintaining the only museum anywhere in the world for a foremost American author of the twentieth century and his legendary wife, Montgomery-born Zelda.

In mid-July, 2005, the remaining Board members honored three retiring board stalwarts, Dr. Wesley Newton, Dr. Robert Delk, and Jim Carrier. Recent board additions include Priscilla Crommelin-Ball of the Montgomery Ballet; Susan Price, Alabama's vice-chancellor of Post-Secondary Education (whom Julian recruited to Princeton twenty-six years ago); and Jeff Free, a businessman-historian.

One exciting new development is the Southern Literary Trail, stretching from the Faulkner Museum in Oxford, Mississippi, through Alabama, all the way to Margaret Mitchell's Gone with the Wind Museum in Atlanta, Georgia. The first organized meeting for this project took place at Montgomery's Fitzgerald Museum in April 2005.

Board member Janie Wall, a landscape architect extraordinaire, has great plans for improving the grounds and gardens of the museum.

We're also fortunate to have a fine new executive director in Alabama historian Mike McCreedy, who lives in the Museum's apartment, providing additional security for the property.

Board member Martha Cassels continues to inspire the annual literary contest, now eighteen years old. Board member Dr. Kirk Cornutt honored the

Fitzgerald Museum by his election to the vice-presidency of the International Fitzgerald Society. Finally, board members Dr. Anne Little, English professor at Auburn University at Montgomery, and Dr. Dorothy Autrey, chairman of the History Department at Alabama State University, have made significant contributions to the museum.

Global Evangelical Christian College and Seminary

Back during the campaign in 2002, given the strong support for my U.S. Senate candidacy in the black church, and given further my record of fighting race discrimination in employment, police brutality, and racial profiling, I was awarded honorary "doctor of religious humanities" degrees from two black seminaries, the Tennessee School for Religion and the Global Evangelical Christian College and Seminary.

Rt. Rev. Frank Bozeman is the founder of Global Evangelical Christian College and Seminary. Due to my continuing activity in black churches, and leadership in healing conferences, the Global Evangelical Accreditation Commission also bestowed upon me a certificate of ordination. They want to call me Reverend now, but I respectfully decline, lightheartedly replying that my title has always been "The Irreverend." That is because I sometimes have had to irreverently stand up against "powers-that-be" in the secular world.

Nonetheless, I have worked with Bishop Bozeman and his wife Hurdis, also a pastor. Dr. Bozeman and I made a trip to Tampa, Florida, in May 2004 to award honorary doctor's degrees to Howard and Kaye Beyer of "We Care for You Ministries." The Beyers had come to Montgomery in late February 2004 to lead our Christ the Redeemer churchmen and others in a "Manna from Heaven" Conference. I have also been with the Bozemans on the "Conversations with Carol" TV program, helping them promote the Global Evangelical Christian seminaries, at seven or eight participating church locations across America, with two campuses in Africa and another in the Bahamas.

Recently the Bozemans connected with Mahesh and Bonnie Chavda about the creation of a seminary campus on their church's property in Charlotte, North Carolina. I have done both legal and ministerial work for Global Evangelical Christian College, and I look forward to continued participation in religious events and spiritual challenges of this body.

David Dixon McPhillips Memorial Scholarship Award

It's hard to believe that it's been twenty-nine years since my dear brother David McPhillips, a year and a half younger than me, died at the premature age of twenty-seven on Mother's Day weekend in 1976. My mother and dad never fully recovered.

To celebrate and commemorate the positive aspects of David's life, Leslie and I created two annual David Dixon McPhillips Memorial Scholarships for good citizenship and academic excellence. The first was started in 1984 at Indian Springs School near Birmingham, where David finished his last two years of high school. The other started in 1986 at Sidney Lanier's LAMP program, just completed its twentieth year.

My brother Frank, and my parents before their deaths, have also contributed generously to this scholarship.

This year's winner at LAMP (now the Loveless Academic Magnet Program) was Justin Hogan, a bright young man who lost his father at an early age, and whose mother is disabled. He plans to be a doctor.

The Indian Springs award, for only the second time in its twenty-two years, had co-winners in 2005, Jenna Caldwell and Jane Latham Hodges. Both were top students and leaders in their class, just like my brother David was. I was tremendously moved to learn that the young Miss Hodges was the daughter of David's best friend, Grey Hodges, at Indian Springs.

Every year, during the scholarship presentations, I have to pray to God at both places to give me the spiritual strength to maintain my composure. Yet every year, in something of a catharsis, I am uplifted by the loving memory of my dear brother David.

Newspaper Columns

Perhaps inspired by my connection to the Fitzgeralds, I have enjoyed occasional writing projects of my own, including this update to my biography. During the fall of 2002, I also wrote several columns that were widely published, in various Alabama newspapers, except for the *Birmingham News*, which ignored them. In November, I stated that Alabama Democrats were at risk of losing their viability if they didn't return to more traditional faith and family values. I concluded that some soul-searching was needed.

In December 2002, I wrote a column defending Roy Moore against "fashionable attacks" in liberal and intellectual circles for his stand on the Ten Commandments. I concluded that Moore was acting out of genuine conviction. Of course, this was before he openly defied a federal court order. Surprising to some, Moore's Supreme Court opinions supported the separation of church and state. His distinction was that the Commandments represented God, and that it is wrong to separate God from state. While Moore is greatly appreciated by many, he is equally disliked by others.

In January 2003, Huntsville's *Speaking Out News* published a column I wrote defending my good friend, Tuskegee Mayor Johnny Ford. I believed he was being unfairly criticized for having switched from the Democratic Party to the Republican Party some years ago. Then a mayor, later a state representative, and now mayor again, Ford has reaped great dividends for his constituents from the move. Too often people engage in unnecessarily partisan bickering between the two parties. First elected mayor of Tuskegee in 1972, and former president of the World Conference of Mayors, Johnny Ford is too astute for that. I'm looking forward to joining Johnny in Benin, Africa, in early August 2005. We'll both participate in an Alabama-Benin reconciliation and trade conference.

I also had another column published in the *Montgomery Advertiser* on February 13, 2003. This time I urged our country to stay out of war with Iraq. I wrote that if our nation could wage war, we could surely lead a fight to wage peace. Like many other voices at the time, mine went unheeded, and Bush invaded Iraq, supposedly to rid that desert country of weapons of mass destruction, which were never found.

In a January 2004 letter to the editor of the *Montgomery Advertiser*, I appealed, as a white Southerner with deep roots in Alabama, for public support for a national museum of African-American history and culture in Washington, D.C. In February 2004, another letter of mine to the *Advertiser* decried the negative impact President Bush's newly signed Medicare bill would have on the nation's elderly poor. In a March 2005 letter to the *Advertiser*, I urged Alabama to promote adoption by funding a program like Florida's where women with unwanted pregnancies could receive counseling against abortions. In an April 2005 letter I spoke out against the starvation of Terri Schiavo, and said that many from the "political left" also wanted to save her.

Wonders never cease. The *Birmingham News*, on July 1, 2005, finally published a column of mine. It took Richard Scrushy's acquittal on all counts for it to happen. I took the *News* to task, for writing so many prejudicial articles, convicting Scrushy. The *News* also belittled his defense, accusing Scrushy of using race and religion to influence jurors out of court. I pointed out the absence of a smoking-gun memo, letter, or email, and how the many HealthSouth officers who testified had ample motivation for lying. I said that if religion played a role, it was through Scrushy's deep faith in God, supported by the prayers of thousands. If race were involved, it was because the white community treated Scrushy like a pariah, while the black community embraced him, I added.

Al Benn of Selma, long-time reporter for the *Montgomery Advertiser*, is my favorite print journalist. I'm not saying this because he wrote a very good review of the first edition of this book in November 2000. Although Benn's stories have "covered the waterfront" during the past thirty years, he nonetheless has a great gift of emphasizing positives about people, while still making the story newsworthy.

Maybe I am a frustrated journalist.

Historic Markers

As is reflected in chapter nineteen of this book, I appreciate history. Leslie and I were pleased to play a role in the 1987 erection of the previously mentioned historic marker in front of the Fitzgerald Museum at 919 Felder Avenue. More recently, we also had a hand in erecting two other markers memorializing three remarkable Alabamians who had a significant impact on history.

After twenty-four years of living in our home on 831 Felder Avenue in the Old Cloverdale section of Montgomery, I finally gave in to pressure to place a historic marker commemorating the fact that Helen Keller was a frequent visitor there. Cooperating with the Helen Keller Foundation, which erected the marker on December 22, 2004, I enjoyed the contact I had with descendants of Mildred Keller Tyson (Helen's sister) who lived in our home from 1923–60, and who came for the marker's dedication. City Councilwoman Janet May presided over a nice ceremony, followed by a Christmas season reception inside the home.

When Leslie and I moved back to Alabama more than thirty years ago in 1975, the first two weeks we were here, we stayed with Clifford and Virginia Durr at their "Pea Level" home in Wetumpka.

Cliff died in 1975, but Virginia, who lived on until 1999, continued to inspire me and many others. Several of my leading civil rights cases were encouraged by her.

Both Durrs played major roles in the history of the United States and of Montgomery. The front side of the marker at 2 Felder Avenue reflects their role in Washington where they worked closely with Frankin and Eleanor Roosevelt. The back side tells the story of their Montgomery work with the "Civil Rights Movement" and especially in representing Rosa Parks during the Montgomery Bus Boycott.

Durr's co-counsel Fred Gray and other local dignitaries spoke at the unveiling ceremony in April 2005. Janet May of the City Council and Ann Durr Lyon, the Durrs' oldest daughter, unveiled the marker before an attentive crowd of about 125 persons. My leadership effort on this project was a labor of love, to honor these two courageous Americans, who were ahead of their times.

Maybe I am a frustrated historian.

Hosting Tours and Receptions

We've also enjoyed hosting tours and receptions. In April 2005, we had two open-to-the-public tours of our home, one sponsored by the Alabama Historical Association, the other by the Old Cloverdale Association, a neighborhood preservation society. Each tour attracted more than a hundred people.

The spaciousness of our ninety-seven-year-old home makes it a good venue for hosting receptions. In Feburary 2005 we had a large gathering honoring distinguished leaders from the central west African country of Benin. In April, we had a reception of one hundred following the installation of the Clifford and Virginia Durr historical marker.

In May we hosted a dinner and reception for a dozen British churchmen who were touring civil rights sites in the South. Present also for the event were local civil rights heroines Mrs. Johnnie Carr (still remarkably vital at age ninety-five, she is a lifelong friend of Mrs. Rosa Parks and has been president of the Montgomery Improvement Association since 1968) and Sheyann

Webb-Christburg (of *Selma, Lord, Selma* fame). The British group was led by Alabama Episcopal priest the Reverend Fletcher Comer, and his wife, Judy.

Oh yes, in November 2004, we hosted about twenty Montgomerians to meet Art, Ellen, and David Sanborn, the uncle, aunt, and first cousin of my new son-in-law, Corbett Lunsford. The Sanborns have for years been Christian missionaries in Southeast Asia. Ellen and David are also a talented acting-singing combination who produced, directed, starred in, and wrote the lyrics and scripts for *Judah Ben Hur*, a musical with a subtle Christian message, performed before tens of thousands (including many Muslims) in Singapore in 2003. Ellen and David did a truncated version of this play before our guests. With costumes and props still intact, these Spirit-filled Sanborns are now aiming for Broadway.

David Sanborn also does an outstanding one-man performance of King David of the Old Testament, Art just finished his inspirational autobiography *Walking Miracle*, and Ellen truly has the most beautiful singing voice I have ever heard. What talent within one family!

Of course, the biggest reception we've ever hosted, with 400-500 guests, was for our daughter Grace's wedding in August 2004. Christ the Redeemer Episcopal Church, site of the ceremony, was resplendent with heavenly flowers by Donna McGuffin. The Capitol City Club, where the reception followed, was stunningly decorated by Janie Wall. By the way, we're delighted that Donna's husband, Dr. Bill McGuffin, is co-chairing again this year a different kind of reception, for the Montgomery community, namely our annual Christmas tree sale at Christ the Redeemer. This event is always a joy to work.

These tours and receptions are a lot of fun and keep us in touch with a number of interesting people.

However, I am not a frustrated host.

33

The Best Things in Life

S OMETIMES ONE has to reach his late fifties before certain truths fully sink in. My journey in life has taken me through thirty-four years of law practice, two statewide political campaigns, marriage, the births of three children, the deaths of two parents and one brother, and the foundings of a law practice, a church, a museum, and an international reconciliation center. Throw in also extensive international and domestic travel, especially with family.

Highlight family trips include skiing in Big Sky, Montana, the last week of 2002, rafting on the Colorado River through the Grand Canyon the summer of 2003, enjoying tropical Aruba in late 2003, and celebrating our thirtieth anniversary in June 2004 traveling with all three kids in Germany, Austria, and Switzerland.

I have had my share of tragedies and mishaps (brother's suicide, three miscarriages, circumstances of parents' deaths, election races stolen or sabotaged, twice broken leg, for instance), but I have been blessed enormously. No doubt much of this blessing has flowed from the strong spiritual heritage of my roots. Simply put, my parents taught me at an early age to love the Lord, and that if we love Him, we must love our fellow man. Basically, that is the Great Commandment. Living it makes a huge difference for the better in the life of anyone.

From the lives and deaths of my parents and brother, from my marriage to Leslie, and from raising my children, I have learned that the best things in life are not professional or political accomplishment. They are relationships with family, and fellow human beings, and most importantly our relationship with God the Father, Son, and Holy Spirit.

Dad was pleased with my running for U.S. Senate, and he encouraged me in it. But I would have gladly passed it all up for a few more years with Dad. Ditto my mother and brother David. I would have gladly passed up worldly success as the "People's Lawyer," if I had been given a choice of more time with them.

Certainly my greatest delights in life, and what touches me most deeply, are to see my children grow and mature, and to enjoy my marriage with Leslie.

Rachel, our oldest at twenty-seven, is a true joy. She is so fine, so very much like her mother. She has lived up to her God-given talents, graduating from Elon University. She has taught school for six years. I am proud also of her recent medical missionary trip to Panama. She is gorgeous on the outside and beautiful on the inside.

Grace is also a great delight to her Dad. What a wonderful wedding we had last summer when she married Corbett Lunsford of Tampa and Chicago. About four hundred people attended, including much extended family on both sides. Grace was a stunningly attractive bride, oozing charm. Eleven bridesmaids, nine groomsmen. When the doors were opened and I began the walk down the aisle to escort Grace to the altar, the many loving, expectant faces beaming at us immediately spawned within me the sensation that we were walking into heaven.

Now living in Chicago with her husband, Grace utilizes her talent well. An actress, singer, and dancer, she can do great things. I pray that God will continue to inspire, protect, and use her. "Goodness Graciosity," I sometimes call her. And Corbett is a mature, considerate fellow who treats Grace well. He is also a great musician with a promising future.

David, my only son. How amazing it is to watch him grow about ten inches in a year and a half, and hear his voice deepen. He's also grown emotionally, mentally, and spiritually. His Citizen Ambassador trip to Australia in June 2005, and his attending Stony Brook School in Long Island, New York, this coming academic year (2005–06) are helping to shape David into the fine young man God intends him to be.

Am I a proud pop? You bet I am.

Leslie and I revel together in watching all three of our children. Isn't it amazing that we are now the oldest generation? Not our grandparents! Not our parents! But us!

We have also enjoyed watching our three outstanding nephews, Jamie,

Alex, and Dixon McPhillips, neighbors at Lake Martin, develop over the years. What a wonderful job my brother Frank and his devoted wife Louise have done as parents.

Frank has developed into one of the top bond lawyers in the state, and was Governor Siegelman's chief negotiator in bringing the Hyundai Motors plant to Montgomery. Louise is a talented architect. Jamie, having finished Harvard and having worked in John Kerry's campaign and then as a paralegal in an international law firm in Washington, D.C., is looking at law schools. Alex, also at Harvard, is a gifted sportswriter. Dixon is developing a multitude of talents as he heads into his final year at St. Paul's School in New Hampshire.

My two sisters Sandy (and her husband, Charlie Pitre) and Betsy, their children, and growing band of grandchildren are always a joy to be with. Family weddings are lively reunions, even without Mom and Dad. Sandy has assumed Dad's role as the "great encourager," a quality my daughter, Grace, has as well.

Speaking of weddings, sister Betsy's children keep expanding our family. In May 2001, her third daughter, Julia, married John Hinshaw, a savvy young executive at Verizon Wireless. In 2003, Julia gave birth to a beautiful daughter, Elizabeth. That same year, Betsy's only son, Gordon Williams, married Anna Davis and moved to Berkeley, California. Betsy's twin daughters, Ann Williams and Eleanor Garver (and her husband Randy) are helping Betsy develop a new business in Virginia Beach, known as "The Little Gym," a motor skills development program for young children. Go Bets! The Garvers, by the way, gave Betsy her first grandson, Ryan, in 2004.

My sister Sandy's family is also a great joy for me as an uncle and great-uncle. Mom and Dad's first grandchild, David Pitre, an organic vegetable farmer in Austin, Texas, turned forty in November 2004. He is happily married to Katie, and their young children, Zack, Julia Claire, and Henry, are sprouting like weeds. My personable niece Lenwood and her energetic husband Mike Anthon are growing their own team of boys in St. Louis, Missouri. The youngest, Michael Jr., entered the world in 2004, joining his older brothers Patrick, Dixon, and Andrew.

I have also enjoyed encouraging Uncle David (Mom's only sibling) and Aunt Mary in writing his forthcoming autobiography, entitled "The Saints, the Superdome, and the Scandal." Is there any chance Mom could get a copy up in Heaven? In June 2003, we had a great time celebrating Uncle Dave's eightieth birthday party in New Orleans, an event for 125 people, which I co-hosted along with their three sons, Frank, Shea, and Stuart.

It has also been fun to stay connected to Dad's only sibling, my dear Uncle Warren and that side of the family. Cousin Libby always enlivens my office when she stops by. Cousin Francie stays in touch with Grace in Chicago, and Warren Jr., John, Emily, Mary Morrow and their families are always delightful to get together with, especially when we celebrated Warren Sr.'s eightieth in 2003.

During the past five years, I have maintained good contact with two second cousins once removed, both in Mobile. They are attorney Rosie McPhillips (of the Harry McPhillips branch) and Dr. Frank McPhillips (of the Joe McPhillips branch). Joe, Harry, my great-grandfather James Jr., and John (who moved to California in 1919) were four brothers born in Mobile between 1870 and 1890 [see photo page A-3]. I also stay in touch with distant cousins on my father's maternal side, including attorney Bill McGowin of Montgomery, a fifth cousin.

On Mom's Dixon side, I enjoy second cousin Michael Smith, an attorney-Anglican priest in West Virginia; second cousin Dean Lindsey, a Presbyterian minister in Salem, Virginia; and Dean's New Orleans parents, Dr. Ed and Margaret Ann Lindsey. The older Lindseys touched me greatly by coming to both my parents' memorial services in Birmingham. On Mom's Sanderson side, I enjoy third cousin David Campbell of Montgomery, a professional photographer; and second cousin Robin Sanderson, a forester in Monroeville, Alabama.

If we go back enough generations, we all tie in somewhere. What a better world this could be if mankind realized that we are all "one big extended family!"

I have also enjoyed the ministries that God has given me. My law practice, not only the clients but the employees, is one big ministry. Our church, Christ the Redeemer Episcopal, though we lost three-fourths of our congregation over an unfortunate issue, still affords many opportunities for ministerial outreach and inreach.

Leslie and I say prayers together twice a day, once in the morning before work, and a second time just before going to sleep. It makes all the difference in the world. Peace of mind, and the presence of the Holy Spirit come from it, and this is worth much more than money.

The older we get the more we realize life's limitations and the more we experience humbling episodes. That is not a bad thing, however. I have come to understand that it is in our brokenness and weakness that God's strength is made perfect, when we call upon Him in prayer.

At fifty-eight years young, I tell people I'm aiming for a hundred and five. I acknowledge that I may not make it, in all likelihood. But maybe I'll get further down the pike for aiming high. It encourages me to keep up good health habits, including daily workouts. That includes running, weight-lifting, neck and back exercises, and, on weekends at Lake Martin in warm weather, swimming and water-skiing.

I believe that we owe it to God, our Creator, to give back to Him every talent he has given us, and to multiply those talents. To echo one of my mother's favorite expressions, and the words of our Lord Jesus Himself, *"To whom much is given, much is required."* I believe that strongly.

I also take my mother's advice, *"Do your best, and to God leave the rest."* Another version she often said was, *"Let go, and let God."*

With this five-year update, in the year 2005, I thank God for life itself, for good health, for peace and for prosperity. These are no small blessings. Much of the world does not have them. I also thank God for a great family, a wonderful church, an enjoyable law practice, a nice home in Montgomery, and a relaxing get-away retreat cottage at Lake Martin.

It is my fervent hope, prayer, and goal to keep giving back to God, and to my fellow man, out of the awesome abundance God has so generously given me. It is not a choice, not an obligation. It is a command. The command comes deep from inside my heart, but I know from Whence it comes.

We honor God when we recognize this and act accordingly.

                              ∾

Index